✴ INSIGHT GUI

THE DOMINICAN REPUBLIC

& HAITI

DISCOVERY CHANNEL

APA PUBLICATIONS   L

Part of the Langenscheidt Publishing Group

INSIGHT GUIDE
THE DOMINICAN REPUBLIC & HAITI

Editorial
Editor
Lesley Gordon
Editorial Director
Brian Bell

Distribution

UK & Ireland
GeoCenter International Ltd
The Viables Centre, Harrow Way
Basingstoke, Hants RG22 4BJ
Fax: (44) 1256-817988

United States
Langenscheidt Publishers, Inc.
46–35 54th Road, Maspeth, NY 11378
Fax: (1) 718 784-0640

Canada
Thomas Allen & Son Ltd
390 Steelcase Road East
Markham, Ontario L3R 1G2
Fax: (1) 905 475 6747

Australia
Universal Publishers
1 Waterloo Road
Macquarie Park, NSW 2113
Fax: (61) 2 9888 9074

New Zealand
Hema Maps New Zealand Ltd (HNZ)
Unit D, 24 Ra ORA Drive
East Tamaki, Auckland
Fax: (64) 9 273 6479

Worldwide
Apa Publications GmbH & Co.
Verlag KG (Singapore branch)
38 Joo Koon Road, Singapore 628990
Tel: (65) 6865-1600. Fax: (65) 6861-6438

Printing

Insight Print Services (Pte) Ltd
38 Joo Koon Road, Singapore 628990
Tel: (65) 6865-1600. Fax: (65) 6861-6438

©2004 Apa Publications GmbH & Co.
Verlag KG (Singapore branch)
All Rights Reserved
First Edition 2000
Updated 2004

CONTACTING THE EDITORS
We would appreciate it if readers
would alert us to errors or out-
dated information by writing to:
**Insight Guides, P.O. Box 7910,
London SE1 1WE, England.**
Fax: (44) 20 7403-0290.
insight@apaguide.co.uk

www.insightguides.com

ABOUT THIS BOOK

This guidebook combines the interests and enthusiasms of two of the world's best-known information providers: Insight Guides, whose titles have set the standard for visual travel guides since 1970, and Discovery Channel, the world's premier source of nonfiction television programming.

The editors of Insight Guides provide both practical advice and general understanding about a destination's history, culture, institutions and people. Discovery Channel and its website, www.discovery.com, help millions of viewers explore their world from the comfort of their own home and also encourage them to explore it first-hand.

This first edition of *Insight Guide: Dominican Republic & Haiti* is carefully structured to convey an understanding of the countries and their cultures as well as to guide readers through the many sights and activities.

◆ The **Features** section, indicated by a yellow bar at the top of each page, covers the history and culture of the Dominican Republic & Haiti in a series of informative essays.

◆ The main **Places** section, indicated by a blue bar, is a complete guide to all the sights and areas worth visiting. Places of special interest are coordinated by number with the maps.

◆ The **Travel Tips** listings section, which has an orange bar, provides a handy point of reference for information on travel, hotels, shops, restaurants and much more.

about the Santo Domingo environs and the Dominican Republic section of the people chapter. **Maxine Rose Schur**, a California-based writer produced *The Old Colonial City*.

Joann Biondi, a regular Insight Guides contributor and a frequent visitor to Haiti, wrote *Haitian Art*. **Monika Latzel**, a talented German writer, contributed *Sporting Passions*, *The Samaná Peninsula* and *The Cibao Valley*. A second German contributor is New York-based **Ilona Weöres**, who wrote *From Caribe to Coco*, *West to Lago Enriquillo* and the box story on scaling Pico Duarte.

Simon Lee is an English travel writer, living in Trinidad. Lee contributed the authoritative essay on the *Origins of Vaudou*, *More than Merengue*, *Back to Nature* and a box story on Haiti's despotic emperors.

A Dominican brother and sister team, **José Velázquez** and **Beatriz Velázquez**, contributed *The Quiet Northwest*, *Cordillera Central*, the Dominican Republic section of the language chapter and *Travel Tips*.

Ellen Sarbone, a travel writer and a former editor at *Lifestyle Magazine* in San Francisco, wrote *The Amber Coast*, *Port-au-Prince*, *Excursions from Port-au-Prince* and *The South*. She also painstakingly compiled the Haiti Travel Tips.

Photographer and journalist **Leah Gordon** wrote *Central Haiti, the West and the Artibonite Valley*, *The North Coast*, and provided additional text for the Haiti Travel Tips and photographs.

Sarah Cameron, writer, editor and Caribbean and Latin America expert, keeps this edition up to date.

Principal photographers include **Yves Fonck** and **Catherine Karnow**. Thanks go to **Caroline Radula-Scott** for her invaluable editorial input.

The contributors

For this edition of *Insight Guide: Dominican Republic & Haiti*, managing editor **Lesley Gordon** assembled an impressive team of experts. **James Ferguson**, the author of *A Traveller's History of the Caribbean*, plotted the island's turbulent history. He also wrote the Haiti introduction, *Island of Magic*, and provided extra editorial assistance.

Florida-based Haitian journalist **Yves Colon** worked at the Miami Herald when commissioned. He contributed *Modern Haiti*, *Haiti's Literary Art* and *Insight on... Architecture*. He also wrote the Haitian sections of the cuisine, language and people chapters.

Talented writer **David Howard** is a Caribbean and Latin America expert, who contributed *The Dominican Republic Today*, *Caribbean Metropolis*

Map Legend

▬ ▬ ▬	International Boundary
▭ ▭ ▭ ▭	Province Boundary
⊖	Border Crossing
▬ • ▬	National Park/Reserve
▭ ▭ ▭ ▭	Ferry Route
✈ ✈	Airport: International/ Regional
🚌	Bus Station
ℹ	Tourist Information
✉	Post Office
⛪ ✝ ✝	Church/Ruins
✝	Monastery
☾	Mosque
✡	Synagogue
🏰 🏚	Castle/Ruins
∴	Archaeological Site
∩	Cave
🗼	Statue/Monument
★	Place of Interest

The main places of interest in the Places section are coordinated by number with a full-colour map (e.g. **❶**), and a symbol at the top of every right-hand page tells you where to find the map.

INSIGHT GUIDE
THE DOMINICAN REPUBLIC & HAITI

CONTENTS

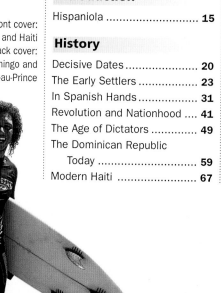

HISPANIOLA

This two-nation multilingual island has a colourful history,
beautiful beaches, distinctive rhythms, Voodoo and rich forests

One island, two very distinct nations – that sums up the complexity of the Dominican Republic and Haiti. History has taken its toll on the island and its peoples, ravaging them with the indignities of slavery, wars, foreign occupations and ruthless dictatorships. Through it all, the cultures have survived and developed, one heavily influenced by Spain, the USA and Africa, the other by Africa and France.

The island was named by Christopher Columbus when he arrived in 1492 to claim the land for Spain. He called it La Isla Española – the Spanish Island – which eventually became corrupted as Hispaniola. Although it's a useful name because it refers to the entire island, Dominicans tend to avoid it in the same way as they avoid anything that associates them too closely with Haiti.

Standing at the back door of the USA, Hispaniola lies around 960 km (600 miles) southeast of Florida and has held a precarious position between stability and instability and the inevitable threat of US intervention – something neither part of the island has managed to avoid in the recent past. To the west is Cuba, southwest is Jamaica and east is Puerto Rico and the chain of the Lesser Antilles. The Dominican Republic covers about two-thirds of the island, totalling 48,734 sq. km (18,816 sq. miles), and Haiti has the remaining third, approximately 27,750 sq. km (10,714 sq. miles).

Volcanic origins

Eight spectacular mountain ranges extend across the length of Hispaniola. The main one within the Cordillera Central in the Dominican Republic has the highest point in the entire Caribbean, Pico Duarte, at 3,087 metres (10,128 ft). The Central range is also home to the longest river, Río Yaque del Norte, and the vast Parque Nacional Armando Bermúdez and Parque Nacional José del Carmen national parks. To the west is the biggest lake, Lago Enriquillo.

The terrain betrays the island's volcanic origins but today no active volcanoes are known to exist. Hurricanes are much more of an issue, bringing with them dangerous tropical storms, high winds of up to 240 kph (150 mph) and flooding during the hurricane season from June to November, although most hurricanes strike in September. The storms can devastate people, property and crops. In 1979 Hurricane David hit the island hard, and in 1998 Hurricane Georges struck, resulting in thousands of deaths.

The tropical climate is warm and humid, with a rainy season in

PRECEDING PAGES: carnival, Haiti; art on every street corner; Haitian musicians; cutting coconuts, Dominican Republic.
LEFT: Las Terrenas, Samaná Peninsula.

the summer and a dry winter season. January and February are the driest months and May and August are the wettest. However, the showers tend not to last too long and, as in all of the Caribbean, once the sun is shining things dry out and warm up again quickly. Daytime temperatures vary between 27°C (80°F) and 32°C (90°F) and at night remain in the region of 20°C (68°F). In the mountainous areas during the winter, temperatures have been known to drop to below freezing.

The island has a rich and colourful natural environment that is home to more than 5,000 plant species, almost half of which are endemic – from ferns and bamboo to frangipani and hibiscus. Protected parts of the coast in the Dominican Republic contain tangles of thick mangroves: red freshwater ones can exist in high water while black mangroves are more comfortable in shallow water and play host to flocks of pelicans, herons and other birdlife that feed off the shellfish, shrimps and small fish living there. There are almost 260 identifiable bird species. Look out for the Hispaniolan woodpecker and the Hispaniolan parrot, the national bird.

In contrast, Haiti's woodland has been devastated by deforestation caused by trees being felled for firewood, charcoal and building. Much of the land is now unable to sustain crops, as there are no trees to protect the earth from the elements. Although Haiti has not embraced environmental protection as enthusiastically as the Dominican Republic, there are reforestation programmes in place, but progress is slow.

Beautiful beaches

There are some very beautiful beaches on Hispaniola, with clear sea water and fine golden sand. The coast and the coral reefs, although damaged by hurricanes, ships anchors and overfishing, still play host to a wide variety of marine life. If you travel to Hispaniola in the winter, you may witness one of the most amazing sights in the Antilles: thousands of Humpback whales migrate to the Atlantic waters north of the Dominican Republic to breed from January to March and many can be seen in Samaná Bay.

Hispaniola is truly a two-nation island; its peoples and landscapes are distinguishably different, yet they share land and history. The Dominican Republic and Haiti offer visitors an intriguing combination of Latin America and the Caribbean – a fascinating opportunity to explore two contrasting traditions.   ❏

RIGHT: life in the Haitian countryside.

Cava de Moua

R. de Maravi

Port de Baracoua

M. de Baracoua

ISLE DE CUBA

aux Espagnols

Pointe de Mayosi

Petye de Tequiry

Porto Descondido

LES FRERES BOU CANIER DE LA T

Cap St. Nicolas
Mole St. Nicolas

Cap aux Four

la Plate forme

DE BARQUEMENS DE CHRISTOPHE COLOMB au Mole St. Nicolas

1492 1697

1697-1804

I. de Navaza

C

ISLE

Pte. de la Seringue

Cap Rose
Trou Bonbon
Trou Jeremie
Grande Ance
Petite Caymite
Caymites
Bu de Marsoin
les Baraderes
R. de Nipe
Pointe

Cap Dame Marie

Pays desert

M. de la Hotte division de la partie du Sud

Ligne de division

Pointe des Irois

QUARTIER
qui avoi

Cap Tiberon
B. du C. Tiberon
Pte. du Vent
Pte. des aigrettes
les Basses
Tapion de la Caouane
les Anglois
Pte des Chardonieres
Pte a Piment
les Damassins
Roche a bateau
l'Ance a Juif
l'Ance a Drie
Port Salut
Pointe a Gravois

Cavaillon
R. de Cavaillon

les Ances
Les 3 Rivieres
Les Coteaux
le Fond de
Cavaillon

Aquin
Fond de

Bu St. George Cave
Grosse Cave
Fort St. Louis
Abaye d'Aquin
Huster

LES CAYES
R. de l'Acul
l'Etron de Porc
Caycalean
la Folle

Baye du Mesle
petit et grand
B. a Diamans

Isle a Vache
Pointe de l'Abacou

Port a Nonet

TOUSSAINT LOUVERTURE GOUVERNEUR GENERAL
1801

ABOLITION DE L'ESCLAVAGE 1793

Decisive Dates

500 BC Arrival of the pre-Ceramic Ciboney people – fishers and foragers from Mexico and Florida.
AD 650–1200 After migrating from what is now Venezuela, the Taínos, reach the Greater Antilles in dug-out canoes, escaping from Carib aggressors.

THE SPANISH ISLAND 1492–1697

For nearly two centuries, Hispaniola (La Isla Española) was a Spanish possession, although competing European nations were soon eager to challenge Spain's ownership.

1492 Christopher Columbus establishes the first European settlement in the Americas on the island he calls La Isla Española.
1493 Columbus's second expedition to Hispaniola brings colonists and gold hunters.
1496 Columbus's brother, Bartolomé, founds the south coast settlement of Nueva Isabela, later moved and renamed Santo Domingo.
1498 Columbus's third voyage; growing tension in Hispaniola ends in revolt.
1500 Columbus's brothers are shipped back to Spain by commissioner, Francisco de Bobadilla.
1509–24 Diego Columbus, the explorer's son, presides as Governor of Hispaniola and Viceroy of the Indies.

1511 Fray Antón de Montesinos criticises the colonists' abuses of the Taínos' human rights.
1551 Publication of Bartolomé de Las Casas' *A Very Brief Account of the Destruction of the Indies*.
1586 Sir Francis Drake sacks Santo Domingo.
1650s French buccaneers settle in the northwest.

RISE AND FALL OF SAINT DOMINGUE 1697–1804

In the course of the 18th century, the French colony of Saint Domingue became the richest in the world.
1697 Treaty of Ryswick officially cedes the western part of Hispaniola (Saint Domingue) to France.
1730 Slave population of Saint Domingue reaches 120,000.
1758 Planned uprising and mass poisoning, led by Mackandal, is foiled in Saint Domingue.
1789 News of French Revolution reaches the colony.
1791 A slave insurrection breaks out in the north; Toussaint L'Ouverture, a former slave, creates his own army to fight the colonial forces.
1793 French republican Commissioner Sonthonax decrees the abolition of slavery.
1798 British expeditionary force withdraws from Saint Domingue after failed five-year campaign.
1801 Toussaint L'Ouverture draws up a new Constitution and proclaims himself Governor for Life.
1802 Napoléon Bonaparte sends in French troops to capture Toussaint and ship him to France.
1803 Death of Toussaint L'Ouverture in France.
1804 One of Toussaint's troops, Jean-Jacques Dessalines, declares the independence of the new state of Haiti and proclaims himself Emperor.

AN ISLAND DIVIDED 1804–1914

Haiti's independence ushered in a century of political turmoil and increased hostility with the Spanish-speaking east of the island.
1806 Dessalines is murdered by mutinous officers; Henri Christophe, who is black, takes power in the north of Haiti; Alexandre Pétion, a mulatto, controls the south.
1809 Eastern part of Hispaniola returns to Spanish control after 14-year French occupation.
1820 Death of Christophe leads to reunification of Haiti under General Jean-Pierre Boyer.
1822 Independence of Spanish Santo Domingo, named "Spanish Haiti". Haiti occupies Santo Domingo under Boyer for 22 years.
1823 US President James Monroe underlines American domination of the Caribbean region.
1825 Boyer agrees to pay indemnity of 150 million francs to France in return for French recognition of Haitian sovereignty.

1838 Founding of underground La Trinitaria movement in Santo Domingo, which pledges to achieve independence from Haiti with the new name of *República Dominicana* (Dominican Republic).
1843 Boyer is overthrown and exiled to Jamaica.
1844 Independence of the Dominican Republic after Haitian troops are expelled. General Santana assumes presidency when La Trinitaria collapses.
1848 Haiti, under Faustin Soulouque, attempts invasion of Dominican Republic; a second invasion in 1859 also ends in failure. Leaders of the Dominican Republic seek annexation with France, Spain or USA.
1861 Spain re-colonizes the Dominican Republic but withdraws in 1865 after "War of Restoration".
1882 Ulises Heureaux begins a 17-year dictatorship in the Dominican Republic.
1905 US takes control of Dominican customs to prevent further interference by European powers.
1914 Opening of Panama Canal.

OCCUPATION AND DICTATORSHIP 1915–86

US interventions in Haiti and the Dominican Republic provoked armed resistance and encouraged the rise of new dictators.
1915 US troops occupy Haiti after a period of extreme political instability, and a year later US forces take control of the Dominican Republic.
1918 Haitian guerrilla leader, Charlemagne Péralte, killed in anti-US campaign.
1925 The US withdraws from the Dominican Republic and leaves Haiti 9 years later.
1930 Rafael Leonidas Trujillo takes power in the Dominican Republic, starting a 30-year dictatorship.
1935 Trujillo orders the massacre of some 15,000 Haitian migrants in the Dominican Republic.
1939 Founding of Dominican Revolutionary Party (PRD) by exiled anti-Trujillo social democrats.
1957 Election of François "Papa Doc" Duvalier as president of Haiti.
1961 Assassination of Trujillo.
1962 Reformist Juan Bosch of the PRD triumphs in Dominican elections but is overthrown by the military a year later, leading to civil unrest.
1965 US occupation of the Dominican Republic.
1966 Joaquín Balaguer of the Social Christian Reformist Party (PRSC) and former Trujillo aide, wins the first of six controversial elections in the Dominican Republic.
1971 Death of Papa Doc and succession of his son Jean-Claude ("Baby Doc").

LEFT: an engraving of Jean-Jacques Dessalines.
RIGHT: Jean-Bertrand Aristide returns to power.

1978 PRD wins election and gains the presidency in Dominican Republic after threatened military coup.
1986 Baby Doc flees Haiti as the military take over; Balaguer returns to power in the Dominican Republic.

TOWARDS DEMOCRACY: FROM 1986

The end of the Duvalier dictatorship pitted the Haitian military against a people thirsty for political freedom, while in the Dominican Republic long-awaited change took place peacefully.
1987 Haitian elections end in bloodshed, as military and paramilitary forces attack voters.
1990 Jean-Bertrand Aristide wins a 70 percent majority in Haiti's first fair elections.

1991 Aristide overthrown in violent coup and exiled.
1994 US-led intervention restores Aristide to power.
1996 Balaguer forced to stand down in Dominican Republic after disputed elections of 1994, and Leonel Fernández wins free and fair elections. Aristide steps down to elected successor, René Préval, the first constitutional succession in Haitian history.
1997 Meeting between Fernández and Préval.
2000 PRD's Hipólito Mejiá wins the presidential elections in the Dominican Republic.
2001 Aristide returns as Haitian president, claiming 92 percent of the vote in a controversial election.
2002 Death of Balaguer aged 93.
2003 A banking scandal in the Republic causes the peso to plummet; the IMF are called in to assist. ❑

THE EARLY SETTLERS

For several centuries the Amerindians led a Utopian existence. Then they welcomed Christopher Columbus and his Spanish fleet to their island

Viewing Haiti's bare, eroded mountains from an aircraft, it is hard to imagine that this was once one of the most beautiful and fertile places on earth. Where now barren hillsides reveal exposed rock and scar-like ravines, there were at one time tropical rainforests and vast expanses of pine. Around the coastal area – today stripped clean by charcoal-burners – mangrove swamps and wooded estuaries flourished, and there was a rich variety of wildlife and exuberant vegetation.

Some of this natural splendour continues to survive in the Dominican Republic across the border, but in Haiti there is little left to suggest what this island once looked like. Crossing the frontier itself makes clear the extent of the environmental catastrophe, for on the Dominican side there are still swathes of forest, pastures and streams. To enter Haiti, however, is to enter a parched and blighted landscape, where hillsides and valleys have been reduced to near-desert and streams have dried up for ever.

A promised land

It is poignant to read Christopher Columbus's breathless words of wonder as he looked at the island's spectacular scenery at the end of the 15th century. It was, he wrote, "fertile to an excessive degree... and filled with trees of a thousand kinds and tall, seeming to touch the sky." At first sight, it was nothing short of the promised land that Columbus had persuaded himself must exist across the Atlantic. Green, well-watered, seemingly full of natural riches, it also held out the prospect of infinite wealth. "In the interior," continued Columbus, "there are mines of metal, and the population is without number."

No records exist to tell us how many people actually lived on the island when Columbus's ships appeared on the horizon in December 1492, but the estimates of early European

LEFT: a portrait of a Taíno Amerindian.
RIGHT: Christopher Columbus and his crew set sail in search of riches in the Americas.

chroniclers range between 100,000 and a million. Modern historians tend to agree there was probably a population of around 500,000.

The arrival of the Taínos

These early inhabitants, who called their island Ayiti, meaning "high ground", were Taínos, the

descendants of a South American, Arawak-speaking people who had originally left the mainland of what is now Venezuela in about 500 BC. The Amerindians had been established on the banks of the Orinoco River for several hundred years before taking to the sea and moving up the Caribbean island chain.

The ensuing process of migration took centuries, as the discovery of one island followed that of another. Starting in Trinidad, the Taínos slowly progressed through the small islands of the Eastern Caribbean, or Lesser Antilles, sometimes sighting neighbouring territories in the distance or perhaps setting off in the hope of finding another island over the horizon. They had formidable canoes, measuring as much as 25 metres (82 ft) and capable of carrying 50 people through treacherous seas. Using these vessels, they moved in successive waves up as far as Cuba, the Bahamas and Ayiti.

Carib enemies

The reasons for this great migration remain unclear, but it seems that the Taínos were pushed out of the Orinoco delta by another group of indigenous people, the Caribs, or Kalinagos as they called themselves. These less sophisticated Amerindians had also originated in the Amazon Basin and were highly aggres-

sive in their dealings with the Taínos. Whether because of competition for natural resources or cultural conflict, the Caribs declared war on them, attacking villages, capturing women and killing men. The Taínos, although well organised, were no match for the war-like Caribs. Escape was the only option.

There is some dispute among historians as to whether the Caribs were really the bloodthirsty aggressors of legend. Certainly, the reports of early European observers should be treated with caution, as should the widespread belief that the Caribs were inveterate cannibals. While there is evidence that Carib warriors did eat

parts of their victims, it is probable that this was an occasional ritual rather than a regular habit. But what does appear clear is that they, in their turn, began moving into the Caribbean from the mainland in about AD 1000.

Again, the Taínos found themselves tormented by their ancestral enemies, as raiding parties arrived by canoe to kill, kidnap and pillage. This only drove the Taínos further west towards the larger islands of the Greater Antilles.

The earliest inhabitants

Here they encountered the earliest human inhabitants of the region, the Ciboneys, who had arrived in Ayiti and other islands around

A LINGUISTIC LEGACY

The ancient Amerindian tongue still lives on in the English language forming the origin of several familiar words: hurricane/*huracan*; maize or corn/*maiz*; canoe/*canaua*; tobacco/*tobaco*; hammock/*hamaca*; savannah/*sabana*; barbecue/*barbacoa*.

Literally translated, other indigenous Caribbean terms are jewels of creativity, for example: father of the fingers = thumb; soul of the hand = pulse; my heart = wife; he who makes me little children = son-in-law; God's plume of feathers = rainbow; the pot is boiling = earthquake.

A European was called a "misshapen enemy" because of his clothing and armour.

500 BC. Originating from Florida or Mexico, they were much less culturally developed than the Taínos and had established small settlements along the shore, living from fishing and hunting. They had no knowledge of pottery and used shells, stone or wood as basic tools. Their diet appears to have consisted of fish, reptiles and wild fruit, since they practised no settled agriculture.

These small primitive communities were soon absorbed or replaced by the Taínos, who came to dominate the whole of the Greater

CIGAR SMOKERS

The Taínos grew tobacco and used a pipe which was forked with two prongs that they inserted in to their nostrils; or they rolled the leaves up into cigars.

Amerindian lifestyle

The Taínos who welcomed Columbus ashore were by no means "savages". They lived in a structured social community, revolving around extended families and grouped into settlements of about a thousand people, normally situated by rivers or on the seashore. Each village had a chief or *cacique*, who doubled as a priest and local law-maker. It was a hereditary position, normally occupied by a man, but women could also be *caciques*. These chiefs were supported

Antilles, with the exception of western Cuba, by about 1200.

So it was that the Taínos had probably inhabited Ayiti for only two or three centuries before Columbus's expedition arrived. The Caribs, meanwhile, were not far behind, having reached what is now Puerto Rico. They were already launching raids across the 100-km (60-mile) passage separating the two islands and would almost certainly have overrun Ayiti in due course.

LEFT: an image of Taíno life, the Museo del Hombre Dominicano, Santo Domingo.
ABOVE LEFT: cabinet detail.
ABOVE RIGHT: Taíno petroglyphs.

and advised by a council of elders, who helped organise communal work according to age and sex. The villages were loosely structured into district chiefdoms, each one ruled by a prominent local *cacique*, which in turn were grouped into regional chiefdoms, headed by the most important district chief.

These tight-knit and ordered communities lived in permanent villages, consisting of large houses made of wood and thatch. Several related families might share such a dwelling, known as a *bohío*. Land was owned and worked communally, and the Taínos were accomplished farmers, raising sweet potatoes, peanuts and beans. Their staple was cassava or manioc which provided a flour for baking after the poisonous juices had been extracted. The surrounding sea and unpolluted rivers were full of fish and turtles, while birds and small animals were hunted and cooked on a *barbacoa* – one of the few Taíno words that still survive today *(see box on page 24)*.

These peaceful Amerindians were seemingly also religious, worshipping a trinity of gods: a male figure associated with cassava and volcanoes; a female fertility god related to the sea and the moon; and a dog-like deity whose role it was to look after the recently deceased. These divinities existed alongside a collective belief in

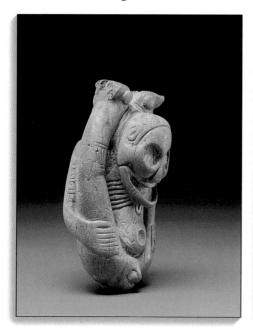

the spiritual power of nature and dead ancestors. Such forces were worshipped in the form of *zemís*, fetishes made from the remains of the dead or from wood, stone and cotton. The *cacique* also played the role of shaman or priest, presiding over religious ceremonies with the help of a sort of hallucinogenic snuff.

Keen ball-players

Skilled potters and accomplished house- and boat-builders, the Taínos were also enthusiastic about games, especially a team sport played with a rubber ball on a court called a *batey*. Columbus and his followers were amazed at the sight of not only a bouncing ball, but of

rival teams of 10 to 30 players propelling the ball to and fro without using feet or hands. These sports grounds were also used for dancing and rituals related to deaths and marriages.

Paradise lost

It is perhaps too easy to romanticise the existence of the pre-Columbian inhabitants of Ayiti and other Caribbean islands, but there is no doubt that their life before the Europeans' arrival was an idyll compared to what was to follow. Across the Americas the "encounter" between indigenous peoples and colonising cultures was to produce terrible dislocations and

human suffering, but nowhere was this process as devastating as on the island that Columbus claimed for Spain on 12 December 1492. The name he gave it was La Isla Española, "the Spanish island", or Hispaniola.

The motives behind Columbus's audacious transatlantic expedition are well known, but nonetheless complex in their ambiguity. The desire to find an alternative to the overland route to Asia, hence bypassing Turkish Muslim control of the eastern Mediterranean, was spurred by the knowledge that contemporary Europe craved the silk, spices and other luxury goods to be found in "the Indies". In this sense, Columbus's project was a simple business proposal, supported financially by powerful bankers from his native Genoa and given official sanction by King Ferdinand and Queen Isabela of Spain. The "Catholic Monarchs" also backed the scheme because they were aware that the rival Iberian power, Portugal, was pulling ahead in the race to reach the Indies by sea.

There was also an ideological dimension to the Spanish involvement. The expulsion of the Moors from southern Spain in early 1492 ushered in a mood of militant

> ### ENRICHING IDEAL...
>
> "Gold is most excellent; he who possesses it may do what he will in the world, and may so attain as to bring souls to Paradise."
>
> — CHRISTOPHER COLUMBUS

by his and subsequent expeditions and the title of "Admiral of the Ocean Sea".

Driven by a blend of political, pecuniary and personal goals, the tiny fleet of the *Santa María*, the *Pinta* and the *Niña* set sail from Palos in southern Spain on 4 August 1492, reached the Canary Islands a few days later and set off into the unknown on 6 September. Thirty-seven days later, after a period of unimaginable doubts and hopes, the expedition arrived at Guanahani in the Bahamas, an island that Columbus

Christianity, and Columbus's assurance that the wealth he found could finance a new crusade to re-conquer the Holy Land fell on receptive ears. He also pledged that his expedition would force the conversion of any "heathens" it encountered along the way.

Columbus sets sail

Among this mix of economic and spiritual considerations stood the explorer's own personal ambitions: 10 percent of all riches brought back

FAR LEFT: an anthropomorphic inhalator made from manatee bone.
LEFT AND ABOVE: Taínos welcomed the Spanish ships.

promptly renamed San Salvador. There, the Europeans were greeted by hospitable Taínos, who informed them that the source of the gold jewellery they wore lay further to the south. "All the inhabitants could be taken away to Castile, or made slaves on the island," noted Columbus. "With fifty men we could subjugate them all and make them do whatever we want."

Believing himself to be in some remote outpost of Japan, Columbus was rather disappointed by the simplicity of Taíno culture and the conspicuous absence of wealth. The expedition pushed on around the coast of Cuba, where first impressions were no more promising, finally arriving off Ayiti two months after the first landfall in San Salvador. It was Ayiti's fortune – or misfortune – to provide the first permanent European settlement in the Americas, for on Christmas Eve 1492, the *Santa María* foundered on a reef off the north coast and Columbus decided to salvage its timbers and build a fort.

A warm welcome

The local Taínos, under their *cacique* Guacanagarí, willingly helped these strange newcomers with rescuing the ship's stores (Columbus was amazed that "not a lace

point" was stolen) and welcomed the construction of Puerto de La Navidad – Christmas Port – on their beach. Their generosity seemed boundless, and a garrison of 39 Europeans eagerly volunteered to stay on the island and collect what gold they could and search for potential mines, while Columbus returned to Spain to mount another expedition.

Leaving Diego de Araña, a trusted associate, in charge of La Navidad, Columbus set sail in early January. Before he left the island, however, he had a brief and violent encounter with another Taíno community at the eastern end of the island, at the Bay of Samaná. Here, attempts to trade European beads and trinkets for the

> **HIGH PRICES**
>
> The Taínos were made to collect a regular amount of gold dust for the Spanish colonists. If they failed, they were either executed or had their hands cut off.

Amerindians' powerful bows and arrows ended in a deadly battle, with the Taínos fleeing "surprised at our courage and the wounds made by our weapons".

Spanish steel and primitive artillery were infinitely more destructive than any weaponry owned by the Taínos, and it may be that this in part accounted for their initial docility. But Taíno patience, it seems, had its limits, for when Columbus eventually returned to La Navidad in November 1493 he found the fort burned down and the entire garrison dead or missing. Guacanagarí explained that his people had not been responsible for the attack, but that another, more powerful *cacique*, Caonabo, had ordered the massacre as a reprisal for the Europeans' violent demands for food, women and gold.

First Spanish settlement

In the meantime, Columbus had returned to Spain to a hero's welcome, telling exaggerated tales of the gold and other riches he had found in what he still took to be some part of Asia. With royal encouragement and a new coat of arms ("To Castile and León Columbus gave a New World"), he was quickly able to organise a second expedition. This fleet of 17 ships carried 1,200 men, animals, seeds and sugar cane shoots; it was an embryonic colonising force, lightly armed and including several priests. Some 200 *hidalgos* or Spanish gentlemen joined the voyage at their own expense, attracted by the prospect of easy wealth.

Finding La Navidad in ashes and relations with the Taínos uneasy, Columbus nonetheless proceeded with his plans for establishing a colony. Founding a settlement named La Isabela near the present-day Dominican town of Puerto Plata, he sent prospectors inland to look for gold nuggets in the Cibao area, where the trusting Taínos had directed him.

So began the first European gold rush in the Americas and with it the first genocide of the modern era. "In all the world no better people," Columbus had said of the Taínos. Within half a century, the indigenous inhabitants of Hispaniola were extinct. ❑

LEFT: gold was abundant in South America.
RIGHT: the Taínos were enslaved to mine for gold.

IN SPANISH HANDS

In Spain's rush for gold and silver, Hispaniola's prosperity rose and fell, destroying the Amerindians in the process. And then the buccaneers moved in...

Hispaniola, so the tourist board slogan goes, was "the land Columbus loved best". But even if the explorer is remembered today as the individual responsible for the first European settlement in the Americas, his influence on the first Spanish colony was nothing short of disastrous. In the modern-day Dominican Republic, superstitious souls prefer not to mention the name of Columbus, for it is widely reputed to carry a *fukú* – a curse.

For the seven years since the second expedition of 1493, the European presence on the island had been dominated by Columbus and two of his brothers, Diego and Bartolomé, and plagued by internal squabbling and violence. Much of this violence was directed against the increasingly hostile Taínos, who, after the destruction of the fort at La Navidad, were openly treated as enemies.

The Spaniards' futile quest for gold, when they discovered that the gold fields of the Cibao had been a mirage, together with their cruel treatment of the Taínos, intensified the situation. In 1495 a Taíno uprising was easily put down by the Spanish, who shipped 500 captives to Seville as slaves. Most died en route or within weeks of arriving in Europe.

Unpopular Columbus brothers

In 1496 Bartolomé decided to abandon the pestilential settlement of Isabela in favour of a new location on the south coast, where he founded La Nueva Isabela, soon to be renamed Santo Domingo. But by now the settlers were restless, suspicious that Columbus's claims had been largely wishful thinking. Even the relocation of the main settlement was viewed as some sort of scheme, designed to reinforce the Columbus brothers' power. An open revolt broke out, led by the former mayor of Isabela, Francisco Roldán, who accused them of monopolising the island's wealth. Desperate to quell dissent, Columbus agreed to share out

land and Amerindian labourers among the colonists in a system known as the *repartimiento*, each being entitled to a number of Taíno villages according to his status.

But disappointment and frustration continued to fuel resentment against Columbus, and in 1500 the Spanish Crown, alarmed at reports

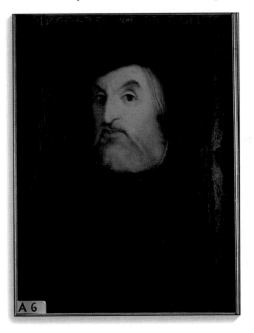

of unrest in its new possession, sent out a commissioner, Francisco de Bobadilla, to investigate. On his arrival, he was met with the scene of seven Spaniards hanging from the gallows. Pardoning any others accused of treachery by Columbus, he arrested the three brothers and sent them back in chains to Seville. Columbus would only see Hispaniola once more, in 1504, as his fourth and final voyage ended in debacle.

Growth of Santo Domingo

In the wake of Bobadilla's intervention, 2,500 more colonists arrived, as well as a new governor, Nicolás de Ovando. Under Ovando, the settlement of Santo Domingo took on the

---

LEFT: a memorial to Columbus, Santo Domingo.
RIGHT: the conquistador Hernán Cortés.

appearance of a town, with stone buildings and the beginnings of a grid system of streets spreading up from the Ozama River.

At the same time, the exploitation of the Taínos continued apace, but with some modifications. Dropping Columbus's *repartimiento* system, he introduced the *encomienda* model of forced labour, in which entire communities, under the leadership of their *cacique*, were allotted to settlers as feudal serfs or chattels. In return for working for six to eight months a year, the Taínos were supposedly protected by their master or *encomendero*, who was also in charge of their spiritual well-being.

deference to her status. By the time Ovando's governorship ended in 1509, there were fewer than 60,000 Taínos left.

Capital of the Indies

The Columbus connection did not disappear with Christopher's death, for Ovando's successor was Diego Columbus, the explorer's eldest son. He arrived in the colony, convinced that he was entitled to the share of wealth negotiated with the Spanish Crown by his late father. As Governor (1509–15) and then Viceroy of the Indies (1520–24), Diego regarded Hispaniola as a family business, to be exploited at will. He

Brutal repression

This system was perhaps marginally more benign than Columbus's wholesale enslavement policy, but it did little to reverse the Taíno genocide. Indeed, Ovando's repression of Taíno resistance was even more brutal than what had occurred before. In 1503, for example, Anacaona, the female *cacique* and widow of Caonabo (who had died in captivity in 1494), invited Ovando to a meeting of Taíno chiefs in the southwestern kingdom of Xaraguá. When the 80 or so *caciques* were assembled in Anacaona's longhouse, Ovando ordered his men to burn down the building with the Taínos inside. Anacaona was hanged, apparently in

liberally handed out *encomiendas* to himself and his friends and supporters and established one of the first sugar plantations on the island, on the outskirts of Santo Domingo.

The *nouveau-riche* Diego also had aristocratic pretensions, having married María de Toledo, a member of the Spanish nobility; he was determined to command appropriate respect. During his periods in power, he presided over the rapid development of the city of Santo Domingo, adding many fine and imposing buildings to those left behind by Ovando. His own *alcázar* or palace, a beautiful two-storey residence on the river bank, was the centre of the Spanish New World empire, acting as administrative headquarters and focus for the colonial elite's social life. Nearby, work began on the first cathedral in the Americas, Diego having laid the foundation stone in 1514.

For a brief period, Santo Domingo was a place of power and prestige. It witnessed a series of architectural firsts: the first permanent hospital in the New World; the first university; the first overseas royal mint. It was the seat of a *Audiencia Real*, a court of appeal answerable directly to the Spanish

ENRIQUILLO'S REVOLT

In 1519, the chieftain Enriquillo led his *encomienda* in a successful revolt, fleeing into the mountains. They stayed there, giving shelter to other runaways and were eventually "pardoned" by the Spanish Crown.

the island, while the rapidly dwindling Taíno population was forced into makeshift villages, theoretically supervised by an *encomendero* but usually neglected. An attempt to bring this rudimentary system under some sort of control failed when priests from the Hieronymite order, dispatched from Spain to oversee a humane reform of the *encomiendas*, met with little cooperation from the colonists. In any case, a devastating smallpox epidemic in 1519 put paid to any prospect of stemming the

Crown and it was soon the base for a growing cast of imperial bureaucrats – military, administrative and ecclesiastical. Religious orders arrived from Spain, establishing their own institutions and teaching centres. Here grew the embryo of Spain's future Latin American empire.

The Church intervenes

Yet outside this tiny enclave, Hispaniola was all but uninhabited. A handful of tiny villages and a few rough settlements connected by mule tracks were dotted around the eastern half of

LEFT: the capture of Amerindian *cacique* Caonabo.
ABOVE: an artist's impression of old Santo Domingo.

Taíno death toll; 3,000 at most survived, pushing them further to the brink of extinction.

By now, the Church was closely involved in the controversy surrounding the treatment of the Taínos and the resulting labour shortage. Mounting official disquiet over Diego Columbus's activities had led to his recall to Spain, but after a five-year period he was seemingly forgiven. In 1520, he returned to a colony where the primitive gold mines were yielding little wealth to their disillusioned owners, and where the economy revolved around little more than informal ranching. Vast areas of otherwise unoccupied land had been turned over to cattle, which often escaped into the wilderness.

Birth of the sugar industry

But one commodity did seem to promise a brighter future: sugar. The cane shoots that Christopher Columbus had transported from the Canary Islands in 1493 had prospered in Hispaniola's fertile soil, and some colonists saw that Europe's insatiable appetite for sugar, sharpened by a shortage of supplies from the Middle East, could be turned to their advantage.

One fundamental problem stood in their way, however: with the decline of the Taínos, there was no available labour to be deployed on the plantations. It was at this point that the colonists and the authorities in Spain began to take notice

of the Dominican friar, Bartolomé de Las Casas, and other advocates of indigenous rights, since he had perhaps inadvertently suggested the solution to their problem. Enslavement of the Spanish Crown's subjects, he had argued, was intolerable, but a Christian conscience could allow "heathens", particularly black Africans, to be used as slaves.

The religious rationalisation of black slavery was nothing new; Portuguese traders had been selling African slaves in Spain since the 1450s, but they were mainly employed as domestic servants and exotic status symbols. Black slave labour was also a feature of the sugar industry in the Canary Islands later in the century. The Catholic Church tolerated this system, as it considered that Africans could be converted to Christianity in the process, and so the Spanish Crown began to allot contracts, known as *asientos*, to those merchants who could guarantee a steady supply of slaves to the New World colonies.

A new slave labour force

In 1518 King Charles V contracted a Court favourite, Lorenzo de Gomenot, to ship 4,000 Africans across the Atlantic each year. According to Las Casas (a man sometimes given to exaggeration), some 30,000 black slaves had entered Hispaniola by 1540. The first slave revolt, meanwhile, was reported in 1522 – on the sugar plantation of Diego Columbus. The slaves, armed with sticks and stones, were massacred by the colony's militia in response.

The early sugar industry faced other difficulties. A lack of expertise, technology and capital created huge problems for the first planters,

---

PROTECTORS OF THE AMERINDIANS

At Christmas in 1511, Antón de Montesinos, a Dominican friar, delivered an unexpected and fiery rebuke to the assembled Spanish congregation in Santo Domingo. "By what authority," he asked, "have you made such detestable wars against these people who lived peacefully and gently on their own lands?" The outraged colonists demanded the plain-speaking priest's immediate return to Spain, where he pleaded directly at the Royal Court for better treatment of the Taínos.

Montesinos's sermon inspired another priest, Bartolomé de Las Casas (1474–1566), who had arrived in Hispaniola in 1502 and had witnessed the Taíno genocide. He renounced his own *encomienda*, realising that the system was inhumane and spent the rest of his life championing the Amerindians' cause. He wrote the hugely influential *A Very Brief Account of the Destruction of the Indies* (1551), and caused deep embarrassment and concern in Spain, where few were aware of the extent of the indigenous disaster.

In theory, the Taínos were subjects of the Spanish Crown, and what had originally been presented as an exercise in evangelisation had in fact resulted in wholesale slaughter. The reforms that followed were too few and came too late, but Las Casas is remembered as the "protector of the Indians" and defender of human rights.

who had to rely on man- or mule-powered mills to crush the cane. But gradually innovations such as the water-powered *ingenio* (mill) began to improve productivity, as did the arrival of skilled workers from the Canary Islands, encouraged by the Spanish authorities.

By 1523 there were 20 *ingenios* and in 1542 Hispaniola recorded exports of 1,200 tons of semi-refined sugar loaves to Spain. According to the contemporary historian and military man, Gonzalo Fernández de Oviedo, there was money to be made, for "there is no island or kingdom among Christians or pagans where there is anything like this industry of sugar."

expedition reached Mexico, from where rumours of vast silver and gold fortunes trickled back to the islands. As the Spanish Empire extended along the Central American isthmus and into South America, Hispaniola held few attractions for the would-be *conquistador*. Its Spanish population, never large, began to shrink from a peak of 14,000 to a mere 5,000 in the 1570s.

Spanish bureaucracy

If Mexico promised instant wealth, Hispaniola was increasingly stifled by Spanish bureaucracy. All trade had to be conducted through the port of Seville, where the state's percent-

Further conquests

However profitable sugar might have been, many Spanish colonists had bolder ambitions. From the outset, Hispaniola had served as a springboard for further conquests: Jamaica (1509); Cuba (1511); Puerto Rico (1512). But as the gold rush swiftly faded, the lure of new horizons became even more irresistible.

Hernán Cortés (1485–1547) was one such adventurer who was unprepared to settle for the humdrum life of a sugar planter. In 1519, his

LEFT: the sugar industry encouraged slavery.
ABOVE: Fray Bartolomé de Las Casas championed the Amerindian cause, Museo de las Casas Reales.

age of gold or sugar was deducted in a special warehouse. All imports into the island came from there, too, but with irritating irregularity. Spain was determined to prevent any other European nation from trading with her New World possessions, and her monopoly was jealously defended with a heavy naval presence, which accompanied the trading galleons across the Atlantic.

Heavily taxed, constantly regulated and yet subject to unreliable supplies, many of the colonists – particularly those who had been born on the island – began to resent the royal stranglehold on trade and the dominance of Spanish functionaries, the *peninsulares*.

Pirates and privateers

By the 1550s, Hispaniola had slipped into a gentle decline. The focus of Spanish activity had shifted to the mainland colonies and the former capital of "the Indies" was largely an irrelevance. As Santo Domingo languished, the Cuban port of Havana grew in importance as the place where the Spanish fleets, laden with bullion from Peru and Mexico, assembled before returning to Europe.

Spanish investment in fortifications poured into Cuba, while Santo Domingo was neglected. The city retained some administrative importance as the seat of the *Audiencia Real* but, in general, life was hard and unrewarding for most colonists. An earthquake in 1562 levelled the few settlements on the north coast, adding to the exodus of disillusioned settlers.

Meanwhile, an even greater threat to the colony was materialising in the shape of the pirates and privateers who began to infest the Caribbean from the 1530s onwards. Since Columbus's first discoveries and the ensuing Treaty of Tordesillas (1494), which had given papal backing to the division of the New World between Catholic Spain and Portugal, other European nations had been following developments closely. England, in particular, was

opposed to any Spanish monopoly of the Americas, while France was also determined to claim its own share of whatever wealth was to be found across the Atlantic. However, the first non-Spanish interlopers were not official navies, but pirates, more often than not operating with the blessing of their government and intent on seizing as much Spanish loot as they could.

Whether privateers (those at sea during times of war and carrying official commissions) or pirates (common criminals), this new breed of maritime terrorist spread panic throughout the Spanish colonies, plundering both ships and settlements on land. In the 1560s, English pirates ransacked what was left of Hispaniola's north coast, forcing the authorities to evacuate the area altogether. Sometimes, however, these sea-borne aggressors could offer a service of sorts, for many of them also worked as smugglers. The traumatised inhabitants of the north coast were relieved and delighted, for instance, to buy 300 African slaves from the English captain John Hawkins, a former pirate, in 1562.

Spain loses its grip

Once the Spanish New World monopoly was breached, Spain's European enemies began to give more serious thought to establishing their own Caribbean colonies. Spain, after all, was

Encouraged by Spanish weakness and the potential of her own sugar industry, England pushed harder against this half-open door. To the consternation of Madrid, an English expedition, dispatched by Cromwell as his "Western Design", took Jamaica with comparative ease in 1655. The English had previously attempted to attack Hispaniola, but had failed through their own conspicuous incompetence. With the capture of Jamaica, the balance of power in the Caribbean tilted further away from Spain.

Cromwell's force may have failed to capture Hispaniola, but Spain's grip on her first colony

over-stretched economically and militarily, often at war in Europe and unable to fend off the swarms of pirates who preyed on the bullion-heavy and vulnerable galleons.

At first, at the beginning of the 17th century, the newcomers settled in the smaller islands of the Lesser Antilles: the English taking St Kitts, Barbados and Antigua; the French claiming Martinique and Guadeloupe. Although, in theory, Spain owned these islands, it did little to prevent their loss.

LEFT: Sir Francis Drake's fleet sails into Santo Domingo.
ABOVE: many battles were fought in the Caribbean.
RIGHT: buccaneers took over as Spanish control waned.

was becoming increasingly feeble and an English and French presence on the island's north coast had been growing steadily.

A base for buccaneers

The new settlers were mainly buccaneers, the successors to the pirates of the previous century, but different in that they were permanently based in the region. Taking their name from the indigenous word *boucan*, the wood-fuelled barbecue pit over which they cooked and smoked strips of wild cattle or pigs, these men were a tough and hard-living mix of deserters, runaway servants or shipwrecked sailors.

Making a living from piracy and smuggling, they first established a base on the offshore island of Tortuga (today La Tortue), from where they could attack Spanish shipping. Attempts to drive them away failed, and by the 1650s they had moved on to the no-man's land of northern Hispaniola, growing maize and tobacco, and ranching.

Piracy was by now a risky business, and many buccaneers opted for a more settled life. As the English buccaneers drifted off to the "pirate

> ### A BUCCANEERING LIFE
>
> There were few female buccaneers and many men lived in pairs, adopting a sort of marriage arrangement known as *matelotage*, possibly as a quasi-legal way of dealing with property rights in the event of death.

capital" of Port Royal, Jamaica, the north coast settlements became overwhelmingly French.

The French move in

With the Spanish unable, or unwilling, to rid themselves of these unwelcome visitors, the northwest of the island became a *de facto* French colony called Saint Domingue. By 1664, it had been incorporated into the French charter. A governor was duly sent from Paris, and the settlement took more permanent shape, with the founding of several port towns. Eventually, the 1697 Treaty of Ryswick officially ceded the western part of the island to France, a paper transaction that merely formalised a *fait accom-*

pli and confirmed Spain's increasingly tenuous presence in the region. The island was henceforth divided, albeit unequally, into what history would reveal as two ill-fitting pieces.

Pearl of the Antilles

The spectacular rise of Saint Domingue was unparalleled in 18th-century colonial history. Within a century, a lawless and backward outpost had been transformed into the most prosperous colony in the world. Where the Spanish side of the island had stagnated for a century or more, the French territory boomed, spurred on by massive state and private investment.

Irrigation was brought to 40,000 hectares (100,000 acres) of land in the 1740s, sponsored by the French government; the latest technology was employed in milling and transporting the sugar cargoes that sailed back to France. Although sugar dominated, there were other lucrative export crops: indigo, cocoa, coffee and cotton.

Saint Domingue gradually became a place of grotesque social extremes. A small cast of white landowners, the *grands blancs*, lived in aristocratic luxury. Towns like the capital Cap Français, Port-au-Prince and Jacmel grew up around the coast, offering all the amenities of European cities. Theatres were founded, newspapers and books were printed, prostitutes, dance halls and gambling dens proliferated.

But this élite's decadent lifestyle depended on the forced labour of a huge majority of black slaves, who arrived at the average annual rate of about 8,000 throughout the 18th century. Brutalised and exploited by a middle stratum of *petit blanc* overseers, these slaves, torn from a number of different West African nations, were the motor of Saint Domingue's economy.

A rigidly hierarchical social structure, based on skin colour and, to a lesser extent, money, grew up: the wealthy planters on top, the poor whites and a minority of mixed-race people in the middle, and the black slaves, locally born or freshly imported, at the bottom. It was a recipe for spectacular profits and dramatic growth. It was also a recipe for disaster. ❑

LEFT: preparing indigo.
RIGHT: several religious men criticised Taíno abuse.

SANTO DOMINGO:
LLAVE, PUERTA Y ESCALA
DE TODAS LAS INDIAS.
FELIPE II

REVOLUTION AND NATIONHOOD

Inspired by the French Revolution, Saint Domingue exploded while Santo Domingo profited. The ensuing turmoil led to independence...

On the eve of the 1789–95 French Revolution, Saint Domingue stood as a monument to European imperialism. It was, wrote historian C.L.R. James, "the most prosperous colony the world had ever known; to the casual eye the most flourishing and prosperous possession on the face of the globe."

In 1787, the territory exported 87,000 tons of sugar, more than all British Caribbean colonies combined. Saint Domingue was also the world's leading producer of coffee. The vast sugar plantations that spread over the fertile northern plain produced fortunes for a few thousand white landowners; in the hilly south, coffee and indigo were grown on smaller holdings. A never-ending succession of ships called at the colony's ports, delivering luxury goods for the planters and salt fish for the slaves before returning to Europe loaded with "white gold".

Tensions in Saint Domingue

Other ships unloaded African slaves: 27,000 in 1786, 40,000 the following year. In 1789, an estimated half million slaves worked in Saint Domingue, the death toll through exhaustion and ill treatment accounting for the annual import of fresh labour. The rest of the population numbered some 40,000 whites, most of them humble tradesmen, administrators or military personnel, and a further 30,000 free coloureds, the result of illicit, often forced, encounters between white men and enslaved women.

All sectors of society hated and feared each other; the whites disdained their coloured offspring, the mulattos envied the whites and despised the blacks. The blacks, meanwhile, awaited the day when they could take their revenge on their oppressors. Attempted slave revolts, escapes, the poisoning of animals and sometimes humans were commonplace.

In 1758, an enslaved man named Mackandal planned to begin an uprising by poisoning the water supply of hundreds of planters; he was betrayed and burned at the stake. The colony lived in constant fear of the slaves.

Santo Domingo recovers

In contrast, Spanish Santo Domingo was greatly poorer but altogether less explosive.

After the decline in the colony's fortunes, it had recovered somewhat in the second half of the 18th century, its population rising from a mere 6,000 in 1740 to 100,000 in 1780. Its modest prosperity was mainly due to the fortunes of neighbouring Saint Domingue, which imported beef and other foodstuffs.

But its social and ethnic composition was entirely different; immigrants from the Canary Islands arrived in large numbers, while black slaves accounted for at most 30 percent of the population. A colony of large ranches and scattered towns, it was a world apart from the industrial-scale plantation system across the mountainous border.

LEFT: Inigo Barlow depicts the revenge of the black army on the French oppressors.
RIGHT: the colonists lived in fear of slave revolts.

The storm breaks

When news of the French Revolution filtered back to Saint Domingue, each sector of society interpreted these distant events according to its own interests. The *grands blancs* were hardly in favour of social revolution, but they believed they could capitalise on disarray in Paris to obtain greater autonomy and a relaxation of the state's control over colonial trade. The free blacks and mulattos felt that the time had come to grab equal rights with the whites, while the slaves absorbed the message of liberty and equality, if not fraternity, entirely literally.

The mulattos were the first to act; an insur-

plantations of the north were reduced to ashes, and a thick pall of smoke covered Cap Français. The colonial militia fought back, and according to the Jamaican planter and witness Bryan Edwards, some 2,000 whites and 10,000 slaves were killed within two months. As the situation grew desperate in the north, a mulatto uprising broke out in the south, while in Port-au-Prince a mob of self-styled revolutionary poor whites went on the rampage.

Into this chaotic state of near civil war sailed an expeditionary force of 6,000 French troops in September 1792. Led by a triumvirate of revolutionary commissioners, its aim was to

rection broke out in mid-1790, led by the black Paris-educated Vincent Ogé, calling for immediate equality of political rights. The uprising was brutally crushed, and Ogé and his associates were tortured and executed, strengthening hostility between the white and mulatto minorities. Increasingly apprehensive, the planters and their political allies contemplated asking for protection from the British.

On 22 August 1791, the storm finally broke, when a secret meeting of slave leaders unleashed the long-awaited insurrection and an orgy of violence. According to legend, the meeting was presided over by Boukmann, a *houngan* or Voodoo priest. Within days the

quell the anarchy by offering equal rights to the mulattos. For the slaves, however, there was nothing on offer. Both Spain and Britain, meanwhile, had been following events closely; the British had long coveted the fantastically profitable colony, and Spanish troops were assembled across the border, ready to reclaim the territory given away in 1697.

Toussaint – a cunning leader

It was at this critical stage that the slaves' main leader, Toussaint L'Ouverture (*circa* 1742–1803), displayed his instinctive genius for strategy. Unexpectedly allying his force of 4,000 men with the Spanish commander, he had no illusions that reactionary Spain would grant the slaves freedom, but realised that this move would place increasing pressure on the beleaguered French commissioners. His guess proved to be right, for in August 1793, the principal commissioner Sonthonax, hemmed in by white counter-revolutionaries and the threat of foreign invasion, unilaterally decreed the abolition of slavery.

Within weeks Toussaint had turned against the Spanish and joined forces with the republican French, aware now that the overwhelming threat to the black majority came from a British force that had landed in September at the south-

succumbed to yellow fever. In 1798, after the recall of Sonthonax, the French commissioner, to Paris and the departure of Maitland's surviving troops, Toussaint was finally able to crush the mulatto insurgence in the south.

By 1800 Toussaint was undisputed master of Saint Domingue, nominally governor-general of a French colony, but in reality ruler of what was really an independent country. He made trade agreements with the United States, encouraged investment in education based on new taxes and urged the ex-slaves to return to the plantations as free labourers. He even courted the remaining white planters (most had

ern port of Jérémie. For their part, the white planters welcomed General Thomas Maitland's expedition as their last hope of re-establishing slavery and ridding the colony of revolutionaries.

In 1795 Spain and France made peace at the Treaty of Bâle and Spain ceded control of Santo Domingo to the French. With the Spanish out of contention, Toussaint turned his attention to the British, who had made an effective start to their campaign, taking Port-au-Prince in June 1794. But this was to be the extent of their success as the British forces

LEFT: revolution on Saint Domingue cost many lives.
ABOVE: English ships sail into the harbour.

TOUSSAINT AND NAPOLEON

Toussaint L'Ouverture's authority was intolerable to Napoleon Bonaparte, who had emerged from France's revolutionary turmoil as First Consul. He was prepared neither to put up with the secession of the most valuable French colony nor to accept a challenge from those he derided as "gilded Africans".

Perhaps spurred on by his wife, the Empress Joséphine, the daughter of a white, slave-owning Martinican family, he sent an imposing force of 22,000 troops to Saint Domingue in December 1801. Their objectives were to remove Toussaint, restore French rule and ultimately to re-impose slavery.

fled during the previous decade to Cuba, Trinidad or other islands), inviting them to help rebuild the shattered economy.

But his rule was also harsh; critics and opponents were not tolerated, and an army of 20,000 forced many back to work. For a short while, Saint Domingue resumed its exports of sugar and coffee, albeit at two-thirds the 1789 levels.

However, Napoleon Bonaparte was not happy with the situation and in 1801 set about restoring the pre-revolutionary

and galvanised the former slaves once more. A fresh insurrection in the north gathered in strength, while yellow fever made its inevitable reappearance. Under the leadership of battle-hardened veterans such as Jean-Jacques Dessalines (1758–1806) and Henri Christophe (1767– 1820), the black fighters began to pin the French down. "It is not enough to have taken away Toussaint", wrote Napoleon's brother-in-law, General Victor-Emmanuel Leclerc, before he died of yellow

status quo. At first, the French appeared to face few serious obstacles. Lured by promises of promotion, some of Toussaint's officers defected, and guerrilla resistance to the massive French military presence soon fizzled out. In June 1802, Toussaint was captured and shipped back to France, warning that the people of Saint Domingue would rise up again.

Black retaliation

A strange stalemate followed. But in July news reached the island that French forces had restored slavery in Guadeloupe, having overthrown the mulatto-dominated government. The revelation confirmed Toussaint's warnings

fever, "there are 2,000 leaders to be taken away." By this time, 24,000 French troops out of a total of 34,000 had died.

French hopes finally faded when hostilities with Britain resumed in May 1803 and the prospect of reinforcements evaporated. Fighting a savage and futile campaign, Leclerc's successor, General Rochambeau, set man-eating dogs on his enemies and turned on the mulattos. Such desperation merely strengthened the black army's resolve, and the fanatical, white-hating Dessalines led a scorched-earth campaign that cut French supply lines and reduced the colony to ashes. *Koupe tèt, boule kay* ("cut off heads, burn down houses") was Dessalines' motto, and his troops wreaked vengeance on the few remaining whites and the tattered remains of the Napoleonic war machine. On 7 April 1803, coincidentally the date of Toussaint's death, Dessalines had ripped the white section from the French *tricolore*, creating the flag of a new nation, symbolically purged of the white oppressor. In November, Rochambeau's men could take no more and, like the British before them, evacuated the island.

Independent Haiti

The birth of Haiti was as sudden as the death of Saint Domingue was lingering. On 1 January 1804, General Dessalines declared the island's independence, restoring the Taíno-derived name meaning "land of high mountains".

"I have given the French cannibals blood for blood", said the country's first ruler, and his constitution expressly forbade *blancs* (foreigners) to own land or property in the new state. It was a nation born in ruins: after 13 years of conflict a huge army of ex-slaves, without land or work, roamed the devastated landscape.

The outside world was either thrilled or appalled by the creation of the world's first black republic. For liberals and abolitionists, it seemed to prove that the oppressed could triumph over tyranny, that slavery's days were numbered. But for the colonial powers and slave societies throughout the Americas, the world's only successful slave revolution offered a fearful example of what could happen elsewhere. As a result, independent Haiti was to be shunned by much of the international community and reviled as a place of unmitigated savagery, as proof that blacks could never be trusted to rule themselves.

The first decades of Haitian independence did not augur well for the country's future. Following Napoleon's example, the autocratic Dessalines declared himself emperor in October 1804. Within two years he was dead, shot by mutinous mulatto officers after a brief and bloodthirsty reign. Dessalines was succeeded by Henri Christophe, a former hotel waiter turned military commander, who, as King Henri I, became the first monarch in the Americas. An eccentric mix of reformer and megalomaniac, Christophe tried to introduce a European-style education system, while imitating court life and surrounding himself with dukes and counts. His most lasting monument is the vast Citadelle Laferrière, a massive fortress built near what had been renamed Cap Haïtien to repel any future French invasion.

By now, the old enmities between north and south, between black and mulatto, had resurfaced. Under the leadership of Alexandre Pétion, the south of Haiti effectively broke away from Christophe's kingdom, forming a separate republic. This bizarre division lasted until 1820, when Pétion's successor, the mulatto General Jean-Pierre Boyer (1776–1850) reunified the

country after Christophe's suicide in the face of a popular uprising. Amid constant power struggles, Haiti remained a country at arms. Independence had been won by force, and the generals continued to wield overwhelming influence well into the 19th century.

In the meantime, the old colonial plantation system crumbled away and the estates were divided up into smallholdings, turning Haiti into a nation of small farmers. And as the rural landscape changed, two separate worlds evolved: that of the peasantry, black, Creole-speaking and mostly illiterate far removed from the towns; and that of the mulatto elite, urban, French-speaking and educated.

LEFT: *Dessalines rides in,* by Philomé Obin.
ABOVE: Henri Christophe ends it all.

Birth of the Dominican Republic

When the French were driven out of Saint Domingue in 1803, they retained a presence in Santo Domingo until 1809 and the *partie de l'est* (eastern part) was returned to Spanish ownership. It was a state of affairs that seemingly neither Spain nor the colonists wanted, and a chaotic period, known as *España Boba* ("silly Spain") followed, in which ineffectual governors tried half-heartedly to impose colonial rule, including slavery, on an increasingly restless population.

In 1821, as anti-colonial movements took root in Spanish South America, a group of

notables proclaimed the territory's independence, choosing the name of Spanish Haiti and asking Simón Bolívar whether they could join his projected *Gran Colombia* federation. They never received a reply, and instead, in February 1822, Haiti's President Boyer led an army into Santo Domingo. It was to stay there for 22 years.

Haitian occupation

Even today, Dominicans are taught that the Haitian occupation was an extended nightmare of brutality. The truth, however, may be slightly different, for although Boyer ruled firmly, the Haitians introduced long-overdue reforms, not least the abolition of slavery. Those who com-

plained loudest were the powerful land-owners, notably the Church and absentee Spaniards, who saw their properties broken up and redistributed. The bureaucrats in Santo Domingo, mostly veterans of Spanish rule, were also resentful when Haitian administrators took their place. On the whole, though, the ranch owners and tobacco growers were left alone, as Boyer recognised their usefulness to the economy.

A more widespread grievance took root from 1825, when the Haitians imposed a number of taxes on the inhabitants of Santo Domingo, to fund an agreement with France, which guaranteed recognition of Haitian sovereignty in return for compensation of 150 million francs, to be paid to the dispossessed planters of former Saint Domingue. Understandably, the Spanish-speaking population was unhappy about contributing to this vast settlement through punitive taxation, and a nationalist movement took root.

Underground movement

But freedom from Haitian rule was a long time in coming. Slowly, a group of nationalists organised a secret network that in 1838 took the name of La Trinitaria. By 1843 the underground movement had extended its influence among Santo Domingo's disgruntled youth and its leaders had settled on what to call their dreamed-of new nation: the Dominican Republic.

The plotters' task was made easier by Boyer's growing weakness. A disastrous earthquake in 1842 had levelled most of the island's north coast towns as well as the east's second city of Santiago. The looting carried out by Haitian forces had deepened hostility, while in Haiti various factions were conspiring against an increasingly corrupt Boyer.

When the veteran president was eventually shipped off to exile in Jamaica in late 1843, La Trinitaria judged the moment ripe for revolt and on the morning of 28 February 1844, the inhabitants of Santo Domingo awoke to find themselves citizens of a new country.

Again the island was divided, but now between two independent republics. This division was more than geographical; already separated by a deep sense of distrust and antipathy, as the two nations entered into a lengthy period of instability and foreign interference, they were often to be the worst of neighbours. ❑

LEFT: Spanish Haiti applied to join Bolívar's federation.

Toussaint L'Ouverture

Paintings and engravings of the period show a dashing figure, usually on horseback, clad in Napoleonic military finery, a true leader of men. Other contemporaries described him as short, ugly and ill-shaped. In his lifetime, Toussaint L'Ouverture was idolised by worldwide progressive opinion as a heroic freedom fighter; when he died, writers such as William Wordsworth and Victor Hugo commemorated his achievements. But others detested him. Napoleon vowed to crush him, and he made many enemies among his own people.

Born a slave around 1742, François Dominique Toussaint Bréda was an unlikely revolutionary. Apparently of noble descent, he was singled out by his master for privileged treatment and another slave, his godfather, taught him to read. Toussaint rose to the trusted position of coachman on the Bréda plantation, near Cap Français, then livestock steward – a position normally held by a white.

But despite his status, Toussaint was receptive to the revolutionary mood growing among the slaves. When the insurrection broke out in 1791, he first protected his master's family and ensured their escape to Cap Français before joining the rebel armies. By now, he was almost 50 and known as "old Toussaint", but he was also widely respected for his learning and wisdom. His years as a senior foreman had given him leadership qualities, but what was more unexpected was his mastery of strategy and tactics.

Throughout the decade of constant unrest that followed, Toussaint transformed an ill-disciplined and ill-equipped rabble into a lethal fighting force. His men, he said, were "as naked as earthworms", but they became formidable exponents of guerrilla warfare, hiding in the mountains. His tactical instincts led him to join forces with the Spanish against the French, only to abandon them when the French republicans abolished slavery. He allowed an epidemic of yellow fever to take its toll on the British invasion force, patiently biding his time while the disease won the war. And he outmanoeuvred his rivals and enemies, earning the nickname *l'ouverture* after the opening or weak spot that he would inevitably find.

Gallant, courteous, even something of a ladies' man, Toussaint had weaknesses as well as strengths. He enjoyed power and authority and was quick to silence critics. As governor-general, he ruled with a firmness bordering on ruthlessness. The plantations resumed production, the former slaves returned to work, any hint of further revolutionary activity was suppressed. At the same time, Toussaint was conciliatory towards the remaining whites, too much so, said his more radical critics. When his nephew, Moïse, led an uprising in protest at the continuing exploitation of the black majority, Toussaint had him shot.

According to historian C.L.R. James, Toussaint finally lost touch with the revolutionary masses, the people whom he had so successfully led and

inspired. When Napoleon's intimidating force finally arrived in late 1801, James depicts Toussaint watching the fleet approach from a mountain peak. "We shall perish. All France is come to overwhelm us", he says. From that moment onwards, the formerly self-confident leader seemed crippled by indecision and in June 1802, he was seized and bundled on to a ship bound for France.

Within a year Toussaint L'Ouverture was dead, found slumped in his chair one morning in his freezing prison cell in the Fort-de-Joux in the Jura mountains. He had written several pleading letters to Napoleon, but never received a reply. "The Black Napoleon", wrote Chateaubriand sardonically, "imitated and killed by the White Napoleon." ❑

RIGHT: a portrait of the skilful Toussaint L'Ouverture.

THE AGE OF DICTATORS

On both sides of the border, political power remained in the hands of despots,
whose tyrannical rule was driven by ferocious self-interest

Bullets have long played a larger part in Haitian and Dominican politics than ballots. Elections in December 1990 were the first to be free and fair in almost two centuries of Haitian history. In the Dominican Republic, it took until 1962 for truly democratic voting to take place – only for the military to step in and overthrow the elected government. So, in both countries, democracy is a recent, and still fragile, commodity.

The roots of dictatorship lie partly in the two nations' transition to independence, a prize won by force of arms rather than negotiation. In both cases, military men were quick to grab the reins of government and the riches that went with political power. The result was chronic instability as electoral niceties went largely ignored. Throughout the 19th century and into the 20th, a succession of strong men or *caudillos* wrestled for control of the Dominican Republic, while in Haiti, only two out of 21 presidents between 1843 and 1915 managed to complete their terms in office. This volatile situation was worsened by the constant interference of foreign powers, a factor which was instrumental in creating two of the Caribbean's longest-lasting and most brutal dictators.

Years of chaos

The history of 19th-century Haiti is one of grinding poverty and perennial political turmoil. The crises that shook the country at regular intervals followed a pattern of sorts: an aspiring president would gather together a mercenary army, march on Port-au-Prince, the capital, and overthrow the existing government, only to be overthrown himself some months or years later.

The vast majority of Haitians knew little, and cared little, about such events, for the political intrigues of Port-au-Prince bore little relevance to their harsh lives, and to them all governments were synonymous only with taxation and oppression. Occasionally, individual presidents made reforming gestures, but these were rare and usually short-lived. Some tyrannies were worse than others. The regime of Faustin Soulouque (1847–59), for instance, is remembered for its longevity and brutality. Ruling with the support of a paramilitary militia, the

zinglins, Soulouque had himself crowned Emperor Faustin I and twice tried to invade the Dominican Republic, in 1848 and 1859.

At the heart of Haiti's malaise was the old conflict between the mulatto minority and the black majority. Some 19th-century presidents were mulattos, but many more were blacks, mostly emerging from the black-dominated military. They often ruled under the watchful eye of the coloured power brokers, who made sure that no government threatened their monopoly on trade and other economic activities. However, most presidents were mainly interested in self-enrichment, with a complete disregard for the welfare of ordinary Haitians.

LEFT: Rafael Leonidas Trujillo Molina in 1955.
RIGHT: Faustin I and the Republic in the 1851 battle.

In the Dominican Republic, the situation was little better. After the idealistic leaders of La Trinitaria had been swiftly sidelined, the new nation was dominated by a handful of regional strongmen, backed by private armies. One such *caudillo*, Buenaventura Báez, had five terms in office between 1848 and 1878, specialising in extorting money from the country's tobacco-growers and, failing that, in printing money to meet government expenses.

As a result, the Dominican Republic – like

> **NO THANKS!**
>
> Only a "no" vote by the Senate in Washington prevented the Dominican Republic from becoming part of the US in 1869, after the country was offered to President Ulysses S. Grant.

Haiti, with its vast compensation payment to France – suffered from rampant inflation and became increasingly indebted to foreign creditors, such as the French, Germans, British and North Americans, who controlled an ever-growing slice of Haiti's coffee-exporting economy.

Spain steps in

Relations between Haiti and the Dominican Republic, meanwhile, were hardly cordial, especially during Soulouque's reign of terror, and this hostility led to one of the most extraordinary episodes in 19th-century Caribbean history.

The leaders of the Dominican Republic had long been interested in securing some sort of foreign protectorate over their territory in order to discourage Haitian expansionism, and Báez and his rival, Pedro Santana, approached France, Spain and the US with requests for annexation. In return, they offered the magnificent natural harbour at Samaná as a military and coaling installation. Finally, Spain agreed to re-annex the territory in what was the first and only voluntary process of re-colonisation in the Americas. In 1861, Spain declared the territory a protectorate.

But the arrangement was a disaster. As before, the Spanish ruled arrogantly and incompetently, discriminating against Dominicans and monopolising state jobs. A second independence war began in 1864, fought largely by black peasants who feared that the Spanish would re-introduce slavery, and by June 1865 the Spanish troops had left for Cuba.

American occupation

It took several more decades of economic chaos in Haiti and the Dominican Republic for the US to become directly involved. As the two countries sank deeper into debt, European powers, notably Germany, began to exert influence on their internal politics. Much of Haiti's coffee was shipped to Hamburg, as were many Dominican cigars, and this burgeoning trade encouraged a large German presence on the island. When German nationals were mistreated or debts were unpaid, Berlin was prepared to dispatch gunboats to seek redress, and Imperial Navy ships appeared in Haitian waters several times between 1897 and 1911. In the Dominican Republic, the unusually long-lasting dictator Ulises Heureaux (1882–99) even offered the Germans a coaling station at Samaná.

None of this was likely to please the Americans, who, since the Monroe Doctrine of 1823, had made it plain that European interference in the region was strictly unwelcome. Anxiously watching the political turmoil on both sides of Hispaniola, the US was determined not to let potentially hostile nations like Germany establish a toehold in the Caribbean. In the wake of Heureaux's assassination, the economic chaos deepened and in 1905 the North Americans decided to take control of the Dominican customs (the only source of state revenue), first paying off debtors and then giving the rest to the Dominican government.

The outbreak of war in Europe and opening of the strategically vital Panama Canal in 1914 merely heightened US suspicions regarding Germany. And as Haiti slipped into near anarchy from 1911 onwards, Washington began to view the country as an unacceptable regional security risk. After President Guillaume Sam was murdered in Port-au-Prince, US Marines landed in July 1915. Almost a year later, US troops were disembarking in Santo Domingo to restore order and "protect American lives".

In the event, the USA remained in the were dismantled, providing US exporters with captive markets. In the Dominican Republic, the antiquated sugar industry received a large injection of US investment.

If the political élite in Port-au-Prince and Santo Domingo were happy to collaborate in this "modernisation", the rural poor were not. Peasant guerrilla armies fought against the occupation forces in both countries and were gradually defeated by superior firepower.

The experience of US occupation, tainted by racism and human rights abuses, was instrumental in reinforcing nationalist feeling, especially in Haiti, where the occupation lasted

Dominican Republic for nine years, and in Haiti until 1934. In that time they could point to certain achievements: an infrastructure was put in place, while primary health care improved.

Peasant backlash

But these were by no means humanitarian missions. The more direct motive was to turn the two countries into client states: suitable for US investment and politically friendly. As a result, land reforms enabled North American corporations to displace peasant farmers, and tariffs

LEFT: Roosevelt and the US entered Dominican domestic politics. **ABOVE:** the USA later invaded.

longer and involved the humiliating imposition of forced labour upon peasant communities.

Papa Doc and the Chief

The Americans left behind them specially trained military forces in both territories, intended to provide stability. In reality, they were breeding grounds for aspiring dictators, such as Rafael Leonidas Trujillo, an ex-petty criminal who rose through the ranks of the Dominican *Guardia Nacional* to take power in 1930. The first truly totalitarian dictator in the Caribbean, he ran the country as his private fiefdom for 30 years, seizing sugar estates and ranches for his own use. When a US journalist asked who owned a particularly fine bull, a startled farmhand replied, *"Es del Jefe"* (it's the Chief's). Murdering and torturing opponents, *El Jefe* was supported by the USA, even when he ordered the massacre of some 15,000 Haitians in 1937 in a "cleansing" operation aimed at stemming immigration across the border. Not a modest man, he had Santo Domingo renamed Ciudad Trujillo and adopted such titles as "the Benefactor". If Trujillo provided a semblance of stability, it was

> ### PAPA DOC'S PRAYER
>
> "Our Doc, who art in the National Palace for life, hallowed be Thy name…Give us this day our new Haiti and forgive not the trespasses of those anti-patriots who daily spit upon our country."
>
> *– 1960s Haitian school prayer*

of the military and proclaimed himself president-for-life. The notorious Fort Dimanche prison was soon full of political prisoners, while thousands fled into exile. Under Papa Doc, Haiti became a byword for poverty and repression, a country memorably described by the novelist Graham Greene as the "nightmare republic".

But Papa Doc had his supporters, too, not least the new black middle class of government workers and political cronies. Before he died in 1971, he simply handed over power and the "family business" to his overweight and slow-witted son, Jean-Claude, better known as "Baby Doc".

at the immense cost of tens of thousands of lives.

In Haiti, the departure of the US Marines was soon followed by a resumption of hostilities between the coloured minority, who had done well out of the occupation, and the black majority. President followed president until in 1957 the military installed a myopic, softly spoken country doctor called François Duvalier.

Yet "Papa Doc", as he was nicknamed, soon showed himself to be nobody's puppet. A militant advocate of African-descended culture and self-styled champion of the black masses, he capitalised on Haiti's resurgent mood of nationalism. Forming a loyal militia, the Tontons Macoutes *(see page 69)*, he reduced the power

Elusive democracy

The grotesque excesses of Trujillo came to an end in 1961 when the CIA and the Dominican military conspired to murder the ageing dictator, whose greed and violence had become an embarrassment. But hopes of a democratic new age were to be frustrated. After a series of short-lived interim governments, a popular social democrat, Juan Bosch, was elected in December 1962 in the nation's first free elections. He promised land reform and greater equality, quickly earning enemies among the armed forces and Church, and was overthrown after less than a year.

As pro-Bosch and anti-Bosch factions in the military looked set to engage in full-scale civil war and angry crowds demonstrated in Santo Domingo's slum districts, Washington feared "another Cuba". In 1965 the US Marines arrived once more to keep the warring sides apart and to make sure that a "safe" politician won subsequent elections. Joaquín Balaguer, formerly Trujillo's confidant and a man versed in political survival skills, was the chosen one.

For 35 years Balaguer dominated Dominican politics, winning elections in 1966, 1970, 1974, 1986, 1990 and 1994. In each case, allegations of fraud were rife and real democracy seemed as remote as ever. Even though a short economic boom, based on bauxite mining and tourism, brought some relief in the 1970s, a growing population faced poverty and exclusion in urban slums or backward rural communities.

By the mid-1980s, the regime of "Baby Doc" Duvalier was also at crisis point. Many who had supported Papa Doc saw his son as weak and incompetent as well as spectacularly corrupt. Mounting discontent shook the country in 1985, and in February 1986 Duvalier was flown into exile in France, leaving the army to take control of a ravaged and expectant country.

With the Duvaliers gone, the Haitian generals expected to fill the void as the country's real rulers. But popular pressure for real change made a military-dominated Haiti effectively ungovernable, and a series of juntas and civilian puppet presidents held ephemeral power during five turbulent years. Finally, however, free elections were held in December 1990 and

US-led military mission restored Aristide to the presidency. Alarmed by the prospect of massive Haitian migration to Florida, the Clinton Administration had no choice but to return the radical to power and unseat the generals.

As a result, the Haitian military was disbanded and political violence waned. And in 1996, Aristide was able to hand over power – for the first time in Haiti's history – to a democratically elected successor. That same year the 89-year-old Balaguer was finally edged out of the Dominican hot seat by domestic and US pressure. A youthful Leonel Fernández took over, promising a fresh approach. ❑

were won overwhelmingly by Jean-Bertrand Aristide, a radical Catholic priest, whose *lavalas* (landslide) movement pledged to cleanse Haiti of its oppression and inequality. The army and the economic elite were horrified. As Aristide's rhetoric became more strident, in 1991 the armed forces moved in and sent "Titid" into exile.

What followed was one of Haiti's darkest periods, as a vicious junta, backed by terrorist gangs, held the country hostage, defying international opinion and victimising Aristide's supporters. It was not until October 1994 that a

LEFT: the military eventually turned against Trujillo.
ABOVE: Jean-Claude "Baby Doc" Duvalier.

WHATEVER HAPPENED TO BABY DOC?

On leaving Haiti in 1986, Baby Doc packed an estimated US$50 million to add to the fortune he had salted away in foreign bank accounts. He then retired to a palatial villa on the Côte d'Azur, in France. But his plans for a comfortable future were thwarted when his wife, Michèle, decamped with their lawyer and a large part of his wealth. Much of the rest was frozen in various accounts, as Haiti tried to recoup the embezzled funds.

Baby Doc had to move into a smaller house and, rumour had it, seek work as a gardener. In 1998, he bizarrely offered to return to Haiti to give the country leadership. After that, he disappeared from view.

TROPICAL ARCHITECTURE AND MONUMENTS

Hispaniola reveals the early influence of its settlers and colonists from the Amerindians to the Spanish, and from the Africans to the French

The religious icons displayed in the houses of worship in the Dominican Republic and Haiti reveal a fascinating blend of African and European cultures. Catholic Spain and Latin America are important influences, hence the richly decorated images of the Virgin Mary. Beautiful cathedrals made of stone are furnished with gold and gemstones, with works of art hanging on the walls, ceilings and ornate altars.

FANCY FRETWORK

In Haiti a few examples of traditional gingerbread architecture survive. Named after the intricate designs of 16th-century German pastry-makers, gingerbread style is based on elaborate wooden latticework. Originally hand-carved, it appeared as a decorative trim to the roofs and verandas of prosperous townhouses. The introduction of the mechanical fretsaw in the 1860s led to the mass production of designs. The fanciful trims, decorative balustrades, shutters and doors of the Oloffson Hotel in Port-au-Prince *(see pages 71 and 282)* are the most elaborate examples of a varied architectural landscape. The wide verandas wrap around the house. Built in the 1880s by a French architect, the hotel served as a hospital during the US occupation at the end of the 19th century.

△ **HOUSES ON THE SEA**
Land for building homes is precious in Haiti and therefore any open space, such as this islet between the mainland and Île de la Gonâve, could be appropriated overnight.

△ **VICTORIAN DESIGN**
The historical town of Puerto Plata is a good place to see Victorian and neoclassic buildings constructed from wood with cooling verandas.

▷ **ICON RESTORED**
Sculptures adorning the Catedral Basílica Menor de Santa María in Santo Domingo were commissioned as part of a 1990 restoration.

△ **COLONIAL LEGACY**
Balconies with delicate iron fretwork add charm to the colonial style of Jacmel in the south of Haiti and Cap Haïtien in the north of Haiti.

FROM CATHEDRAL TO COTTAGE

The Catedral Basílica Menor de Santa María *(see page 183)* is the oldest cathedral in the Americas. It was built between 1514 and 1544 of grey limestone in an ornate architectural style and originally included sculptures of the apostles. The building was badly damaged during an attack by Sir Francis Drake in 1586. The most recent renovation was in 1990.

In the countryside many homes – most commonly in Haiti – still resemble those built by early settlers using techniques inherited from Africans and Amerindians. Farmers braid palm trunks covered with clay to make walls and use palm fronds as thatch for roofs. Modern roofs are usually made of corrugated iron and steel.

▽ **DOOR DECORATION**
Brightly coloured and detailed decoration of the doorways that line the streets of Cap Haïtien in northern Haiti are some of that city's treasures.

△ **EUROPEAN STYLE**
Jacmel has a wonderful collection of European-inspired architecture, with walls made from stone and corrugated iron roofs.

▷ **COUNTRY COLOUR**
Even the most modest of country homes are adorned with fanciful trims and bright colours that are evocative of the Caribbean.

THE DOMINICAN REPUBLIC TODAY

*The future is looking brighter for Dominicans as the tourist industry
expands, but there are plenty of creases still to be ironed out*

Some 32 km (20 miles) southwest of Barahona on the Caribbean coast stands the rundown town of El Paraíso. The beach is littered with debris, while gangs of scruffy children search for "treasure" along the tide line. The multinational tourist industry has yet to arrive here. Back from the beach, a cluster of low-level apartment blocks, built in the 1970s and now slightly decrepit, are covered with fading slogans. "Balaguer again 1994–1998", says one, "Balaguer gave us these homes", proclaims another. All around the initials and symbols of the former president's Social Christian Reformist Party, the PRSC, are stencilled on to every home.

Personality politics

This everyday scene is testimony to the political system that has shaped the Dominican Republic and which was operated to perfection by the veteran Joaquín Balaguer. Homes for votes, jobs for votes, land for votes; the deal was straightforward. In return for electoral loyalty, Balaguer and his party machine handed out favours and distributed resources.

At countless ceremonies, the president personally handed land titles to grateful peasants or front door keys to families. *L'état, c'est moi* was Balaguer's guiding principle, as he controlled up to half of the national budget and sacked ministers at whim. The Dominican economy boomed briefly in the 1970s and fell into recession in the 1980s before recovering again in the 1990s. Balaguer controlled inflation, but the national debt rocketed as he spent millions on his pet projects.

It was this old-style personality politics that Leonel Fernández pledged to abolish when he took power in 1996. After several controversial elections and three decades dominated by Balaguer, the country seemed ready for a fresh start. And yet, ironically, this new beginning was itself largely the work of Balaguer. Unable to stand in the 1996 elections he had urged his

supporters to vote for Fernández. Fearful that his old adversary, José Francisco Pena Gómez of the PRD, might take power, Balaguer cynically joined forces with Fernández in yet another manipulation of the system. Despite blindness and old age, Balaguer even managed to stand in the elections of May 2000, aged 93,

although he came third. The PRD, led by Hipólito Mejía, finally returned to power after 14 years in opposition. Balaguer died in 2002.

Party games

Party politics are an obsession, a matter of life and death in the Dominican Republic. Loyalties run deep, since electoral victory spells opportunity. When a party loses power, its supporters can expect to lose their government jobs, just as the winning party rewards its rank and file. Members of the three main parties have fought lethal battles in the past, not just against one another but among themselves. The country seems to be in the grip of a permanent electoral

---

PRECEDING PAGES: a Punta Cana seascape.
LEFT: enjoying a sunny day in Las Terrenas.
RIGHT: Joaquín Balaguer ruled with an iron fist.

campaign. No sooner has a presidential election been settled than congressional campaigning begins. At the same time, the parties look forward to the next presidential contest, starting the drawn-out and usually bitter process of selecting their candidate. Almost every wall and lamp-post in the country is festooned with posters, streamers and slogans from the last election.

From the early days of independence, politicians have been expected to be charismatic and hard-hitting. Some, like Balaguer and Juan Bosch, ran their parties as vehicles for their own ambitions, establishing a sort of personality cult. "*Lo que diga Balaguer*" ("Whatever

commercials, featuring frenetic drumming and Voodoo ceremonies, were intended to alert voters to the supposed threat from across the border.

When not engaged in character assassination, politicians are just as likely to enter into the most unlikely and opportunistic alliances. The three-party structure means that there is constant strategic manoeuvring between those in and out of power. A familiar tactic is the congressional boycott, in which a president finds himself confronted by an obstructive majority. Under these circumstances, presidents find it hard to pass the smallest item of legislation, and quickly become unpopular.

Balaguer says") was a PRSC slogan in the 1990s, emphasising the party's unconditional loyalty to *El Jefe*. When Juan Bosch left the PRD in the 1970s to form a new, more radical, organisation, a fierce battle broke out over his succession – even resorting to shoot-outs.

Dirty tricks are part and parcel of the Dominican political scene. In 1994 a bogus medical report was leaked to the media, suggesting that Juan Bosch was suffering from Alzheimer's disease. That same year, the PRD's Pena Gómez was the target of an intense racist campaign, suggesting that as a black Dominican of Haitian ancestry he was conspiring to allow Haiti to take over the country. Ominous television

Privatisation and corruption

One of the most obvious legacies of the Trujillo dictatorship is the extent of the state sector. The *Generalísimo* literally owned most of the country, and when he was murdered, his land, business interests and assets passed to the state. This centralisation of economic power proved very useful to politicians such as Balaguer, who could fill the boards of the sugar or electricity companies with cronies, and provide unskilled jobs for party stalwarts. But most state corporations were spectacularly unprofitable, draining the government's coffers.

If Balaguer resisted calls to privatise the key industries (sugar, electricity, banking, insurance),

Fernández seemed more receptive to the idea of modernising the economy and divesting the state of some of its biggest loss-makers. Here, however, he faced the wrath of the opposition majority, who claimed that he was selling the national patrimony for short-term gain. As a result, progress in privatisation has been painfully slow.

The existence of a huge state sector, however bankrupt, has also been an irresistible magnet for the country's less honest politicians and businessmen. Hand-outs and kickbacks proliferate at every level of Dominican society, from multi-million dollar frauds to bribe-taking police officers. And the military has been persistently accused of involvement in the lucrative drug transhipment business, enabling South American cocaine to reach the US via the Dominican Republic.

In 2003 the country was rocked by a banking scandal, which led to the collapse of the Baninter bank and the arrest of some of its directors. Confidence in the government's handling of the economy fell to an all-time low as the peso plummeted. A dramatic increase in public-sector jobs after Hipólito Mejía took office in 2000 pushed up government spending and new borrowing of US$1.1 billion in early 2003 put further pressure on the fiscal accounts. Inflation rose to around 25 percent and consumer spending fell as the poor got poorer.

From plantation to vacation

Despite the vested interests of the old-style politicians, the Republic's economy has undergone a revolutionary transformation since the 1960s. Then, the country was almost entirely dependent on sugar exports, with a tiny manufacturing sector and very little tourism. Today, the canefields are rapidly giving way to golf courses and hotel complexes, while purpose-built factories have sprouted around Santo Domingo and other towns. Once-deserted idylls like the Samaná Peninsula or Punta Cana now welcome tens of thousands of visitors each year.

Agriculture still has a role in the Dominican economy, especially the deluxe cigar industry, which brings in annual sales exceeding

LEFT: political dissent around Lago Enriquillo.
RIGHT: local news.

US$400 million. The country also has important gold deposits (as Christopher Columbus guessed) and is a major exporter of ferronickel. But the biggest money-spinner is tourism, accounting for revenue of US$2 billion or more each year and employing more than 150,000 people. The Republic averages over 2½ million arrivals. Most go to the large all-inclusive resorts, operated by multinational chains, but many are beginning to see the attraction of the scattering of smaller, independent hotels.

> **NO QUALMS...**
>
> President Fernández discovered that Balaguer's associates had been selling land destined for small farmers under an agrarian land reform project to developers for tourist complexes.

The tourist invasion has changed the face of the country, particularly the north coast around Puerto Plata where intensive development has brought ecological and social problems in its wake. Some are unhappy about hotels monopolising land and scarce water but the benefits in terms of employment and income are so obvious that critics are in a small minority.

More controversial has been the spread of "industrial free zones" – manufacturing plants set up to assemble goods for the US market. Since the 1970s, Dominican governments have encouraged foreign companies to establish factories, offering tax concessions and a supply of extremely cheap labour. Conditions in the zones are often harsh, but workers and managers alike are aware that other countries also attract investors with low wages. Half of all the free-zone companies are located in the Cibao Valley. Total free-zone exports exceed US$4 billion a year but the removal of quotas in 2005 is expected to lead to greater competition from China and Central America.

> ### CHEAP LABOUR
> For as little as US$20 a week, a largely female workforce assembles clothing and electrical goods for North American and Asian companies who take the profits.

Pastures abroad

Walking the streets of New York's Washington Heights district, you could believe yourself to

be in Santo Domingo – apart from the climate. Dominican restaurants offer chicken, rice and ice-cold Presidente beer; *merengue* music blares from shop fronts, postal agencies guarantee next-day delivery of money transfers anywhere in the Republic – the regular influx of US dollars is a lifeline for many families.

About a million Dominicans live in the US, mostly in and around New York, and they send an estimated US$1.5 billion home each year. They are the second-largest immigrant community and the fastest-growing. Most are legally there, engaged in conventional, if often ill-paid, jobs, but a small minority has earned the majority an undeserved reputation for law-

lessness. Drug-dealing and other criminal activities are part of the expatriate scene, but only a part. Many are there for educational and professional reasons: former president Leonel Fernández was brought up and educated in New York.

Dominicans are prepared to take huge risks to reach the "promised land" if official channels are closed. Queues for US visas are endless, so some prefer to board the rickety boats that ply the shark-infested Mona Passage between the Republic and Puerto Rico, from where they furtively make their way to the US mainland. Many die in the process. The sight of wealthy returning Dominicans, sometimes enviously known as *Dominicanyorks*, inspires more young people to take the gamble.

Caribbean role

The Dominican Republic has often seemed contradictory in its regional identity, sometimes slavishly pro-US, sometimes stridently nationalistic. Its animosity towards neighbouring Haiti is well known, and it has not enjoyed easy relations with other Caribbean nations, identifying more with other Hispanic states in Central and South America.

For many years, the English-speaking Caribbean distrusted the Republic, suspicious of its volatile politics and separated by language and culture. But the widespread fear of economic marginalisation has prompted better relations as leaders across the region see the future increasingly in terms of cooperation and a common market. In 1998 President Leonel Fernández signed a landmark trade agreement with members of the Caribbean Community (CARICOM) promoting free trade and investment in the region.

The Republic looks towards Europe and the US for trade and aid. As a member of the Africa-Caribbean-Pacific group of developing countries, it is entitled to special treatment from the European Union, and also enjoys preferential trade status from the US. The potential for economic success is there; the problem, as Dominicans will tell you, is the politicians. ❏

LEFT: upmarket resorts provide entertainment.
RIGHT: a touch of luxurious living on the beach at Arena Gorda on the Costa del Coco.

MODERN HAITI

Although the overthrow of the military and the restoration of constitutional order
opened up political freedom, social conditions have been slow to improve

Dozens of US helicopter blades beat away the last of the darkness, as the sun began to make its way in the sky above Port-au-Prince on 19 September 1994. The helicopters circled the white presidential palace and the army's mustard-coloured headquarters as a delegation of US officials, headed by the former president Jimmy Carter and including General Colin Powell, shuttled between the two buildings, trying to squeeze an agreement from Haiti's military men to leave peacefully, and allow the country's democratically elected president, Jean-Bertrand Aristide, to return.

Three years earlier, the Haitian militia backed by the rich upper echelons of society and led by General Raoul Cédras, had staged a coup that sent Aristide into exile in the USA. They said they did not trust the former priest's "liberation theology" brand of politics.

Punishing economic sanctions by the US did not destabilise the new government, as Haitians, particularly the military, earned small fortunes running food supplies, fuel and other goods through the Dominican Republic. A right-wing militia called FRAPH was doing the military's bidding, hacking Aristide's supporters into silence. Tensions were high. Every day, radio stations were reporting another mass grave on the Route Nationale 1 to the north.

Not one shot was fired

After three years, the USA had lost patience. More and more Haitians were fleeing to North America, mostly illegally in boats that were barely seaworthy. They wanted Aristide – who had been living in exile in Washington – returned to power. They told the Haitian military to put an end to the theatrics. They were bringing the helicopters full of troops to back them up.

Following a three-week transition, during which time 20,000 US troops arrived and no shots were fired, Aristide returned to Port-au-

PRECEDING PAGES: baby's baptism is an important day.
LEFT: the locals travel by brightly coloured *tap-tap*.
RIGHT: the army continues to be a powerful force.

Prince in October to gigantic street celebrations. And it was the military leaders' turn to flee into exile – Cédras went to Panama, where he still lives. The chief of police, renowned for his brutality, is now in Honduras, which has refused several requests to extradite him. Others are scattered about in Florida, New York and elsewhere.

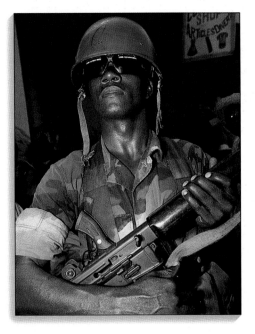

They did not leave Aristide a country in great shape. Foreign businesses that had taken advantage of Haiti's cheap labour had all left during the embargo. More than 40,000 people had lost their jobs, shooting the unemployment rate to catastrophic heights. The few paved roads had become deeply rutted, and tourism, once a major source of revenue, was dead. What the junta had left Aristide was a broken toilet in the president's office, along with a heap of social ills.

One of the agreements with the USA was that Aristide would only serve a year as president – the remainder of his term. To eliminate the threat of long dictatorships, the constitution of 1987 had been changed so that no president could serve more than one five-year term at a time. So in early 1996, Aristide handed over the presidency to his democratically elected former prime minister René Préval. Haitians say Préval and Aristide were *marassa,* Créole for twins, and critics say that Aristide remained behind the scenes pulling Préval's strings.

THE CREOLE PIG

Until the early 1980s, Haiti had 1.7 million indigenous Créole pigs, but due to an outbreak of swine fever, every one of them was killed and a whole breed was wiped out.

High hopes with Baby Doc

During Jean-Claude Duvalier's dictatorship (1971–86), Haitian hopes had run high as he

plane landed at the Port-au-Prince airport, and for several hours, truckloads of Louis Vuitton suitcases were taken from the presidential palace to the plane. Later that morning, Jean-Claude, his wife Michèle, his mother and other family members were taken to exile in France *(see page 53).*

The next day, and for several weeks afterwards, a mixture of happiness and chaos pervaded the capital. Truckloads of revellers waving tree branches as a symbol of peace crossed the streets of the capital. In the alleys, however, it

courted international aid by easing repression. As a result, foreign businesses started to establish factories in the country, creating more jobs. But the economy took another dive in the early 1980s after Baby Doc's extravagant US$7 million wedding to a high-society mulatto woman which lost him a large chunk of support from the black middle classes.

So the Tonton Macoutes, the freewheeling thugs his father had set up, were put back into top gear. Tourism went into decline, civilian unrest escalated, egged on by the Roman Catholic radio station, Radio Soleil, and by February 1986, Baby Doc had lost the support of his army and the USA. On 7 February, a US

was time for revenge, and the targets were the Tonton Macoutes who had been left powerless.

The irony was that Jean-Claude's father, François "Papa Doc" Duvalier, had stood above the crowd as one of the most respected men of his generation. He had been elected in 1957, taking over the presidency from Paul Magloire, who had installed himself as president without a vote. Civil liberties had been eliminated and arbitrary arrests had been on the increase.

Papa Doc's regime

Duvalier senior was a country doctor and a poet whose popularity had been increasing among the masses. A black man in a country ruled by a light-skinned elite who spoke French, this quiet-spoken man set out to shift the balance of power. His model was Toussaint L'Ouverture, who fought the revolution so that blacks like himself could govern themselves.

He painted himself as a descendant of those slaves who nearly 200 years before took an oath in a clearing at Bois Caiman to end the white man's cruelty and slavery on the island. He believed that the same spirit that fuelled the slaves to revolt would push Haitians to remake their country. In telling his own story later on, images of his face were superimposed on a map of Africa. Americans, he said then, had pilfered

goal, he said, was to fight against social inequities and encourage Haitians to believe in themselves. By 1958, he had invalidated the regular army by creating the Volontaires de la Securite Nationale (VSN), better known as the Tontons Macoutes *(see box below)* – a force that would respond only to him. He no longer trusted the light-skinned army officers who were still loyal to Magloire.

Mulatto power

Only about 5 percent of Haiti's nearly 8 million people were mulattos (people of mixed black and white ancestry). But these light-skinned

the country during the occupation from 1915 to 1934. Later, he would establish an on-off relationship with Washington, as the USA were playing a tug of war with Moscow over Cuba. Duvalier made his people believe that the US were about to invade Haiti, and warned them away from anyone who did not want to see his "Duvalierist Revolution" take root.

After several coup attempts, Duvalier tightened the noose on his critics, declaring himself an "authentic leader of the Third World". His

LEFT: a mural celebrates Aristide's return in 1994.
ABOVE: Haitian people feared the Tontons Macoutes but dreamed of rising against them.

PAPA DOC'S HENCHMEN

François Duvalier was determined not to be the puppet of the military élite and created his own private armed group to protect his position. They took the name Tontons Macoutes from a character in Haitian folklore who carries off "bad" children in his "macoute", the Créole word for a bag made of palm leaves. They wore denim shirts and jeans, and a red bandanna, and at first they could be seen with a machete tucked into their belt. Then they began to carry guns.

Fiercely loyal to Duvalier, the Tontons soon did away with the denim uniforms and became the stereotypical henchmen in shades portrayed by Graham Greene.

people controlled politics through the army and the economy, and set the intellectual and social calendar for the country. Their clubs were closed to black Haitians and their children were trained in France. They controlled the debates as well, as they mostly spoke French, while everyone else spoke Creole. Duvalier, a *noiriste*, wanted to reduce their power substantially and started by attacking the Church, a heavyweight in the balance of Haitian politics. He demanded, and the Vatican ceded, that the European clergy in

COUP ATTEMPTS

There were nine attempts on Papa Doc's regime, the last being by a coastguard officer in 1970, the year before he died. All rebellions were quickly put down.

page 128) expertly captured the country's mood in his 1966 novel *The Comedians*, in which an idealistic young doctor who complains about the brutality of the Macoutes is gunned down in the pool of the Hotel Oloffson.

Duvalier set out to usher Haiti into the modern age, promising a new airport and port, and a dam that would bring electricity to the countryside. Symbols were equally important to him, and he commissioned a large statue to the unknown slave and had it placed opposite the palace.

Haiti be replaced by a black archbishop and three black bishops. Duvalier's partisans defined Duvalierism as the end of privileges for a minority class that was exploiting the masses and the middle class.

On the streets, they said that Papa Doc had re-edited the 1804 revolution. He declared himself Haiti's eighth president for life, promising to bring changes to workers and farmers, with the Tontons Macoutes as his private army. It was the beginning of another dark period in Haiti's history. All civil rights were revoked; family members became suspicious of each other; open critics of the regime were beaten up, imprisoned or killed. The British writer Graham Greene *(see*

Failed promises

Some of his promises for a better life came true, but failures littered the landscape. One of them was a city for workers outside the capital that he aptly named Duvalierville, which eventually fell into disrepair. The settlement was later renamed Cabaret.

Haitians' hopes were deflated. He closed ports throughout the country, routing all traffic through the capital. He centralised all aspects of Haitian life, leaving the smaller towns to their own devices. Companies closed as nepotism ruled. The only people who could get jobs in government were related to someone in the Tontons Macoutes.

The brain drain

That period saw one of the greatest migrations of Haitians overseas. Intellectuals, teachers, engineers, accountants and others began to flee to the newly independent French-speaking countries in Africa, or to Canada. A few left for France, too. As work dried up further, and the grip of the Tontons Macoutes on the country got tighter, middle-class Haitians began to head to New York, Chicago and Boston, where they have settled in large communities.

AWAY FROM IT ALL

Around 1½ million Haitians live abroad – mainly in Florida, New York, Boston and Montreal – and send more than US$300 million a year to their families at home.

Bachelor prince

The only fact Haitians knew about Jean-Claude, when his father, on his death bed in 1971, bestowed upon him the role of president-for-life, was that he drove fast cars and owned a stable of European sports machines in the palace. Baby Doc was the 19-year-old bachelor prince, with his father's private army of volunteer thugs still the power behind the presidency.

His administration brought some breathing room for Haitians, with foreign companies

That flow of Haitians to other shores continues at both ends of the spectrum. Throughout the 1970s and beyond, poorer Haitians went to the Bahamas, where they found work in the service and construction industries. Those islands, less than 80 km (50 miles) from the Florida coast in some parts, would become the launching point for the Haitians who would later settle in Florida, whose tropical climate and strong economy makes it a popular choice.

coming to Haiti to take advantage of the country's cheap labour rates. Life was getting better, especially for the middle class. The diaspora was travelling to the homeland, bringing money and goods. They seemed to be willing to forgive the past, albeit grudgingly.

All that turned sour when Jean-Claude took a mulatto, light-skinned wife who, along with her family, became an icon of rapaciousness in a country known as one of the poorest in the Western Hemisphere. Haitians began to take notice of her shopping trips overseas, which they considered obscene. She appeared to be Haiti's Marie Antoinette and Imelda Marcos rolled into one.

LEFT: on parade at Fort Dimanche, Port-au-Prince.
ABOVE: Hotel Oloffson, Port-au-Prince.
RIGHT: statue of the *Le Marron Inconnu* .

And Michèle was not the only one in her family to profit from her elevated position. Her father, well-known businessman Ernst Bennett, became the sole distributor in Haiti for cars and agricultural goods, amassing a fortune.

The outspoken priest

Haitians kept their grumbling pretty low, going with the flow. But one person who refused to keep quiet was Jean-Bertrand Aristide, a young priest who began to win a loyal following among the

> ### BIG SPENDER
>
> It is said that Baby Doc's wife, Michèle, would hold parties in the palace, turning up the air conditioning to its coldest so that she and her friends could wear their fur coats.

poor results. A constitution adopted in 1987 provided for presidential and national assembly elections by the people, but the Government still tried to shift control to the army.

Presidential elections that were going to be held on 29 November that year had to be cancelled after a massacre by right-wing militias of more than 30 voters at a polling station. In January 1988, new elections were held and a civilian president took power. But not for long. Namphy grabbed his posi-

poor for his candour and courage in the pulpit. He spoke about children dying of malnutrition, half of the population still without access to education and clean water, the lack of decent roads, endemic poverty, and he railed against corruption. Public demonstrations at the time were violently crushed, until finally, in 1986, the pressure that had been bottling up for 40 years erupted and forced Baby Doc into exile.

The first to fill the void was an army general named Henri Namphy. He became head of the Government, tried to disband the remaining Macoutes and failed. Several other military personnel followed, but with equally

tion back in June, only to be ousted three months later by officers of Haiti's Presidential Guard. While Namphy was in power, it is believed that cocaine worth around US$700 million was processed through Haiti each month, of which many senior officers reaped the benefits.

Prosper Avril, a Duvalierist general, then declared himself president and began to rule as a dictator, until March 1990 when, as protests and violence shook the country anew, he fled the country. And in December 1991, Haitians elected Aristide ("Titid") when he stood for the presidency at the last minute, giving him a landslide victory.

Aristide in exile

After Aristide was overthrown in September 1991, the Organisation of American States (OAS), an association of North and South American nations, led a trade boycott against Haiti designed to force Aristide's return to power. And the UN followed with its own boycott. It was important that he be returned to stop the flood of refugees arriving in the United States, which was causing embarrassment to the US government.

Eventually, on 3 July 1993, Cédras, the military leader, agreed to allow Aristide to return to office and restore a democratic government by 30 October. But he failed to carry out the agreement and barred Aristide from returning, despite demands from the UN and the United States. In September 1994, the US began sending troops to Haiti to enforce the agreement and Cédras caved in. A combination of 500 US and UN soldiers remained in Haiti after Aristide returned, to help keep order and rebuild the country's infrastructure. At the end of 1995, René Préval, a member of Aristide's Lavalas coalition, was democratically elected president.

An anarchic society

Between the end of 1999 and March 2000, the peace-keeping forces finally left their base beside Haiti's international airport, terminating a presence that has bitterly divided Haitians. The troops had worked in healthcare and construction projects while they were there, but although some say they provided a stabilising presence in a still unstable nation, others say the invasion did little for the country, as Haitians were still poorer, hungrier, less literate and still getting shot down in the streets.

As Max Cherie, an unemployed mechanic, said, "When they came, we thought things would get a little better. Instead, people are still being killed all the time. Maybe they built a couple of schools, but I think considering all the people who are dying, they could help us more with security. People can't walk safely to go to market, you can't have five cents on you, you can't carry a watch, can't have nice clothes, or the thieves will rip them off."

The 4,000-strong Haitian National Police force received some training from UN civilian police trainers but remains understaffed, under-funded, undertrained, and few consider the force capable of combating crime. Tainted by drug scandals and human rights abuse, it has been caught within a power struggle by political parties vying for its control.

In May 1999, police shot 11 detainees in Carrefour-Feuilles, a neighbourhood south of the city centre. A former Port-au-Prince Police Commissioner and several other officers were arrested in connection with the killings. More recently, in 2003, Aristide, who returned to power in 2001, appointed a new Chief of Police to investigate police crimes and abuses of human rights. Officers, including the police

THE BOAT PEOPLE

Haitians took to small boats and left in their thousands in 1994 soon after the military takeover that sent Aristide to exile. Heading for Florida, they were fleeing repression, no prospect of jobs, and land that could no longer produce food. The US Coastguard picked up as many as 30,000 people from the sea that year and held them at the Guantanamo Bay naval base in Cuba. Others died due to their flimsy craft.

At first, the refugees were sent back to Haiti, but later many were resettled in Florida. Today, Haitians are still trying to escape hardship – 400 tried to sneak into Miami in one boat at the end of 1999 under cover of Millennium Eve.

LEFT: view from fisherman's wharf in Port-au-Prince.
RIGHT: a political mural criticises foreign intervention.

chief of the southeast, were arrested for involvement in cocaine trafficking. The judiciary has been charged with rooting out police corruption but many crimes remain unsolved.

New political parties

The overthrow of the military and the restoration of constitutional order briefly opened up political freedom in Haiti. More than 60 legal political parties sprang up but intimidation remains a troubling aspect. Politicians have been gunned down and some have sought asylum abroad, while opposition parties boycotted elections and results have been flawed and disputed.

Deep parliamentary divisions

For much of Préval's presidency Haiti was embroiled in a political crisis. The deep division was exacerbated by Préval's support for an International Monetary Fund (IMF) structural adjustment programme, including limited privatisation of state companies.

Aristide had reluctantly agreed to the programme in order to facilitate his return, but he subsequently opposed it. In 1997 Prime Minister Rosny Smarth resigned, causing international concern that commitment to reform was faltering. Millions of dollars of aid was prevented from reaching the needy as political squabbling and violence continued.

A new Prime Minister was not formally appointed until January 1999 after considerable political infighting. Much-delayed legislative and municipal elections were held in May 2000, producing a landslide victory for the Fanmi Lavalas (FL). Opposition parties denounced the results, claiming that their candidates and supporters were harassed and some murdered in the run up to the election.

The disputes continued to simmer and opposition parties boycotted the November 2000 presidential elections, while the USA, Canada and the EU declined to send official observers. In fact, none of the six candidates who stood against Jean-Bertrand Aristide actually campaigned. Aristide and the Fanmi Lavalas (FL) claimed 92 percent of the vote and he was returned to power in February 2001. The FL controlled 80 percent of the seats in the Legislature and nearly all the municipalities.

Despite such an overwhelming majority and apparent political control the shocking violence continues. In 2001 there was an attack on the National Palace in what was believed to be an attempted coup. The former police chief of Cap Haïtien was arrested but he later fled to the Dominican Republic, claiming his innocence.

Today, Haiti is the poorest country in the Americas with the gross domestic product (GDP) per capita at only US$460 and half of the population is undernourished. UN statistics show life expectancy is only 49.5 years and the infant mortality rate is 79 per 1,000 live births. In 2001 more than 6 percent of the population were infected with HIV or have Aids. Only 46 percent of the population have access to clean water and 28 percent have access to good sanitation. About half of the islanders are illiterate, and unemployment runs at about the same level.

So what of the future for Haiti? In 2002 Yvon Neptune took over as Prime Minister, his brief was simple: to do more to help the poor. The government struck yet another deal with the International Monetary Fund (IMF) in 2003, the aim was to cut fiscal spending and stabilise the country's currency, the gourde. But disbursement of loans from the InterAmerican Development Bank and the World Bank has been put off until Haiti's arrears are paid. ❑

LEFT: market politics.
RIGHT: Haiti relies heavily on agriculture to survive.

PEOPLE

Despite the many cultural and racial divisions between ordinary Haitians and Dominicans, they share a common heritage in their African-inspired beliefs

Although the Dominican Republic and Haiti share the same land – the island of Hispaniola – their peoples are markedly disparate. The differences are displayed in the language, the physical features – more importantly race – and most of all in the culture. The historical influence of the Spanish in the Dominican Republic, the French in Haiti, an African heritage and US domination have led to divergent cultures from a common base.

A question of race and colour

The last "pure" native Taíno in Hispaniola probably died before the end of the 16th century, but today many Dominicans still like to classify themselves as *indio* or "Indian". This might seem like nothing more than a quaint and harmless affectation, but it points to a more serious issue in the countrys' collective psychology – that of race and colour. The problem is that the vast majority of Dominicans are of at least part African descent, and many are quite obviously black. But in Haiti, more than 90 percent of the population is black, and ancestral suspicions of the neighbouring state mean that blackness tends to be equated with all things Haitian, and hence disparaged.

THE DOMINICAN REPUBLIC

In the Dominican Republic, "good" hair is straight hair, "normal" features are European ones. Women spend hours straightening their hair and trying to lighten their skin, since the country's popular culture values non-African looks and promotes an image of light-skinned beauty. TV commercials and press advertisements depict almost exclusively pale-skinned models, while black people are normally portrayed in menial roles. A whole vocabulary exists to describe skin colour and ethnic identity in this most race-conscious of countries: most

desirable is to be *blanco* (white), followed by *trigueno* (olive-skinned). Further down the social hierarchy come *mulattos* (mixed white-African) and *morenos* (meaning dark or swarthy), and at the bottom is *negro*, sometimes used affectionately but more often than not as a mark of disapproval or even as an insult.

Hence the term *indio*: historically absurd, but revealing in the way that it provides a non-African racial category for people who are not white. Many Dominican identity cards describe their bearers as Indians, colour-coded as *oscuro* (dark), *quemado* (burnt), *canelo* (cinnamon) or *lavado* (washed). The important thing, irrespective of colour, is not to be African, and by extension, Haitian. Consequently, Dominicans have looked back into the country's past to find a cultural identity that explains their colour but denies an African heritage. Many Dominicans would deny any prejudices, but attitudes are deep-rooted, particularly towards the poor nation next door.

PRECEDING PAGES: a little Haitian girl with clever hair decoration; an old lady watches the world go by.
LEFT: selling oysters in Puerto Plata.
RIGHT: welcome to San Pedro de Macorís.

Us and them

More than a range of mountains separates the Republic from Haiti. The frontier is largely a psychological and cultural one, in which most Dominicans tend to view Haitians as everything that they are not – and do not want to be. The official ideology suggests that the Dominican Republic is an Hispanic, Catholic nation, European in composition and Western in outlook. Haiti, on the other hand, is considered to be African, Créole-speaking and Voodoo-worshipping, with an alien set of cultural values. As a result, Dominicans have been taught to see their neighbours as potential invaders,

live in the Republic, mostly employed in low-wage agricultural jobs or in the informal sector, but they are vulnerable to abuses, including arbitrary arrests and deportations. Balaguer used to specialise in rounding up "illegal" (and often legal) Haitian migrants and expelling them in times of political tension.

In theory, anyone born in the Republic is entitled to Dominican citizenship, but children of Haitian ancestry have often been expelled and sometimes separated from their parents. Haitians have few rights and face constant harassment, yet thousands are prepared to take their chance across the border each year since

who pose the threat of diluting the Republic's identity. This perception often borders on a sort of racist paranoia, in which Haitians are portrayed as being inferior, barbarous and biologically dangerous. Take, for instance, the best-selling *La Isla al Revés* (The Upside Down Island), written by Joaquín Balaguer during his eight years out of office and published in 1983: "The Black... left to his own instincts and without the restraints which higher living standards impose in all countries on reproduction, multiplies nearly as rapidly as plants."

Racism of this sort has fuelled a long history of violent discrimination and exploitation. About half a million Haitians are thought to

any kind of work, however badly paid, is preferable to the unemployment and hunger felt at home.

The 1937 massacre of 15,000 Haitians by President Trujillo's *Guardia Nacional* was the worst episode in this dark history, but injustices continue. Many Haitians are still confined to ramshackle and insanitary barracks *(bateyes)* in the sugar-producing areas, where they carry out back-breaking work for as little as US$5 a day. International human rights organisations have long criticised the Dominican Republic's authorities for tolerating this exploitation, but reforms have been slow in coming.

Migrant nation

Although present-day Dominicans may like to romanticise a long-gone indigenous heritage, in reality the majority of the country's 8 million people are actually descended from the later arrivals, most notably those from Spain and Africa, but also some other, smaller groups of incomers.

The first Spanish settlers were hardly numerous, and many were only too eager to abandon the colony for greener pastures elsewhere. It was

> **RACIAL CENSUS**
>
> Some 15 percent of Dominicans regard themselves as black in official census forms (the same percentage define themselves as white, while the great majority are of mixed race).

A history of black inhabitants

The black population has always been small compared to Haiti's, yet despite Dominican delusions of racial superiority, people of African descent have been present in the country in large numbers since the mid-1550s. But whereas neighbouring French Saint Domingue owed its prosperity to half a million black slaves, Spanish Santo Domingo's poverty forced many landowners to let their slaves go free as they simply could not afford to feed them.

only at the end of the 18th century that the colony's population stabilised, helped by a large influx of immigrants from the Canary Islands. Subsequent European migration came in fits and starts, encouraged by government efforts to "whiten" the population; some Spaniards stayed after the brief recolonisation of 1861–65; a significant Italian community began to arrive from the 1870s onwards; and a small, but conspicuous mix of Europeans settled in the 20th century, some escaping persecution by Nazi Germany.

By the end of the 18th century, some 30 percent of the population officially comprised of enslaved men and women, with many more blacks classified as free citizens. The 22-year occupation of the territory by Haiti inevitably added to the black population, as large numbers of Haitians married and stayed across the border. More recently, migrant cane-cutters from the smaller English-speaking Caribbean islands of St Kitts, Nevis and Anguilla came in the early 20th century to work on plantations around La Romana. Traces of an English dialect and distinctive musical forms left behind by these *cocolos* can still be heard around San Pedro de Macorís.

LEFT: a 20th-century family portrait in Las Salinas.
ABOVE: friends.

Immigrant impact

Several small migrant communities have made a significant impact on Dominican society. From the late 19th century a substantial group of Syrians and Palestinians, commonly known as *turcos*, established themselves as traders in Santo Domingo and other major towns. Mostly Maronite Christians, they rapidly earned a reputation as shrewd business operators, and several family names – Majluta, Wessín y Wessín, Isa Conde – now have strong political connections.

> ### CITY OF CONTRASTS
>
> In Santo Domingo, the wealthy live in the northern suburbs, the middle classes share the city centre, and the poorest inhabitants have been forced out towards the edges.

Haves and have nots

A few residential districts of Santo Domingo or Santiago rival the plushest suburbs of Florida or California. TV satellite dishes and swimming pools can be glimpsed behind high walls, while armed guards and trained dogs protect lavish mansions.

But just a few miles away, in areas like La Ciénaga (the Swamp) or Capotillo, are some of the Caribbean's worst shanty towns, where poverty, crime and disease are all too common. Some of these slums cling to the banks of the

A Jewish community has also contributed to Dominican life – first the Sephardic Jews who settled in the early colonial period, and more recently refugees from Hitler's Germany who put down roots in the northern town of Sosúa. Jews from Curaçao settled in Hispaniola in the 19th century, but did not form a community, and the oldest Jewish grave site dates to 1826.

Perhaps the oddest experiment in immigration policy involved some Japanese farmers brought over by Rafael Leonidas Trujillo in the 1930s to populate the territory adjacent to Haiti. This attempt to create a *cordon sanitaire* around the border failed due to government neglect, and the disgruntled Japanese soon moved on.

River Ozama, visible from Santo Domingo's main bridges, and face the constant threat of flood. Tiny huts of wood and corrugated iron are crammed together without sanitary facilities or services of any sort. It is here that serious, violent crime, often drug-related, reaches epidemic proportions.

Yet in the past few decades literally hundreds of thousands of Dominicans have willingly moved into slum areas in the capital, leaving behind a life of poverty and boredom in the countryside. Outside the large export-orientated farms producing bananas or pineapples on an industrial scale, agriculture is neither profitable nor sustainable. Young people, in particular, are not prepared to accept a life of rural drudgery. For them, the move to the city is a search for employment and excitement, and perhaps a first step towards their dream of life in the USA.

Average per capita income in the Republic is about US$1,600 per year (compared with US$460 in Haiti), but this average conceals a sharp difference between the wealthy top 10 percent, who account for 40 percent of income, and the bottom 10 percent – who receive less than 2 percent. The rich are a mix of old and new. "Old money" takes the form of ranching, sugar and tobacco interests, controlled by traditional light-

For the majority of poor Dominicans, education and migration offer the only escape routes out of poverty. Unfortunately, education is in short supply, especially in the rural districts, where schools are usually overcrowded and under-equipped due to lack of finance. As a result, large numbers of children do not manage to complete even their primary education and an estimated quarter of adults cannot read or write. The wealthier Dominican families face no such difficulties, however, since they can afford to send their children to prestigious privately funded schools and to universities in North America.

skinned families, some of whom can trace their lineage back to the *conquistadores*. These are mostly the lucky ones, who avoided expropriation by the insatiable Trujillo clan. "New money", on the other hand, is more likely to derive from tourism, the new manufacturing sector and the sometimes dubious activities of Dominicans in the United States. Needless to say, the old élite despises the *nouveaux riches*, who are not welcome in traditional upper-class establishments like the Country Club.

LEFT: cooking for Haitian cane-cutters.
ABOVE: large cruise ships dock in the harbour near the Zona Colonial, Santo Domingo.

Visa for a dream

Migration provides the slim prospect of upward mobility that is lacking in the Dominican Republic. In his song *Visa para un Sueño* (Visa for a Dream), the Dominican *merengue* singer, Juan Luis Guerra expresses the fears and yearning felt by so many of his compatriots as they balance separation and homesickness against the hope for a better life. Often it is the brightest who leave in search of fortune, thereby impoverishing the country's future. Conversely, their remittance payments sustain families and communities that would otherwise find it hard to survive.

The reality of life in the USA often fails to match up to the dream, but North American culture continues to exert a strong fascination for many Dominicans, especially the young. Ever since the country's early independence leaders tried to sell their sovereignty to Washington, the Republic has had a love-hate relationship with a nation that has twice invaded it. Older Dominicans may remember the humiliations of the 1965 occupation, when Marines searched passers-by at checkpoints, but younger generations are attracted by the fast lifestyle that they see daily on satellite TV. To some extent, this generational difference is reflected in the personalities of Joaquín Balaguer, proud of his Spanish parentage and

those who live in Santo Domingo. A Criollo mixture of many influences, *dominicanidad* (Dominicanness) may be under threat from North American cultural dominance and remain overly fearful of Haiti, but it has strong roots in its own history and experience.

Acts of faith

Every year on 21 January thousands of pilgrims make their way to the vast modern cathedral in the eastern city of Higüey to pay tribute to Our Lady of Altagracia, patroness of the Republic since 1922 and reputed to perform healing miracles. It is one of the strongest manifesta-

attached to a Hispanic cultural model, and Leonel Fernández, who promised in an election speech to "turn the Dominican Republic into a little New York". As more and more Dominicans experience life in the USA, so North American tastes and habits become increasingly commonplace. But the Dominican Republic is not yet entirely Americanised. While baseball and Coca-Cola are almost ubiquitous, the popularity of rum and cock-fighting points to another cultural dimension, both Hispanic and Caribbean.

Regional identity also remains important; many people in Santiago, for instance, consider themselves different in a variety of ways from

tions of religious faith in a society that claims to be 90 percent Catholic. While Catholicism is an important element in Dominican cultural identity, in reality the Church is politically weak, conservative and in desperate need of priests and money. As elsewhere in the region, Protestant churches are making gradual in-roads and competing with traditional Catholicism, but the Church still has influence in education and social welfare. In some of the most deprived areas, priests have also been at the forefront of organising community self-help groups.

But if devout Dominicans deride their Haitian neighbours for their Voodoo practices, they cannot deny that large numbers of their compatriots are also attracted to African-inspired beliefs. *Brujería*, which encompasses worship, spiritual magic and even witchcraft, has many followers, although generally their activities are not widely publicised. Dominicans of all backgrounds consult *brujos* – priests and medicine men – who offer advice and sometimes spells to counteract the effects of *mal de ojo* or the evil eye.

Ironically, then, while the Dominican Republic officially proclaims its Catholicism and its Hispanic heritage, it is precisely in folk religion and popular beliefs that its common culture with Haiti is most clearly revealed.

as their ticket to an easier life in this country of eight million people, where 50 percent of the population is considered illiterate. Families from the countryside see it this way: the child who goes to school might be able to secure employment in Port-au-Prince. That child will then become an example of what is possible and will be expected to give help to everyone else within that family.

There are no universal retirement benefits in Haiti. For countless families, the only welfare is to have one of their children attend medical or law school, or one of the professional colleges. Every year, thousands of young men and

THE HAITIANS

A world away from the relative prosperity of the business centres and fashionable cities in the Dominican Republic are the steamy and crowded slums along Port-au-Prince's waterfront. The anxieties are more basic here. They are about jobs, food, healthcare and education. Despite their poverty, most Haitians will do their utmost to secure an education for their children and get them through school: it is seen

FAR LEFT: religious icons at Santiago market.
LEFT: baseball is big business for the Dominicans.
ABOVE: education is seen as a way out of poverty.
RIGHT: preparing maize.

women from all over the country go through the ritual of taking a national high school exam. The students with the highest grades gain admittance to the school of their choice. It's an investment in human capital for the future.

A crucible of all things good and bad in Haiti, Port-au-Prince best illustrates the disparities that exist in the country, with pockets of wealth surrounded by vast expanses of poverty. Pétionville, as well as dozens of suburbs that have mushroomed in the hills above the capital city, seems to be fenced off from the rest of the country. The conception of the people who live in these enclaves is that although they speak Créole, just like everyone else, they prefer to use French or English and have probably studied abroad. Their homes are larger, their schools are better, and every night they watch North American and European programmes on satellite TV.

Racial divisions

Most of the suburbanites belong to Haiti's light-skinned élite, scions of a world where colour meant everything. It wasn't too long ago, years after the Revolution of 1804, that Haitians were classified by how much white blood was in their

> **PORT-AU-PRINCE**
>
> It is difficult to find your way around Port-au-Prince and street maps are hard to find in advance. However, once there, good maps published by the Shell Oil Company can be bought at Shell petrol stations.

Today the Arabic community has earned a reputation as successful entrepreneurs and they now own banks and factories, among various other thriving businesses.

Class divisions

Over the years, the strict racial divisions have given way to class partitions based to some extent on education and family ties. Black people who benefited from François "Papa Doc" Duvalier's black revolution began to buy better homes in the hills, setting them-

veins. The original slave owners, from small towns in France, settled in places like Jacmel, Cap Haïtien. More than 7,000 families fled to New Orleans in the USA a few years before the slave revolt, but many others stayed behind. At the turn of the 20th century, a few German adventurers settled in Haiti, along with some North American whites who stayed on after the US occupation of Haiti in 1919.

The Arabs, mainly Christians from Syria and Lebanon, were the last to arrive in Haiti, mostly after the 1940s. Refugees from a French-speaking country, they began doing business where "educated" Haitians would not dare venture, in downtown Port-au-Prince.

selves apart from the millions of poor and uneducated Haitians living below.

These distinctions certainly still exist. Young Haitians, now living in New York, Miami or Paris, speak of the "name-game" they have to play whenever they return home. Someone from an older generation will invariably try to place them by reference to their family name. Who was your grandfather? Who's your mother?

Life on the affluent hills is a world away from where most Haitians call home. Out of Haiti's total population, about 2 million currently live in Port-au-Prince, the capital. Except for the tiny proportion of the élite there, most live in cramped housing or in slums on the city's waterfront, such as Cité Soleil, La Saline and Boston.

The majority of Haitians, who are descendants of the African slaves brought to the island from the 15th century, still live in the countryside, where they scratch a living from small plots of land. Arable land is increasingly in short supply in the mountainous regions, as the population increases and deforestation spreads like wildfire. They live in one of the secondary cities like Gonaives, Jacmel, Cap Haïtien, Les Cayes, or in small municipalities such as Las Cahobas, a town on the border with the

owning communities such as the United States, England, Spain, and especially France, did not want it made public knowledge that a band of slaves had indeed defeated the great general, Napoleon Bonaparte's men – at the time one of the most powerful armies in the world.

"We spent too many hours looking at each other instead of looking at other people." Laguerre says. "As a country, we had a small-town mentality. It's all about gossip. People only talked about each other."

This introspective world still exists in many rural localities in Haiti today, and in plenty of neighbourhoods in the capital, too. These places

Dominican Republic where Michel Laguerre spent the first few years of his youth.

"I never heard of Paris or New York," said Laguerre, now a professor of anthropology and sociology at the University of California at Berkeley. "We were one step above La Saline." Haiti's turbulent past should explain this kind of disparity. Like natives of a country that has been forcibly fenced off from the outside world, Haitians spent many years looking inward. They were isolated after the Revolution, as countries with their own powerful slave-

LEFT: washing in the river.
ABOVE: Voodoo is a powerful influence in Haiti.

THE BIG BAND SOUND

Everyone loved the music of celebrated composers Nemours Jean-Baptiste and Weber Sicot, big-band leaders of the 1950s. They introduced a special kind of recreational dance music called *compas direct* or *cadence rampa* with a beat that refuses to die. At carnival time, the Jean-Baptiste and Sicot float always attracted the biggest crowds who would dance to their music and follow the float as it wound its way through the city. "There was common understanding, a common bond," Michel Laguerre, professor of anthropology and sociology at the University of California at Berkeley, says. "We were on the boat together."

have yet to join the global village, untouched as they are by Internet technology and multiple-channel television. In their world, the small-town grocer becomes the synthesiser of neighbourhood news, continually repackaging it as the day wears on.

Growing diversity

Until the end of World War II, Haiti was practically a homogeneous country, with a shared culture. Everyone in the countryside practised Voodoo, and though city folk attended church, they were familiar with the gods worshipped by their servants. (Although Voodoo has been

portrayed in literature and the arts, it is still considered as belonging to the working classes.)

When François "Papa Doc" Duvalier rose to power in 1957, Haiti became more complex, more culturally heterogeneous. In among the islanders who never left, there are those who lived abroad and have now returned – along with their own distinct backgrounds – from the United States, Canada, France, Africa, and the Dominican Republic. There are an estimated 1 million Haitians overseas, mainly in the United States and Canada.

In the late 1950s and early 1960s, as Papa Doc was tightening his grip on power, many French-speaking intellectuals left for teaching positions in Canada and the newly independent countries of Africa. When someone who lived in New York – which has the largest Haitian community anywhere overseas with 600,000 people – talks about democracy, and a native islander talks about democracy, they're often discussing two very different things.

Looking to the USA

In the past, ambitious Haitians in the country-side could climb up the social ladder by moving to Port-au-Prince, where there were job opportunities and good schools. Now, they're looking to the USA. Well-off Haitians send their kids to American schools, such as Union School, or Quisqueya, where they learn English. In less well-off families, children pick up English wherever they find it: on television, in books and from advertisements.

"They're getting ready for Miami," Laguerre says. Over the years and through the often difficult changes, the Haitians have remained warm and fundamentally honest. Hospitality is a strong feature of their culture. In villages, more so than in Port-au-Prince, Haitians are likely to welcome foreigners into their home for a meal and a place to rest their head.

They're hard-working people, with strong family ties and extended linkages overseas. Many families live on money sent from relatives overseas. Contact with abroad has fundamentally changed Haiti, moving it towards being a transnational culture. Television and music comes from powerful cultures in the USA, Canada and France. ❑

ENVIRONMENTAL PROBLEMS

Environmental problems are very difficult to solve in Haiti. Overpopulation and poverty have resulted in severe stress on the land, and while some limited agricultural plans are being put into operation, more agrarian reform is needed, including technical and financial assistance for the peasant class. Irrigation systems need to be built to increase the export of legitimate crops, but there are obstacles in the form of massive deforestation and much corruption among the ruling classes. The international cocaine trade is important in Haiti, with government officials in the past often raking in huge profits, running into millions of US dollars.

LEFT: a Dominican elder.
RIGHT: at home with the family, Samaná Peninsula.

LANGUAGE

The island of La Hispaniola is linguistically diverse: Dominican Spanish has five different dialects, while on Haiti you will hear both French and Créole

From the beginning, the Spanish language brought to America by the conquerors was enriched with the characteristics of four different regions of the Iberian peninsula: León, Castilla, Extremadura and Andalucía. Contact with the Taínos led to the incorporation of several indigenous words in to the various Spanish

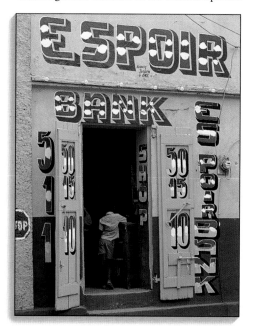

dialects. Despite this, the indigenous tongues did not influence the Spanish language in a significant way, mostly because the few Amerindians that still survived by the mid-16th century already spoke Spanish.

The Taínos, however, left a legacy of widely used words such as *huracán* for hurricane, *hamaca* for hammock, *bohío* for house and *maíz* for corn. Even though the quantity of indigenous terms known and documented is broad, the truth is that their use and validity in Dominican Spanish is minimal.

Due to the historical circumstances of the "discovery" and to the geographical reality of being an island, Dominican Spanish was also influenced by the nautical terms brought by the navigators that colonised the island. Those terms were later applied to mundane objects and situations, and their sense drifted slowly from the original meaning. A good example of this is the word *tolete* which means *thole* and is used as a synonym for *stick*, *peso* (unit of Dominican currency), and even for the male sexual organ.

Dominican dialects

The Dominican Republic is divided into regions, each one with its own linguistic characteristics. There are five areas that can be perfectly distinguished:

● **Northern Zone** or "**Cibao**". Close to the pure-blooded Spanish brought here many centuries ago, it keeps verbs, terms and phrases that are archaic in Spain. This is especially true in the mountainous rural areas. A distinctive seal of the dialect is the vocalisation of "i" as in "faida" instead of "falda" (skirt) or "caig**ai**" instead of "car**gar**" (to carry or to charge).

● **Southwestern Zone**. Predominance of the consonant "r", leading to the pronunciation "farda" for "falda" (skirt).

● **Southeastern Zone**. The assimilation of a consonant which follows another, producing "fadda", instead of "falda".

● **National District** (includes Santo Domingo). Predominance of the consonant "l" which leads to the pronunciation of words such as "puelta" instead of "puerta" (door).

● **Oriental Part of the Samaná Peninsula**. This region is more complex due to the influence of the eastern part of the Cibao region as well as the influence of the English language and the Haitian dialect.

Santo Domingo, like other parts of the Caribbean, distinguishes itself by the strong use of its Castilian (Spanish) vocabulary as well as its syntax. But the vocabulary used in Santo Domingo has a more phonetic similarity to the Andalucian region than to the Castilian region.

Santo Domingo was the first centre of the Americanisation of the Spanish language in the

Dominican Republic. One characteristic of the Dominicans is the use of idiomatic sayings and phrases. These sayings and phrases add a picturesque and refreshing flavour to the daily use of the Spanish language.

The African influence on Dominican Spanish has not been significant, since the integration of black slaves only occurred during the first half of the 16th century. This integration happened at the time when the island's earliest inhabitants – the Taíno Amerindians – were in the process of being exterminated.

Haitian Créole

If you want to converse with people while in Haiti, bring along both a Créole and a French dictionary. Everyone in Haiti speaks Créole, but about 10 percent of Haiti's 8 million people know French well enough to use it comfortably in any situation. The French dictionary will come in handy in dealing with any members of Haiti's élite, who sometimes are reluctant to use Créole with foreigners. Some might even be insulted if a foreigner attempts to use Créole, given the low status of the language.

In the early days, a large number of these black slaves were not brought directly from the African mainland, but from Spain, where they had been acquired from Portugal and were therefore already hispanicised.

Examples of some incorporated words from African languages include *cachimbo* (smoking pipe), *can* (party), and others which have also been extended to the Antilles, such as *naqueru* (child's funeral) = *naquine* (child's funeral) in Puerto Rico; *bembe* (lip) in Puerto Rico = *bemba* (lip) in Cuba.

LEFT: a corner shop in Cap-Haïtien.
ABOVE: every *tap-tap* tells a story.

Although related, Créole is not a dialect of French. It belongs to a group of languages called French-based créoles in which the majority of the vocabulary is taken from French. Other French-based créoles are found on Mauritius and the Seychelles, and in Louisiana in the US. Approximately 80 percent of Haitian Créole's vocabulary comes from French, but the words do not necessarily have the same meaning, form or function as French. For example, *neg* in Créole means a man, but in French *negre* means a black man, a negro. Structurally, however, Créole is very different from French, having more in common with the other créoles. It has a simple grammar that doesn't require conjugating verbs according to the subject, as in French and English. Instead, key words are placed before a verb to indicate a tense.

French was declared the official language in the 1918 constitution. It wasn't until 1987 that Créole was made one of the two official languages. Until then, French was the only language in public service and in schools, and therefore only a small number of people were able to communicate with officials and educators, read newspapers and legal documents. The élite spoke French with each other, and also used it with their children to make sure they grew up at an advantage. Créole was – and still

is in some circles – reserved for family and close friends, for speaking with servants and for Voodoo ceremonies. Many classes are still taught in French, although most students are not as proficient at the language as they could be, and many of the teachers speak it badly.

It wasn't until 1964 that the government allowed people who spoke only Créole to use it for any official purpose. Because of the social stigma, many Haitians think that Créole is not a viable language, going as far as saying that it has no grammar, that they don't have a native language. That's because few know how Créole came to them. It came to Haiti with the Africans, who brought along about 30 lan-

guages from their homes in West Africa. Before independence, according to Michel DeGraff, a linguist at the Massachusetts Institute of Technology, Créole had prestige. There was no prejudice towards Créole, as whites preferred to deal with slaves who knew the language.

"An African who spoke Créole commanded respect," says DeGraff. "More so than one who spoke French or one who spoke neither. Those who didn't speak Créole fast were sent to plantations." *Neg Bosal* (rough man) was the phrase used for slaves who were not acclimatised, who could speak neither French nor Créole. Africans spoke languages that belonged to the Niger-Congo family of languages, which came into contact with the dialects of provincial France. The French slave-owners, merchants and tradespeople did not speak Parisian French, which did not exist at that time.

A common language

Over the years, the Africans took the syntax from their own languages, borrowed French words from the whites, and cobbled a common language. That ability to communicate in the same language can be partly credited for the early and successful emancipation of Haitians.

It was only after independence that Créole lost its prestige, when the neo-colonial class looked on French as a privilege; the African languages disappeared and French became a symbol of education and prestige. Mulattos, whose fathers were French, sent their children to France to study, and Créole became a reflection of the social and political situation. Language had become a symbol of class. "Créole is a disadvantage in certain places," DeGraff says. "In the countryside, people will be more than happy to speak Créole."

There are distinct regional variations in pronunciation and grammar, and it is only recently that Créole has become a written language in a meaningful way. The long-term neglect of the language means there are no "official" rules of grammar, only this one: if a native Haitian Créole speaker says it's OK, then it's OK.

Morisseau the saviour

Poet-playwright Felix Morisseau-Leroy's name burns bright in the consciousness of generations of Haitians. He made Créole "respectable" to those who thought of their language as a disreputable patois incapable of expressing much beyond the most basic human needs. Morisseau wrote *Antigone in Créole*, and performed it in Port-au-Prince in 1953; it was the first time Créole-speaking Haitians saw a play in their own language. Morisseau was forming his ideas at a time when people like François "Papa Doc" Duvalier was talking about black power. Créole was as good as classic French, he said. Morisseau's adaptation of the Greek tragedy was a revolutionary act, the tremors from which can be felt today in the words of populist activists like singer Manno Charlemagne, the mayor of Port-au-Prince and priest-turned president Jean-Bertrand Aristide. Morisseau, who died in Miami in 1998, became an almost mystical and mythical figure.

"He was the inspiration who allowed me and others to continue the work he started doing," said Jan Mapou, a friend who has directed *Antigone in Créole* abroad. Now, several more works, including teaching manuals and other reading material are available in Créole, as Haitians continue to debate whether children should be taught in Créole instead of French. At the same time, universities in the United States and elsewhere offer doctorate programmes in Créole. Several dictionaries are available, including *Créole Anglais* by Joel Laguerre and Bryant Freeman and a Haitian-English dictionary by Albert Valdman of Indiana University.

An organisation known as Sosyete Koukouy was set up in Haiti in 1965 by a poets and playwrights to promote the use of Créole as the national language. It has representatives in North American cities, such as Boston, Montréal, New Jersey and New York, while its headquarters, founded in 1986 by Jan Mapou as a Haitian cultural centre, are in Miami. It also works closely with groups in other Créole-speaking countries such as Dominica, Guadeloupe and Martinique.

As a young language, Créole has absorbed words from several other languages besides French. A smattering of English words have made their way into Créole, including:
● shoe black *(choublak)*, the common name for hibiscus. It comes from the American occupation of 1915 when hibiscus was used to shine shoes and American soldiers requested "shoe black" when they wanted their boots polished.
● coat *(kot)* – also jacket *(jaket)*.

● many words derived from brand names, such as *Clorox* for bleach, *Delco* for generator, *frijide* for refrigerator, and *kleneks* for tissues.
● the ubiquitous hotdog, as well as "chips" for potato crisps.

Getting a feel for Haitian Créole

Most words don't change their form, meaning there are no endings to signal grammatical distinctions such as singular or plural for nouns, or tense for verbs. For example, "the book" is translated as *liv la* and "the books" as *liv yo*. Grammatical relations between words are signalled by the word order. For example, the order for a

declarative sentence is: subject, verb, indirect object, direct object. Other examples of word order: Yves *renmen* Marie means Yves loves Marie (possession is shown by placing the possessor immediately after the thing possessed); and *Kay* Marie, which translates as Marie's house. To express negation in Créole, the marker *"pa"* comes immediately before the verb.

As in English, there are three persons in the singular (*mwen, ou* and *li*) and two in the plural (*nou* and *yo*). The first person *nou* corresponds to we and you, and can refer to more than one person, if at least one of them is a participant in the conversation. *Yo* is more than one person or thing *not* participating in the conversation. ❏

LEFT: Voodoo images adorn a building.
RIGHT: butcher's store front in San Cristobal.

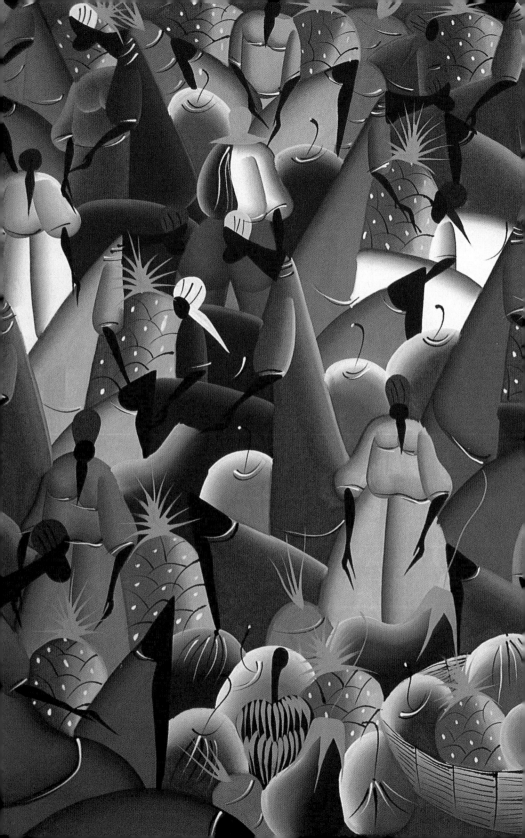

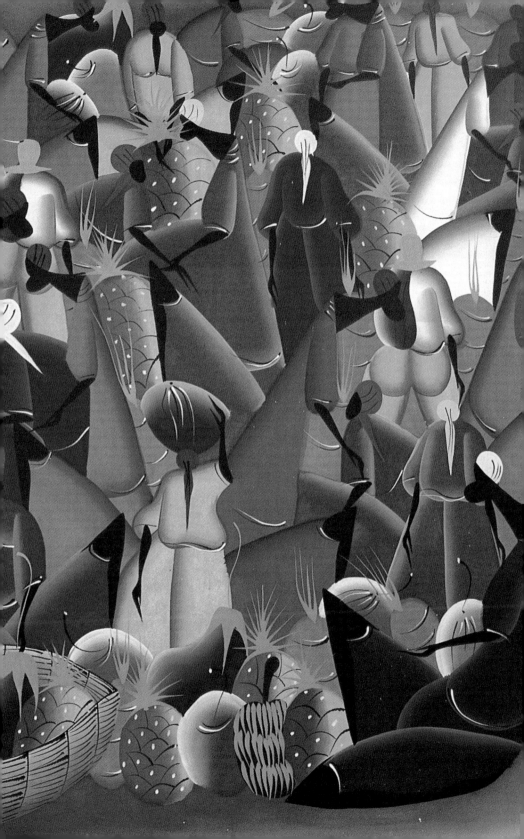

HAITIAN ART

Local paintings lie covered in dust while talented artists go hungry. The artists who are successful divide their lives between Haiti and North America

When a country has very little in terms of material wealth, art is not just a vibrant means of expression, it's an affirmation of identity, the hard currency of hope, and a potent agent for social change. As one of the richest resources of this poverty-stricken nation, Haitian art is recognised throughout the world by its bold primary colours and its primitive motifs, and is traditionally regarded on the island as a symbol of the long, tumultuous struggle of the country's soul.

Art in Haiti is present everywhere: at the airport, in restaurants and hotels, on *tap-taps* (buses) and street corners, inside markets and modest homes. But at Port-au-Prince's teeming Iron Market, colourful oil paintings, covered with a layer of dust, sit stacked in piles as high as the ceiling while hungry vendors wait for customers and barely earn a living. The Iron Market was once a popular shopping stop where cruise ship passengers loaded up on Haitian art, but now, along with many art galleries on the island, it has fallen on hard times.

Dwindling sales

"In the past, Haiti depended on upper-class, well-educated and liberal tourists, who were very good buyers of our art," explains Michel Monnin, a Swiss-born art critic and dealer who has lived in Haiti since the late 1940s. "When tourism fell off back in the 1980s, the day-to-day dealing of art fell off with it. We also have the problem of collectors who are stuck on one image of Haitian art. Art in Haiti, like art everywhere in the world, is in constant evolution. Often, when buyers see the new art being produced by some of our young artists, they say, 'This isn't Haitian art. We want the real thing.'

"There are a few big name artists who are able to sell their work to collectors in Europe,

and lesser-known artists who sell their work to diplomats, journalists and UN employees, but in general, Haiti today is a country full of artists and most of them are starving".

Whether most artists in Haiti are actually starving is debatable, but Monnin is right in saying that Haiti is a country full of artists. Whether rich

or poor, almost every family has at least one member who works as an artist. It is commonly said that Haiti has more artists and poets per capita than most other countries on earth.

Georges Nader Jr, owner of art galleries in Petionville and Santo Domingo, paints a more promising view of the current status of art in Haiti. "In our gallery, a bunch of modern painters – Alix Roy, Calixte Henry, Galland Semerrand, Gesner Armand, Luckner Dasmangles, Lyonel Laurenceau, Henry Jacques and Bernard Segourne – are getting the highest prices ever for their work, and I believe that we are entering a period when we are going to see another great boom in Haitian art."

The early masters

The history of the first Haitian art boom can be traced back to the early 1940s when US teacher and aspiring artist DeWitt Peters went to Port-au-Prince to teach English. A conscientious objector during World War II, Peters was awed by the "self-taught and instinctive" artists he encountered in the cities and throughout the countryside of Haiti.

In 1944 he opened the Centre d'Art in Port-au-Prince, still in existence today. The Centre's

Other great artists who came out of the Peters era include Philomé Obin and Riguad Benoit, who both died in 1986; Castera Bazile (d. 1964); Wilson Bigaud (b. 1931); Préfète Duffaut (b. 1923); Jasmin Joseph (b. 1924); Georges Liautaud (1899–1991); and André Pierre (b. 1916), who still produces exuberant art at his Croix-des-Missions home, some of which sell abroad for up to US$50,000 a piece. "Haitian art is mystical because Haiti is mystical," Pierre once told *Art & Antiques* magazine. "Everything comes from the spirits."

VOODOO INFLUENCE

Voodoo has been a major factor in Haitian art. Inextricably linked to the unseen world, Haitian artists served *Voodoo* spirits by decorating temple walls and flags used in ceremonies.

goal in the early days was to arouse Haitians' interest in the arts, provide needed supplies, and nurture the talent of hundreds of impoverished artists on the island. Peters is credited with "discovering" Voodoo priest Hector Hyppolite, the legendary Haitian master whose dramatic paintings were marked by Voodoo rituals, symbols and gods, along with prominent Christian figures amid Caribbean landscapes. Before he met Peters, Hyppolite was an obscure artist and financially strapped house painter, so poor that he used chicken feathers as paint brushes. In the last three years of his life, with the financial assistance of Peters, he produced over 250 paintings. He died in 1948.

Throughout the late 1940s and 1950s, this early generation of Haitian artists attracted international acclaim and put Haiti on the world map for its visual arts, making the genre widely popular. French surrealist André Breton and Cuban master Wilfredo Lam also helped raise interest by bringing attention to Haitian art in Paris and arranging European shows to highlight their work.

After buying five Hyppolites to take back to Paris in the late 1940s, Breton reportedly told Peters, "This should revolutionise modern painting; it needs a revolution." What resulted from all this international attention was a virtual art explosion of what became known in the art world as the "naive-primitive" or "instinctive" genre. Described by critics as lush, bold, pastoral, whimsical, lyrical, romantic and exotic, these naive-primitive oil paintings for the most part emphasised Haiti's African heritage, but also had an overlay of classical French influences. Lush jungle landscapes, wild animals, towering mountains, exotic flowers and plants were common themes.

Eventually, this pleasing-to-the-eye style became synonymous with Haitian art throughout the world. Isaa El Saieh, a Palestinian art dealer who has lived in Port-au-Prince all his life, started selling naive-primitive art in Haiti

Haiti and will go out of his way to help them find exactly what they want. One of his former clients was the writer Graham Greene, who, after a round of shopping for art, asked El Saieh to take him to one of Haiti's most notorious brothels for a late-afternoon tryst.

Haitian art goes commercial

During the next few decades the blossoming of art in Haiti continued, promoted by local merchants and sold under the generic "Haitian Art" label to tourists. From the start, Haitian art was created for the export market and artists were encouraged to produce work that fitted into this

in the 1950s and has never stopped. A gregarious old man with a thick moustache and barrel chest, he has a stable of modest-to-good artists from whom he regularly buys work. His home in Port-au-Prince, a rambling hillside mansion on Avenue Chile that also serves as a gallery, has a massive storage area that's always packed with canvases. Along with claiming to know more about Haitian art than "all the so-called experts in the world", El Saieh still makes himself available to tourists shopping for art in

LEFT: André Pierre at work in Croix-des-Missions.
ABOVE: the painting of wild animals at a jungle watering hole by Blanchard reveals common themes.

mould. Although credited with "discovering" naive-primitive art in Haiti, what DeWitt Peters actually did was create a mass market for Haitian art, much of which was clone-like and predictable, the product of a formula that worked and easily made money. Haitian art became stereotyped in the process, assumed to be of interest only to folk art collectors or souvenir-hunting tourists. In essence, it turned into a clichéd art form marked by commercialism and tailored to feed tourist consumption.

Haiti's upper classes never considered their own art valuable, and looked instead to Europe to decorate the walls of their plush, tropical homes. There are few Haitian collectors of

Haitian art; most of the work of the early masters, such as Hyppolite and Obin, is in the hands of private European collectors. Obin, however, spawned an art revolution in his own family, and today there are dozens of his close and distant relatives producing art in Haiti and abroad.

Throughout the 1960s and 1970s, the Haitian art market thrived on a constant flow of well-heeled tourists. The galleries in Port-au-Prince, Petionville and Jacmel prospered. In addition to the paintings, fine mahogany wood carvings, beaded flags and iron sculpture crafted from oil drums, became common art commodities.

But when the tourist market collapsed in the

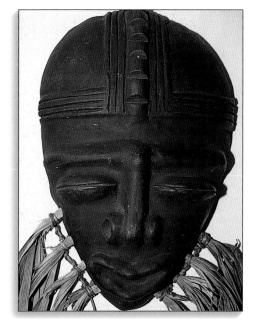

1980s, so did many of the country's galleries. And when the hardships of the post-Duvalier/ economic embargo years followed, the art scene in Haiti got even worse. There were shortages of food and fuel, as well as paint, canvases and brushes. Some artists had only latex house paint, which cracked on their canvases in about two years. Others worked with just a few colours, and their art, referred to as "embargo painting", was evidence of the scarcity of supplies. Some gave up painting altogether and turned to sculpture, using scrap metal, tin cans and wire found on the streets.

After the election of Jean-Bertrand Aristide in 1990, the streets of Haiti saw a proliferation of street art, political graffiti in the form of joyous murals. Bold and provocative, most appeared as a spontaneous celebration of political and social liberation unleashed by the downfall of the Duvalier regime. Rich with the patriotic colours of red and blue, the common themes of these murals included the number 5, Aristide's number on the ballot; a crushed guinea head, a bird that once symbolised the Duvalier regime; and the horrific practice of "necklacing" – placing a petrol-soaked tyre around a victim's neck and setting it on fire.

After the 1991 coup forced Aristide into exile, most of these murals were obliterated by the Haitian military. When Aristide was returned to power in 1994, Haiti's political street art came back to life. And today, although democracy remains fragile, the country is seeing a renewed cultural vitality, and an intense period of expression that is relatively free of fear.

A contemporary generation

"Artists are a tormented species, no matter where you come from," said Edouard Duval-Carrié, a prominent Haitian artist who divides his time between Miami, Florida and Port-au-Prince. "And artists in Haiti for generations have been tormented by what they saw around them."

Among the current community of Haitian artists, Duval-Carrie (b. 1954) is one of a handful – including Burton Chenet (b. 1958), Philippe Dodard (b. 1954), Mario Benjamin* (b. 1964)* and metal sculptors Serge Jolimeau (b. 1952) and Gabriel Bien-Aimé* (b. 1951) – who have gained international recognition for their work, and who have also been able to earn a decent living from it.

This *generation explores Haitian roots and culture with a new, freer form of expression, transcending the stereotypical image of naive-primitive art usually associated with their country. Most have been educated in Europe or North America, are well-travelled, multi-lingual, urbane, and willing to take greater risks in their work.

*Duval-Carrié creates lush, colourful and intense paintings that are definitely Haitian, but far from being clichéd. Full of both beauty and despair, they are portraits of paradise with a hint of violence and a tinge of terror. The subjects of his work range from mythical gods to bourgeois matrons, Voodoo spirits, political brutality, and even Jean-Claude Duvalier in drag. Like his contemporaries, Duval-Carrié resists being categorised. "One look at me and you can see that I am neither primitive nor naive," he explains. "I am a contemporary Haitian artist with a political agenda who is trying to analyse my country and figure out why it is in such a mess.

"My biggest complaint about Haitian art today is that it is still lumped together under this one broad category. We have had several great artists who should have received recognition as individual masters, not just regional or Haitian painters. And we have never had a retrospective show at a major museum, or

Although Duval-Carrié admits that there are hundreds of fine artists in Haiti today who have little choice but to sell their work to dealers for a few dollars, he is optimistic about the future*: "The years ahead look very promising for Haitian art. We have a democratically elected government, the organised terror has gone, artists are no longer afraid to express themselves politically, and there is great demand for the discussion of our country's problems. And even though the tourist market is very weak, all of the current circumstances will mean that a finer quality and more original form of art will be coming out of Haiti in the years to come." ❑

even a catalogue collection of our masters."

Calixte Henry, a Haitian artist in his seventies, echoes Duval-Carrié's sentiments. "There has always been a problem with Haitian painting because of the concentration on Voodoo," he once told *Art & Antiques* magazine. "I say there is more: there is what the painter feels within. I'm not going to do Voodoo just because it sells." Instead, he has turned to European Impressionism for inspiration, while resolutely expressing scenes of Haitian life.

LEFT: a mask influenced by African tradition.
ABOVE: many political murals carry a strong message and so some are destroyed during political unrest.

DANGEROUS ART

Artistic censorship has always existed in Haiti, especially during such turbulent times as the post-Duvalier years. Musicians whose music challenged the status quo have been jailed and executed, their performances threatened or halted by a spray of bullets.

Because visual artists don't regularly make public appearances like musicians, they have fared somewhat better, but they too have been threatened by the powers that be. Over the years, many have left the island out of fear and now live and work in Paris, Montréal, New York and Miami, where controversial and political art is usually tolerated and often actually encouraged.

THE ORIGINS OF VOODOO

Outlawed as dangerous superstition, it has taken hundreds of years for Haiti's most popular religion to gain official recognition

The saying that "Haiti is 80 percent Roman Catholic Voodoo" may be close to the truth, rather than an exaggeration. What started out hundreds of years ago in west Africa as simply ancestor and spirit worship has developed in Haiti into a unique syncretic religion, with its own world view, philosophy, healing system and artistic expressions. As the Voodoo master drummer and emperor (high priest) Aboudja Derenoncourt says: "Voodoo is not just a religion, it's a way of life."

A misunderstood religion

Voodoo permeates the Haitian psyche, operating at all levels of society. Along with Créole, it is fundamental to cultural identity and for any kind of insight into this extraordinary country. Voodoo has been a significant factor in Haitian history since the first slaves arrived in 1503, inspiring fierce resistance, which culminated in the final rebellion against France.

Jean-Jacques Dessalines, the rebel slave leader who declared independence in 1804, was an *oungan* (priest) who would be elevated to the Voodoo pantheon after his assassination. Despite prescriptive legislation and a series of anti-superstition campaigns aimed at wiping it out, Voodoo has survived and was recognised as an official religion in 2003. This strategic move allows *oungans* to legitimately accept money for their services, a practice which had been carrying on illegally anyway. It was also considered a political move against the spread of Protestantism by zealous North American missionaries.

Yet the Voodoo of Haiti is a far cry from the spine-chilling version of the movies in which possessed devotees wreak havoc with Voodoo dolls riddled with pins. This stereotype resulted from confusing Voodoo with the magical practices of the *bokor* or sorcerer, which were not part of the religious system. The misrepresen-

tation of Voodoo and the paranoia this caused was fuelled by the precedent set when the slaves won their independence in 1804. The Haitian revolution sent tremors of fear through all the slave colonies of the Caribbean as well as the southern slave-owning states of the USA. The plantocracy of the entire Americas felt

threatened, and the fear of similar uprisings was transferred to Voodoo – certainly a unifying factor among the rebel armies. Besides the isolation which followed independence, Haiti has also suffered from misconceptions about Voodoo. Some of these, based on the taboos and mystification of the past which sought to maintain the survival of Voodoo, unfortunately contributed to its negative image.

But Voodoo is essentially a polytheistic religion of harmony and tolerance, based on the relationship between the natural and supernatural worlds and the ties between the living and the dead. Since State recognition, there has been a movement, in Haiti and elsewhere, to give

LEFT: a popular Voodoo ceremony on All Saints Day, Port-au-Prince.
RIGHT: Voodoo flags with their symbols and detailed beadwork are considered by some to be works of art.

Voodoo more positive exposure. As Aboudja Derenoncourt points out: "This is a tradition open to the world. Everyone can come and look into Voodoo and see the positive things we're doing and see we're not hanging people upside down or eating soup with fingers in it."

Voodoo originated in the religious practices of the Fon, Yoruba and Ewe tribes in the area of west African which now covers Ghana, Nigeria, Togo and the Republic of Benin, formerly Dahomey. The word Voodoo (French: *Vaudou*) comes from Vodu, the Fon

NEW WORLD SURVIVAL

Uprooted from their different tribal homelands and shipped off to St Domingue, the west African slaves took their beliefs with them as a means of survival in a hostile world.

their help and guidance. Priests mediated between the initiates and the spirits who, when ready to deliver their messages, would possess or "ride" a dancer, hence the term "horse" for an initiate who is possessed. Regular communication with the ancestors and spirits meant the living could benefit from the accumulated tribal wisdom of the past and contact with supernatural forces.

For slaves arriving in the New World, Voodoo evolved as much as a system of survival and resistance as a link to "Guinee", the

word for God. *Loa* – the Congo word for spirit – survives in the Haitian Creole "*Lwa*" – a term used interchangeably with *les mystères*, *les anges* and *les saints* to mean "the spirits".

Although the African religions recognised a supreme being and creator, he or she was considered beyond human affairs, so the living turned for guidance to the dead and the spirits. The soul of a recently deceased family member would in time reach the status of ancestor and could later become a spirit and eventually come to represent an archetype. The *vodun* or "ancestors and spirits" were honoured and summoned by ceremonies of drumming, dance and song, while animal sacrifices were offered to solicit

ancestral homeland. The spirits of the various tribes or nations were accepted into the Voodoo pantheon with the same characteristic tolerance as were the Roman Catholic saints. The French *Code Noir*, introduced to regulate slavery in 1658, required slaves to be baptised as Catholics and banned all other religions. Voodoo embraced the saints and assimilated them: the Virgin Mary became Erzulie, goddess of love; St Patrick was equated with Dambala, the life force, and St Joseph with Loko, spirit of healing.

While the deities of the culturally dominant Kingdom of Dahomey and the Dahomean Rada rites formed the African tradition which survives to this day, a new nation of aggressive spirits was born in St Domingue as a response to the intolerable conditions of slavery.

Spirits of rebellion

The Petro nation of spirits was born from the meeting of runaway slaves *(marrons)* and surviving Taínos, the Amerindians with whom they shared many beliefs and a hatred for the genocidal European colonisers. The Petro spirits expressed the rage and subsequent rebellion of the slaves, which the benign, protective Rada deities were unequipped for. Although it was a Petro ceremony at Bois Caiman in 1791, presided

oldest surviving Voodoo tradition – white-clad *ounsis* (initiates) make their way from mud-walled, millet-thatched huts towards the temple. Some are already in a state of trance induced by hours of chanting inside one of the temple's inner rooms. Led by the *oungenikon* (chorus leader) – a hunched old man whose voice still has amazing vigour – the *ounsis* break into songs of welcome. Cowskin drums begin to charge the night air with surging polyrhythms that change with each song. By the end, one man has collapsed, possessed, falling to the floor. Catching himself he rises, brushing the dust from his head, and joins the other *ounsis* who have gathered at

over by the Jamaican *oungan* Boukman, that signalled the start of the rebellion against France, it is the Rada rites that are still celebrated annually at Souvenance, a few miles from Gonaïves, where independence was declared in 1804.

Imagine it is Easter Saturday night. The darkness engulfing the Plain of Gonaïves signals the start of an ancient ceremony, which will continue day and night until the following Thursday. In the Lakou Souvenance, a spiritual compound revered as the seat of the Dahomey rites – Haiti's

---

FAR LEFT: food offerings on an altar.
LEFT: a painting of the black virgin in a temple.
ABOVE AND RIGHT: Voodoo flag and ceremony.

a building at the entrance to the Lakou. Fernand Bien Amie, the grey-haired, stately high priest or *Serviteur* stands solemnly erect. In one hand a candle, which flickers in the night air, in the other, a large enamel mug for pouring libations.

The *ounsis* begin to chant for Papa Legba, the spirit who guards the gate to the realm of the *Lwas*, the spirits who will be invoked and to whom sacrifice will be made over the following days: "Papa Legba open the gate for us."

The *Serviteur* steps slowly out into the dusty track leading to the Lakou, pouring a libation to Legba in the dirt. Re-entering the compound he pours a libation before the "admirals of the drums" – the master drummers whose inconceivable energy will keep the *ounsis* singing and dancing for the following five nights. The ceremony has now begun and in the peristyle, the communal room of the *ounfor* (temple), the *ounsis* dance until long after midnight. By five in the morning they are back in an inner room, emerging after dawn, their white vestments – worn to summon energy and power for the ceremonies – splashed with the blood of slaughtered goats, ready for a day of sacrifices to the *Lwas* of the compound.

Various spots in the compound represent towns in the ancient kingdom of Dahomey. The ceremonies and dances performed at each of the

the failing daylight the colours are vibrantly intense, as the ceremony becomes a beautiful fusion propelled by the drums, sustained by the call-and-response songs. Many *ounsis* and spectators alike have been possessed by the different *Lwas*, yet in this context of devotion and joyous celebration, possession is the norm and not in the least intimidating.

The fact that the Souvenance ceremony has survived (some think for over 200 years) is proof of how deeply rooted Voodoo is. The religion of the slaves retains its validity for their descendants, the Créole-speaking peasants who account for 90–95 percent of the Haitian popu-

locations are those of the *Lwa* associated with each town. Many of the songs are sung in *langaj*, an African devotional language that is no longer understood. By dusk, the sacrifices to Ayison, Ogou, Zamadonn, Atchasou and Dambala are complete, and the *ounsis* have exchanged their white vestments for a riot of individual colour.

The crowd in the compound has been growing all day and there are several thousand people packed tight to see the *Serviteur* – dressed in his satin sash of blue and red, fringed with gold, flanked by the Haitian flag and the pale blue flag of La Société Belle Etoile, the Souvenance congregation – lead a procession round the tamarind tree of Ogou, the warrior spirit. In

lation. Yet although Voodoo has played such a significant role in Haiti, it has also suffered the same oppression meted out to similar African-derived belief systems in the Caribbean. While it was a motivating force in the war of independence, when the slaves believed that if they died in battle, their spirits would return directly to the ancestral homeland of Guinee, Voodoo soon became an embarrassment to both the mulatto and to the black political élite. These two factions, which temporarily put aside their hatred and rivalry to defeat the French, only to resume hostilities after victory, still shared the 19th-century belief in the supremacy of European culture and the backwardness of Africa.

So while politicians could speak of Haiti as "the cradle of African independence", their sons were educated in France and the Roman Catholicism of their former French masters remained the official religion.

Voodoo was allowed to flourish under black president Soulouque but was subsequently suppressed by the mulatto president Geffrard, who signed a concordat with the Vatican in 1860 as part of his attempt to "remove from our land these last vestiges of barbarism and slavery, superstition and its barbarous practices." These sentiments are echoed by the position of fundamentalist Protestants who are making inroads in Haiti. It was the period of US occupation from 1915 to 1934 which saw the start of the ideological shift away from cultural Eurocentricity, the eventual re-evaluation of Africa, and Voodoo's rehabilitation. Faced with US political and cultural imperialism, writers like Justin Dorsainvil and Jean Price-Mars founded the ethnological movement which defended both the relevance of Voodoo and West African traditions.

State recognition at last

Although ideology was shifting, Voodoo was still suppressed or exploited. Declared illegal in 1935, the Protestant convention established with Haiti in 1949 led to the massacre of *oungans*, and the destruction of *ounfors* and sacred trees. The last massacre of Voodoo priests was in the 1986 "Deshokage", or uprooting of Duvalierists, following Baby Doc's flight to France. State recognition in the constitution of 1987 finally acknowledged Voodoo and in 2003 it became the official religion (see page 105).

The Nacyonal Zantray, founded in 1986, is an organisation of Voodoo institutions with a government mandate to promote the re-evaluation of the sacred cult and to equip it as an agent of social, economic and environmental development. Projects have been set up aimed at making rural Voodoo communities self-supporting, establishing *ounfor*-based primary schools and literacy schemes, as well as much-needed reforestation schemes. The religion is also being promoted as a tourist attraction.

Despite the harsh realities Haiti still faces, the official recognition given to both Voodoo

and Créole reveals a new mood of embracing essential elements of the nation's identity. Voodoo rhythms and songs play an important part in the repertoire of a whole new generation of "racine" or roots musical groups.

As the religion of the majority, Voodoo has consistently been tolerant of Catholicism and other Christian sects (all Voodoo ceremonies begin with Catholic prayers). The Catholic and Anglican church in Haiti now view Voodoo in a more favourable light, and it is only the growth of evangelical Protestantism – which often holds out the lure of employment – that continues to condemn the sacred cult. ❏

LEFT: Voodoo priest and flag-maker Edgar Jean-Louis.
RIGHT: a painting of Jean-Claude Duvalier on the side of a temple; he used Voodoo to maintain power.

DEFENDERS AND EXPLOITERS

Price-Mars' seminal collection of lectures *Ainsi parla l'oncle* argued that Voodoo could not be dismissed as mere superstition but was in fact a religion of "dynamism or animism". The *noiriste* writers of the Griot group (including the young François Duvalier who would later become the notorious Papa Doc), founded after the US occupation, developed this re-evaluation, calling Voodoo "the transcendent expression of racial consciousness before the enigmas of the world". The Duvaliers, father and son, exploited Voodoo connections to maintain power. Papa Doc especially, manipulated peasant sensibility, dressing at times like the spirits of death and rebirth.

MORE THAN *MERENGUE*

They may not be politically in tune, but Haiti's African-rooted beats and the
Dominican Republic's eclectic dance music provide a musical bond

The musical spectrum of Hispaniola ranges from Haiti's neo-African forms, some of the Caribbean's oldest surviving African music, to the manic mayhem of *merengue*, the Dominican national music, which is a serious contender for the fastest music in the Caribbean.

At first glance, these uneasy neighbours appear to have totally different musical traditions and styles (Haitian French- and Créole-influenced as opposed to the distinctive Latin sound of the Dominican Republic), but there are musical bonds linking the two political entities.

A common link

Periods of occupation by the French and then by independent Haiti did not endear Dominicans to Haitians. Consequently, despite their equally antagonistic relationship with Spain, Dominicans have always identified culturally with Spain or other Latin American countries. Their African heritage, symbol of the Haitian enemy, was rejected to the extent that blacks even now often refer to themselves as "Indios oscuros" (dark-skinned Indians).

Yet the West African heritage is there, both indigenous and imported by thousands of Haitians who came, and still come, to cut sugar cane. The Dominican folk religion, with its worship of West African spirits, drum-led songs, dances and spiritual possession, is close to Haiti's Voodoo, while *gaga* (a Dominican version of Haiti's *rara*, a raucous Lenten street-procession music featuring bamboo and zinc trumpets) is popular on the western border with its large Haitian immigrant community.

Even *merengue* links the two. Ironically it is still the national dance of both countries. The Haitian and Dominican versions both originated in the first half of the 19th century. These were only two variants of a whole family of creolised European dance forms based on the

contredanse, mazurka, polka, quadrille and waltz, which were fairly popular throughout the Greater and Lesser Antilles.

As might be expected, controversy and rivalry surround the origins of the *merengue* (*méringue* in Haiti), with the Haitians claiming they introduced it east of the border during the 1822–44 occupation. During the 20th century, the Dominican form became dominant largely due to the actions of the Rafael Trujillo, who made it the national music and commissioned bands to sing his praises. *Merengue* was also borrowed in the 1950s to form the basis for Haiti's enduringly popular *konpa* dance music.

Caribbean interaction

Another significant yet more subtle musical bond between the two countries comes from their constant exposure to other Caribbean styles of music. The migratory experience of both populations has involved them in cultural interaction in neighbouring Cuba and Puerto Rico and through-

LEFT: playing the maracas at a beach bar on the Samaná Peninsula.
RIGHT: Feet of Rhythm reveal the importance of dance to the culture.

out the greater Caribbean. In the past, Cuban *son*, *bolero*, *guaguancó* and *mambo*, and more recently *salsa* from Puerto Rico, influenced both Haitian and Dominican music, while the Haitian-derived *tumba francesa* became a distinct genre in Cuba's Oriente province, and *merengue* has been a huge hit as far south as Venezuela. Beyond these links, however, the two countries have their own distinctive music. What is so surprising is that both countries (especially Haiti, the poorest nation in the western hemisphere) have produced such vibrant, powerful music, considering their long histories of oppression and devastation.

Haiti is unique for its sacred Voodoo drums

rhythms are altered, the spirits do not answer.

Voodoo evolved as a clandestine and syncretic religion under colonialism. The slaves came from an area in West Africa stretching from Senegal to the Congo River basin and on arrival in St Domingue, members of the same ethnic group were deliberately separated in order to prevent communication and rebellion.

The ancestral spirits and deities of the many different tribes were integrated into a new, extended pantheon, which also embraced the Roman Catholic saints of the French slave masters. In the isolation of the plantations and the mountain communities of runaway slaves, the

and vast repertoire of songs and dances (many still undocumented and unrecorded) performed to worship and invoke the *Lwas*, or spirits. Although similar neo-African religions exist throughout the Americas (Santería in Cuba, Kumina in Jamaica, Shango in Trinidad and Candomblé in Brazil and other South American countries), Haiti's early independence in 1804 meant the survival of African musical forms to an extent unparalleled elsewhere.

Some of these forms are now unknown in Africa. It has been suggested that their survival is not due simply to the conservatism of religious music but rather to the fact that specific rhythms are used to summon the spirits. If those

religion and its music developed some regional variations. Even the sacred drum – the voice of the spirits – comes in many shapes and sizes, from the 3-metre (10-ft) *asoto* to the bongo-sized *tanbou kout*. Most of the other instruments are percussive (rattles, bells and tambourines), but the European violin and flute are used by southern *menwat* (minuet) groups, a legacy of the days when slaves played in orchestras at the colonists' concerts, operas and balls.

Among the many different rites, the Rada of Dahomey (the oldest African tradition in Haiti), the Kongo, Petwo (a new nation of militant spirits called into being to combat slavery) and Bizango (secret society) are best known. All these rites have their own specific instruments, rhythms, song and dance cycles.

Rada instruments include three single-headed cowskin drums: the largest, the *manman* (mother drum) is played with one hand and the hammer-shaped *agida* stick. The *manman* leads the dance with its low-register rolling, indicating choreographic or song changes by breaking against the rhythms of the other drums. The mid-sized, middle-register *segon* is played with one half-moon-shaped *abara* stick and a straight

music, with its beautiful interplay between drums and call-and-response songs, is the most sophisticated Voodoo music.

For Westerners accustomed to the concept of sheet music, the experience of listening to the master drummers leading the five-days-and-nights Rada ceremony at Souvenance which begins on Easter Saturday *(see page 107)*, is incredible. The rhythms, passed down from generation to generation, are never repeated and there are no scores to play from. Sera Jean-Baptiste, one of

MERENGUE FESTIVAL

Santo Domingo's annual Merengue Festival is held in the last week of July and the first week of August, and features some of the world's best *merengue* bands and dancers.

stick, answering the *manman* with intricate patterns, while the smallest, high-pitch *boula* – played with two straight sticks – continues a regular beat in time with the *ogan* (bell). The *ason* (rattle) can only be handled by *oungans* and *mambos* (priests and priestesses) or the *oungenikon* (chorus leader). Occasionally, a *bas* (large tambourine) supports the *manman*.

The foremost Rada rhythms are the trilogy of *yanvalou*, *mayi* and *zepol*, and the *nago gwan kou*, *kongo-rada* and *dyouba-matinik*. Rada

LEFT: the brass section of Orquesta Septentrional play at home and abroad.
ABOVE: Kanpech on stage.

the Souvenance "admirals of the drums", jokingly admits, "You have to know how to play drums here. You really have to know what you're doing, otherwise they'll eat you!"

Marathon ceremony

The main rite for the Kongo spirits is the marathon 15-days-and-nights ceremony at Sukri Danache. The Kongo rhythms of *kita* and *boumba* are played on two single-headed goat skin drums, which answer each other, while *tchachas* (rattles) play in counter rhythm and the bell maintains a continuous time. Southern Kongo groups may use up to eight drums.

Besides the sacred music of Voodoo, Haiti also

has a rich folk tradition and a variety of urban-based European- and Caribbean-influenced dance styles. The traditional folk song "*Choucoune*" provided the melody for "*Yellow Bird*", a long-time favourite throughout the English-speaking Caribbean.

Many of the folk forms, work songs of the *konbits* (communal field gangs), play, story, praise, protest and political songs are simply continuations of African traditional forms. *Mizik twoubadou* (troubadour music), which is performed by small ensembles of guitar, maracas, *gwaj* (scraper), *tanbou* drum and *marimba* (a wooden box bass fitted with metal keys which are plucked

occasionally saxophone and trumpet. Those without instruments beat time on empty bottles.

The most significant dance music since the 19th century has been the *méringue* or *mereng*, a créolised version of an old European dance, although other forms, such as the *mascarón*, *quadrille* and *contredanse* have also enjoyed popularity. Based on the quintuplet, a five-note rhythm, the *mereng* originally developed in two forms: one for the salon and one for the streets.

European-trained Haitian composers like Occide Jeanty, Ludovic Lamothe and François Manigat wrote *merengs* for piano, sometimes using violins or woodwind instruments. The

by the player who sits on the box), was introduced by cane-cutters returning from Cuba.

Rara music

Another folk form which is just as popular as carnival music in countryside and city alike is *rara*. This exuberant music, which has Voodoo connections, accompanies the vividly costumed bands that parade through the streets from Ash Wednesday to Easter day. While the bands sing songs with themes ranging from topical events to political satire and the outrageously obscene, a skilled hooting accompaniment is provided by *vaksins* and *kones* (bamboo and pressed zinc trumpets), *big* (bugle), *gwaj*, *tchacha* and

Afro-Parisian sound is reminiscent of ragtime and Puerto Rican dances of the same era. Street *mereng* was especially popular with the 19th-century carnival crowds, as it was used to mock and ridicule prominent or powerful figures.

As a popular dance, the *mereng* acted as a barometer of musical and ideological fashion, absorbing any number of influences. During the American occupation of 1915–34, dance bands began incorporating jazz into their repertoire and from the 1920s onwards Cuban *son* was a major influence. Aspects of Voodoo music were introduced as part of the movement rejecting US culture and affirming Haitian values.

While classical composers like Justin Elie

and Werner Jaegerhuber utilised Voodoo-inspired melodies, the dance bands, now in a big swing band format, introduced Voodoo ceremonial instruments to their line-up and Voodoo rhythms and melodies to their compositions. The Super Jazz de Jeunes, the most famous of the Voodoo-jazz bands, dressed in colourful folk style and their stage show included dancers moving to the well-known *yanvalou*, *kongo* and *ibo* Voodoo rhythms.

By the mid-1950s, the craze for the accordion- and sax-led Dominican *merengue* swept Haiti, altering the course of its cousin for ever. In 1955, saxophonist Nemours Jean-Baptiste introduced his new dance rhythm, *konpa-direk* (direct rhythm), which, while slightly altering the beat, owed much to the *merengue*.

This was the start of *konpa*, which would dominate Haitian popular music until the 1980s and which is still played by foreign-based bands, notably Tabou Combo and the Magnum Band. In 1958, Weber Sicot, Haiti's leading saxophonist, produced his *Kadans-rampa* (rampart) rhythm (identical to *konpa* except for a minor variation in beat) in direct competition with Nemours. It was the contrived rivalry between the two bandleaders that marked the start of modern commercial Haitian music, lasting until Sicot's 1965 song of truce, *Polemik Fini*.

Mini-djaz bands

In the early 1960s, the influence of US and British rock and pop spawned a proliferation of Yeye combos (after The Beatles' *Yeah Yeah Yeah*) among the children of middle- and upper-class Haitians. Although the Yeyes were popular at youth concerts, the non-contact dances which went with the music were too much of a break with the traditional *tet kole* (heads glued together) dance style. Combos began including *konpa*, with its close-couple dance style, in their repertoires. These groups were known as *mini-djaz* (big dance bands were known as *djaz*, while *mini* referred to the miniskirt craze).

With the success of *mini-djaz* bands like Shleu-Shleu and Tabou Combo, the established *konpa* bands scaled themselves down in order to compete. Through the 1970s, *konpa* – with its guitar and percussion sound augmented by

sax or organ – was a major influence in the French Antilles, French Guiana, and Dominica and St Lucia (both English-ruled islands with Créole-speaking populations).

But with the emergence of hi-tech *zouk* in Martinique and Guadeloupe in the early 1980s, that influence waned as it did back home where *konpa*, the popular music of the repressive Duvalier era, made way for a new cultural thrust. One of the few island-based *konpa* bands to survive the change was Coupé Cloué, led by the late great troubadour Gesner Henry (1925–1998).

The most significant development of the last two decades of the 20th century was the *mizik*

LEFT: a variety of percussion instruments on sale at Mercado Modelo, Santo Domingo.
RIGHT: Tabou Combo.

rasin (roots music) movement, which some see as a development of the Voodoo-jazz of the 1940s. *Mizik rasin* was produced by the generation who, at the end of the 1970s, were influenced by roots reggae, funk and rock.

While the novel *generayson* cultural movement of the 1980s stressed the importance of the Créole language and the utilisation of rural music as inspiration, *mizik rasin* explored Rara and ceremonial Voodoo music. Foula, led by the Voodoo master drummer Aboudja, experimented with a

> **POPULAR PERFORMER**
>
> Manno Charlemagne is a satirical troubadour who sang protest songs in the Duvalier era. He spent years in exile but returned to serve as mayor of Port-au-Prince 1995–9.

huge following. Their live performances, with Jimi Hendrix-like guitar soaring over the battery of Voodoo drums, are intense and cathartic. It's not unusual for members of the audience at a Boukman Eksperyans concert to become possessed. Theodore "Lolo" Beaubrun, founder and leader of Boukman explains: "This music is engaged, for the revolution. We have to go back to the spirit level, beyond intellect, ideology, religion."

The contemporary music scene reflects some of the current trends in the Caribbean and the

fusion of both Voodoo drumming and American-influenced jazz.

Bands like Boukman Eksperyans, Sanba-yo, Sakad, Boukan Ginen, Kalfou Lakay and then Koudjay, Ram, Zobop, Alowi Jaweh and Kampech use traditional songs and Voodoo rhythms in a vibrant new fusion incorporating transnational influences from rock, funk, jazz and more recently rap and hip hop. The *rasin* bands are probably the first Haitian representatives on the World Music scene.

With conscious lyrics which champion the poor and oppressed in Bob Marley-style, the *rasin* bands, who have suffered their share of persecution at the hands of the military, have a

US. *Zouk*, *salsa*, *merengue*, soca and especially reggae are all popular. King Posse, the dance-hall reggae band, even sing in convincing Jamaican patois. Rap and hip hop artists have been on the scene since Master Dji's 1987 "Sispann", a call for the end of political violence. This style has received a tremendous boost from the success of Haitian-born, US-based Wyclef Jean, one-time Fugee, whose debut solo album *The Carnival* included four Créole tracks.

There are two young guitarists who are highly respected at home and around the world: Beethova Obas for his gentle troubadour songs, which draw on traditions from Brazil and the entire Caribbean, and the composer Amos Coulange for virtuoso renditions of his new arrangements of folk themes from Haiti and the French Antilles. An impressive and much-travelled guitar trio is Strings, which plays a happy blend of *konpa*, flamenco and Latin rhythms, accompanied by a group of three virtuoso percussionists.

A few hours on the bus takes you from the home of Voodoo rhythms across the border to the capital of *merengue*, the northern provincial town of Santiago de los Caballeros, which is the Dominican Republic's version of Nashville. Musically, the Dominican Republic may be synonymous with *merengue*, but there are many other styles to discover. These range

instrument with purely African origins, is still used in parts of the country, where it is known as a *gayumba*, and the tall *palo* drums of the Afro-Dominican folk religion which are played throughout the Republic are Yoruba in design. The *palo*, which is carved from a single piece of wood and then hollowed out, comes in two sizes: the *mayor* is 1.5 metres (5ft) long and 30 cm (1ft) across the single goatskin head; the *menor* is nearly 1 metre (3ft) long and 23 cm (9 inches) across. While one drummer beats the skin with bare hands, another hits the body of the drum with a stick, a recognisably African practice.

from the distinctly African-style *cantos de hacha*, chopping songs of the south, and *plenas*, or work songs, to the almost pure Spanish *tonadas* and *salves* of the Cibao Valley, whose melodies resemble those of ancient Castille.

African influences

Even though the African heritage has been denied or rejected by the cultural mainstream in the Dominican Republic, it continues to survive. The mosquito drum or earthbow, an

LEFT: Lolo Beaubrun, the lead singer of Boukman Eksperyans, one of the most popular *racines* bands.
ABOVE: Richard Morse in his younger days with RAM.

Fiestas celebrating saints' days often feature *palo*-driven music, which takes the form of call-and-response song and dance. In the north-coast town of Samaná, where many of the black American immigrants who arrived in 1824 were settled, the feast day of the Republic's patron saint, the Virgin of Altagracia (21 January), is preceded by the *Novenas* – nine nights of celebration. The festivities start at 9pm each night, finishing at six the following morning, and the focus of these all-night parties is the *palo* drumming, with its accompanying Dance of the Palos (a circular couples dance) and improvised songs, sung by a lead singer with a call-and-response chorus. In Samaná, the *bambulá*, an Afro-Caribbean dance widespread throughout the Caribbean, is also performed.

Another obvious example of African and Roman Catholic syncretism is the *saradunga* festival, held for John the Baptist on the night of 23 June in the southern town of Baní. Here the *Capitana*, the *Bomba* (the major African dance of Puerto Rico) and the *Jacana* are all carried out to the accompaniment of the double-headed, barrel-shaped *tambora* drum, the *güira* (metal scraper) and the characteristic and ubiquitous call-and-response singing.

Only 19 km (12 miles) from Santo Domingo in Villa Mella, a popular legend exists explain-

imported by immigrants from the English Leeward and Windward islands and the Momise dance dramas, Créole versions of the English Mummers plays, were brought from St Kitts and Nevis in the 1920s. In San Pedro, *la danza del padre invierno* (a Father Winter dance based on the St George and the dragon legend), *la danza salvaje* (wild dance) and *la danza del Codril* are performed on St Peter's Day (29 June) and at other festivals on the island.

Even the basic five-note rhythm of the *merengue* probably has African origins. This rhythmic pattern is common to much of the black music of the Americas, from the Cuban

ing the arrival of the *palo* drums, which are used by the Congos del Espíritu Santo, who play at the feast of the Holy Ghost and throughout the year at wakes and secular dances. Folklore has it that in the mid-19th century a saint was found playing the drums in a guava field. A more mundane theory is that this tradition derived from the African *kalinda* dance, which was banned a century before.

Other folk rhythms, like the *mangulina* from the mountains and the *carabine,* may well have African origins. One unique Afro-Caribbean tradition, the *ritmo guloya* of the San Pedro de Macorís region on the south coast, deserves special mention. The *guloya* dances were

habanera, Puerto Rican *danza* and Argentine tango, to the early Trinidadian calypsos.

The origins of *merengue* are undocumented. One theory suggests that the original dance was based on the popular *upa* from Cuba, which travelled to Puerto Rico where it was banned as immoral in 1848. After adapting steps from the *contradanza*, it was then referred to as the *merengue*. An account of its first performance in the Dominican Republic goes back to the 1844 war against the Haitians, when the victorious Dominicans sang and danced to a song about a deserter: *Toma' Juyo con la Bandera* (Thomas Fled with the Flag).

Despite its obscure beginnings, *merengue*

developed from folk forms before going on to establish itself not only as the national dance music but as an international genre, which even eclipsed salsa as *the* Latin dance sound of the 1980s. Of the many Creolised European dance forms to originate from the Caribbean, *merengue* has probably travelled the furthest and certainly moves the fastest.

In its early form the *merengue* was played by ensembles of guitar (or the smaller four-string cuatro), *güira* (a perforated metal cylinder scraped with a metal stick, a

UBIQUITOUS SOUNDS

The big band sound of *merengue* can be heard all over the Dominican Republic – in bars, restaurants, taxis, on the street – and mostly played at full volume.

dance soon took on the Afro-Caribbean features of vibrant rhythms and the call-and-response final section of the accompanying songs, with their wide-ranging topics. Predictably spurned by the white and mulatto élite as being vulgar, *merengue* was enthusiastically embraced by everybody else.

By the end of World War I (1914–8), the modern form of *merengue* had been established: the short introductory *paseo* followed by the two longer sections, the *merengue* or song section which

modern version of the gourd scraper is still used in Cuba today), *tambora* (double-headed barrel drum, the left head made from male goatskin played by hand; the female goatskin right head played with a stick), and *marimba* (a metal key box bass).

By the 1870s, the guitar had given way to the melodeon, the button accordion brought by German immigrants, which was to give the *merengue* its defining sound.

What began as a very restrained European

segued into the call-and-response improvised *jaleo*. The structure of the two main parts is very similar to Afro-Cuban forms such as the rumba or *guaguancó*, where the melodic European-style first part is followed by some percussion-led improvisation.

Of all the regional variants, the *merengue típico* of the Cibao region became the most influential. This classic style, known as *Perico Ripiao* (after The Ripped Parrot bar in Santiago's red-light district), was popularised by bandleaders like Nico Lora and Tono Abreu in the 1920s. Galvanised by the runaway tempo of the *tambora*, the accordion is played with staccato stabs to the harmonising saxophone.

LEFT: *merengue* was made for dancing.
ABOVE: music can be heard everywhere – in the bars, restaurants, clubs and on the street.

A late addition to the line-up, the sax would blare out *merengue*'s international success, but the accordion-led style is still very much alive in Santiago with players like Francisco Ulloa and Fefita de la Grande.

The American occupation of 1916–24 fuelled growing nationalism and with it bourgeois acceptance of the *merengue*. Although the Dominican Republic has little to be grateful to Rafael Trujillo for, during his dictatorship *merengue* was elevated to the status of national music and dance by a 1936 decree. Urban dance bands were legally required to incorporate *merengue* in their swing band repertoires. These bands,

heavily influenced by Cuban *mambo*, added the exhilarating trumpet and sax arrangements which still feature in contemporary *merengue*.

Ironically, Trujillo's 1961 assassination was celebrated with the *merengue* "*El Muerte del Chivo*" (Death of the Goat). While the 1970s saw *merengue* competing with salsa and US pop, the emergence of bandleaders like Johnny Ventura, Cuco Valoy and Wilfredo Vargas pioneered the speed-defying modern version of *merengue*, which would sweep the heartlands of salsa in Puerto Rico and New York City.

Ventura, with his James Brown-like stage presence, pared down the ensemble, giving the lead role to the sax and the horns, replacing the accordion with guitar and keyboards or synthesizer, and emphasising the automatic fire of the *tambora*. Vargas has made the *merengue* a truly Caribbean mélange of drawing-room *konpa*, *zouk*, reggae and even rap.

Rival to *merengue*

The most outstanding figure of what some would call neo-*merengue* is the extraordinary singer/songwriter Juan Luis Guerra. After training at the National Conservatory and studying jazz at Boston's prestigious Berkley College of Music, he returned home to form the vocal quartet 440, performing Manhattan Transfer-style jazz songs.

In the 1990s, Guerra tackled both *merengue* and *bachata*, traditional, sentimental, guitar-based country music. With influences ranging from The Beatles to the great Panamanian *salsero* Ruben Blades and the Cuban *nueva canción* singers, particularly Silvio Rodríguez, Guerra's nasal delivery perfectly matches the popular timbre of the Latin style. His vocal sophistication, intelligent and often socially conscious lyrics, and command of diverse styles, make him – along with the brilliant jazz pianist Michel Camilo – the Dominican Republic's most significant contribution to international music.

Although it has not yet gained the international exposure of *merengue*, *bachata* (songs of bitterness) is the highly popular soul music of the Dominican *barrios* (neighbourhoods), the voice of the displaced rural peasant driven by poverty to the slums of Santo Domingo, New York City or any major Caribbean port. It is easy to identify a Dominican bordello in Antigua, Curaçao or the Virgin Islands by the steady stream of sweet melancholic *bachata* drifting from it at all hours of the day and night.

Bachata developed from the guitar-led folk ensembles of the 19th century, which by the 1950s played a repertoire of Cuban *sons*, *boleros* and Mexican *rancheras*, with their sentimental appeal. Although dismissed by the middle classes, who in the 1970s labelled it *bachata* after the raucous lower-class fiestas, singers like Luis Segora and Julio Angel popularised the form to the extent that it now rivals the *merengue* at home. ❏

LEFT: innovative band leader Johnny Ventura has been compared to James Brown on stage.
RIGHT: Emeline Michelle gets in the groove.

HAITI'S LITERARY ART

Haitian authors are making their mark at home and abroad with serious novels written in various languages, including Creole

The new voices in Haitian literature are speaking in different languages: English, French and Créole. In the US, the strongest of those voices belongs to Edwidge Danticat, a young Haitian American author who has earned the respect of literary critics and a devoted following among lovers of new Caribbean feminist literature *(see page 126)*. Her short-story collection, *Krik? Krak!*, was nominated for the prestigious National Book Award in 1995.

In French-speaking Canada, it's the voice of Dany Laferriere that's being heard. His *How to Make Love to a Negro* – the fanciful musings of an out of place immigrant – caused a sensation when it hit the bookshops of Montréal in the autumn of 1985. Most of Laferrière's work has now been translated into English.

Immigrant voice

A lot of serious literature is being created in Haiti as well, by authors such as Rodney St Eloi, Yanick Lahens, Margaret Papillon, Paulette Poujol and Lyonel Trouillot, who all write in French. Among them is Gary Victor, who served as a deputy minister under President Jean-Bertrand Aristide, before the military coup of 1990. Voodoo, politics and acerbic social comment are blended in his novels.

Edwidge Danticat's stories, however, have struck a chord that resonates deeply among women and immigrants in the United States. Her voice is fresh, honest, caring and respectful of the past. She speaks eloquently and realistically about the experience of moving to a new land.

Danticat grew up in New York City, but all her stories have deep roots in the Haitian soil of her childhood. It is in Haiti that she began to notice, and nurture, the magic of storytelling – as much a part of the Haitian landscape as its mountains and blue seas. "In telling stories to my mother and me, my grandmother gave us a gift, a treasure trove of beautiful memories…"

LEFT: reading at Hostal Nader Hotel, Santo Domingo.
RIGHT: Voodoo rituals continue to be a common theme in Haitian storytelling.

Danticat writes in the foreword to *The Magic Orange Tree and other Haitian Folktales*, a collection by Diane Wokstein. "For once you are granted the remembrance of a story, it never stops with you. You find yourself anticipating your next opportunity to retell the tale."

It is in that spirit that she wrote her novel,

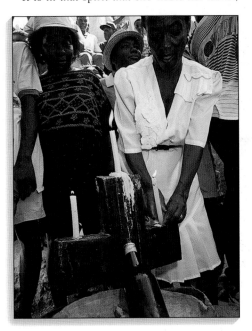

The Farming of Bones. Set in 1937 in the Dominican Republic, the story turns over soil that has been soaked over decades with Haitian blood. It is the story of one kind of immigrant, Haitians too poor and unable to find work in their own country who cross over to the other side of the island to cut sugar cane. Danticat creates characters that could have walked out of any history book, or any painting depicting that migration. *The Farming of Bones* is fiction, but it could have been fact.

Set on the comfortable plantation of Alegría, not far from the border with Haiti, the novel begins on an August morning in 1937. The protagonist is Haitian-born Amabelle Désir, who serves as light housekeeper and companion to Señora Valencia, Alegría's young matron. Amabelle and Señora Valencia have been friends since they were little girls, since the day Valencia's father found Amabelle in tears on the banks of the Massacre River. Amabelle's parents, herbal healers, perished after they were caught in the river's current and swept away.

So the girls grew up together, Amabelle sharing a room with Valencia, but that changed when Valencia married the ambitious Pico Duarte, a rising star in the army of dictator Rafael Leonidas Trujillo Molina. What united them in the past is now forgotten. Their blood

and class differences are now all that matters. Amabelle is banished from Valencia's bedroom, and shares a room with a sugarcane worker who arrived looking for work after a hurricane destroyed his home in Haiti.

When Valencia gives birth to twins, a boy and a girl, the boy, light-skinned, is named after the dictator. The girl's skin is deep bronze. "Amabelle, do you think my daughter will always be the colour she is now?" Valencia asks. "My poor love, what if she's mistaken for one of your people."

Against this background begins one of the most appalling chapters in Dominican history.

THE ART OF STORYTELLING

Darkness falls in Haiti, and everything turns to magic. Around the countryside, the only visible light is a yellowish glow from small kerosene lamps inside small huts. Mothers put their babies to bed. Everyone whispers as they move around, large shadows on the walls. The only noises are the mournful sounds of livestock bedding down for the night.

There are no TVs here, only a storyteller who gathers children around him to hear his folktales. "Krick!" says the storyteller, a signal that the story is about to begin. "Krack!" they answer, meaning they're ready. And so the story begins.

Haitians believe that nightfall is the right time for stories. Telling a story in daylight only brings bad luck. Tonight,

maybe they'll hear about the *loupgarou*, the werewolf who eats children alive. Or they'll hear about Bouki, a dumb character who gets into all kinds of trouble, or Malis, the smart fellow who gets Bouki out of those troubles.

Some stories are about the church and God, others are about Voodoo. In Haiti's oral tradition, these stories occupy an important place. Watching the faces of the children and their wide, bright eyes, they certainly entertain. They're also used to educate, to tell right from wrong. They've been passed down through the centuries, often with little change. Some tell what life was like during slavery, and others go all the way back to Africa.

In October 1937, thousands of Haitian labourers are shot by Dominican troops and police. The killings go on all over the country. Dominicans support the effort. Haiti's president, Stenio Vincent, remains silent in the face of such horror. "The poor man, no matter who he is, is always despised by his neighbours," someone tells Amabelle. "When you stay too long at a neighbour's house, it's only natural that he become weary of you and hate you."

As a child, Danticat lived through her own

THE 1937 MASSACRE

President Trujillo was angry at the number of Haitians settling in the DR. Thousands were herded up in courtyards, forced to lie face down, then shot in the back of the head.

Luckily, she survived that dark period in history, joining her family in New York three years later. Like all young immigrants of that age, Danticat spent a period floating between languages – in her case, Créole and English.

It didn't take her long to find her voice, though. In her first published work, an essay that appeared in a New York newspaper, she talked honestly about her immigrant experience. Graduating from Barnard College with a degree in French literature didn't leave many options: it was either teaching

version of madness and terror under Jean-Claude Duvalier, who was named Haitian president for life after his father François Papa Doc Duvalier died in 1971. Danticat was nine years old at the time. Dissent was not tolerated.

When Danticat first started writing down her poems in her little schoolgirl notebooks, "a lot of people who were in jail were writers. They were journalists, they were novelists, and many of them were killed or "disappeared". It was a very scary thing to think about," she said.

LEFT: many remember hearing stories at their grandmother's knee.
ABOVE: imagery in art is mirrored in literature.

or nursing. She chose writing, translating her experiences into tales of universal appeal.

Danticat was only 25 years old when *Breath, Eyes, Memory* was accepted for publication. Next came *Krik? Krak!*, which includes stories about life in Haiti during the Duvalier years. Characters range from a man attempting to leave the island in a faulty boat to a woman who doesn't want her son to discover she's a prostitute.

The well-received collection competed for the National Book Award with works by writers such as Madison Smartt Bell, whose own *All Souls Rising* explored the Haitian revolution in all its gory details.

Edwidge Danticat

There's no mistaking Edwidge Danticat's voice. It's strong, immigrant, female and black, and it's unsettling. In her novel, *The Farming of Bones*, she leads readers through a nightmarish landscape of brutality, where labourers from Haiti are treated as less than human on the sugar cane plantations of the Dominican Republic.

Danticat may be the most celebrated Haitian-American writer of her young generation, but she knows about pain. She was only an infant when her father left the family's native Haiti for New York,

in search of a better life. Her mother followed soon after, leaving her to be raised by an uncle. Danticat hardly knew her family when she and a younger brother were reunited with their parents in the USA more than eight years later. A shy 12-year-old, her accented English stood out at Clara Barton High School in Brooklyn. She quickly assimilated.

Raised in a culture that teaches its women to be mute and obedient in a male-dominated world, Danticat now lays bare painful issues once taboo in her homeland. In her first novel, *Breath, Eyes, Memory*, Danticat shares a young twisted world, between love and sexual deviousness, as she traces the mental steps a young girl goes through as her mother tests her virginity. Is this sexual abuse? Would she have

thought those thoughts in Haiti? The US creates the space that makes it possible to raise those questions, and Danticat's character, Sophie, begins to distance herself from her family and her culture.

Her recent novel, *The Farming of the Bones*, also explores the great divide of exile, this time between families and between countries. Seminal moments in the story take place along the Massacre River, which separates Haiti and the Dominican Republic. Generations of Haitian farmers have crossed over to cut sugar cane, live on plantation-style shacks, and get miserable wages. Those who have stayed behind illegally live in fear of border-town army patrols that can send them back to Haiti at any time. Haitians say that as black Créole speakers, they are treated shabbily. Some elderly Dominicans tell their grandchildren stories of legendary cruelty from Haiti's army of freed slaves who occupied the Spanish side of the island for 20 years after their revolution.

It is against this background that Haitian-born Amabelle Désir, the protagonist in *The Farming of Bones,* serves as light housekeeper and companion to Señora Valencia, a plantation's young matron. Amabelle's parents drowned in the swirling waters of the Massacre, where the plantation owner picked up the orphan. The girls grow up together, but worlds apart. Amabelle's Haitian roots in 1937 force her to flee the house where she was raised, as Rafael Leonidas Trujillo's army leads a pogrom against Haitians in his country. More than 30,000 Haitians are said to have died at the hands of Dominican soldiers, militias whipped up into a frenzy, the waters of the Massacre flowing red.

Seventy years on, the genocide continues to find deep resonance in Haiti, a country still seeped in blood and tears. Danticat's voice has found recognition in international circles, her work getting the attention it deserves, both in her adopted country and in her homeland. Her collection of short stories, *Krik? Krak!*, was nominated for a National Book Award and in 1998 the *New York Times Magazine* picked out Danticat as one of the USA's most promising young artists. She was an honoured guest at Haiti's Festival of the Diaspora in 1999.

Although she writes about deeply hurtful episodes, Danticat draws readers in with sparse words presented in a gentle style. But don't mistake that gentleness for anything less than what it is: a writer of exceptional talent sharing a rich heritage with her fellow Haitians and opening a new world to readers throughout the globe. ❑

LEFT: Edwidge Danticat: a novelist who knows pain.

Dany Laferrière made his mark as a writer early on, too. His satire *How to make Love to a Negro* became wildly popular in Canada and was quickly adapted and made into a film when he was still in his early 30s. Like Danticat, Laferriere was born in Port-au-Prince, but left Haiti for exile in North America for different reasons.

He was working as a radio journalist in the mid-1970s at a time when the younger Duvalier was actually creating more openings in Haitian society for press

GUEST OF HONOUR

Although she writes in English, Danticat's fame has reached her homeland. She was a guest of honour at the 1999 Festival of the Diaspora in Haiti.

him long to produce *How to Make Love to a Negro*, a book about an immigrant determined to move ahead in a new culture without losing his identity.

The beauty of Laferrière's writing is that he didn't swallow this new culture whole. He set out to look at it with a critical eye. David Homel, who has translated Laferrière's works into English knows the author well. "That first novel," Homel says, "is not what one would expect to find by just reading the title. It is much more complex.

ABOVE: escape is a common theme in literature.

freedom. However, Laferrière soon saw the door of opportunity firmly closed when he stumbled upon the body of a murdered colleague on the side of the road. He decided it was time to move on and headed to Montréal. The year was 1978.

He followed the well-trodden immigrant path and found work as a labourer in various factories throughout the city. By night, he wrote about his experiences as a black man who grew up in Haiti, whose professional life took a curve, and who now was living among a minority in a city of French Canadians. It didn't take

"Once one gets past the effective teaser title," he continues, "sex becomes mostly an indicator of class, ethnic and historical conflict. When the hero fails to score, it is because he has committed not a romantic but a historical gaffe. Whether it is his praise of carbohydrates to a Scarsdale dieter, or his admission that, in his country, people eat cats, the results are hilarious and usually result in the hero sprinting out of his prospective lover's apartment to try to catch the last subway of the night. Even in the most sensual moments, the hero's calm, collected consciousness is evaluating the acts of love-making in terms of class and colour."

The book became an international best-seller,

making Laferrière Canada's best-known Haitian writer. He went on to work as a journalist for Canadian TV, while continuing with his fiction. Other works include: *Why Must a Black Writer Write About Sex?*, a look at race, sex and class in North America; *Dining With the Dictator*, a tale of a young boy's foray into the lives of daring and beautiful women in Port-au-Prince; *An Aroma of Coffee*, the magical story of a 10-year-old boy spending the summer with his grandmother in a small town in Haiti, listening to her stories; and *Eroshima*, a contemplation on sex, death, beauty and the Bomb.

Laferrière and his family live part of the year

in Canada – where he has a loyal following – and part of the year in Miami.

Many other young Haitian writers are finding their literary voices in exile, too, some even writing in Créole, which has been gaining wider acceptance as a written language in Haiti and elsewhere around the world.

A wider audience

In Haiti, most writers trying to reach an international audience continue to write in French. Among them is Marguerite Papillon, whose novels about class, colour and child abuse, among other issues, are gaining a small fol-

GRAHAM GREENE

In his 1966 novel, *The Comedians*, Graham Greene revealed Haiti's descent into a terrifying orgy of lawlessness under François "Papa Doc" Duvalier and his Tontons Macoutes. On one of his frequent visits to Haiti he took a room at the Hotel Oloffson, a creaky building in Port-au-Prince. A former "summer home" for a vice president, then a hospital during the US occupation, the hotel was later immortalised by Greene in his novel. In recognition, one of the rooms bears Greene's name. That tradition has been followed for several other artists who have graced the old hotel with their presence, such as the Rolling Stones' Mick Jagger.

lowing among Haitians in the United States and Canada. Papillon has written a selection of short stories, along with a novel for adolescents. She's married to the famous Haitian painter Albert Desmangles, and is reportedly also a talented painter herself.

The issues Papillon raises in her novels were first brought up by another female writer, Marie Chauvet. She was nurtured by the same egalitarian principles that were the hallmarks of other authors, such as Seymour Pradel and Jacques-Stephen Alexis, who rang the bell for writers of their generation to become engaged in the immediate world around them through their writing. Alexis' work laid the groundwork for the school of writing that would later be known as negritude.

Chauvet, who grew up in a world where women had limited roles, wrote passionately against all kinds of abuse committed against women and the poor. All her novels are dominated by the question of equality and justice. Her writings didn't have many fans, including her second husband, who apparently bought all remaining copies of *Amour, Colère et Folie*, (Love, Anger and Madness) – published in 1968 – and immediately had them burned. Chauvet died in New York City in the early 1970s.

These writers, whether in exile or still living

reproduce French literature in the Caribbean, with the subject of Haitians themselves being worthy of only cursory interest.

It took the US occupation in 1915 to change that. White US Marines from the American South did not deal in subtle racial categories. To them, Haitians were black, whether mixed race or pure Africans. And that included the writers, who were treated as blacks who spoke French.

This state of affairs spurred Haitian authors to begin looking at themselves differently. Led by Jean Price-Mars, they began to seek their identity in Haiti's African roots. They started to write about the people of Haiti, the peasants

in Haiti, are following a path first laid out at the turn the 20th century by others like Jean Price-Mars. He put down the demarcation line in 1919 with his essay *Ainsi Parle Oncle* (Thus Spoke Uncle) about the need to recognise Voodoo and Créole as the essence of Haitian life.

There was no Haitian literature to speak of before Price-Mars. The Haitian experience was limited to writers of mixed race who had turned their backs on their African roots. It was part intellectual snobbery – they were trying to

LEFT: Hotel Oloffson in Port-au-Prince, made famous by Graham Greene's novel, *The Comedians*.
ABOVE: read in French, Creole, Spanish and English.

who live *en deyo* – a Créole term for "in the countryside" – away from the snobbery of city life. Créole words and Voodoo began to appear alongside each other in their books.

Political writers

Soon, some of these writers started dabbling in politics. In 1922, Price-Mars wrote a poem calling on Haitians to resist the occupation, which ended in 1935 with the withdrawal of US troops. Price-Mars became a national figure and later went on to occupy important positions in numerous administrations, including Minister of Foreign Affairs and Ambassador to France under François Duvalier in the 1960s.

But it would take writer Jacques Roumain to humanise the countryside Haitians, the pure descendants of Africans, who spoke only Créole and practiced Voodoo rather than Catholicism. Born in 1907, Roumain belonged to the same generation as Price-Mars. He founded the Haitian communist party, and died at the young age of 37. His novel, *Gouverneurs de la Rosée (Masters of the Dew)* may be the best-known Haitian novel of all time, translated into countless languages around the world and the subject of a feature film.

It is a universal story: a family's small plot of land turns into hard dirt from a brutal dryness

that has gripped the country. Crops are dying. The prodigal son crosses the border into the Dominican Republic – just like Danticat's characters in *Farming of the Bones* – where he can work as a labourer on a sugar plantation. He keeps his family alive by sending money home, and on his return, actually brings them life itself, by going on a quest to find water. In the end he succeeds, and the whole community blossoms once more.

Besides *Masters of the Dew*, few other works by Roumain have been translated into English, although there are some famous poems of note, including *Langston Hughes*, *Madrid* and *When the Tom-Tom Beats*.

While *Masters of the Dew* celebrates the power of the human spirit over environment, Roumain the doctrinaire Marxist seethes with anger in his other work. Listen to the opening section of his poem *Filthy Negroes*, when he says, "we filthy negroes, we won't take any more, that's right we're through being in Africa, in America, your negroes, your niggers, your filthy negroes, we won't take anymore, that surprises you, to say: yessuh, while polishing your boots, oui mon pe to the white missionaries, or master, while harvesting your sugar cane, coffee, cotton, peanuts, in Africa, in America, poor negroes, filthy negroes, that we were, that we won't be anymore, we're finished, you'll see…"

Passing on the torch

When the Catholic Church and the Haitian government began their campaign against Voodoo in the mid-1930s, with soldiers going about from village to village destroying altars and sacred symbols, Roumain was one of the first writers to oppose it. Strangely enough, he recognised the important place of Voodoo in Haitian culture, but was opposed to Voodoo itself. As a communist, he regarded it as a superstitious religion.

Roumain's literary activism didn't die out with his death. He passed the torch to other poets and novelists, such as Felix Morisseau-Leroy and René Dépestre. Morisseau-Leroy stunned the Haitian élite with his *Antigone in Créole*, an adaptation of the Greek tragedy to Haitian conditions in a language that other intellectuals of his time had deemed incapable of conveying complex ideas. ❑

LEFT: a rural image of rice harvesting.

A Writer in Exile

René Dépestre is arguably one of Haiti's greatest living writers. A political activist, Dépestre lived in Cuba, where he used to broadcast communist propaganda targeted at Haiti. His political activities led to him being exiled from Haiti, Czechoslovakia, Brazil and Cuba. He has since renounced communism and now lives in France.

Born in 1926, he came from a poor family in Jacmel, a city southwest of Port-au-Prince that has produced its fair share of writers and is a refuge for artists from all over Haiti, the United States and even Europe.

Dépestre's parents could barely afford to send their children to school. But within the grinding poverty of their existence, there was also a certain dignity. And his family's dire economic condition did not stop the young poet from enjoying the beauty of the world around him.

He published his first work as early as 1945, when he was only 19 years old. His circle of friends include the Cuban poet Nicolás Guillén and Aimé Césaire of Martinique, and he once served as secretary to the famous Spanish poet, Pablo Neruda.

Dépestre's love of life shines through all his poems. They're filled with a sensuality, a love of things around him and of living beings.

His novel, *The Festival of the Greasy Pole* (1979), takes an overt stab at the François "Papa Doc" Duvalier regime. The main character, Henri Postel, owns a small shop in a working-class neighbourhood of Port-au-Roi, above which a sign reads "Closed for dezombification." Postel is 49, of mixed race, a former senator and political agitator. He drinks too much.

The president condemns him to death – by boredom. Postel is expected to fall apart in this process of internal zombification, but he manages to resist.

Life becomes interesting when Postel enters the annual contest of climbing the greasy pole, which takes place in the national park. President Zoocrates Zachary sees Postel's challenge as a personal threat to his own control, and decides to face him head-on.

Dépestre was transparent in his attempt to ridicule Papa Doc Duvalier's closest supporters, giving the characters in the book cover names

that anyone living in Haiti at the time could easily match to the real people: Clovis Barbotog, Angel Boipiraud, the president's married daughter, the local bishop, Monsignor Wolgonde, and even the revolutionary Jean-Jacques Brissaricq. Haiti's infamous Fort Dimanche (Fort Sunday) becomes Fort Samedi (Fort Saturday).

Postel puts up his morally courageous battle against the forces of darkness and attempts to wake the Haitian people from the lethargy of their long-term hopelessness.

Dépestre has said in the past that the novel is not an historical chronicle, a *roman à clef*, or one based on his own life.

However, he was also quoted as saying that, "The events and the characters of the narrative therefore belong to the realm of pure fiction. "Any resemblance to persons, animals, trees, living or having lived, any similarity, close or distant, to names, situations, places, systems, cogwheels of steel or fire, or to any other scandal in real life, can only have the effect, therefore, of coincidence that is not only accidental, but downright scandalous."

Dépestre writes with passion and profound insight into the politics of Duvalierism and the penetrating influence of the practice of Voodoo on everyday Haitian life. Like others before and after him, what he does best is simply, but beautifully, expose the fun and eroticism of what it means to be Haitian. ❏

RIGHT: René Dépestre spent many years writing in exile, unable to return to his homeland.

SPANISH AND AFRICAN CUISINE

The fusion of European and spicy African influences has produced
Dominican and Haitian cookery with their own distinctive flavours and colours

Dominican cuisine owes much to its rural roots. Indigenous, African and Spanish heritages encouraged a varied harvesting of foodstuffs and cooking techniques which still flavour today's tastes. Rosy images of peasants farming homesteads or *conucos*, cultivating the staple crops of yam, plantains and sweet potato often romanticise a bucolic culinary past. But the severity of the colonial plantation system and the associated slave trade has similarly been a catalyst for contemporary Dominican dishes. Many modern-day food crops arrived from Africa on the slave ships, while the ill-fated indigenous groups already propagated plants such as the yucca.

Similarly, the lineage of traditional agricultural produce can be traced directly to the experimental dabbling of early Spanish settlers. Cattle, goats and chickens were domesticated, and the introduction of coffee and cocoa beans and their subsequent cultivation occurred only after the mid-18th century.

Perhaps the most significant new crop during colonial times was sugar cane. The arrival of Columbus on his second voyage with two bundles of cane later fuelled a sugar-based economy that not only shaped the historical development of the Caribbean region as a whole, but also redirected established trade routes. First cultivated during the 16th century, sugar cane remains the dominant crop. The failure in recent times, however, to stem the challenge of high fructose corn syrup and artificial sweeteners threatens to knock sugar off its throne. New pretenders are encroaching, and enforcing their status as consumer and economic staples. Many of the former canefields are now carpeted by pineapples or forested with citrus and banana plants. The cultivation of traditional and arriviste foodstuffs closely parallels national development and forms the basis for the current *comida criolla* (Créole cuisine).

LEFT: a *fritay* vendor preparing *banan peze* (fried plantain) for sale, at the market in Charlette.
RIGHT: chickens on the way to market.

La bandera Dominicana

If you are invited to dine at a Dominican home, you will probably be treated to one of several favourite platters. Stories of *merengue*, politics and national pride will be nourished by *la bandera Dominicana*: flying the flag at dinner refers to the national dish of rice, beans,

chicken or meat, with avocado, plantain, yucca and salad. Tasty, wholesome and heavy, rice and beans, *arroz con habichuelas*, form the foundation of most meals – good news for vegetarians.

Sancocho, a delicious meat and vegetable stew, is frequently employed in more poetic parlours as a metaphor for Dominican society. The pleasing potpourri of sausage, pork, chicken, beef, goat, vegetables, herbs and spices parallels the social blending of Spanish, indigenous and African influences. Conjured up for family occasions and friendly reunions, *sancocho* is a tasty potion for togetherness.

Another standard, *mofongo*, is a plantain-based dish served as a Dominican classic. A word of warning – many culinary adventurers have confused *mofongo* during their à la carte forays and ordered substantial helpings of another traditional favourite, *mondongo*, an action-packed stew of tripe and entrails.

Not so easily confused, *pipián* is another favourite stew, this time presenting the palate with goat's offal. Goat *(chivo)* is served in a variety of forms and often makes an interesting variation for the visitors' tastebuds.

The less adventurous may settle for *asopao de pollo*, a deliciously filling chicken and rice soup or risotto. Extras include chicken's foot –

a delicacy in the republic. Many dishes are served with green plantains, either boiled and mashed as *mangú*, or sliced and fried as *tostones*. Ripe or yellow plantains are also fried, but are much sweeter. *Ropa vieja*, "old clothes", generally fails to live up to its name and is usually a tasty dish of seasoned fried shredded beef served with rice and a side salad of lettuce, shredded cabbage, tomato and avocado.

Festivals are an excuse to eat, particularly during *Las Navidades*, the Advent run-in of food, booze and merriment. Yuletide excesses commence in earnest on Christmas Eve for those who can afford the season's festivities.

HERBAL CURE-ALLS

Traditional remedies for a variety of maladies make full use of hundreds of local ingredients growing in the wild and widely available throughout Hispaniola. There are alleged natural cures for everything from the common cold to catarrh.

● To combat colds, a tea made from mint, limoncilla and guanábana (custard apple) leaves with lemon slices cut into the shape of a cross is recommended.

● For stomach aches, a tea of aloe leaves or cloves, cinnamon and aniseed will ease troubles away.

● Catarrh can be counteracted by a powerful concoction of shark and cod liver oil, chives and honey.

Lechón asado (roast suckling pig) traditionally draws family and friends together at house parties. *Pasteles en hoja*, savouries wrapped in plantain leaves, and *niños en vuelta*, minced meat swaddled in rice, complement the feast.

A sweet tooth is more than catered for by the sugar-laden range of desserts. Traditional cakes – *bizcochos* – combine sweetness with a highly adhesive and delicious white cream-like topping. *Dulce de leche* is made by caramelising sugar in milk, or reducing sweetened condensed milk by boiling. It is often flavoured with coconut or fruit to make a cloyingly sweet candy. For those wishing to keep the sugar-rush at bay, *queso de hoja*, a moist white cheese from Bonao served with flat cassava bread, *casabe*, acts as the perfect antidote.

On the hoof

Much of Dominican culinary life occurs on the street. Fried foods are readily served up from mobile vats. A sampling of *yaniqueques* (Johnny cakes), *pastelitos* (meat or cheese-filled pastry turnovers) and *quipes* (ground beef encased in cracked wheat) provide a good entrée. *Chimichurris* are more substantial pork sandwiches off the spit. After a few roadside fry-ups, even the most reticent of healthy eaters will be scrambling for an

temporary relief. Shavings of ice are scooped into a cup and topped with a variety of fruit syrups. Sliced coconuts provide a refreshing gush of *agua de coco*, and the gentle purr of a miniature mobile thresher will guide you to an energy-restoring glass of sugar cane juice.

Bars and cafés

Café society has found its tropical home in the Dominican Republic. Cafés cater for all tastes – coffee-fuelled morning reviews of the newspapers, sober afternoons of delicious ice creams and outrageously divine fruitshakes, or rum-soaked cocktail evenings. *Batidas con leche*, a

appointment with the nutritionist. Fortunately, they come to you. The itinerant fruit stalls (greengrocers on tricycles) offer a luscious cascade of fresh produce – mangoes, pineapples, oranges, *guineos* (bananas) – all peeled and presented for you. *Quenepas* may provide a handy new taste sensation. Sold in bunches, the brittle green skin of the fruit is broken open, revealing a white pit surrounded by a sweet pulp.

When the heat takes its toll, *frío fríos* provide

rich mixture of milk, sugar, crushed ice and a bewildering range of fruits will keep you nourished until supper. *Lechosa* (papaya), *zapote* and the unusually named orange-based *morir soñando* ("to die dreaming") are particular favourites. If fruit juice alone suffices, then *jugos* will be the order of the day. You may wish to ask the waiter to go easy on the sugar, or leave it out altogether. *Jugo de china* and *chinola* – orange and passion fruit juices – frequently top the taste polls.

People-watching on a central plaza, such as the capital's Plaza de la Hispanidad, provides a relaxed start to an evening's café entertainment. Whether cruising later to swish down-

LEFT: Sunday lunch includes fried plantain.
ABOVE: a *frío frío* stand in the Dominican Republic offers temporary relief from the Caribbean sun.

town bars, or meandering quietly homewards and stopping off at a *colmado*, the choice of beverages for the evening will be either the excellent domestic beer or locally produced rums. The former option is ruled by Presidente, by far the most popular bottled beer and of outstanding quality. Attentive brewing and razor-sharp marketing has made this beer a national icon. Always served ice-cold, Dominicans will view with distaste anyone who accepts a lightly chilled bottle.

Rum is sold in three general categories – *blanco*, *dorado* and *añejo*. The former lighter rums are used in cocktails and with mixers. The

darker blends are more suited to less vigorous adulteration. True *añejos* are best taken neat. *Un servicio* consists of a bottle of rum, a bucket of ice and *refrescos* (soft drinks) as mixers. Given the strength, quality and abundance of Dominican rums, the ability to hide alcohol within sweet fruit flavours, as exemplified by the ubiquitous *ron ponch*, is a dangerous trait among Dominican bartenders. Many a happy hour at sunset can slip smoothly through to a melancholic dawn.

Unmissable Haitian *griyo*

It's hard to miss the smell and sight of *griyo*, or *griot*. If Haiti had to have a national dish, *griyo* would carry the banner, and proudly. It's everywhere. It is part of what Haitians call *fritay* – Créole for fried food. There is no better word to describe those pieces of pork, sweet potatoes, bony fish, *akra*, fried plantain and *taso*, on sale on street corners throughout Haiti. Customers pick up a dollar's, or a few cents' worth, of *griyo* or *banan peze* (fried plantain) as a snack on the way to the Champs de Mars across from the National Palace in Port-au-Prince.

Fritay vendors are invariably women. They travel far and wide to get the best prices on *malanga* and *patates*, pork and snappers. To cook, they dip the flour-coated meat and vegetables into a vat of hot oil bubbling over a charcoal fire. On offer are tempting morsels including crispy pork rind, sweet potato, blackened fish, rice and beans. To accompany *griyo* ask for *pikliz* – shredded cabbage, carrots and peas pickled in hot peppers, although it's not advisable to order *griyo* if your stomach is not used to eating street food in Haiti. Nearby, a

GRIYO: ALMOST A NATIONAL DISH

To make traditional Haitian griyo you need only a selection of some simple ingredients:

8–10lbs of cubed pork
1 sour orange and the juice from another orange
1 lime and the juice from 4 additional limes
2 tablespoons of salt
2 hot green peppers

Wash the pork under running water then pat dry. Rub the pork with the lime and the sour orange, ensuring that the orange rind does not touch the meat. Mix together the salt, orange juice, the juice of two limes and one green pepper in a large bowl. Add the pork to this mixture, then stir and

coat the meat with the marinade. Cover the bowl and leave the meat to stand for at least half an hour.

Place the pork in a casserole dish and add enough water to cover the meat. Stir well and cook uncovered over a medium heat. When the water has reduced, remove and discard the hot pepper. Skim off the oil and fry the pork in a separate pan until crispy.

Combine the remaining fresh green pepper with the juice of two limes and add some of this mixture to the pork. Serve with salad using the gravy as a dressing.

Note: be careful when handling the hot pepper, be sure to avoid contact with your face and eyes.

man, usually the *fritay* vendor's husband, sells pieces of sugar cane, another sort of fast food.

In the city, most Haitians seem to eat on the run during the day. This is odd in a country where unemployment, or under-employment, is the highest in the Caribbean. But the night belongs to the *fritay* vendors – a good business for thousands of women. Their twinkling lamps are sometimes the only lights visible on the streets at night, even in the capital.

The demise of the Créole pig

Griyo is a good, cheap protein alternative to beef: there is little grazing or arable land in mountainous Haiti. Fish, too, is pricey due to deforestation, when silt runs down hills during the rainy season and covers the reefs. As a result, fishermen need to go further afield to find a good catch.

Pigs, on the other hand, are good business in Haiti. Low-maintenance animals, they roam freely, foraging for vegetable and fruit scraps. To use a cliché, the little *cochons* are a piggybank of sorts for Haitians. Valued highly, children are given piglets as gifts. Others buy a few animals, fatten them and sell them for a hefty profit. There's always a demand, so there's always plenty of money to be made.

Back in the early 1980s, though, it was difficult to find any pigs in Haiti. They were all slaughtered as part of a US government project to prevent the spread of swine disease. After scientists discovered some of the Créole pigs in Haiti carried porcine fever, they feared the disease would spread to the Dominican Republic, and eventually to the hog population of North America. Although those pigs have since been replaced (by a different breed), Haitians complain that varieties introduced from the United States are more finicky eaters and don't taste the same as their old, small, black Créole pigs.

Local produce

There are few farms in Haiti, just garden-sized plots that dot the mountainous landscape. Most rural Haitians work these smallholdings growing beets, aubergines, carrots, hot peppers, tomatoes, corn, millet, beans, plantains, okra, spinach, tomatoes, avocados, manioc and other tubers like *malanga*. Fruits include mangoes, papayas, oranges and mandarins. Spices are also

nurtured wherever there's a space to grow them.

Saturdays at the vegetable market could be from a scene in a Haitian painting. Women balance bright baskets of fruits and vegetables on their heads, and sway their hips as they come down the hills. Some catch the *tap-tap* (bus) from the mountains to the towns and cities, where they offer their colourful produce for sale. In Port-au-Prince, one of the biggest markets is held on Avenue John Brown, not far from where the road crosses Martin Luther King. The air is cooler here, quite different from the wilting heat of downtown Port-au-Prince. Haitian farmers also raise chickens, goats and some cows,

LEFT: Dominican Brugal rum is sold in most bars.
RIGHT: a greengrocer on wheels.

although they don't eat them. They are raised with the specific intention of selling them on to *fritay* vendors. The majority of rural Haitians only butcher their livestock for very special occasions such as baptisms or weddings. And a few use them in animal sacrifices to their Voodoo gods.

When they can find it, Haitians love to eat shellfish, such as crabs and conch – the latter is a delicacy that Haitian men believe helps their sexual performance. Mounds of the huge shells are piled high in coastal villages, testament to their great popularity. The conch, known as *lambi*, is either grilled, or simmered in a tomato-based créole sauce. Restaurants also serve conch fritters, a Caribbean favourite that requires chopping or grinding the conch meat, mixing it with onions, celery, green pepper, hot pepper, thyme, tomato purée, salt and pepper in a soft batter, then frying it in golfball-size pieces.

Imported foodstuffs

Most foodstuffs in Haiti are imported, including the very popular codfish. Prepared in a batter with onions and hot peppers, then fashioned into a ball, the *akra* as the dish is called, is fried.

Haiti has been awash with imported dark chicken meat from the US, which has been dis-

A TYPICAL CRÉOLE *LAMBI*

The ingredients, to serve 4 people:
1½ lb conch, shelled, cleaned and skinned
2 limes, juice and grated rind
1 onion, sliced
3 cloves garlic, minced
2 shallots, minced
¼ cup of butter
1 tomato, peeled, seeded and chopped
¾ cup of water
2 tsp of thyme, chopped
¼ tsp red pepper flakes
salt and pepper, to taste

Pound the conch meat into 3mm (⅛-inch) thickness with a wooden mallet. Cut into 4cm (1½-inch) square pieces. Place in a bowl and squeeze over the lime juice. Add the lime rind and completely cover with cold water. Refrigerate for approximately 3 hours.

Sauté the onion, garlic and shallots in a heavy saucepan until soft and opaque, keeping the heat low and taking care not to brown them. Stir in the tomato, water, thyme, red pepper flakes and conch meat. Bring to a vigorous boil, then reduce the heat. Simmer, partially covered, stirring occasionally, until the conch meat is fork-tender (about 1 hour). Season to taste with salt and pepper.

carded from the fast food outlets. Local chicken farmers can't compete. Rice, one of the staples in the Haitian diet, is shipped from overseas, competing with the native variety produced in the Artibonite Valley. All processed food comes from either the Dominican Republic or the US. However, most Haitians cannot afford such products, maintaining a daily diet based on locally grown food.

Much of a muchness

Variety is not the spice of life in the Haitian kitchen. The only experimentation to be found in their cuisine is believed to be taking place in the large Haitian communities in Miami, New York City and Montréal.

For those who can afford it, the Haitian menu does not vary much from week to week, or from home to home. It is usually a two-course meal, starting with beef either grilled on charcoal, or cooked in tomato sauce, mixed with cabbage and other vegetables. Every meal is accompanied by plantain, either boiled or fried. Wealthier middle-class families also eat goat meat, which is cooked in a similar way to beef.

The second course is either rice and beans, or cornmeal and beans. The beans are either red or white, and are cooked in a sauce, or stirred into the rice. Some Haitians serve up rice and beans with every meal.

There are only subtle geographic variations in the Haitian menu. For example, cooks in the northern part of the country cook their rice and beans with a head of clove, while in southern areas they don't. Haitians are not big beer drinkers – they prefer their meals accompanied by a local sweet cola drink or freshly squeezed fruit juices.

Outside influences

Slowly, as a result of contact with the Syrians and Lebanese who have settled here over the years, some Haitians have began to incorporate Arab dishes such as stuffed vine leaves into their dishes, but this practice is limited to a few restaurants and a small number of homes.

Besides picking up a piece of *griyo* from a street vendor, Haitians don't eat out much.

Those who can afford it will go out for exotic food such as pizza or hamburgers. These can be found in Pétionville, the wealthy suburb above Port-au-Prince with bars, cafés and clubs. They cater mostly for wealthy Haitians, as well as tourists and foreign workers.

Pétionville has enough multi-star French restaurants to satisfy the most sophisticated palate. Restaurants such as Chez Gérard and Plantation serve a menu that would rival any European four-star establishment. Restaurants that have managed to combine the two cultures have achieved remarkable results. Just don't expect to find a plate of *griyo* in these places.

Haitian homes come alive on special occasions, such as a child's first communion and New Year's Day, when pumpkin soup is usually served. On Christmas Eve, the favoured dish is *griyo*, prepared with rice and beans, *lambi* and sweet-tasting food. Christmas is also one of the times to bring out the *Rhum Barbancourt*, locally produced from sugar cane. A bottle of five-star aged Barbancourt is reserved for special occasions and is mixed with lime juice, sugar and crushed ice. No festive occasion is complete without sharing a bottle of *cremasse*, a home-made concoction of rum and sweet, thick condensed milk. Before you know it you'll be feeling mighty happy. ❑

FAR LEFT: a Haitian girl carries grapefruits to market.
LEFT: fresh fish is not always easily available.
RIGHT: a colourful fruit stand.

SPORTING PASSIONS

Baseball dominates, but athletics, horse racing, polo and watersports
are all popular. So, more controversially, is cockfighting

There is one great passion which runs through all classes of Dominican society, and that is baseball. This is a game in which two teams of nine players each try to win points by hitting a small ball so hard with a bat that the one or more runners spread out across the field – in a diamond marked by white cushions – can manage to run to safety before the opposing team recovers the ball. The movements on the field will long remain a mystery to the uninitiated spectator, but the Dominicans, just like the North Americans, love the game.

Baseball remains without doubt the nation's favourite sport. Six teams compete for the national championship: the Tigres del Licey (blue) and the Leones del Escogido (red), both in Santo Domingo, the Aguilas Cibaeñas (yellow) in Santiago, the Estrellas Orientales (green) in San Pedro de Macorís, Gigantes del Cibao (brown) in San Francisco de Macorís and Azucareros del Este (purple) in La Romana. They compete six days a week, and the main season runs from October to January.

In winter, the *Quisqueya* in Santo Domingo and the other stadia on the island are often sold out for weeks in advance. In summer, baseball fans settle down in front of the TV to follow the competitions of the North American Major League. After all, many of their compatriots can be seen running, hitting and catching across the flickering screen. No other Latin American country can claim as many top-rate players in the US as the little half-island in the Caribbean. More than 50 Dominicans currently take to the field for the Major League teams, and another 500 or so play for the Minors.

A North American import

In the early part of the 20th century, from 1916 to 1924, US troops occupied the Dominican Republic for the first time, in support of the Monroe Doctrine. The "Americanos" brought

their favourite game with them to the island – baseball. It seems that the young islanders took to the game as well, for it wasn't long before they had formed a team which was good enough to take on the international competition. During the 1950s the first Dominicans successfully played the game in the Major League

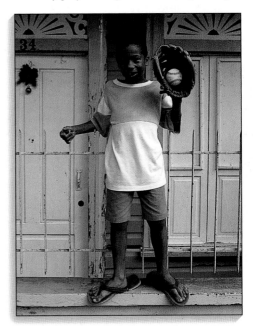

of the United States. The Alou brothers and Juan Marischal are famous names to this day.

The Dominican Republic has now become a paradise for talent scouts working on behalf of the Major League clubs. Every winter, US scouts occupy the stands of the island's baseball stadiums, on the lookout for future home-run record-breakers. The Los Angeles Dodgers, Cleveland Indians, Chicago Cubs, Boston Red Sox and other clubs run training camps in many locations throughout the Dominican Republic. In some of them, the young hopefuls undergo intensive training for three months without a break, while other US clubs send coaches into schools every day, where they spend their

LEFT: Manny Ramirez in action.
RIGHT: baseball has been a national sport in the Dominican Republic since the Americans arrived.

afternoons teaching boys how they can best hit the ball into the invisible strike zone.

A large number of the players who have made it to the top in the United States grew up in the *bateyes*, the impoverished barrack-like settlements around San Pedro de Macorís where the sugar-cane workers live. There, as small boys, they played on uneven ground with sugar-cane bats, an unripe orange and gloves made from old cement bags or milk cartons. On Sundays, these same children would flock into the Tetelo Vargas Stadium to learn a few tricks by watching the *Estrellas Orientales* (the Eastern Stars). Sammy Sosa, Pedro Martínez, Raúl Mondesí, José Martínez, Tony Peña, Tony Fernández and Manny Ramírez are all top stars in the baseball firmament of the USA. The legendary Matty Alou once joked about the remarkable success of the Dominicans: "It must be the water".

No doubt the warm climate on the island plays a part by supplying ideal conditions for year-round training. But probably the most important incentive for the youthful talents is the fact that a sports career in the United States still remains the best way of realising the American Dream. Stars like Sammy Sosa earn millions of dollars every season in the US, and plenty of pesos in their homeland as well, by flickering across TV

"SLAMMIN" SAMMY SOSA

For 37 years, the baseball legend Roger Maris held the single-season home run record – until 1998, when Mark McGwire and Sammy Sosa had a neck-and-neck race on the long run home. "Big Mac" of the St Louis Cardinals was the first to make it, and a few days later, "Slammin' Sammy" of the Chicago Cubs also broke Maris's record.

Sammy Sosa, the enterprising boy from the Consuelo slums near San Pedro de Macorís, contributed to his family's income as a shoe-shine boy. Today he is a multi-millionaire sporting superstar whose international fan club has been growing ever since he began his career with the Texas Gulf Coast in 1986. His sporting prowess and winning smile

have resulted in several magazines voting him Sportsman of the Year and he was invited to watch the then US president, Bill Clinton, light the Christmas Tree at the White House.

Sosa also donates a percentage of his earnings to good causes. In December 1997, as "Sammy Claus", he toured schools and hospitals in the US and the DR, distributing gifts to thousands of children. A father of four, Sosa founded the bi-national Sammy Sosa Foundation for underprivileged children. The baseball player, who reputedly gave his first contract payment of US$3,500 to his mother Lucrecia, except for a few dollars that he used to buy his first bicycle, epitomizes the universal dream of the poor boy made good.

screens in advertising campaigns. Many boys dream of following in Sosa's footsteps.

Hoop dreams

Basketball occupies the second position in the Dominican Republic sports league. Most schools have a basketball court, and many professional baseball players started life playing basketball. Today though, the popularity of basketball has diminished in the face of the huge success of Dominican baseball players. However, young

At the end of the 1980s there were only four golf courses in the republic; today there are more than two dozen with more planned. Many of them enjoy lovely locations near the seashore, where you can hit a ball clear across the cliffs, ravines and bays. Locals and visitors alike agree that the best courses on the island are the Pete Dye course, known as "Teeth of the Dog", in the grounds of Casa de Campo, and the Playa Grande course on the north coast near Río San Juan, designed by Robert Trent Jones Senior.

local hopefuls can still be seen frequently aiming the ball into the net. Felipe López, who plays for the Minnesota Timberwolves, provides the island's basketball fans with a famous star to admire.

Golf

It cannot be denied that golf is enjoying a boom in the Dominican Republic. As elsewhere in the Caribbean, the grassy sport is in season all year round, unlike in parts of Europe and the USA.

LEFT: basketball has been somewhat overshadowed by the success of baseball.
ABOVE: polo at Casa de Campo.

Sport of princes

Prince Charles plays it, as do a whole galaxy of the world's aristocracy and everyday folks too. Devotees of the ancient sport of royalty – polo – are varied. Perched on horseback, they wield long sticks which they use to try to manoeuvre a small white ball into the opposing team's goal. Polo is one of the fastest team games in the world. It is played by two teams of four on a field which is more than three times the size of a football pitch. Each game lasts about an hour, for which each player will need five or six polo ponies (hence the great expense), because according to the Hurlingham Rules, which originated in the English club of the same name, the horses have to be changed every seven-and-a-half minutes.

There are four polo fields within the grounds of the luxurious Casa de Campo resort near La Romana. Champions from around the world look forward to meeting here during the season, which runs from November until May.

The Maharajah Jabbar Singh brought the game to the Caribbean. Porfirio Rubirosa, a famous Dominican playboy, had met the Indian aristocrat in Europe and encouraged him to visit the Antilles in 1954. Singh was an excellent player with a handicap of nine, who brought with him his knowledge of the game

the visitors on their narrow boards. The prevailing wind in the Bay of Cabarete is an invigorating northwest trade wind measuring force five or six on the Beaufort scale. The entire Atlantic coast of the island also provides excellent conditions for the sport.

Kitesurfing

Cabarete is also a mecca for lovers of a different kind of wind-assisted sport – kitesurfing – which takes place about 1 km (½ mile) downwind of the windsurfers on Kite Beach. When the wind is favourable the whole area is a riot of colourful sails and kites flitting about on the water.

as well as trainers and horses and soon built up a pretty good team.

A windsurfing paradise

Canadian windsurfer Jean Laporte discovered the Dominican Republic in general, and the Bay of Cabarete in particular, for the sport in 1984. "One of the best windsurfing places in the Caribbean," was the champion's verdict. Before long, his international fan club arrived hot on his heels.

In the early days, the people of Cabarete were torn between admiration and amusement for Laporte and his companions, whom they christened *mariposas* (butterflies); nowadays, large numbers of young Dominicans compete with

Deep-sea fishing

Boca de Yuma in the southeast Dominican Republic is the traditional angling centre. It was the place where international fishing competitions were held every year until Hurricane Georges more or less blew away the little village at the mouth of the Río Yuma. So the fishermen planning to hook sea-dwelling creatures, such as the blue and white marlin, sharks and tuna, currently have to make a detour to Cabeza de Toro in Punta Cana. High season runs from January until June, but fishing continues throughout the year. Further information can be obtained from *Clubes Náuticos* or *Actividades Acuáticas*.

On Avenida de la Salud

In Santo Domingo it seems incongruous that, in the heart of a metropolis of 3 million people, a city where traffic chaos reigns, there should be a smooth, wide tarmac road running through the middle of the *Parque Mirador del Sur* on which not a single car can be seen. Avenida de la Salud, "Health Avenue", is out of bounds to all motorised vehicles. Here, joggers, inline skaters, skateboarders, roller skaters, cyclists and walkers can expend excess energy. The extensive parkland means that the air here is considered to be better than elsewhere, and the little drinks stalls by the wayside provide welcome refreshment.

contain the arenas. The cocks are weighed and measured to determine which birds should be pitted against each other, then the owner attaches spurs of metal or bone to the claws of his bird and ensures the requisite adrenaline rush by repeatedly propelling the creature across the 6-metre (20-ft) wide arena towards its opponent. Meanwhile, the bookmakers clamber across the rickety spectator stands, accepting bets, which are placed in a mysterious sign language. The sums of money involved are often quite large; a man will sometimes wager a whole month's wages. A successful fighting cock can cost US$500–1,000.

Dominican sportsmen and women flock to the park, especially on the weekend.

Cockfighting

Before baseball conquered the country, cockfighting was the most popular spectator sport in the Dominican Republic. Even today, there is scarcely a village without its own *galera* or *club Gallistico*. Every weekend, an air of excitement with a hint of scurrilousness pervades the windowless circular buildings which

LEFT: windsurfing and white-water rafting are popular watersports in the Dominican Republic.
ABOVE: there is a cockfighting arena in every town.

Violent pecking and scratching with razor-sharp claws results in a bloody battle during virtually every encounter, although it is by no means always a fight to the death. The struggle often ends when one of the sparring partners gives up; sometimes both animals refuse to fight on.

Cockfighting, which was invented over 3,000 years ago in Asia, has been the subject of much controversial debate in the Dominican Republic, but so far the attempts to ban the bloody sport have been no more than half-hearted. It remains a popular sport supported by Dominicans from every walk of life. Once forbidden from attending, women, are still rare visitors to the arenas.

Horse racing

No blood flows on the race track which is located between Santo Domingo and the airport, but the atmosphere is just as exciting as a cockfight. At weekends whole families flock to the *Hipódromo Quinto Centenario* to enjoy an afternoon at the track with a carnival atmosphere among the snack and drinks stands. Even those who speak no Spanish and have no idea how the betting works can enjoy a visit to the modern, spacious racing complex with its

> **DOMINICAN GOLD**
>
> Félix "Super" Sánchez, the 400-metre hurdler, won a gold medal for the DR at the 2003 Pan American Games, he won again just a few weeks later at the World Championships in Paris.

when the country was seeking financial assistance from the IMF, it was argued that the benefits of having the most modern sporting facilities in the Caribbean would outweigh the costs. The games were a resounding success with Dominican athletes winning 41 medals, including 10 golds.

No sporting paradise

Haiti is not exactly a sportsman's paradise. For example, the country has only one golf course, the *Pétionville Club* near Port-au-Prince. In this

1,600-metre (1,750-yard) track. The system is based on the North American one, and regular race goers are usually happy to help novices fill out betting slips.

Putting athletics on the map

The popularity of athletics was elevated to new heights when, in 2003 the Dominican Republic hosted the XIV Pan American Games. At a cost of US$57 million, facilities built for the games included a stadium in the Parque del Este, an athletes' village and specialist sporting pavilions. The stadium at Juan Pablo Duarte Olympic Centre was also remodelled. Although there was controversy over the cost of staging the Games

desperately poor country, sporting activity remains a privilege of the upper classes. Their favourite forms of exercise include golf, horse riding and tennis. Ronald Agenor has even provided Haiti with a player who has competed on an international level in what some consider to be a white sport – tennis.

The ordinary people satisfy their competitive instincts primarily through cockfighting. As with their next door neighbour, there is virtually no village without its own arena constructed of wooden planks. In the bigger towns, there are large circular stone buildings where even wealthy Haitians can be seen taking their place in the stands to watch the fray.

In Haiti the cocks fight without spurs. At the beginning of each fight, the birds are intoxicated with *Clairin*, an alcoholic beverage consisting of partially distilled rum which is passed directly from the owner's mouth. He forces the liquid through his lips so that the cock is enveloped in a fine, mildly inebriating mist. Bets start at 1 gourde (15 cents) and a fighting cock can cost up to an average month's pay of around US$30.

Ball skills

Football (soccer) can't compete with baseball across the border, but in Haiti it causes many a was the only one scored by the Haitians in Munich and the moment of glory is remembered in Haiti to this day. Patrice Dumont, author of *Haiti to Munich – 20 Years On* marked the anniversary by recounting every detail of that sensational event. Today, the Haitian national side takes on other teams from the Caribbean and fans follow their favourite teams – Brazil and Argentina – on the TV screen. There is little interest in the football skills of their former colonial rulers, France. When Brazil was defeated by France in the final of the 1998 World Cup, Haiti was engulfed in mourning. ❑

heart to beat faster. You will see a leather ball being kicked around everywhere – in school playgrounds, along a path through the fields, and of course in the major stadiums, the Sylvio Cator in Port-au-Prince and the Parc St Victor in Cap Haïtien.

The last major international victory of the Haitian football team was in 1974, when the national team qualified for the World Cup in West Germany; they even managed to score a goal against the indomitable Italy. The Italians may have won the game, but that famous goal

LEFT: large crowds turn out for local baseball games.
ABOVE: A game of chance on a Haitian street corner.

A GROWING SOCCER SCENE

Despite the lack of financial investment in football in Haiti, there are many small clubs who play unofficial contests all over the country. The National League of 57 teams is divided into three divisions. Only league finals and international games are played at the refurbished Sylvio Cator Stadium. The atmosphere is loud with lots of singing and drumming. The official league season runs from November to May, while other games are played during the summer. There is also a project called Athletique d'Haitiand, which trains talented young players from the slums. It is next to the motor racing track which is located 4 km (2 miles) from the centre of Port-au-Prince.

BACK TO NATURE

The tourist brochures focus on the beaches, but this fertile, mountainous island

has much more to offer outdoor enthusiasts and the ecologically aware

Hispaniola offers ecologically minded, nature-loving and adventure tourists some of the Caribbean's most exciting prospects. Haiti is the region's most mountainous country and the Dominican Republic is home to the region's highest mountain, Pico Duarte, at 3,087 metres (10,128 ft). The north coast of the Republic is also one of the world's major whale-spotting and windsurfing destinations. The country already has a well-developed eco and adventure tourism infrastructure with many established tour operators and activities ranging from hiking and diving to kayaking, rafting, tubing, climbing, abseiling, caving, canyoning, cascading, paragliding, mountain biking and horse riding.

The Dominican Republic's landscape is both dramatic and varied: spectacular mountain ranges; long rivers winding through forests or rushing through ravines and over high waterfalls; fertile valleys; mangrove swamps and white sand beaches fringed by the clear blue waters of the Caribbean.

Wildlife

Flora and fauna are abundant with over 5,600 plant species (including more than 300 endemic orchids); 258 bird species (including the Hispaniolan parrot and parakeet); four species of sea turtles and two freshwater species; reptiles like the American crocodiles of Lake Enriquillo and the rhinoceros iguana; 33 land mammals (among which are the endangered *solenodonte* and *jutia*) as well as marine mammals: the endangered Antillean manatee and the humpback whale.

Humpback whales come to the Silver Bank (Banco de la Plata) 140 km (87 miles) off the north coast during the breeding season from December to March. The Silver Bank is part of a protected marine area and the most important humpback sanctuary in the Atlantic, with up to

3,000 whales visiting annually. From January to March there are excursions to Samaná Bay, where pilot whales, bottlenose, spinner and spotted dolphin can also be seen.

With 31 national parks, five scientific reserves, natural monuments, protected areas (islands, bays, river estuaries, lagoons) and ecological

corridors, the Dominican government is taking a systematic approach to preserving the environment. Construction is forbidden in the protected areas. Establishing the central national parks of Armando Bermúdez and José del Carmen Ramírez has saved the last extensive areas of forest, and the Plan Sierra reforestation project is onstream at nearby San José de las Matas.

The Dominican national park system covers the republic's range of bio diversity and offers many adventure options, from the relaxation of camping to the more strenuous activities of climbing, hiking or river sports.

Los Haïtises park on the south coast of Samaná Bay has mangroves, wet forest and

PRECEDING PAGES: devastating deforestation on the road to Forêt des Pins, Haiti.
LEFT: a humpback whale in the waters at Silver Bank.
RIGHT: Taíno petroglyphs at Las Caritas.

subtropical rainforest, and is a major habitat for the Hispaniolan parrot, owls and gannets. Some of the caves here are decorated with Taíno petroglyphs and pictographs.

The highest peaks in the Caribbean (Pico Duarte, 3,087 metres/10,128 ft; La Pelona, 3,070 metres/10,072 ft; La Rucilla, 3,045 metres/9,990 ft; and Pico Yaque, 2,760 metres/9,055 ft) are found in the central region in the Armando Bermúdez and José del Carmen Ramírez parks, where temperatures can fall below freezing point in December and January. Besides the Dominican Republic's national bird – the *cigua palmera*, palm chat

south west. The 12-km (7½-mile) long island is below sea level and supports a large crocodile population, 10 species of cactus and 62 species of birds, including the tiny *manuelito*, the great hummingbird and the *cu-cu*.

Jaragua, further south, is the largest park in the republic, and includes Beata and Alto Velo islands. Geological formations discovered here date back 50 million years. The Oviedo Lagoon is home to the country's largest population of flamingos. Also in the southwest is the Sierra de Bahoruco highland park where more than 50 percent of the orchid species known in the Dominican Republic can be found. One of the

(Dulus dominicus) – there are woodpeckers, kestrels and other rare species.

Coniferous trees provide vegetation on the lower ground, while pine covers the higher slopes. Mammals include wild pigs, while lower down, savannah snakes make their home. This area is also the source of the Yaque del Norte and Yaque del Sur rivers.

In the southeast, the Eastern National Park, includes Saona Island and supports subtropical wet and dry forest. Saona is the habitat of the rare, white-headed dove and the manatee. Its extensive cave system also features many examples of pre-Columbian art. The smallest park is Isla Cabritos in Lake Enriquillo in the

most important national monuments is the Bahía de Calderas, established to protect the great Las Salinas sand dunes.

The north coast

The north coast is a haven for divers, windsurfers, kitesurfers, mountain bikers and horse riders. Cabarete is classed as one of the best windsurfing beaches anywhere, and hosts World Cup competitions. A protective reef and varying wind conditions make Cabarete ideal for both beginners and world-class windsurfers.

Neighbouring Sosua, with its shallow reefs, has the best diving for beginners, but there are also sites for the more advanced, such as Las

Palmitas, the Airport Wall and the interconnecting tunnels of La Pirámide. In the south, close to Santo Domingo, La Caleta national underwater park has reef and wreck dives. Saona Island is a good site for spotting big fish and Punta Cana on the east coast has the DR's longest coral reef, at nearly 30 km (19 miles), which is protected.

The north coast and the northern mountain range have mountain bike trails ranging from easy to advanced off-road or single-track mountain passages.

SUBMERGED TREASURE

West of Puerto Plata are wrecks to explore off Cofresí and Montecristi. Qualified divers can join salvage parties that are searching shipwrecks, including those of the 1563 Spanish treasure fleet.

down the middle of the cascade to the bottom, where you jump into the water. The best cascading sites are El Salto del Jimenoa, Cascada del Limón, Cascada Ojo de Agua and El Salto de Baiguate.

Canyoning takes you up the wall of a river gorge with rope and harness. When you're high enough you jump into the river. The best sites are in La Damajagua in Imbert and the Jarabacoa area. You can paraglide over mountains and rivers from any convenient ridge, given the appropriate wind conditions.

Those who prefer to tackle mountains on foot can try the strenuous hike up Pico Duarte (or cheat by riding a mule) and the easier climb up Mt Isabel de Torres in Puerto Plata.

If you want to get wet, try rubber rafting on the Río Yaque del Norte in Jarabacoa. You can go solo without a paddle in an oversized rubber tube on the same river, or the Río Jamao al Norte or Río Isabela in Santo Domingo.

For the truly adventurous there's cascading and canyoning. Cascading involves climbing to the top of a waterfall and then abseiling

LEFT: riding in the Dominican Republic's countryside.
ABOVE: rafting down the Río Yaque del Norte.

(Ecosport packages are offered by Rancho Baiguate in Jarabacoa in the centre of the country and by Iguana Mama Adventure Tours, situated in Cabarete on the north coast.)

Haiti's natural heritage

Despite extensive deforestation, soil erosion, crippling political and economic problems, Haiti is making slow steps to arrest its ecological decline. There are a number of reforestation and eco-tourism projects already onstream aimed at preserving and developing the natural heritage.

UNESCO and the UNDP, in conjunction with other international organisations and the Haitian Institute for the Protection of the National

Heritage, initiated the Route 2004 project in the late 1990s. This aimed to celebrate the bicentennial of independence, with a programme restoring and preserving major natural and cultural resources with tourism in mind. The first stage focused on the historic area from Fort Liberté to Cap-Haïtien on the north coast, with its national history parks, where tours have been developed.

While Haiti cannot compete with its neighbour as yet in terms of organised ecotourism, there is still a wide range of activities available and sites to visit. Besides the peaks of La Selle (2,674 metres/8,770 ft) southeast of Port-au-

Prince and the Pic de Macaya (2,347 metres/ 7,700 ft) on the southwest peninsula, there are the Forêt de la Visite and pine forests above Port-au-Prince. There are caves in the north on Ile de la Tortue and Dondon; and in the south near Les Cayes at Camp Perrin, Port-à-Piment and Île-à-Vache, and Les Îles Cayemite, Vol Drogue, Anse d'Azure and Anse Duclerc near Jérémie.

Coral reefs can be found on the Côte des Arcadins and Labadie north of Port-au-Prince, Île de la Gonâve and south at Cayemite near Pestel and at Île-à-Vache. In contrast to the lush central Artibonite Valley and most of the southwest peninsula, parts of the area from Gonaïves stretching northwest to Port-de-Paix is virtually desert. There are waterfalls at Seguin in the Pine Forest, the famous Voodoo pilgrimage spot at Saut D'Eau, Artibonite in the centre of the country, and at Étang Pichon and Belle Anse in the southeast near Jérémie.

Although the best beaches are found on the Atlantic coast in the north (Labadie), or on the Caribbean coast near Les Cayes (Port Salut and Port-à-Piment), or near Jacmel (Mouillage, Raymond les Bains and Cyvadier Plage), the marine park of the Arcadin Cays 3 km (2 miles) off the Côte des Arcadins, has excellent diving.

Ecological degradation has destroyed many wildlife habitats and adversely affected fauna but there are two mountain parks which eco-tourists will want to visit. Parc La Visite is on the high Massif de la Selle, a five-hour hike from the hilltop resort of Kenscoff. Covered in pine and montane cloud forest, the park is home to 80 species of birds and endemic mammals – the *nez longue (solenodon)* and the Hispaniolan *hutia*. The black-capped petrel nests here and the migratory North American warbler winters here.

Virgin cloud forest

The Macaya National Park at the tip of the southwest peninsula is the site of Haiti's last virgin cloud forest. There are pines 45 metres (148 ft) high, 141 orchid species, 102 fern species, 99 moss species and 49 species of liverwort. There are 11 species of butterfly, 57 snails, 28 amphibians, 34 reptiles, 65 birds and 19 bats.

The most spectacular fauna are the Grey-crowned Palm Tanager and the Hispaniolan *trogon*. The endangered peregrine falcon also winters here. From Les Cayes it takes about half a day to reach the University of Florida base at the edge of the park, where there are camping facilities. The university has a project for visitors wishing to scale Pic de Macaya.

Étang (Lake) Saumâtre east of Port-au-Prince is the habitat of more than 100 species of waterfowl, flamingos and crocodiles. Although organised tours and activities are few, both the national parks offer good birdwatching sites and there is horse riding in La Visite Park and the Bassin Bleu near Jacmel. ❏

LEFT: coral around Île de la Gonâve.
RIGHT: relaxing by the stunning Salto Aqua Blanco.

THE HUMPBACKS OF SAMANÁ BAY

The mating season of the majestic humpback whale is a major attraction for visitors to the Dominican Republic who come to see the mammals

Thousands of North Atlantic humpback whales *(megaptera novaeangliae)* migrate to the waters around the Dominican Republic at the beginning of each year. Such is their environmental importance that 24,000 sq. km (9,250 sq. miles) of sea to the north east of the country is protected as the Marine Mammal Sanctuary of the Dominican Republic, which includes the Banco de la Plata (Silver Bank), Banco de la Navidad (Christmas Bank) and the Bahía de Samaná (Samaná Bay). The whales come here from the cold waters of the North Atlantic to mate and breed in the warm waters further south, a journey that gives their offspring a better chance of survival.

AROUND THE BAHÍA DE SAMANÁ

It is estimated that some 300 whales are resident in the Samaná Bay in February, although up to 1,500 cruise the area during the January to March mating season. Visitors to the waters can witness fantastic visual displays of lobtailing and fin slapping; it is an exhilarating sight to see a 40-ton male heave himself out of the sea before throwing his body down again with an enormous splash, a practice known as breaching. Male humpbacks are also well-known for communicating through song; they develop refrains on the migratory trip to keep in touch with each other and to attract a mate. It is not unusual to see a mother and calf close to the surface of the water. Female whales suckling their young have to transfer their fat reserves to their calves, who gain weight at an amazing rate of 45 kg (100lb) a day by drinking up to 200 litres (350 pints) of milk.

△ **SEARCHING**
A number of tour operators run well-organised whale-watching tours in the Caribbean where humpbacks head during the winter.

▷ **HEADS AND TAILS**
A humpback whale *(megaptera novaeangliae)* lobtailing in the waters around the Banco de la Plata (Silver Bank).

WHALE-WATCHING EXCURSIONS

Whale watching tours are popular in the warm waters of the Bahía de Samaná (Samaná Bay) in the northeast of the Dominican Republic. Tour boats can offer breathtaking sights of migrating humpback whales. In an effort to protect the breeding area excursions are strictly regulated, with just 40 boats licensed to operate around the Bay; visitors are not allowed to swim in the water with the mammals, as in the past. With powerful binoculars the whales' mating rituals and calving can be seen from dry land at Bahía de Samaná, but it is nothing like the view from a whale-watching boat.

An adult can grow up to 12 metres (40 ft) and weigh about 40 tons. So it is an impressive sight when the animals (usually male) breach – rush out of the water at great speed, hit the surface and fly through the air. Access to the protected Banco de la Plata is severely restricted.

For tour details contact Victoria Marine, which has an office on the Malecón in Samaná (tel: 809 538 2494; email: kim.beddall@usa.net), or Transporte Marítimo Minadiel, located further along the coast road from Samaná (tel: 809 538 2556).

△ SPECTACULAR DISPLAY
To capture the amazing sight of a humpback whale tail breaching in the waters around Silver Bank Sanctuary be sure to take a camera and waterproof clothing.

◁ ON THE LOOK OUT
The clear Antillean waters off the Dominican Republic's coast are a treasure trove for snorkellers. But take note, visitors cannot swim with the whales and dolphins around the Bahía de Samaná (Samaná Bay).

◁ BAYWATCH
Whale Watch Bay on the Samaná Peninsula is a great spot on dry land from which to observe the great mammals in the ocean.

▷ GOING BELLY-UP
A Caribbean humpback whale swims belly-up just below the surface. It can make acrobatic displays above the water too.

THE DOMINICAN REPUBLIC

A detailed guide to the entire country, with principal sites clearly cross-referenced by number to the maps

Think of the Caribbean country of the Dominican Republic and visions of palm-fringed strips of wide golden sand lapped by warm water are sure to appear. Indeed there are many miles of fine beaches to enjoy along the north coast, on the Samaná Peninsula and on the eastern tip – though not all have escaped the nastier effects of mass tourism. But scratch the surface of this mountainous land and there is so much more to see.

Protected within the national parks are cascading waterfalls, rivers and vast forests – the habitats of varied flora and fauna. The wildlife includes some found exclusively on the island within its fertile valleys and dry, arid desert conditions in the west around Lago Enriquillo. The highest points in the Caribbean are here too and some visitors are attracted by the challenge of hiking through the mountain ranges and scaling the peaks.

In the tranquil northwest, the agricultural Cibao Valley and the lush hills of the Cordillera Central, country life continues in much the same way as it always has. Sugar cane and fruit plantations, paddy fields and fragrant alpine forests dominate the landscape, while the hills offer relief from the tropical temperatures inland.

Experience the hurly-burly of the nation's colourful capital city, Santo Domingo. Rich in the historical monuments of the founding fathers, beautiful centuries-old architecture stands side by side with modern structures. The capital is the commercial and cultural centre of the Republic, where local people rush about their everyday business. But typical of the Caribbean and Latin America, there is always time to stop, relax and chat in the pretty squares and parks.

Elsewhere in the Republic there are interesting sights, including the ruins of La Isabela in the north between Puerto Plata and Monte Cristi: this was the first permanent settlement in the Americas. There is also evidence of the effect of a rapid rise in tourism development with luxury resorts and crowds of sun- and fun-seeking visitors. All-inclusive hotels jostle for space along the south coast from Boca Chica to Punta Cana, and on the north coast from Puerto Plata to Río San Juan. Sosúa and Cabarete on the north coast have some of the best scuba diving and windsurfing, and the infectious rhythms of *merengue* music, played at ear-splitting volume, can be heard almost everywhere. ❏

PRECEDING PAGES: the lush Constanza farmland; a pony and mule trek through the Cibao Valley; girls running through the clear waters that lap Isla Bonita beach, Las Terrenas on the Samaná Peninsula.
LEFT: Carnival characters in La Vega.

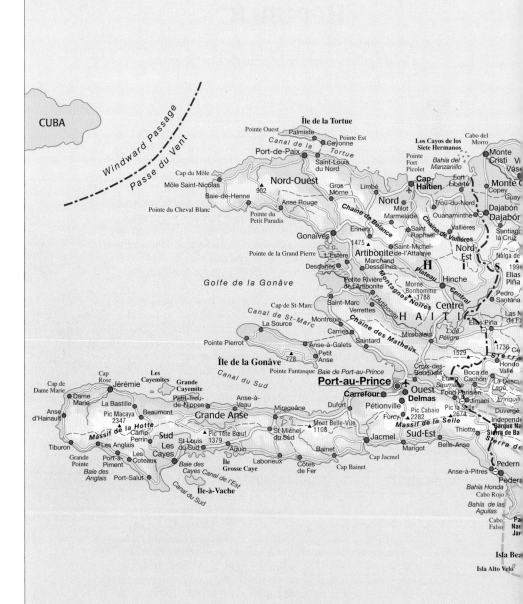

CUBA

Windward Passage

Passe du Vent

Île de la Tortue
Pointe Ouest Palmiste Pointe Est
Canal de la Cayonne
Port-de-Paix *Tortue*
Saint-Louis
du Nord

Los Cayos de los
Siete Hermanos
Cabo del
Morro
Pointe
Fort
Picolet
Monte
Cristi Vi
Vás

Cap du Môle
Môle Saint-Nicolas
Nord-Ouest
902
Gros
Morne
Limbé
**Cap-
Haïtien**
Bahía del
Manzanillo
Fort
Liberté
Monte
Copey Guay

Baie-de-Henne
Pointe du Cheval Blanc
Anse Rouge
Pointe du
Petit Paradis
Nord
Milot
Chaîne de Bélance
Marmelade
Saint-Michel-
Trou-du-Nord
Ouanaminthe
Vallières
Dajabón
Dajabón
Guay

Gonaïves
Ennery
1475
Artibonite
L'Estère
Saint
Raphaël
Chaîne de Vallières
Saint-Michel-
de-l'Attalaye
**Nord
Est**
Nalga de

Pointe de la Grand Pierre
Marchand
Dessalines
Hinche
199
Elías
Piña

Desdunes
Petite Rivière
de l'Artibonite
Montagnes Noires
Morne
Bonhomme
1788
Plateau
Centre
Pedro
Santana
Las N
de F

Golfe de la Gonâve
Cap de St-Marc
Saint-Marc
Verrettes
Artibonite
Chaîne des Mathieux
H A I T I
Elías Piña
Ce

Canal de St-Marc
La Source
Montrouis
Carries
Mirebalais
L'de
Péligre
1529
1736 Ce

Pointe Pierrot
Anse-à-Galets
Saintard
Croix-des-
Bouquets
Boca de
Cachón
1529
Hondo
Vallé

Île de la Gonâve
778
Petit
Anse
Canal du Sud
Pointe Fantasque
Baie de Port-au-Prince
Port-au-Prince
*Étang
Saumâtre*
Fond Parisien
La Descu
Lago
Enriquill

Cap de
Dame Marie
Cap
Rose
Jérémie
**Les
Cayemites**
**Grande
Cayemite**
Anse-à-
Veau
Miragoâne
Dufort
Carrefour
Delmas
Ouest
Pétionville
Furcy
Pic Cabaio
2282
Pic la Selle
2674
Massif de la Selle
Jimani
Duvergé
Independ
Parque Na
Sierra de Ba

Anse
d'Hainault
Dame
Marie
La Bastille
Pic Macaya
2347
Beaumont
Grande Anse
Miragoâne
Mont Belle-Vue
1108
St Michel
du Sud
Jacmel
Thiotte
Sud-Est
Sierra de

Tiburon
Camp
Perrin
Les Anglais
Sud
**Les
Cayes**
Massif de la Hotte
Pic Tête Bœuf
1379
Aguin
Bainet
Marigot
Belle-Anse
Cap Jacmel
Pedern

Grande
Pointe
Port-à-
Piment
Les
Coteaux
St Louis
du Sud
Laborieux
Côtes
de Fer
Cap Bainet
Anse-à-Pitres
Peder

*Baie des
Anglais*
Port-Salut
*Baie des
Cayes*
**Île
Grosse Caye**
Canal de l'Est
Bahía Honda
Cabo Rojo

Île-à-Vache
*Bahía de las
Aguilas*
Cabo
Falso
Pa
Nac
Jar

Isla Bea

Isla Alto Velo

CARIBBEAN SEA

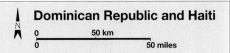

Dominican Republic and Haiti

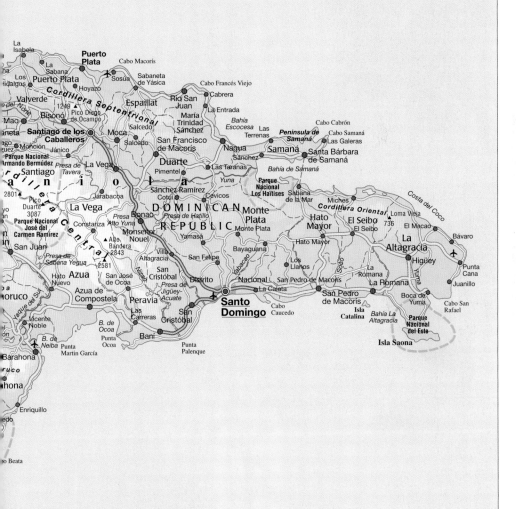

ATLANTIC OCEAN

CARIBBEAN METROPOLIS

Sprawling out from the Zona Colonial, Santo Domingo, the Dominican Republic's capital city, is a vibrant, noisy place. Its parks, palaces and museums offer some respite

Map on page 170

Santo Domingo

More than 4 million Dominicans live in the sprawling metropolis and bustling hubbub of the nation's capital. At any one time, the bulk of residents seem to be out and about – negotiating cracked pavements or gushing along the arterial roads which crisscross the city and lend a semblance of order to the urban bustle. Street corner sentinels, neighbourhood regulars and observers on home turf decorate the vibrant streetscape, diligently watching fellow citizens fly by. Santo Domingo is alive and kicking.

The combustion engine, in all its various stages of evolution, provides the background growl that accompanies every roadside chat and shopping transaction. Infrequent lulls of activity are readily dissipated by the fleets of overloaded buses or *guaguas, carros públicos,* thundering trucks and private cars which career along the main drags. Internationally flavoured avenues – Abraham Lincoln, Winston Churchill, John F. Kennedy and Bolívar among others – hold the key to unlocking citywide travel. While much can be covered on foot, some places will require a taxi fare or a double-dime adventure in the *públicos* – the mainstay of the popular transport system. These cars traverse the city along fixed routes, stopping to pick up and set down on request.

At the mouth of the Río Ozama, the **Zona Colonial** peacefully reflects its important historic past behind ancient thickset walls *(see pages 183–190).*

LEFT: "El Macho" obelisk. **BELOW:** guarding the Palacio Nacional.

Monument to liberation

The western limit of the old city is marked by the solid stonework of the **Puerta del Conde ❶**. Originally built in the mid-17th century to commemorate the successful repulsion of British troops from Spanish territory, the former city entrance evokes stronger emotion in Dominican hearts as the site of the declaration of Dominican statehood in 1844, signifying the population's imminent liberation from Haitian control. In front of the arch, an underfoot brass plate marks "kilometer zero"– the locus for measuring inter-provincial distances and the starting point from which to explore a hectic, vibrant city that always seems to be on the edge of chaos.

While the Puerta del Conde heralds the colonial chapter of the tour, the past is never far away outside the imposing gateway. The old city walls on either side form the eastern edge of the **Parque de la Independencia**, a popular spot for resting and people-watching. Surrounded by swirling traffic, which re-groups and warms up for the westward race along Avenida Bolívar, or an eastward dash down Avenida Mella, the park's relaxed atmosphere is all the more apparent and welcome. The occasional shoe shiner or street vendor seem almost amateurish in their persis-

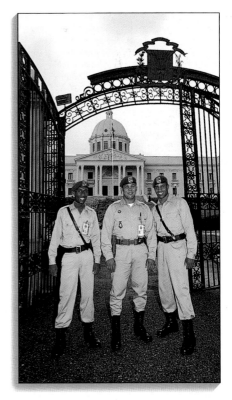

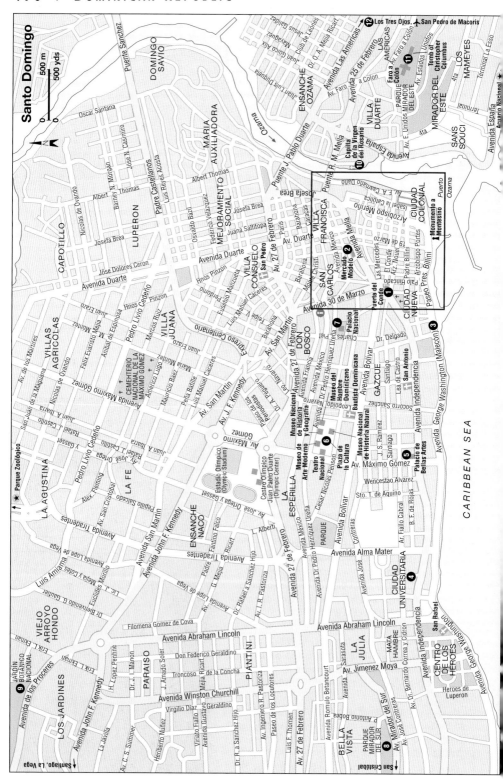

Santo Domingo

tence compared with the well-practiced assault of those garrisoned in the colonial quarter. Perhaps the presence of the **Altar de la Patria** (open daily; entrance free) exudes an element of tranquillity and respect for the three famous founding fathers enshrined in the park. Built in 1976, the mausoleum houses three towering white marble statues and the remains of the statesmen who engineered the fledgling republic during the 19th century: Francisco del Rosario Sánchez, Juan Pablo Duarte and Ramón Matías Mella. Stern-looking military sentries guard the monolithic solemnity of the site seven days a week.

Leaving a shady park bench induces a change of pace, not least while negotiating a crossing of Avenida Bolívar on the north side of the park, then heading east along the consumer-driven Avenida Mella. Before plunging into the shopping mêlée, you can recall the past at the **Fuerte de la Concepción**. The contrast between old and new is never clearer than after a visit to the ruins of this fortress, built in 1543 at the corner of Avenida Mella and Calle Palo Hincado. Formerly the northwest outpost of the colonial city, a morass of brightly coloured overhead signs greets today's gaze along the Avenida Mella.

The **Mercado Modelo ❷** lies a short walk down this heaving, jumbled concoction of clothing shops, tourist trinket stalls, superstores, banks and camera shops – markedly more up-beat than the parallel pedestrian strip of El Conde in the Zona Colonial. This busy covered craft market focuses largely on the tourist trade, but it is also used by locals. A plethora of stallholders eagerly divert passers-by, proffering woodcarvings, paintings, T-shirts, amber jewellery, dolls, ornaments, ironwork… a veritable lion's den, treasure trove and old curiosity shop combined. Be prepared to bargain, be seduced and leave with a purchase. Beyond the indoor maze of merchants is Little Haiti where vegetable and fruit sellers pack the back streets, jostling for space with the colourful Haiti-bound buses or *tap-taps* and several *botánicas* – bright, perfumed shops selling religious icons, potions, candles and images for the faithful.

Down along the Malecón

Avenida George Washington, otherwise known as the **Malecón ❸**, which skirts the seafront from the port, is a welcome escape from the buzzing throng of shoppers and pedestrians. A 20-minute seaward stroll down Calle Santomé from the market takes you through the Zona Colonial to the **Ciudad Nueva**, a neighbourly mixture of 19th-century townhouses, noisy mid-street baseball games, sociable corner shops and beautiful glimpses of a dilapidated architectural past. Gingerbread lattices of ironwork lace tumbling balconies. Rocking chairs creak on stone-tiled floors. Approaching the sea, the imposing statue of the indigenous peoples'-rights petitioner, **Fray Antón de Montesinos** *(see page 34)*, looms to the left, overlooking the harbour entrance and marking the head of the Malecón. A healthy walk westwards follows the contours of the rocky seashore, usually refreshed by a welcoming sea breeze and occasional mists of spray.

The relative inactivity of the afternoon rolls over to the dusk arrival of the jogging set, to be replaced by a busy nightlife clientele. Roadside bars spring up and

Map on page 170

You will not be permitted to pay your respects to the three national heroes in the Altar de la Patria if you are in shorts.

BELOW: liquor for sale.

Merengue *can be heard in restaurants, bars, even taxis, and is usually played at full blast.*

BELOW: directing the traffic in Santo Domingo. **RIGHT:** service with a smile.

merengue blasts forth from straining stereo systems at the weekends. The volume increases impressively for the annual *merengue* festival during the last week of July and first week of August *(see page 113)*. Thousands gather on the Malecón to dance, drink and party some more. *Carnaval*, at the end of February, is another occasion for a boisterous seafront gathering. The pre-Lenten celebrations coincide with the anniversary of Dominican independence, fuelling vivacious parades, non-stop music and the copious flow of rum.

A westward trek along the 3-km (2-mile) long Malecón leads past two self-congratulatory obelisks erected by Trujillo and ends up at the uninspiring **Centro de los Héroes**, renamed to commemorate those who fought the former dictator. Once the site of the Free World Fair for Peace and Fraternity during the 1950s – another of the dictatorship's ironic financial follies – the area now houses a green-painted concrete forest of government buildings. For those wishing to play postal roulette, the main Post Office is located nearby.

A city ramble

Inland, sandwiched between the Zona Colonial and Avenida Abraham Lincoln, the neighbourhoods of Gazcue and Ciudad Universitaria provide interesting glimpses of city life. Both areas house a variety of educational and cultural centres, mixed within pleasant residential zones.

Gazcue lies directly west of the Parque de la Independencia *(see page 169)*. Formerly the home of the city's élite before they headed for the hills of the newer northern suburbs, this catholic cluster of architectural styles dates from the 1930s. Beautiful leafy streets and the distinguished array of homesteads wrapped in a veil of sleepy decay lay the foundations for a pleasant ramble.

Occasional modern apartment blocks juxtapose urban designs, while the arrival of several fashionable restaurants, cafes and businesses have threatened to wake up this twilight zone in recent years. The relatively lively thoroughfare of Calle Santiago leads to the **Ciudad Universitaria** ❹, the adjoining residential neighbourhood that is home to one of the oldest universities in the Americas.

It may lack funds and architectural longevity, although originally founded in 1538, but the Autonomous University of Santo Domingo (UASD) makes up for material shortfall with a proud reputation and a history of vigorous student activism that consistently challenges the political and social inequalities evident in Dominican society. A range of concerts, films, and theatre productions, not to mention demonstrations, are regularly held on site.

The **Palacio de Bellas Artes** ❺, an impressive building that dominates the intersection of avenidas Máximo Gómez and Independencia, promises more architecturally than it offers culturally. There are occasional events and art exhibitions held in the spacious halls, but generally little happens on the inside. The grand stairway murals of José Vela-Zanetti are worth a peek, though.

A concentration of culture

The **Plaza de la Cultura** ❻ (the museums are open Tues–Sun; separate entrance fees), just a few blocks to the north on Avenida Máximo Gómez, soon provides a feast of opportunities to satiate the cultural appetite. Set amid pleasant lawns and landscaped gardens, the complex was constructed during the 1970s in the finest modernist style, and houses the most important arts institutions in the country. Fronting the main entrance, the **Teatro Nacional** *(see Travel Tips, page 357)* is the imposing home of classical arts in the Dominican

Map on page 170

TIP

Carros públicos – old minivans or cars, which traverse fixed routes – can take you from one area of the city to another and sometimes beat the taxi. Flag down a ride for the princely sum of 5 pesos *(see Travel Tips, page 351).*

BELOW: the impressive Palacio de Bellas Artes.

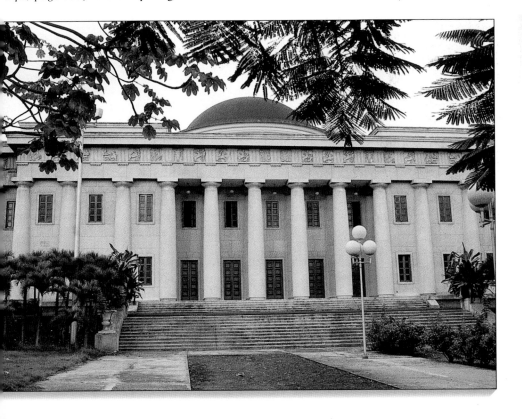

Exhibition of pre-Columbian artefacts plot the early history of the Dominican people.

BELOW:
the interior of the Museo del Hombre Dominicano.

Republic. National and international artists regularly perform ballet, opera and orchestral performances here. A smart dress code is expected and enforced. At the top occasions, the well-to-do descend, bib-and-tuckered, from their gated uptown villas to join a who's who *soirée* of social flurrying.

The **Museo de Arte Moderno** (tel: 685 2153) houses an excellent exposition of contemporary Dominican art which more than compensates for any shortcomings of the Palacio de Bellas Artes. Even sceptics cannot fail to be aroused by the vivacity, depth and quality of the work on display. Representations of country life, evolving from the 1930s *costumbrismo* movement headed by Jaime Colson, Darío Suro and Yoryi Morel, provide a feel for the rural traditions that infuse longstanding notions of *dominicanidad*, which can seldom be experienced during a short stay in the country. Between museum hops, the cafe by the side of the Museo de Arte Moderno, provides a well-stocked retreat for a reflective drink or meal.

The **Museo del Hombre Dominicano** (tel: 687 3622) has fascinating exhibits of pre-Columbian artefacts and illustrates the history of the Conquest and slavery, demography, folklore, rural life and religious beliefs. The *Carnaval* display includes brightly coloured masks and garish costumes, and offers a good taste of a festive atmosphere. Unlike many aspects of Dominican society, the museum provides a reasonably balanced and unbiased amalgam of Hispanic, African and indigenous influences.

The two remaining museums ignite fewer sparks of enthusiasm. The **Museo Nacional de Historia y Geografía** (open Tues–Sun 9.30am–5pm; free admission; tel: 686 6668) constructs a loose chronological journey around 19th-century Haitian-Dominican tussles, and the assorted memorabilia and personal

DOMINICAN JEWS

The author Peter Furst describes his arrival by boat on the north coast of the island: "We glided past a shanty-town whose roofs of corrugated iron, catching the sun's first rays, exploded into a roaring, mind-expanding van Gogh of Dominican parentage" (*Don Quixote in Exile*, 1996).

Similar tropical landscapes greeted the 300 Jewish families who, like the writer, were fleeing Nazi Europe for the promised sanctuary of Dominican shores. Centuries earlier Jewish moneylenders had financed Columbus's first expedition, while the advent of Sephardic Jews during the 19th century consolidated interests in the island's import and export trade. It is the later arrivals, however, who have charted the most apparent changes to Dominican society.

A Jewish enclave was established in Sosúa, east of Puerta Plata *(see page 211)*, following moves by Trujillo to encourage European immigration in the late 1930s. Though many of the settlers moved overseas during the 1960s, they left behind a thriving dairy and meat industry that still serves the island. Few visible remnants of the Jewish presence remain, but the Sinagoga de la Comunidad Judía de Sosúa (synagogue) and the Museo de la Comunidad Judía de Sosúa (Museum of the Jewish Community of Sosúa) survive as records of their time here.

effects from the two longest-lasting dictatorships of Ulises Heureaux (1886–99) and Leónidas Rafael Trujillo (1930–61). The **Museo Nacional de Historia Natural** (entrance fee; tel: 689 0106) similarly hawks a lacklustre display of gems, rocks, basic ecology lessons and a stuffy array of taxidermists' treats. Additional enlightenment is restricted to those who are able to understand the Spanish display notes. Finally, and also of more interest to Spanish readers, the neighbouring **Biblioteca Nacional** (National Library) houses a significant collection of books encased in an impressive modernist block.

Wander eastwards along Avenida Dr Pedro Henriquez Ureña for about five blocks to refocus the tour on the nitty-gritty of everyday political reality, headquartered in a pink, domed baroque fantasy at the intersection of avenidas Doctor Delgado and México. The **Palacio Nacional** ❼ combines neoclassical style, presidential grandeur, regal decadence and keen security. It was designed by Italian architect Guido d'Alessandro during the late 1940s to match the magnificence of the dictatorship, and Trujillo's troubled ghost allegedly whisks through the ornately mirrored and heavily furnished salons, haunting present incumbents.

Around the city parks

Santo Domingo is fortunate in having its fair share of well-maintained, attractive and accessible park space. Bordered to the north by affluent suburbs and adjacent to the foreign diplomatic missions dotted along Avenida Anacaona, the **Parque Mirador del Sur** ❽ (open daily), in the western reaches of the city, is a popular location for in-line skaters, cyclists, runners, and people out for a stroll. The 7-km (5-mile) stretch of paths and lawns is a much-appreciated retreat from rush-hour traffic fumes. Police close the through road to vehicles

Map on page 170

TIP

The Palacio Nacional is not generally open to the public, but free guided tours can be arranged on Monday, Wednesday and Friday by calling 686 4771. If you are given a tour, you are expected to be smartly dressed.

BELOW: the Palacio Nacional.

Schedule park visits to avoid the afternoon heat and regular rainy season downpours – early morning or evening visits will prove more pleasant, especially during the summer.

BELOW: the shuttle shades visitors from the heat.

during morning and evening peak hours (6–9am and 4–8pm). The park lies along a limestone ridge that is home to a series of caves: the Cueva del Paseo de los Indios has a notable bat population, but perhaps the best-known cave is the **Guácara Taína** on Avenida Mirador del Sur. Converted into a lively subterranean music venue, this is where *capitaleños* dance and make merry until dawn at the weekends.

The **Jardín Botánico Nacional** ❾ (open daily 9am–6pm; entrance fee; tel: 567 6211) on Avenida República de Colombia is fair reward for journeying to the northwestern edge of the city. Nestled among Santo Domingo's wealthiest households in the residential suburb of Arroyo Hondo, the botanical gardens cover 180 hectares (450 acres) and exhibit a wide variety of tropical and aquatic plants, ferns, a herbarium and 200 species of palm. Within minutes of arrival, the buzz and belch of distant traffic is easily discarded for a tranquil few hours among the vegetation.

The Japanese garden receives worthy praise, but perhaps just as striking are the floral and faunal national emblems: a pavilion houses the famous collection of over 300 indigenous orchid varieties; fine examples of the national plant, the *caoba* or mahogany tree, have survived hurricane damage; and the national bird, the palmchat, is often visible among the royal palms. A huge floral clock adds a note of eccentricity. More reliable and useful perhaps is the shuttle that ferries visitors around the gardens when the heat distracts even the most avid gardening enthusiasts.

A natural companion to the botanical gardens and a short drive east along Avenida los Reyes Católicos, the **Parque Zoológico** (Tues–Sun; entrance fee; tel: 562 3149) is an undervisited attraction. The park, in the northwest of the city,

comprises 160 hectares (400 acres) of landscaped gardens and a collection of animals and is generally not considered worth going out of the way for.

Across the Río Ozama

Beyond the **Río Ozama**, the eastern section of the capital is noticeably less affluent than many of the western suburbs. The low-income settlements along the river bank are alarmingly worlds away from the city's wealthy neighbourhoods. Crossing over on Puente Mella, the Zona Colonial downstream on the west bank seems an ever isolated patch of urban antiquity.

The rainbow-striped **Molinos Dominicanos** are eye-catching kaleidoscopic silos that have gained their own prominence on the city's low-level skyline. A great sight for homesick prairie folk, the huge canisters also cast their shadow on one of the first churches constructed in the Americas. The **Capilla de la Virgen del Rosario** ⑩, at the end of Avenida Olegario Vargas, is a quiet drop-in chapel en route to the capital's largest architectural venture, Columbus's lighthouse or the **Faro a Colón** ⑪ (open Tues–Sun; entrance fee; tel: 592 5217), a five-minute walk to the east. Dreamed up in the 1920s to honour the conquistador's arrival in the Americas, original plans were penned by British architect, J.L. Greave, who won the international competition for its design. Funding and interest languished for almost six decades, until President Balaguer resurrected the idea to construct the Faro a Colón in order to commemorate the 500th anniversary of Columbus's landfall in 1992. Originally to be financed with donations from around the Caribbean, the Dominican government eventually dug deep into national coffers.

Material expenses aside, controversy has engulfed the project. Hundreds of

Map on page 170

Where's the smallest "P" on a bottle of Presidente beer? Scouring the label will generally not reveal the tiny golden letter printed alone below the writing. But if you find it, you'll have the chance to impress, even the regulars, with your local knowledge.

BELOW: pink flamingos around the lagoon at the Parque Zoológico.

Map on page 170

People need to wear shoes, but they also need to wear a tie. The lighthouse is that tie.

– ATTRIBUTED TO JOAQUÍN BALAGUER ON THE CONSTRUCTION OF FARO A COLÓN

BELOW: guarding Columbus's tomb at the Faro a Colón. **RIGHT:** a manatee *(trichechus manatus)* can be seen at the Acuario Nacional.

low-income families were forcibly removed to clear space for construction, or later shovelled aside to hide unscheduled human shabbiness.

The construction of the Faro a Colón prompted demonstrations and riots as people protested the extravagant spending and disregard for human rights. Several people lost their lives during disturbances, drawing international attention to the dispute. As disapproval of the project increased the Pope decided against inaugurating the building and the Spanish royal family stayed away from the celebrations. Despite all of his resistance to opposition and his grand plans, not even Balaguer was able to attend the ceremonies. The president's sister died just a few hours after inspecting the completed building and he went in to mourning. The tragic event led the public to speculate that the edifice was, in fact, the target of a curse, or *fukú*, by Columbus himself.

The lighthouse itself is a striking 800-metre (875-yard) long concrete edifice, shaped as a recumbent cross which projects a laser image of the crucifix into the heavens – when funds allow it to be lit. The monument is best viewed on a cloudy night.

At the centre, the tomb of Columbus is guarded by a military vigil. In addition, reproductions of documents and colonial artefacts and exhibitions from other countries highlight the path of the Conquest.

Built as a mausoleum, ongoing debate contests the veracity of its namesake's remains. A great voyager in life and in death, Columbus's relics were shipped on a variety of occasions between Cuba, Spain and the Dominican Republic, after an initial Spanish burial in 1506. Custodians of a tomb in Seville, however, also lay claim to his remains, and Italian and Cuban petitions have similarly jockeyed for pole position as the final resting place on the Grand Navigator's celestial cruise. The remains were DNA tested in Spain in 2003, in a final effort to resolve the question of authenticity.

The Three Eyes

The lighthouse is situated at the western end of the **Parque Mirador del Este**. Heading across the 5-km (3-mile) long narrow park (a short taxi ride), similar in layout to its western twin, the paths and perimeter roads eventually lead to three sinkhole caves called **Los Tres Ojos** ⓬ (open daily; entrance fee) where Taíno princesses and their companions went to bathe. Flanked to the north by the *Autopista de las Américas*, the main thoroughfare to the airport, "The Three Eyes" is a popular stop for coaches making rapid detours en route to the airport. If time permits it is worth hanging back from the crowds to savour something of the beauty of the underground caves and the three deep lagoons. Roughly hewn steps lead down to these karst sinkholes, adorned by stalagmites and stalactites, while a raft (extra cost) assists passage between the last two lagoons. Humidity levels soar as the day progresses, so arrive early, beat the crowds and enjoy what should be a natural wonder.

Located a few blocks to the south of the Parque Mirador del Este on the Avenida España, the **Acuario Nacional** isn't really worth an extended trip, in spite of the manatee rescued off the southwest coast of the island near Barahona. ❏

THE OLD COLONIAL CITY

At the heart of Santo Domingo is the Zona Colonial, the preserved reminders of Columbus's first town in the New World. A tour of the old quarter provides a sense of life in those early days

Map on page 187

This is where colonial life in the New World began – in the narrow streets of old Santo Domingo on the west bank of the Río Ozama, and it is here that you can experience the vibrancy and grandeur of 16th-century living in the New World as you walk around the Zona Colonial, the first overseas town to receive a royal charter from the Spanish Crown. Founded in 1498 after several false starts, the old city has a rich colonial past with many beautiful buildings still intact. Authentic and atmospheric, colonial Santo Domingo is a joy for the history buff, as well as for shoppers, art lovers and romantic types, who stroll the cobblestone streets, dine in fine restaurants and chance upon delightful historic attractions on every corner. Santo Domingo was laid out in a grid pattern, and this pattern became the model for town-planning in North America. The logic of this layout makes a walking tour of old Santo Domingo an easy and pleasurable experience.

A good place to start a walking tour of the Zona Colonial is at **Parque Colón ❶** on the corner of the bustling, pedestrian shopping street, Calle El Conde and Arzobispo Meriño. The park is named for its bronze statue of Christopher Columbus, made in 1897 by the French sculptor, Gilbert. This is where you can opt for a guided tour or a bus tour of the old city. But, with map in hand, discovering the delights of the old city of Santo Domingo on your own is a breeze.

The first of many firsts

Situated on the south side of the park, east of Arzobispo Nouel, stands the **Catedral Basílica Menor de Santa María ❷** (open Mon–Sat 9am–4.30pm; no shorts). Built 1514–1544, it is believed to be the first cathedral in the Americas. From the outside, the grey limestone cathedral is a majestic sight with massive gates which were originally carved with sculptures of the apostles. When Sir Francis Drake attacked the city in 1586 *(see page 36)*, these were destroyed – as was much else in the building he used as his headquarters – and it wasn't until 1990 that they were replaced with sculptures representing indigenous people.

Inside, the cathedral is a dizzying mixture of Gothic, Spanish Renaissance and baroque architecture that's surprisingly harmonious. The beautiful stained-glass windows have been recreated by the contemporary Dominican artist, Rincón Mora, using the original 12th-century method, and other treasures include the 18th-century carved mahogany altar, the silver carillon created by Italian sculptor Benvenuto Cellini (1500–71) and the oil painting by the 17th-century Spanish artist, Bartolomé Murillo; 14 distinct chapels line the interior of the cathedral, and the treasury contains the emerald-studded crown of Queen Isabela. The queen was forced to pawn her precious crown to meet the expense of Columbus's first voyage.

PRECEDING PAGES: an aerial view of the old city and the Río Ozama. **LEFT:** altar detail inside the cathedral. **BELOW:** chess on the Calle El Conde.

Religious icons were often crafted from gold and precious stones.

Facing Parque Colón on the east side of Calle Isabel la Católica is the 19th-century **Palacio de Borgella**. Once the home of the governor, today it houses a tourist information office. A half block south of the palace, and a right turn on to Calle Padre Billini, brings you to the **Casa de Tostada** ❸ (open Thurs–Tues 9am–2pm; entrance fee), the home of the writer, Don Francisco de Tostada. The first university professor born in the colony, he was murdered by Sir Francis Drake's raiding party in 1586. Later, the graceful house became the Archbishop's Palace, and the double Gothic windows are the only surviving examples in the New World.

Today, inside the well-restored palace, the **Museo de la Família Dominicana** (Museum of the Dominican Family) portrays how a typical well-to-do Dominican family lived in the 19th century. The lovely inner courtyard is a good place for a rest.

First seat of learning and some early churches

The majestic **Convento de los Domínicos** ❹ (open Tues–Sun; free admission) stands at the corner of Calle Padre Billini and Calle Duarte Macorís another block to the west. Founded in 1510, the convent was visited by Pope Paul III in 1538, and, impressed by the theology lectures that he heard here, he granted it the title of university, making it – you've guessed it – the oldest university in the New World. Its unusual ceiling depicts both the classical gods and the Christian saints and angels in a single pantheon. The Sun represents God while Mars, Mercury, Jupiter and Saturn are the four evangelists.

The **Iglesia de la Regina Angelorum** ❺ (open Mon–Sat), two blocks further along in Calle José Reyes, was constructed in 1537 and is a delicate

BELOW:
the Convento
de los Domínicos.

plateresque-style building that was badly damaged during Haitian rule from 1822 to 1844, but some of the original structure survives. Today, the church of the Queen of the Angels is a small convent which has an exquisite wooden altar inside the simple chapel and a wall made from silver. On the same street, half a block north at No. 6 is the **Museo de Porcelana** (open Tues–Sun; entrance fee). Built in the 19th century and modelled on the Alhambra in Southern Spain, this very small museum has a lovely collection of antique porcelain.

Around the corner, and one block to the west on Calle Arzobispo Nouel, is the **Iglesia del Carmen** (open at varying, unscheduled times). Built around 1615 at the side of Capilla de San Andrés, the chapel contains a lovely wooden sculpture of Jesus. A 10-minute detour down Calle Sánchez with a right turn on to Calle Arzobispo Portes will bring you to the **Puerta de la Misericordia ⑥**. Forming part of the old wall of Santo Domingo, its name, "the Gate of Mercy", was bestowed upon it because the local population always fled to this point for protection during hurricanes and earthquakes. It was at this site, on 27 February 1844, that Ramón Matías Mella, one of the country's founding fathers, fired the shot that began the struggle for independence from Haiti after 22 years of occupation *(see page 46)*.

Lovely Ladies Street

Located directly east from the Gate of Mercy, after about 800 metres (just over ½ mile), the lovely **Calle Las Damas** leads northwards parallel to Río Ozama. This Street of the Ladies is the oldest in the western hemisphere and its name honours the elegant noblewomen of the Spanish Court who promenaded along it in their finery each evening. Today it is the visitors who

Map
on page
187

The Museo Mundo del Ambar, which has a gift shop, can be found at 452 Calle Arzobispo Meriño and is open Mon–Sat until 6pm; admission is free. See page 215 for more information about this amazing gem.

BELOW:
a tobacco shop on
Calle Las Damas.

TIP

When visiting the Fortaleza Ozama, if you decide to hire one of the many guides offering their services at the door, make sure that you agree on a fee before you start.

promenade, delighting in the street's beautifully restored colonial buildings. Doña María Toledo, wife of the fourth governor, Diego Colón, and niece of the King of Spain, brought 30 ladies of the court with her when she sailed to the colony and the street is named after them.

The imposing buildings of the **Fortaleza Ozama** ❼ (open Mon–Sat 9am–7pm, Sun 10am–3pm; entrance fee) dominate the southeastern end of the Calle Las Damas. Also known as the Fortaleza de Santo Domingo, the fortress was built in 1503 to protect the eastern border of the city overlooking the mouth of the Río Ozama, and it forms the oldest military complex in the New World. Inside the massive stone walls is a pleasant square with the munitions building to one side, guarded by a statue of the Virgin Mary.

At the opposite end of the plaza is the **Torre de Homenaje** (Tower of Homage). Built in 1505, the tower, despite its name, was the cruel holding pen for condemned prisoners. Today it is a museum and gallery with changing exhibits, and from the roof, at the top of a spiral staircase, there is an all-embracing view of the city.

Situated to the north of the fort, the **Casa de Bastidas** (garden only, open daily; free admission) was constructed in the early 16th century for Don Rodrigo Bastidas, the king's tax collector. Bastidas went on to found the city of Santa Marta in Colombia. The house has a neoclassical portal and an inner court resembling a cloister. Inside, there are two pretty gardens with huge, shady caucho trees, but the building is undergoing renovations and is closed to the public.

Across the street is the Gothic **Casa de Francia** ❽, which today is occupied by the French Cultural Alliance, part of the French Embassy. It was originally built in 1503 and is where the famous explorer and conqueror

BELOW:
guard of honour at Panteón Nacional.

ADVENTURER EXTRAORDINAIRE

Hernán Cortés (1485–1547) was only 19 years old when he arrived in Santo Domingo from Spain in 1504. Desperate for adventure, he was intelligent, ruthless and ambitious. His prayers were answered when he met the conquistador Diego de Velázquez, whom he helped in his successful expedition to conquer Cuba in 1511.

Fired with the conquering spirit, Cortés was given the command of an expedition to Mexico in 1518. After founding Vera Cruz, he arrived at the magnificent Aztec capital of Tenochtitlán in 1519 with fewer than 400 Spanish soldiers, 16 horses – never seen before in the New World – 10 heavy guns, four lighter pieces of artillery and plenty of ammunition. The Aztec emperor Montezuma II thought Cortés was a messenger from the god Quetzalcóatl, and welcomed the explorer with many gifts, but the Spaniards repaid the emperor by taking him prisoner and attacking the city. Forced to retreat, Cortés didn't conquer the city until 1521, when he completely destroyed it and laid the foundations for Mexico City.

In 1522 he became governor of New Spain. After more conquests he went back to Spain in 1528 and was returned to Mexico City as Captain-General in 1530. In 1540 he went home a sick man, where he died.

of Mexico, Hernán Cortés, is alleged to have planned his conquests. The Alliance often holds art exhibitions of modern Dominican artists.

A few steps more on the opposite side of the street is the elegant **Hostal Nicolás de Ovando**, once the home of the city's first governor and where Christopher Columbus himself was a guest. Following years of renovation work the Hostal reopened as a luxury five-star hotel. Next door is the **Capilla de Nuestra Señora de los Remedios** (open Mon–Sat; Sun for Masses beginning at 6am). Rebuilt in 1884, the Chapel of our Lady of the Remedies is where the Spanish colonists first worshipped before the cathedral was constructed, and has Castillian-Romanesque-style blind arches and a barrel-vaulted ceiling.

Resting place for real heroes

The neoclassical grey limestone facade of the **Panteón Nacional ❾** (open Tues–Sun 9am–4.30pm; free admission, but it's customary to tip the guide; respectable dress required) dominates the opposite side of the street. Constructed

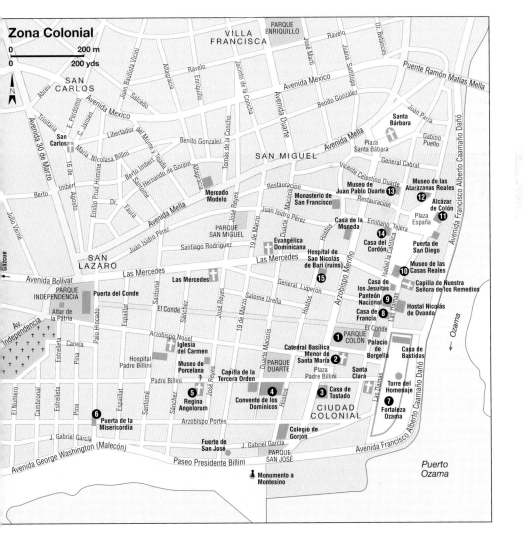

between 1714 and 1745 as a Jesuit monastery, the building was given to the Spanish Crown in 1767 when the Jesuits were expelled from Hispaniola and it has served as a tobacco warehouse and a theatre since. In 1950, the dictator Trujillo mandated that the building be transformed into a memorial to the country's national heroes, thinking that he himself would one day be interred here. Ironically, it now contains the remains of the martyrs who assassinated him. In fact, on the ceiling above the altar a commemorative scene of the assassination is painted. Note the sculpted Dominican coat of arms that graces the entrance and the exquisite copper chandeliers, a gift from Spain's own dictator, General Franco (1892–1975).

Behind the Panteón Nacional is the Plaza María de Toledo, named for Diego Colón's wife.

Just around the corner in Calle Luperon is the **Casa de los Jesuitas** (open Mon–Fri 8am–4.30pm; free admission), which houses not only the Institute for Hispanic Culture but also an excellent library of colonial history.

Spanish treasure – a royal inheritance

A fascinating treasure chest of eclectic, colonial objects fills the **Museo de las Casas Reales ⑩** (open Tues–Sun 9am–6pm; entrance fee) across Calle las Mercedes on the other side of the Panteón. In two 16th-century Renaissance-style mansions, the Museum of the Royal Houses was where the Royal Court or *Audiencia Real (see page 33)* for the colony sat. On display are antique coins (pieces of eight) and dolls, coats of armour, coaches, a Royal Court room, treasure from shipwrecks, gilded Spanish colonial furniture, an apothecary shop and Taíno Amerindian artefacts. In the cartography room, an enormous map marks the voyages of Columbus. The museum also puts on exhibitions of contemporary Dominican art.

BELOW:
interior of Museo de las Casas Reales.

To know the time of day, the judges sitting in the *Audiencia Real* in the Casa Reales merely needed to glance out of the window at the **Reloj del Sol** (sundial) across the Calle Las Damas. The strategically placed timepiece was built in 1753 and is a perfect spot for a pause to savour the fabulous view of the Ozama River.

Map on page 187

Colonial splendour in the Plaza España

The Calle Las Damas enters the **Plaza España**, where you come face to face with the **Alcázar de Colón** ⓫ (open daily 9am–6pm; entrance fee; guided tours in English), the most spectacular colonial site in the city. This was the palace of Christopher Columbus's son, Diego, who succeeded Ovando as governor of Hispaniola in 1509. Diego lived here with his beautiful wife, María de Toledo, King Ferdinand's niece, until 1523. It is where Pizarro, Cortés, Ponce de León and Balboa charted their future conquests. Four generations of the Colón family lived here until 1577 and it was later used for official purposes until it was abandoned in the 18th century. Having been built without nails in 1509–14 the palace gradually collapsed in ruins until the 1950s and 1960s, when it was restored. The coral-stone palace's graceful arched facade is magnificent, and each of the 22 rooms has been carefully refurbished with period furniture and paintings donated by the University of Madrid.

In the 18th century, the Alcázar de Colón was in such a bad state that it was used as the city's unofficial dumping ground. It has since been restored three times.

The palace also houses the **Museo Virreinal** (Viceregal Museum) that displays religious items and furnishings of the colonial period, and from the second floor you can enjoy a grand view of the river and the entire Zona Colonial. Venture around the back of the building and you'll come to the **Puerta de San Diego**, the original gate to the city which still stands in a part of the old city wall built to discourage a riverside attack.

BELOW: playing dominoes on the plaza at the Alcázar de Colón.

Map on page 187

The ruined fortress and church of Santa Bárbara (open Mon–Fri am, Sun for Masses starting at 6am) lie in the northernmost part of the old city. Completed in 1574, the church is a mishmash of architectural styles including baroque and Gothic.

BELOW: cathedral gateway detail.
RIGHT: a beautiful bride at Hospital de San Nicolás de Bari.

A flight of steps down from the front of the Alcázar takes you to a narrow street called **Las Atarazanas** (Royal Mooring Docks), which was once the colonial commercial district and where naval supplies used to be stored. Today, the small white houses lining the street are home to craft shops, art galleries and restaurants, providing the ideal spot for rest and refreshment.

A little way north stands the 17th-century **Puerta Atarazanas** and the **Museo de las Atarazanas Reales** ⑫ (open Mon, Tues, Thur–Sat 9am–5pm, Sun 9am–1pm; entrance fee). This maritime museum tells the story of the most famous shipwrecks around the Dominican coast, and has some marvellous exhibits of recovered treasure such as silver and gold coins, porcelain, antique bottles and all manner of interesting contraband.

Duarte – father of the *República*

One of the Dominican Republic's founders was born in 1813 at the house which now contains a museum in his honour. The **Museo de Juan Pablo Duarte** ⑬ (open Tues–Sun 8am–noon and 2–4.30pm; entrance fee) can be found at 308 Calle Isabel La Católica, two small blocks to the west of Las Atarazanas. The national hero was one of the three patriots who liberated the Dominican Republic from Haitian domination in 1844, only to see it come under Spanish rule again in 1861. He fought hard against it but was forced to leave the country and died in Venezuela in 1876. The museum is dedicated to the life of Duarte who is considered to be the father of the Dominican Republic.

Two blocks south down Calle Isabel La Católica, on the corner with Calle Emiliano Tejera, stands the **Casa del Cordón** ⑭ (open daily; free admission) where Diego Colón lived when he arrived in 1509. Built in 1500, it is the oldest European-style residence with two floors in the New World. On the facade, the sculpted sash and cord is the symbol of the rope-belt worn by the Franciscan order.

Overlooking a small hill, another two blocks to the west, lie the evocative ruins of the **Monasterio de San Francisco** (open daily; free admission). Built in 1508, it was the first monastery in the New World, but Drake destroyed it in 1586 *(see page 36)* by setting it on fire. After rebuilding, it was then levelled by an earthquake in 1673. Restored again, it was damaged by a hurricane in 1751 and converted into a lunatic asylum in 1881 – the chains that used to hold down the hapless patients can still be seen. Just as poignant, during the 20th century, artists took refuge here from the Spanish Civil War. Today the ruins often serve as a venue for cultural events.

A couple of minutes' walk south on Calle Hostos and Calle las Mercedes are more ruins. The **Hospital de San Nicolás de Bari** ⑮ was ordered to be built by Nicolás de Ovando, to serve the city's poor, and was the first hospital in the Americas. You can still make out the shape of the hospital in the form of a cross.

The church of **Nuestra Señora de las Mercedes**, three blocks west on Calle las Mercedes, was built between 1555 and 1576, but after being plundered by Drake and suffering earthquakes and hurricanes, the cloister is the only original feature that remains. The baroque carved wooden altar is a masterpiece. ❑

FROM CARIBE TO COCO

Rural primitiveness rubs shoulders with luxurious holiday resorts around the southeast coast, offering stunning beaches, an underwater world and a national park teeming with exotic birds

Map on page 198

Santo Domingo

P rovincial peacefulness and professional power-tourism? The island's beautiful southeast coast is living proof of such a strange marriage. Peasants driving their cattle alongside fields of waving sugar cane are just as typical as tourists relaxing in high-end luxury resorts.

However, it is a big mistake to categorise the eastern part as mainly a "mecca for charter tourists". True, the endless white sand beaches of the Costa Caribe in the southeast and Costa del Coco in the far east are skirted by hundreds of hotels, some of them small and basic, some of them lavish and ready to be featured in design magazines. But the eastern interior, especially in the provinces of San Pedro de Macorís, Hato Mayor and La Romana, is still dominated by rural simplicity. Raising cattle and cultivating fields of grass-green sugar cane are major aspects of Dominican life and many a farm worker can be seen riding a horse against a backdrop of pale purple mountains. In contrast, the industrial cities of **San Pedro de Macorís** and **La Romana** are abuzz with *motoconchos* (taxi motorcycles). Here are the nation's largest sugar processing plants and free-trade zones.

Nevertheless the east *is* a major destination for package tourists and independent travellers alike. The Government is proud of its supply of more than 13,000 hotel rooms in the region. The scenic Costa Caribe has at least 50 beaches – half of which are clustered with fancy accommodation. Yet there are still a few inexpensive inns where individual travellers prefer to stay and don't need to book in advance. The spectacular Costa del Coco (40 km/25 miles of pure white sandy beaches), on the other hand, caters solely to charter tourists. The eastern tip's up-market beach resorts resemble one gigantic satellite village, where the all-inclusive set-up satisfies every need possible. It's heaven for both beach bums and sports enthusiasts, but for the more adventurous tourist it might just seem like wasted time in an isolated golden cage. Except for some tiny hamlets, the area is sparsely populated and therefore poor in infrastructure; the nearest large city is 50 km (30 miles) away.

The world's largest bathtub

East of **Santo Domingo ❶** on the *Autopista* Las Américas, before the turning to the international Las Américas airport, is **La Caleta ❷**, where the Parque Nacional Submarino lies beneath the waves. Here, an intact reef and three wrecks provide a fascinating day's diving. To reach the park's waters, you must travel with a group organised by one of the dive shops at Boca Chica, a 10-minute drive away, since there are no facilities at La Caleta.

Beyond Las Américas airport lies the stronghold of

PRECEDING PAGES: boats tied up at Playa Bayahibe. **LEFT:** fun in the sun at Costa del Coco. **BELOW:** Jesus and Sammy Sosa.

Sadly the small Museo Ceremonial La Caleta is derelict. Taíno skeletons, curled in the foetal position with their belongings, were discovered here. The graves are believed to date from the 13th century.

Euro-Canadian party-tourism. **Boca Chica** ❸ offers all the hustle and bustle a fun-hungry person can desire – 24 hours a day. At the weekend, when the city dwellers join the foreign visitors and descend into the "world's largest bathtub", the reef-protected **Playa Boca Chica** in Bahía de Andrés is a mecca for families with children. Hustlers offer everything from manicures to fake amber jewellery to hair-braiding – in every language. Musicians serenade the crowds with hits like *Bambolero*, while revellers practise their clumsy *merengue* steps until the dawn.

Founded as a port for exporting sugar cane in the 1930s, this one-time idyllic *pueblo* gained fame when the gruesome dictator Trujillo built a beach villa here. After his dispatch in 1961, Boca Chica grew into a fancy and exclusive resort earning itself the name "Playa St Tropez". Nowadays, every business-savvy local rents out rooms, and the busy **Calle Duarte**, the main strip, is lined with souvenir shops, cappuccino bars and open-air restaurants. At night though, it reverts to a red-light district with persistent soliciting girls. Watch out for their exuberant hugs – most of the time it's a trick to pick your pocket.

In a way, Boca Chica is a crazy human zoo. Yet away from the all-inclusives and the seedy Calle Duarte, you can still enjoy its simple attractions and low-price guesthouses. The beautiful and inviting reef-protected lagoon does not go beyond 1.5 metres (5 ft) deep and is ideal for children. At low tide you can wade all the way to the island **La Matica** just offshore.

All-inclusive isolation

About 14 km (9 miles) eastwards along the coast is the all-inclusive settlement of **Juan Dolio/Villas del Mar** overlooking the flawless white coral beaches of the Caribbean and presenting quite a mishmash of architectural styles. Busy at

weekends, this 10–12-km (6–7-mile) stretch is completely isolated from Dominican life and is quiet out of season. The many luxurious all-inclusive hotels dominate the beaches, and the cheaper guesthouses are closer to the Las Américas highway with a 10-minute walk to the shoreline. Juan Dolio was created as a tourist development in 1987 and there is no village *per se*, just a long road with lots of speed bumps.

Map on page 198

The drive to **San Pedro de Macorís** ❹ (pop. 212,000) is via an *autopista*, renamed Avenida Presidente Antonio Guzmán. Crossing the large bridge over the **Río Iguamo**, the industrial clouds hang like tinted cotton balls above the city. San Pedro is synonymous with sugar cane, yet the real money comes from the baseball team Estrellas Orientales and their permanently sold-out stadium **Tetelo Vargas** during the season from October to February. Sammy Sosa, a US *beisbol* hero *(see page 142)*, is one of the players exported from the San Pedro team.

The port town, named for the Macorís Amerindians, was founded in 1822, and it soon grew into a centre for the sugar processing industry. With the outbreak of World War I, sugar prices shot up, turning San Pedro into a prosperous haven for entrepreneurs. European and Middle Eastern immigrants swarmed into the so-called "Sultan of the East", American sugar honchos landed in Pan Am seaplanes on the Río Iguamo, and majestic villas with neoclassical and Victorian ornamentation started to spring up. Nowadays, their splendour has almost entirely flaked off – yet it's still worth having a look at the neo-Gothic church of **San Pedro de Apóstol** (1913) on the river bank, and the **San Pedro fire station** and mansions near **Parque Duarte**. However, this university town is loud and rather unfriendly towards visitors. Be prepared for heavy traffic caused by the *zona franca*. Unfortunately, the road out to La Romana leads right through the chaos.

BELOW: friendly chat at the salon in San Pedro de Macorís.

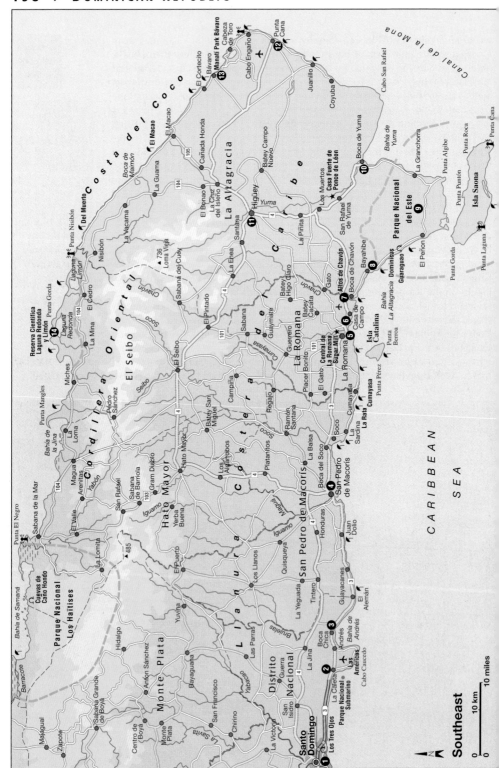

Southeast

CARIBBEAN SEA

Canal de la Mona

La Romana – a friendly sugar town

The *autopista* shoots like an arrow across the flat landscape, through fields of swaying sugar cane and grazing cows, reminiscent of a classic Dominican oil painting. Taking the little dirt road to your right, after the village of **Soco**, the **Soco**, **La Sardina**, **La Rata** and **Cumayasa** beaches appear languidly behind the fields. In the distance, **La Reina Cumayasa** *(see Travel Tips, page 352)*, one of the most stunning hotels of the southeast, stands aloft like a Mediterranean castle above the mouth of **Río Cumayasa**.

Map on page 198

Cockfighting is a popular pastime in the southeast.

La Romana ❺ (pop. 101,350), the financial capital of the southeast, is a sprawling town dominated by the country's biggest sugar mill plant (Central de la Romana). The factory belches smoke and even at the night you can hear the rumble and hooting of the company's sugar trains. In the town centre is the large and open **Parque Central**, and just north of it, on a rise, is the pretty church of **Santa Rosa de Lima**, which overlooks a smaller park. Nearby the church is the **Mercado Modelo**, a busy place from where buses leave for outlying villages and towns.

La Romana, established as a port by the Spaniards in 1502, is named after a Roman scale there, used for weighing sugar. But it was only in the 1920s that the town came into its own, when the North American company Gulf & Western invested in the sugar production industry and poured US$20 million into La Romana in an attempt to turn it into "the showcase of the East".

In 1974, Charles Bluhdorn, founder of G&W, built **Casa de Campo** ❻ (the "house in the country"), just 10 km (6 miles) along the coast. In the 1980s, after Bluhdorn's death, it became an exclusive retreat. One of the most sumptuous holiday resorts in the Caribbean, the complex spans over 30 sq km (12 sq miles) with more than 950 palatial villas and smart *casitas* (cabins). Oiling this leisure machine are three golf courses, a marina, a polo club, 15 swimming pools, 17 tennis courts, a riding stable with several hundred horses, but only one small beach.

BELOW: market day in La Romana.

Sitting on a plateau in a spectacular position above the "house in the country" is the international artists' village of **Altos de Chavón** ❼. Spoilt Europeans used to sympathetic architecture might trash this mock Italian settlement, yet undeniably, the beauty of the picturesque limestone buildings and panoramic view over the **Río Chavón** has to be an inspiration to all. Part of this US$40-million project, created in the mid 1980s, is the excellent **Museo Arqueológico Regional** (open daily; entrance fee), which houses an extensive collection of Taíno artefacts. The **Church of St Stanislaus**, containing the ashes of Poland's patron saint, is also here, as well as a 4,000-seat amphitheatre, where international stars often top the bill (Frank Sinatra was the first) and there are fancy boutiques and restaurants. Be warned, however, the prices are exorbitant.

A Robinson Crusoesque isle

Lying in an idyllic bay, backed by the Parque Nacional del Este, **Bayahibe** ❽ (pop. 2,400) is a sleepy fishing village only 30 minutes drive away from La Romana. There are several all-inclusive hotels along the coast, pushing into the border of the

national park, but the village is still charming, with pastel-coloured huts, seafood restaurants, small hotels and a dive shop. The locals rent out their homes as guesthouses, sometimes for under US$25 a night, making it popular with back-packers, while the owners live in extensions at the back. They also offer boat rides to **Playa Dominicus**, further around the coast, to neighbouring lagoons and to the Robinson Crusoesque Isla Saona off the southern tip of the island.

Part of the Parque Nacional del Este and fringed by virginal, coral sand beaches, the mangrove-lined lagoons of the beautiful 117-sq km (45-sq mile) **Isla Saona** are home to endangered birds such as the Hispaniolan lizard cuckoo and zillions of mosquitos (insect repellent is highly recommended). Unfortunately, the island is suffering from the damaging effects of mass tourism. Speed boats, catamarans and smaller *lanchas* bring around 1,000 tourists to the beach for a swim and buffet lunch, washed down with plenty of local rum. Pollution from the boats' engines and the tourists is a growing problem.

An Amerindian stronghold

The **Parque Nacional del Este** ❾ covers most of the Dominican Republic's southeastern peninsula and incorporates a total area of 41,900 hectares (103,500 acres). Established in 1975, the Eastern National Park is one of the older conservation areas of the Dominican Republic. Bird watchers and nature lovers who are not unduly bothered by the intense and dry heat can explore the park's tropical deciduous forest for glimpses of around 112 exotic birds. Wild olive, mangroves, Hispaniolan mahogany and coconut palms provide shelter to rhinoceros iguanas and all sorts of reptiles and endemic mammals, such as the endangered solenodon and hutia.

TIP

Guests staying at Casa de Campo can reach the artists' enclave of Altos de Chavón by a free bus service that leaves the resort every 30 minutes.

BELOW:
an aerial view of Altos de Chavón.

OSCAR DE LA RENTA

Fashion designer Oscar de la Renta was born in 1932 in Santo Domingo where he studied art. He left the Dominican Republic at the age of 18 to study painting at the Academy of San Fernando in Madrid. While in Spain he landed a job at the world-famous fashion house of Cristobal Balenciaga, whose elegant gowns were the coveted apparel of the 1940s and '50s. In 1937 Balenciaga moved his operation to Paris but de la Renta remained in Spain until 1961 when he too moved to Paris to join the house of Lanvin-Castillo as a couture assistant. By 1963 he had settled in New York, designing the couture collection for Elizabeth Arden.

Unable to let his imagination run wild with his designs, he started his own fashion company in 1965 and throughout the 1960s he built up a reputation – and a fortune – for his opulent, ornate evening dresses.

Although he is an American citizen, he has remained loyal to his roots in the Dominican Republic, and spends most of the year at the beautiful beach villa he built in the exclusive Los Corales in Punta Cana. He and his great friend, Spanish crooner Julio Iglesias, have not only invested in the Casa de Campo resort, but also co-own the Punta Cana airport and much of the surrounding area.

The few beaches can only be reached by boat, and you may spot manatees and bottlenose dolphins playing in the waters. In the **Guaraguao** area there are several pre-Columbian caves with Taíno carvings and drawings on the walls, and many artefacts have been found at La Aleta, once a large ceremonial site that was discovered in 1997. It is believed that this was the settlement that the priest Bartolomé de las Casas *(see page 34)* witnessed being destroyed in 1503.

The northeastern entrance to the park is near **Boca de Yuma ❿** which was reduced from a quaint fishing village to a deserted ghost town by Hurricane Georges in 1998. Ruined hotels and tourist villas are up for sale and the seafood restaurants overlooking the splendid Bahia de Yuma have closed. The famous deep-sea fishing tournament, which attracted blue marlin hunters from all over the world every June, had to be moved to Playa Cabeza de Toro further north, and the dirt road to the Taíno Cueva de Berna was inaccessible. However, restoration work is in progress and the road is in excellent condition again, but it is still only worth visiting the village on a day trip.

Between Boca de Yuma and the provincial capital of Higüey, a turn-off at San Rafael de Yuma leads to the **Casa de Ponce de León**. This early fortified house *(casa fortaleza)* was built by enslaved Taínos in 1505–08 for the administrator of the province, Ponce de León, when he came to pacify the region. The two-storey square stone building has a few, tiny windows and large wooden doors; inside are items that are thought to have belonged to the conquistador. Historians believe that there was an escape tunnel running from the house into what is now a sugar cane field. It isn't an easy place to find, since there are no road signs to direct you to this edifice, but it has been lovingly restored and the immaculate gardens are tended by a guardian, who will show you around for a tip.

Map on page 198

A 5-minute boat ride from La Romana port takes you to the picture-perfect Isla Catalina. Belonging to an Italian shipping company, the icing-sugar beaches serve as a spring board for divers to a magical underwater world.

LEFT: Playa Saona.
RIGHT: the entrance to Parque Nacional del Este.

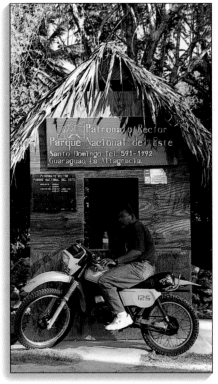

Higüey – a miracle town

Carretera 4 provides a smooth trip north through wide swathes of sugar cane and vegetable fields to **Higüey ⓫** (pop. 120,000), 32 km (20 miles) away. *Motoconchos* buzz like flies through the streets of this thriving town, which has a lively market and a rum factory nearby. Founded in 1494 by Spanish *conquistador* Juan de Esquivel, the capital of the province of La Altagracia developed in the early 1500s under the infamous governor of Santo Domingo, Nicolás de Ovando, who chose Ponce de Léon (1502–08) as his administrator.

TIP

No one is allowed in the Basílica de la Nuestra Señora de la Altagracia wearing shorts or a mini-skirt.

The true attraction of this drab city is the **Basílica de la Nuestra Señora de la Altagracia**, built to replace the cathedral *de la Merced,* where Columbus's forces planted their cross while fending off an Amerindian attack. The soil is attributed with mysterious miracles: allegedly, Columbus and his posse were on the point of defeat by the Taínos when a vision of the Virgin appeared on the cross allowing the Spaniards to repel the attack. In 1922, *La Altagracia* (Virgin of the Highest Grace) became the country's patron saint, and ever since pilgrims have been coming to the site on 21 January and 16 August. In 1954–72, the French architect André Jaques Dunoyer de Segonzac built the modern church, so the old church is seldom used now. With a 60-metre (200-ft) high pointed arch and the tallest bell-tower in the Americas, the cathedral is easy to spot from miles around.

LEFT: Higüey's "new" cathedral. **RIGHT:** sailing in the waters around Punta Cana.

Beautiful beaches of Costa del Coco

¿*Vamos a la playa*? No problem in **Punta Cana ⓬**, 45 km (28 miles) east of Higüey on the 60-km (37-mile) long Costa del Coco, as this stretch of coastline has the most stunning beaches in the Dominican Republic. Every one of them could be a film set for *The Blue Lagoon*. Thanks to the coral reefs that protect

Map
on page
198

the bays from the might of the Atlantic, the conditions are ideal for swimming, with bathwater temperatures (77°F/25°C), and the forests of coconut palms behind give the desired shade. The idyllic **Playa Punta Cana** stretches for over 2 km (1 mile) and, apart from two all-inclusives and a luxury villa development, there is little else in the area. An international airport serves Punta Cana and Playa Bávaro, with charter flights loaded with tourists.

    Cabo Engaño, the easternmost point above Punta Cana, provides ideal conditions for both surfers and windsurfers. The cape juts out into the dangerous **Mona Passage**, which separates Hispaniola from Puerto Rico – and the wind whips around it. Northwards, the mega-luxurious hotel resorts along the 24-km (15-mile) coastal stretch between Bávaro and Punta Arena Gorda are a complete contrast to the poverty-stricken local life outside the fences. These palatial satellite villages (up to 1,200 rooms each) offer everything from psychiatrists to casinos to shopping malls. A plethora of sports are on offer, from water skiing, surfing and sailing to horse riding, golf and tennis, and more. Children are well catered for in "kiddie clubs" and can play in the clear, warm, shallow sea.

    The **Bávaro Beach Resort Complex** (*see Travel Tips, page 352*) is the biggest on the Costa del Coco. With an 18-hole golf course, its five hotels are categorised by their names (Palace, Golf, Garden, Beach, Casino). If a mega-resort isn't your style then there are more hotels along the coast, run by international chains or Dominican companies, which offer visitors a relaxing beach holiday. Higüey, more than 50 km (30 miles) away, is its nearest town, so the international-style restaurants and bars in the resort are the only choices. The **Manatí Park Bávaro** ⓮ (Plaza Bávaro, daily; entrance fee; tel: 552 0807) is popular with visitors to the Costa del Coco, being the only attraction in the area. The zoo houses almost every indigenous animal of the *república*: flamingos, manatees, rare birds and spiders, crocodiles and performing parrots. For an additional fee, you can swim with the dolphins, an increasingly controversial practice opposed by conservationists who object to the capture of the mammals for this purpose.

On the Costa del Coco, wealthy Dominicans craving fresh seafood eat at Capitán Cook (Playa del Cortecito, tel: 552 0646). The Spanish owner serves up delicious paella, lobster and jugs of sangría.

BELOW: beautiful beaches stretch along the Costa del Coco.

Dream bays and Atlantic waves

North of **Playa Arena Gorda**, the charter meccas are left behind glinting like shiny oyster pearls in the sun, and the Atlantic waves provide lots of fun. From here, there is one lonely dream bay after another – **Playa El Macao**, **Boca de Maimón**, **Punta Sabena** and **Playa del Muerto**. The enchanting lagoons of Boca de Maimón are postcard material, where you can walk for hours without seeing any other visitors except dozing sea turtles. The numerous potholes on the shabby coastal road are the only setback and you should seek local advice before driving, if it has been raining.

    A better road is the drive further north to the **Reserva Científica Laguna Redonda y Limón** ⓯, where you can watch magnificent seabirds stalk through the mangroves and experience the sensation of being deep in the jungle. About 20 km (12 miles) further on lies the quiet little, poor and forgotten port of **Miches**. Outside the town the beaches are wild and superb, and there is a pleasant hotel on a hill overlooking miles of unspoilt coastline. ❏

THE AMBER COAST

Rich in precious amber, the northeast coast is blessed with beautiful beaches, coral reefs and rolling countryside which attracts both sun worshippers and adventure tourists

Maps:
Area 212
Town 208

The Dominican Republic's northeastern region has a varied topography – fertile valleys with forested, inland mountains soaring to breathtaking vistas, and 120 km (75 miles) of dazzling beaches. Known as the Amber Coast because of its extensive deposits of the ancient resin, the area's amber is among the most desirable in the world.

The north coast has the Atlantic Ocean for its front door and a chain of majestic mountains as its backyard. In between are some of the most beautiful beaches in the Caribbean, interspersed with historic towns and modern resorts.

With such a felicitous natural environment, the north coast offers a range of active and high adventure sports. The exhilaration of the Atlantic's strong currents and on-shore winds makes for excellent windsurfing at Cofresí, Playa Dorada, Playa Grande, Sosúa, and particularly Cabarete. Scuba diving is outstanding all along the north coast with lots of reefs and wrecks to explore. Unfortunately the water is not always clear – currents can whip up the sand and the outflow from rivers can reduce visibility for divers, especially if there has been rain in the mountains. Opportunities abound for diving among beautiful reefs, underwater pinnacles, walls with swim-throughs and a number of historic wrecks. Popular dive areas on the Amber Coast include Sosúa, Río San Juan and Cabrera and the Samaná Peninsula in the far east. West of the main city of Puerto Plata are Costambar, Luperón and Monte Cristi *(see page 222).*

Other northern adventures include traditional mountain hiking, horse riding and caving; the largest concentration of caves in this region is between Río San Juan and Cabrera, and there are some fascinating pictographs and petroglyphs depicting the lives of the Taínos. Cascading involves plunging down a 55 metre- (200 ft-) high waterfall, and canyoning aficionados climb high into the steep rocks, then jump into a river far below. Exciting white-water rafting is available at Jarabacoa in the nearby "Dominican Alps", within the Cordillera Central, so called because of its mountains, rivers, waterfalls and fragrant pine forests.

PRECEDING PAGES: a a ride on the beach at sunset, Cabarete. **LEFT:** poolside playtime, Sosúa. **BELOW:** rollerblading on the Malecón, Puerto Plata.

Golfers paradise

There are numerous golf courses on, or near the coast. The two championship 18-hole courses are **Playa Dorada**, designed by Robert Trent Jones (tel: 320 4262), and **Playa Grande** at Km 9 on the Río San Juan-Cabrera road, with 10 of its 18 spectacular holes along the reef-lined shore (tel: 582 0860). There are also several 9-hole courses including: **Los Mangos** in Costambar, mostly used by residents and guests of Hacienda Resorts (tel: 970 7143); **Costa Azul** between Sosúa and Cabarete (tel: 571 2608) and **Loma de Chivo** in the far east on the Samaná

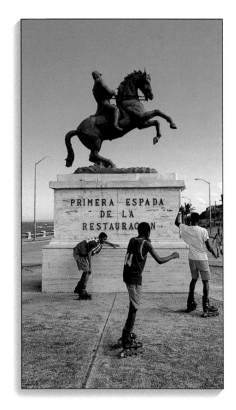

The teleférico is the best way to reach the summit of Pico Isabel de Torres.

BELOW: view of Pico Isabel de Torres.

Peninsula (tel: 538 3111). Further afield in Jarabacoa, there is a 9-hole course in the pine forest at the entrance to the town (tel: 573 2474) and Las Aromas has 18-holes designed by Pete Dye in the hills of Santiago (tel: 276 5396).

Puerto Plata

Outside the confines of the popular all-inclusive resorts which pepper the coastline there is plenty to discover. Historically significant Puerto Plata, literally "port of silver", is the natural starting point for a tour of the Amber Coast.

Founded in 1502, **Puerto Plata ❶** is the largest city on the Atlantic coast and a focal point of the north. It is steeped in history dating from the arrival of the conquistadors, who came in search of gold, and events in the 16th century to the harsh Trujillo years and beyond. The lively *malecón* (seaside promenade) extends about 6 km (4 miles) along the waterfront from Fortaleza de San Felipe at the tip of the peninsula, past the downtown area – where there are restaurants and bars – as far as Long Beach at the eastern end (Avenida Circunvalación Norte). The *malecón* is the venue of some of the city's biggest annual events including Carnival (February or March) and the *Merengue* Festival in October. Outside fiesta time there isn't much to see since it is run down and the beach here is polluted.

The city was once an important port because of its close proximity to the neighbouring agricultural region of the Cibao Valley and the northwest. **Fortaleza de San Felipe ❹** (open daily 9am–5pm; entrance fee) at the end of Avenida General Gregorio Luperón (part of the *malecón*) was built between 1564 and 1577 on **Bahía de Puerto Plata** as a northern defence against invasion by sea. In recent history the fortress was a prison during the Trujillo years and has been home to the Brugal rum factory. Today it is a museum with a

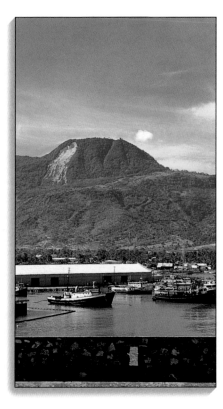

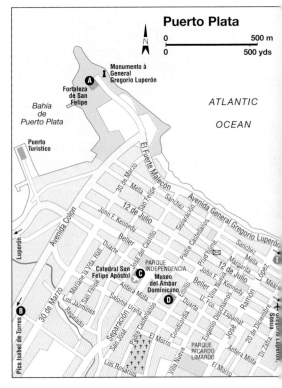

istorical photographic exhibition and a display of guns and canon used in independence battles. Alongside the fortress, on the highest part of the promontory,
s a spectacular iron **lighthouse**, built in 1879 and restored in 2002. An octag-
onal iron cupola, supported by mustard-coloured columns, used to house a
revolving light fuelled by kerosene, but it is no longer in service.

The **Brugal Rum Factory** (daily tours 9–11.45am, 1–3.45pm; free admission;
tel: 586 2100) is now on Avenida Luis Ginebra on the road heading out of Puerto
Plata towards Playa Dorada. Established in 1888, the factory bottles 360,000
litres (634,000 pints) of rum every day, of which only 5 percent is exported.

Pico Isabel de Torres ➒ towers 850 metres (2,800 ft) above the city and the
Parque Nacional Pico Isabel de Torres (open daily; tel: 586 2122). Known
locally as Loma Isabel de Torres, the peak can be reached by the *teleférico*
(cable car). For a small fee the cable car carries visitors from the city to the
extensive **Botanical Gardens**, providing a spectacular view of Puerto Plata
Bay below. Queues for the cable car can be long during high season and it may
not run if there are high winds. At the summit of Pico Isabel de Torres is a 16-
metre (52-ft) statue of Jesus Christ similar to the one in Rio de Janeiro, Brazil.
Hiking to the top is possible, but difficult as there are no cut trails, so it is best
to go with a guide. Visitors can also access the peak by four-wheel drive vehicle, or grab a ride from a local (unofficial) guide on the back of a motorbike.

Back in the centre of Puerto Plata, the beautifully restored Art Deco **Catedral
San Felipe Apóstol** ➌ on Calle José del Carmen Ariza, stands opposite **Parque
Independencia** – also known as Parque Central – a pretty park bound by José del
Carmen Ariza, Separación, Beller and Duarte streets. At the centre of the park is
an attractive two-storey Victorian-style wooden bandstand called **La Glorieta**.

Maps:
Area 212
Town 208

*The Museo del
Ambar Dominicano
in Puerto Plata has
tours in several
different languages.*

BELOW:
the pretty Parque
Independencia is
known locally as
Parque Central.

Masks are an important part of African tradition and are still used at Carnival time.

Many of the other gingerbread buildings, which line the streets, date from the 19th century, when Puerto Plata's thriving port attracted German merchants dealing in tobacco. Today the buildings house restaurants, bars, shops and offices.

The mountains around Puerto Plata contain the world's richest deposits of amber, believed to be up to 20–60 million years old. A lustrous vegetal resin containing prehistoric fossils, it is often fashioned into jewellery and ornamental items *(see page 215)*. The **Museo del Ambar Dominicano** Ⓓ (open Mon–Sat 9am–5pm; entrance fee; tel: 586 2848) is a private museum in a beautiful Victorian mansion southeast of Catedral San Felipe Apóstol at No. 61 Calle Duarte. The first floor is a large shop and one of the best places to buy amber with confidence. Exhibits on the second floor include some of the most prized prehistoric animal and plant specimens encased in honey-coloured resin. Dominican amber comes in a rainbow of hues from translucent, golden-yellow, green, red and brown to a deep blue. The rare blue amber is volcanic, found only in the east of the Amber Coast and is unique to Hispaniola. It contains no fossilized insects.

Displaying replicas of items made by the first inhabitants of Hispaniola, the small **Museo de Arte Taíno** (tel: 586 7601) is virtually unknown. It offers a look at the culture of the Amerindians who lived peacefully on the island for 1,500 years before the Europeans arrived. An excavated tomb provides fascinating insight and Taíno art reproductions are on sale.

An exclusive playground

BELOW: fun in the sun, Sosúa.

The private gated resort complex of **Playa Dorada** is around 5 km (3 miles) east of Puerto Plata. It consists of 14 large oceanside all-inclusive hotels sharing a substantial strip of sandy beach with casinos, discos, numerous restaurants and bars,

a shopping plaza, swimming pools and a wide variety of sports facilities available to hotel guests only. In addition there is a championship 18-hole golf course. Guests can (and some do) spend a whole week here without leaving the compound.

Heading east along the Amber Coast, pretty beaches in the suburbs and villages stretch around tranquil bays and coves. An extensive selection of first-class resorts and casinos, mid-size hotels and guest houses is available all the way around the eastern end of the coast. Just before Sosúa, on Carretera Sosúa, 20 km (12 miles) east of Puerto Plata, **Columbus Aquapark** (open daily 10am–6pm; entrance fee; tel: 571 2642) beckons children of all ages. There are five Olympic-size swimming pools and a diving tower, a slow-flowing "river", water slides, volleyball courts and places to eat. Lockers can be rented for the day and the park is popular with local families, especially on Sunday.

Sosúa

A sleepy hillside fishing village only 10 years ago, **Sosúa ❷** has morphed into a hotel-laden tourist mecca, albeit more relaxed than other Caribbean mega-resort complexes. The beach is lined with rows of bars, restaurants and souvenir shops. Popular activities include sailing, scuba diving and snorkelling around the coral reefs just offshore. A favourite with European travellers – many of whom have stayed or returned to open guest houses, restaurants and open-air bars along Calle Pedro Clisante – Sosúa is divided into two neighbourhoods, separated by a sheltered bay with a distinctive half-mile long, white sandy beach.

Los Charamicos, to the west, has grown into a business and residential area for the many Dominicans who moved here to work in the local tourist industry. It has a typically Dominican ambience, its centre filled with crowded, rambling

Maps:
Area 212
Town 208

Pretty pastel-coloured buildings line the streets of the Amber Coast.

LEFT:
Sosúa synagogue.
RIGHT: on the beach at Cabarete.

The flag of the Dominican Republic in rich, mosaic tile, symbolizing the mix of people who make up the nation.

streets lined with old characterful buildings and noisy *motoconchos* constantly riding up and down. Most restaurants serve local dishes, and some are well-known for their excellent fish specialities.

El Batey, across the bay to the east, has blossomed into a tourist centre with hotels, bars and souvenir shops located mainly along Calle Pedro Clisante. It was founded by Jewish refugees in 1939 *(see page 174)*. After the Dominican dictator, Trujillo, ordered the massacre of 15,000 Haitians in 1937 *(see page 52)*, he tried to repair his international image during World War II by offering political asylum to Jewish refugees fleeing persecution by the Nazis in Germany. In fact it was a cynical move to "whiten" the population by encouraging European immigration. A small group of settlers began the areas' now famous dairy and smoked-meat industries that continue to flourish. Some of the Jews intermarried with their new neighbours, while maintaining their religious customs, but over the years most of the original group of refugees left the island. Ironically, many German expatriates took their place, together with migrants from Austria and Eastern Europe.

Although few of the descendants of the original settlers remain, the Jewish community in El Batey maintain the one-room **Sinagoga de la Comunidad Judía de Sosúa** on Calle Dr Alejo Martínez near Calle Dr Rosen. Next door, the small **Museo de la Comunidad Judía de Sosúa** (Museum of the Jewish Community of Sosúa; open Mon–Fri 9am–1pm; tel: 571 1386) chronicles their sojourn. Exhibits include photographs from the 1940s and the first telephone in the town. The museum reopened in 2003 following renovations funded by donations, some of which came from the original settler families.

Sosúa's lively nightlife encompasses dance floors, which don't get crowded until around midnight, plus bars and restaurants. The whole area hots up in October during the annual Puerto Plata Jazz Festival, which attracts performers from the US and throughout the Caribbean. Events are held at venues in Puerto Plata, Playa Dorada, Sosúa and Cabarete.

After dancing the night away many visitors want to spend some of the daylight hours relaxing on the sand. The beautiful neighbouring beaches of **Puerto Chiquito**, **Playa Chiquito** and **Playita** are ideal, and they also provide a plethora of

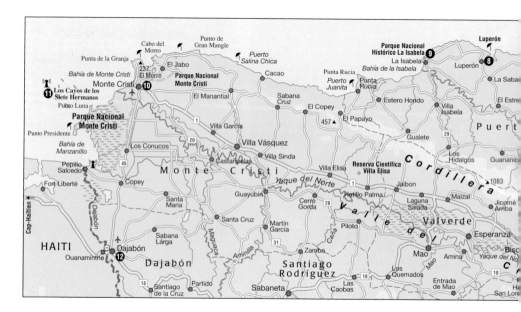

water sports including sailing, waterskiing, jet-skiing and surfing. **Sosúa Bay** is considered to be one of the best areas on the north coast for scuba diving thanks to the vibrant coral reef which lies close to shore. A little further from the beach, outside the bay, a second reef referred to by local divers as the Tropical Garden offers more experienced divers an interesting area to explore. New divers can arrange to take lessons in Sosúa which can lead to a PADI certification.

Map below

Cabarete, the windsurfing capital

About 10–15 minutes drive east of Sosúa, **Cabarete** ❸ is one of the world's premier windsurfing locations. Trade winds here produce the conditions that attract the sport's best surfers from around the globe for the annual **Cabarete Race Week** in June. The town has also hosted the Professional Windsurfing Association's World Cup several times, also held in June – the best month of the year for excellent winds ideal for windsurfing and sailing. West of the windsurfers' area is reserved for kitesurfing, off a beach renamed **Kite Beach**. There is flat water for 500 metres (1,640 ft) and a reef with waves. On the outskirts of Cabarete is **El Encuentro**, a beach with waves ideal for surfing with a consistent "break" off the right and left. Instruction and equipment hire is available from a variety of reputable outlets.

See delicate fretwork on the balconies of gingerbread-style buildings.

Cabarete was a sleepy fishing village until the tourist industry took hold in the Dominican Republic in the 1990s and transformed the place into a well-developed, busy leisure centre. However, the easy-going friendliness of the townspeople remains. In addition to sites for advanced scuba divers other active sports include tennis, horse riding and mountain biking. With its national parks, mountains perfect for hiking, 15 km (9 miles) of beach and sheltered sandy bays, Cabarete and its neighbours are a hub of activity all year round.

Ecotourism is growing. A few local companies offer adventure tours that don't cause long term damage to the environment, including Iguana Mama (tel: 571 0908; *see page 358*) and Freddy Tours (tel: 571 0829). Both have offices in town. Cabarete is a starting point for guided tours to Pico Duarte, Jarabacoa and a fantastic trip around the north coast.

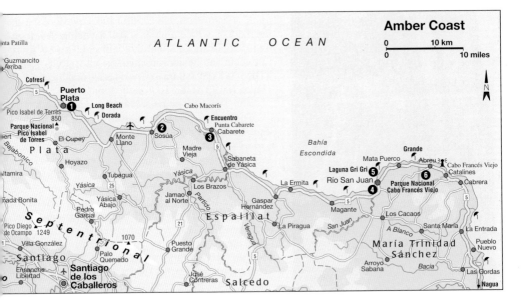

Map on page 212

The dancing and partying start late (typical for this part of the world), sometimes in the wee hours of the morning, and continue until breakfast. The bars are often brimming with a happy mix of local people, holidaymakers and wind-surfers all enjoying the loud *merengue* and a cocktail or two while discussing the events of the day. There is often live music on the sand and regular beach parties and barbecues. The town is really one long street running along the bay with hotels, restaurants and bars opening on to the sand. The less expensive places to stay and eat are located on the other side of the road backing on to a lagoon.

Río San Juan and Cabrera

Continuing east from Cabarete, some of the Dominican Republic's most spec-tacular, virtually deserted beaches unfold. Long stretches of powdery sand mean-der around Bahía Escondida. Picturesque **Río San Juan ❹**, about a 1 hour drive southeast of Sosúa, is home to the cool mangrove-shielded **Laguna Gri Gri ❺** where visitors can explore a series of mysterious marine caverns during a leisurely 2-hour boat trip. Board the boat at the end of the main street, Calle Duarte. The caverns were formed by the erosion of the soft karst layers and the largest one con-tains striking stalagmites and stalactites. Scuba diving offshore is excellent. The boat passes **Cueva de las Golondrinas**, a 10-metre (32-ft) deep, 12-metre (39-ft) high cave, and stops at **Playa Caletón**, a popular beach known locally as La Playita. The village of Río San Juan has notable fishing and dairy traditions.

The restful atmosphere of Río San Juan is exemplified by the main street, which is lined with pretty pastel-coloured gingerbread-style architectural gems. After-dark activities centre around the small restaurants, ice cream parlours, swinging jazz clubs and discos where visitors can learn to *merengue* – the vibrant national dance. The communities of Río San Juan and its neighbour **Cabrera** were jointly re-named **Costa Verde** in 1999, a sure sign that this is one of the next areas to receive mega-resort treatment and tourist-related development.

About 5 km (3 miles) outside Río San Juan is one of the most beautiful beaches in the country, **Playa Grande**. This is also the home of the Playa Grande golf course, with its beautiful links overlooking the reefs. The whole area is gradually being developed with hotels, resorts, holiday villas and sports facili-ties, but the beach remains free for public access. There is a tiny nature reserve nearby, and local people have set up small food and drink stalls along the beach. The seafood on sale is definitely worth a try.

Continuing along the coast towards Cabrera, look out for **Parque Nacional Cabo Francés Viejo ❻**, which preserves a small area of precious rainforest with a variety of flora and fauna. The area has exten-sive freshwater caves where advanced scuba divers can dive through the wide tunnels. At Cabrera, in the province of María Trinidad Sánchez, is **Cuevas de Lago Azul**, three beautiful lagoons that flow under-ground to the sea. The water is clear, blue and cool, and ideal for swimming. The next main town is **Nagua**. There is little of note in the town, or along this route, until one reaches the Peninsula de Samaná (*see page 227*) at the far eastern tip of the country. ❑

BELOW: the steamy mangroves at Laguna Gri Gri.

Amber

A mber is formed out of sticky resin from the flowing sap of a now extinct tree called *Hymenaea Protera*, a relative of the *algorrobo*, or carob. Over the passage of time, the resin hardens, creating the amber as we know it today. The *Hymenaea Protera* grew in prehistoric times, up to 50 million years ago. Tiny lizards, flies, spiders and other creatures were trapped in the sap and their fossilized remains, known as "inclusions," are preserved intact in the hard, translucent material. The rarest amber specimens are embedded with these fossils.

Amber from the Dominican Republic is not as well known as the amber that comes from the Baltics formed from the resin of the *Pinus Succinifera*, but experts now consider it to be among the best and most valuable in the world because of its translucence and wide variety of colouring.

The amber deposits are found in a grey sandstone and seashell mixture in the mountains along the northeastern coast (eponymously named "The Amber Coast"). This is mined by hand to protect the delicate contents. Skilled craftsmen carefully extract and examine the amber to see if it contains any fossils.

If they find fossils in the resin, the craftsmen use special cutting and polishing techniques to best display minute details of the creatures inside the translucent material of the gemstone. Amber that doesn't have inclusions is processed into jewellery. Some of the unusual shades of amber are blue, green, red and a beige-yellow, called cognac.

Although varicoloured amber is found in many countries all over the world, the colours from the Dominican Republic's northern mountains are among the most desirable. Collectors around the world put the highest value on the rare blue amber of volcanic origin and on pieces containing animal fossil inclusions. Some dealers claim that even sapphires can't match the distinctive purple amber from the Dominican Republic.

As Paolo Costa, director of the Amber Museum in Puerto Plata, noted, "Amber has an important history, which many people aren't familiar with". Indeed, American movie director Stephen Spielberg conducted background research into amber in the Dominican Republic for his movie blockbuster *Jurassic Park*. The film featured a mosquito preserved in amber which had fed on dinosaur blood. The blood provided the DNA which the fictional scientists used to recreate the prehistoric dinosaurs.

Before 1950, Dominican amber was not very well known. When the Soviet Union lowered the Iron Curtain and shut down the Baltic supplies, suddenly everyone turned to the Dominican Republic. That was when the world's experts and European dealers first discovered the high quality and beauty of Dominican amber.

For 30 years, this amber dominated the market. Then the Soviet Union collapsed and newly independent Baltic countries – Latvia, Estonia and Lithuania – started exporting large quantities of amber. Consequently, Dominican production dropped drastically in the early 1990s, but it is again the predominant source of this beautiful "transparent gold." ❑

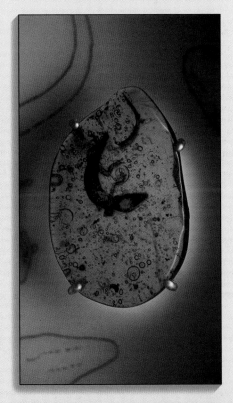

RIGHT: amber with a fossilized inclusion.

THE QUIET NORTHWEST

Christopher Columbus chose this coast as the location for his first colonial town in the New World in 1493. Outside the confines of a holiday resort, not a great deal has changed

Map on page 212

Puerto Plata

Santo Domingo

The extreme northwestern corner of the Dominican Republic, to the west of Puerto Plata, is bordered in the south by the magnificent mountain range of the Cordillera Septentrional. Only two main roads (*Carreteras* 1 and 5) serve the region with any efficiency, passing through small ramshackle towns and villages on the way. In between the mountains and the Atlantic coast the rolling landscape provides grazing for cattle alongside fields of rice, tobacco and sugar cane. Wild orchids grow in profusion on the old trees of the sub-tropical dry forest that covers large areas, particularly in the Parque Nacional Monte Cristi in the far northwest. This stretches almost as far as the colourful border town of Dajabón, a crossing-over point to Haiti. The further northwest you travel, the more arid the land becomes. Goats can be seen everywhere, looking for food among the scrub and cactus.

Protected by wide stretches of coral reef, busy with marine life, the Atlantic coast beaches of the Dominican Republic are mainly grey and gravelly and not up to "paradise" standards, apart from a few in resorts such as Cofresí, where scuba diving, fishing and other watersports are good value. This is the coast where Columbus decided to settle his first group of New World colonists, and remains of the historical site can be seen in the Parque Nacional Histórico La Isabela. Out in the ocean, dolphins and humpback whales can sometimes be spotted during January and February. Very little has changed in this undeveloped region and the people, many of whom are descendants of immigrants from the Canary Islands in the 18th century, are laid back and friendly.

PRECEDING PAGES: country life in the northwest. **LEFT:** on the road to Monte Cristi. **BELOW:** ready for the beach.

Waterfalls and a sheltered bay

It may be difficult to leave the comforts of a holiday complex where everything is at your fingertips, but it's worth venturing outside the resort gates where you may experience the sensation that time has stood still for decades. In a taxi or hired car, organised through your hotel *(or see Travel Tips on page 351)*, take the *Carretera* 5 southwest out of **Puerto Plata** *(see page 208)* towards the mountains. After about 10 minutes, take a left turn at the crossroads and continue to Imbert 22 km (14 miles) away.

Surrounded by sugar cane fields and farmland, the little town of **Imbert** ❼ is named after José María Imbert, a hero of the Restoration of the Republic and is mainly a busy intersection for picking up transport connections – be they *motoconchos, guaguas,* buses or taxis – to surrounding areas and the south. The town has a restaurant and a petrol station and nearby at **Damajagua** is a spectacular series of 20 small waterfalls each with a pool, eight of which are accessible to the public. Here you can wallow in the

This plaque at the Parque Nacional Histórico La Isabela commemorates the first colonial town in the New World. However, there are a couple of villages nearby that also call themselves La Isabela, which can cause confusion.

cool waters before heading west to Luperón, 25 km (15 miles) away on the *Carretera* 30, just off the road that brought you into Imbert.

Luperón ➑ is a small fishing village set in a beautiful natural bay of the same name, which is well protected from the hurricanes that can strike between June and November. For this reason, the bay has become a haven for yachts from all around the world. The local people mainly earn their living from farming and fishing in the Atlantic waters, making it a good place to stop for a lunch or dinner of seafood and the delicious Dominican speciality of creole fish in any one of the little *comedores* (informal restaurants). Just outside the village is the modern **Luperón Beach Resort**, an all-inclusive hotel complex which has a lovely beach and offers a wide range of watersports.

La Isabela – Columbus's first colonial town

After Columbus had returned to Hispaniola in 1493 to find the Spanish garrison at Puerto La Navidad obliterated *(see page 28)*, he established the town of La Isabela – named after the queen of Spain – further along the coast, 12 km (7 miles) west of where Luperón is today. But it was doomed from the start, as the first colonists succumbed to disease and the strains of hard manual labour, or became disillusioned and returned to Spain when no gold could be found. Violence and discord, hurricane and fire all added to the demise of the town and by 1498, the remaining colonists had left to start Santo Domingo *(see pages 169–190)*.

Some of the remnants of this short-lived town have been unearthed and preserved in the **Parque Nacional Histórico La Isabela ➒** (open daily 8am–5.45pm; entrance fee). Here you can see the foundations of Christopher Columbus's original house, and a cemetery containing both Taíno and Spanish

burial chambers. Unfortunately much of the site was bulldozed and some of the ruins thrown into the sea a long time ago, when an enthusiastic official was told to clean it up prior to a visit by General Trujillo. A museum contains some interesting artefacts, believed to have belonged to those early colonists, and provides information about the Taínos in pre-Columbian days.

Excavation of La Isabela began in the 1950s and archaeologists have placed stones to indicate the outline of the main buildings. The reconstructed **Templo de las Américas** (Temple of the Americas) is on the spot where the first Mass in the New World was celebrated on 6 January 1494. La Isabela is also believed to have had the first City Hall in the Americas.

Map on page 212

Estero Hondo – battleground for liberty

Further along the coast to the west you come to **Estero Hondo**, which has a quiet beach. However, in 1959 the peace was broken when a boatload of exiled Dominican anti-government activists disembarked here in an attempt to bring down Rafael Trujillo's regime. The dictator learned of the rebels' plans and sent the army to ambush them, resulting in a bloody battle. Since then Estero Hondo has remained a symbol of the Dominican Republic's struggle for liberty and democracy.

A short distance further along the rough coastal road, on the border of the province of Monte Cristi, is the small fishing village of **Punta Rucia**, where brightly coloured fishing boats lie on the pretty, sandy beach. Framed by coconut palms and shallow waters, it may not the cleanest but it is one of the favourite beaches on what Dominicans call the *Línea Noroeste* (Northwestern Line); on Sundays it comes alive with picnickers and the sound of *merengue*.

From Punta Rucia boat trips go to the Laguna Estero Hondo mangrove swamps and the white sandy island of Cayo Arenas, 10 km (6 miles) off shore.

BELOW:
a mural for Máximo Gómez y Báez.

Because the roads on the coastal side of the mountains are generally poor, it may be best to go to Monte Cristi via Carretera Duarte, the main road running from Santiago to Monte Cristi, 90 km (55 miles) along the southern slopes of the Cordillera Septentrional above and almost parallel to the Río Yaque del Norte.

The rises and falls of Monte Cristi

As you approach **Monte Cristi ⑩**, the capital of the province of the same name, the landscape becomes much drier due to low rainfall and temperatures that can reach 35°C (95°F). Flattening out into the delta of the Yaque del Norte, the only relief is the flat-topped **El Morro** to the northwest of town, washed by the sea on one side and waterways with mangroves on the other.

Founded in 1533 by 60 farming families, the original village of Monte Cristi, along with other towns on the northwest coast, was evacuated in 1606 by Hispaniola's governor Antonio Osorio in order to end illegal commerce between the villagers and foreign pirates. For 150 years Monte Cristi lay abandoned until it was resettled by farmers from the Canary Islands. It became an important seaport, handling goods such as timber, honey and tobacco that were carried down the Río Yaque del Norte from Santiago *(see page 239)* and La Vega *(see page 245)*. The city flourished, attracting European businesses, until the construction of the railway which connected Puerto Plata to the towns of the Cibao Valley and the Restoration War in the 1860s caused its downfall as a centre of commerce.

The Victorian buildings lining the streets of Monte Cristi reflect the town's European influence. Here too, on Avenida Mella, is the former house of Baní-born Máximo Gómez y Báez, where he and José Martí signed the manifesto for Cuba's independence, alongside the historic homes of Restoration War generals.

The old colonial shipwrecks and reefs off the beaches of La Granja and El Morro, just north of Monte Cristi, provide good diving. Deep-sea fishing expeditions can be organised through Club Nautico Monte Cristi Inc. (tel: 579 2530). Every June a blue marlin fishing tournament is held.

BELOW: a one-stop shop for a taxi or a refreshing drink.

The beaches, El Morro and the waterways and lagoons either side of town form the **Parque Nacional Monte Cristi** along with the **Los Cayos de los Siete Hermanos ⓫** (Islands of the Seven Brothers). These seven tiny islands provide a sanctuary for seabirds and turtles who come here to lay their eggs; sadly poaching has taken its toll. Closer to the shore in front of Juan de Bolaños beach, and just a five-minute boat ride away, lies **Cayos Cabras** (Cabras Key). Lapped by the Atlantic Ocean, it provides a window on a world of tropical fish and starfish. An old lighthouse and a salt pond can be seen on the western side of the key.

Map on page 212

Dajabón – a colourful border town

A 30-minute drive south from Monte Cristi through subtropical dry forest and bush, past coastal lagoons, is **Dajabón ⓬**, right on the border with Haiti. Only the **Massacre River** (Río Dajabón), which can easily be crossed on foot, separates the two nations. Founded on 4 July 1776 by a Spanish soldier named José Solano, Dajabón became an important point of commercial traffic between the colonies of French St-Domingue and Spanish Santo Domingo after the Aranjuez Treaty was eventually signed by France and Spain in 1777, defining the boundary between the two.

Today hundreds of Haitians pour across the border every day to sell their wares at the daily market here, at rock-bottom prices. Pots and pans and other kitchen utensils, secondhand clothes and shoes, and perfumes are all spread out on colourful cloths on the dusty ground for people to inspect. Then with their day's takings, the vendors buy rice, beans, plantain and other produce before crossing back to Haiti. Here in one small town, the differences and contrasts between the two countries are plain to see. ❑

BELOW: the sun sets over the cemetery at La Isabela.

THE SAMANÁ PENINSULA

*Fringed with soft white beaches, this beautiful peninsula
juts out into the clear blue Atlantic Ocean, making
it an ideal vantage point for whale-watching*

Map
on page
231

Dense forests of palm trees shading a carpet covered with bromeliads and orchids clothe the gently rolling green hills; little vegetable gardens frame the brightly painted cottages; rivers and waterfalls plunge through lush tropical vegetation. On the Samaná Peninsula lie lonely beaches of sand as fine and white as icing sugar, where the sea is warm and as blue as on a picture postcard. Here, seeing the world through rose-coloured spectacles does not require the assistance of a rum cocktail.

More than 80,000 people live in and around the villages and little towns of Samaná, which covers both sides of the Bahía de Samaná. The Dominicans like to live life in the open air, for all to see. *Merengue* music blares out of the open-sided bars; elderly men click their dominoes in front of a *colmado* (neighbourhood bar) apparently without a care in the world; a group of young boys in baggy baseball shirts shoot pool under a leafy roof; a grandmother, sitting in a rocking chair on her veranda, peels a mango, and a couple of teenage girls have their hair braided in the shade of a huge tree next to the cocoa beans and coconut shells spread out on the asphalt to dry in the hot Caribbean sun. Samaná seems a peaceful place, remote and like a small universe on its own.

For a long time the region was separated from the rest of the island by a broad area of marshland and waterways where pirates used to flee. It was necessary to take a boat trip in order to reach the main island, which was 60 km (38 miles) long and 20 km (13 miles) wide, until the waterway silted up and was turned into dry land in the 19th century. For hundreds of years after the arrival of Columbus, Samaná remained uninhabited until, during the 18th century, a few migrants from the Canary Islands settled here. At the beginning of the 19th century, during the Haitian occupation, land was made available to former slaves from North America and the English-speaking islands of the West Indies. The descendants of these settlers spoke a strange mixture of English and Spanish known as *inglés del muelle*. Reminders of the origins of the inhabitants of Samaná can still be seen in the large numbers of Smiths, Kings and Greens in the telephone directory, and the handful of Protestant sects, not to mention such culinary specialities as *yaniqueques* (Johnny Cakes).

An individualistic approach

Samaná is still a place for individualists. Some visit the peninsula because of the picturesque beaches on the north coast, while others take delight in the Parque Nacional Los Haïtises and its seabirds, mangrove swamps and secret caves across the bay. Between

PRECEDING PAGES:
fishing boats off
Playa Bonita.
LEFT: colourful
column, Las
Terrenas.
BELOW: a milliner
selling his wares in
Sabana de la Mar.

January and March, humpback whales *(megaptera novaengliae)* gather near the *Banco de la Plata* (Silver Bank), 60 km (38 miles) north of the coast, and also in the bay. Thousands of the huge marine mammals migrate each winter southwards to the Dominican Republic from the cold North into warmer waters, to mate and give birth to their young, which would freeze instantly if they remained in the chilly North Atlantic. *(See pages 156–7).*

In the 1990s the Government hoped to establish a high-class, luxury tourist industry in Samaná, and invested in infrastructure: the airport of Arroyo Barril on the peninsula's south coast has been open to international traffic since 1999, although the runway is still too short and the concrete surface too thin for the large transatlantic aircraft. Another airport is now being planned elsewhere. However, a good-quality tarmac road leads from Sánchez to as far as Las Galeras on the northeastern tip. Las Terrenas, on the north coast, is also easily accessible over a winding mountain road. Builders are also paving the road from Las Terrenas across the mountains to Santa Bárbara de Samaná.

Victorian cottages and spectacular views

Sánchez ❶ is usually considered no more than a stopover by visitors but it's worth taking time out for a stroll past the brightly coloured wooden Victorian cottages down to the harbour of this little port. The railway line which once ran from La Vega to Sánchez no longer exists, and the tracks are completely overgrown with vegetation. In the town itself you can see the remains left from the early years of the 20th century, when the bustle between the railway station and the port brought a little life to this remote corner.

A steep and winding road climbs northwards from Sánchez into the hills,

TIP

Samaná Bay (Bahía de Samaná) is part of the protected Marine Mammal Sanctuary of the Dominican Republic, which also includes the Banco de la Plata (Silver Bank) and the Banco de la Navidad (Christmas Bank).

BELOW: a hillside view on the road between Sánchez and Las Terrenas.

RAINFOREST AND MANGROVES

The Parque Nacional Los Haïtises covers an area of more than 200 sq km (nearly 80 sq miles) on the southern side of the Bahía de Samaná, opposite the peninsula. The karst soil is covered with sub-tropical humid forest, bordered by extensive swampland containing red and white mangroves. The natural habitat of frigate birds, vultures, sea swallows and pelicans, the park is accessible only by boat and as you approach it you pass a number of striking *mogotes* – flat-topped columns of rock formed by erosion – which rise out of the sea like emerald-green mushrooms. Young fish, crayfish, crabs and mussels abound in the shallow waters between the mangrove roots.

Travellers taking an excursion to the Parque Nacional Los Haïtises will start their journey from Sánchez, Sabana de la Mar or Samaná – the tour also includes a visit to the park's karst caves. In the Cueva de la Línea there are some fascinating rock carvings left by the Taíno Amerindians – sadly interspersed with modern-day graffiti. La Arena offers stalactites and bats, while the San Gabriel impresses by virtue of its size, its bizarrely shaped stalactites and stalagmites and a subsidiary cave, open to the sky.

which reach an altitude of over 400 metres (1,300 ft). From **Naranjita** – the highest point on this stretch of road – there is a spectacular view of the largest continuous coconut palm forest in the whole of Hispaniola, as well as sweeping panoramas of the shimmering green meadows that billow out as far as the Atlantic coast and the three tiny offshore islands known as **Las Ballenas** (literally meaning the whales). Their form, as the name indicates, is reminiscent of the back of a whale as it rises out of the sea.

Map on page 231

Samaná's main holiday centre

A few dozen bends later, after a total journey of 17 km (11 miles), you reach **Las Terrenas ❷** on the north coast. It was only at the end of the 1980s that the first houses were built alongside the beach here. Today, the approach road, the Calle Principal, is flanked over a distance of around 2 km (over 1 mile) by souvenir shops, cafes and bars, and bureaux de change. Numerous small hotels, restaurants and diving stations are mushrooming along the lovely beachfront from where you can walk out to the coral reefs at low tide.

    The little town has grown into Samaná's main holiday centre, and the number of inhabitants has expanded rapidly as a result, with the international community now comprising some 14,000 residents – many of the well-heeled arrive by private plane at the airstrip located outside town at El Portillo. The French make up the largest minority group in Las Terrenas, then the Italians, the Swiss and the Germans.

    Las Terrenas is the place for those people who are not at ease among large crowds of holidaymakers, but like to be kept occupied. Distractions of all kinds, especially outdoor pursuits, are available around the clock: diving,

TIP

In Las Terrenas' El Paseo de la Costanera shopping complex, you can not only go shopping, but also get a new hairdo, a beauty treatment, air tickets or even have a tooth crowned.

BELOW: a mobile shoe salesman, Las Terrenas.

snorkelling, sailing a hobie cat or riding a horse. As night descends, you can relax over a sundowner in a beach bar.

Gerard, the chef at the Hotel Atlantis (tel: 240 6111) in Playa Bonita, once served as chief chef to President François Mitterrand of France. Today, he ensures that not only fine food, but also fine French wines, are served in the restaurant.

Peace and quiet at Playa Bonita

The road west out of Las Terrenas is no more than a sandy track. But it is worthwhile enduring the 5 km (3 miles) of bumps and ruts to get to **Playa Bonita ❸**, the perfect destination for those in search of complete peace and the opportunity to do nothing more than relax beneath the palm trees. Pretty little hotels and restaurants nestle under palm trees in tropical gardens, and from time to time a horse canters along the sandy track by the beach, or a *motoconcho* rattles past. Further along lies the magnificent 6-km (4-mile) **Playa Cosón** and a string of unnamed beaches, where you can walk along the shore for miles on the soft white sand in the shade of the coconut palms. In the opposite direction, you can walk along the beach all the way back to Las Terrenas.

En route to Santa Bárbara de Samaná

There has long been a road link between Las Terrenas and the provincial capital of Santa Bárbara de Samaná about 30 km (19 miles) away on the south coast, but it is only recently that is has begun to be improved. Travelling eastward out of Las Terrenas, after a few kilometres you pass **El Portillo Beach Club**, an attractive all-inclusive holiday resort offering a wide range of sporting facilities. Across the road there is a runway for small charter planes.

BELOW: the inviting pool near El Limón.

The road continues for about 5 km (3 miles) into the hills and eventually reaches a little village where, at the **Casa Berca** (tel: 240 6261), you can lunch on spicy Creole specialities before setting out on mules or horses with a

Dominican guide to **El Limón** waterfall. This is just one of several starting points for the ride; many local families hire out horses and you can get refreshments along the way. The ride takes about one hour, crossing alarmingly steep hills, bridle paths and muddy cattle tracks. The water plunges over 40 metres (130 ft) into a pool which provides an inviting opportunity to cool off. Depending on the season and the weather conditions, the ground may prove to be quite slippery, making this ride correspondingly adventurous.

The route through the hills is just one of three ways of reaching **Santa Bárbara de Samaná ❹**. Another way is by ferry across the Bahía de Samaná from Sabana de la Mar, which affords the most attractive view of the little port as it chugs into the harbour. However, the ferry is for foot passengers only.

Should you approach the capital along the coastal road from Sánchez, then pause briefly at **Las Garitas**. On the left-hand side is the **Balneario La Fuente**, a natural swimming pool beside a little stream, where you can plunge into the refreshing green water and then enjoy a snack or an iced drink on the shady terrace. At weekends the *balneario* belongs to the Dominicans, and loud *merengue* music is likely to drown out the birdsong. And during the week, tour groups sometimes stop here for light refreshment; it is usually busy but the decibel level is lower.

Motoconchos which pull small trailers are ideal for taking the shopping home.

Seagoing migrants

Samaná, as the provincial capital is invariably known, comes to life during whale watching season, when visitors descend on the town and take to its waters to watch the mating rituals of the whales. For many years, yachts from all the corners of the world have dropped anchor in the little bay, overlooked by the port

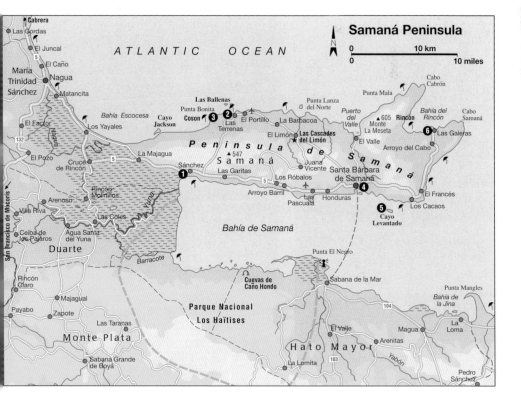

that clings to the shore between two hills. These international sailors added a touch of worldly flair to the provincial charm.

On 12 January 1493, Columbus and his fleet reached the peninsula here and discovered that the Ciguayo Amerindians were waiting to receive them armed with bows and arrows rather than a welcoming smile. The *Gran Almirante* immediately christened the bay *Golfo de los Flechas*. Once all the Amerindians had been killed or enslaved, the remote region remained silent and abandoned for a long time. In 1756 the Spanish governor, Francisco Rubio y Peñaranda, settled migrants from the Canary Islands here in order to prevent this section of the coastline being captured by pirates and smugglers. In the 1820s, another wave of immigrants arrived: English-speaking, freed slaves from Philadelphia who were known as "Los Ingleses" (the English). In 1946 the town was destroyed by a major fire, and only a few of the houses, which were mostly built of wood, survived the flames. One building which escaped was the 19th-century Methodist church, **La Churcha**, imported from England and donated by the Methodist Church for the benefit of the settlers from Philadelphia . Today, most of the houses are made of concrete.

A multitude of marine mammals

The **Malecón**, the wide harbourfront promenade all along the town's seafront, is where the ferry docks, linking Samaná with Sabana de la Mar on the other side of the bay. It is from here, too, that the excursion boats set out for the idyllic island of Cayo Levantado *(see opposite)*, and from mid-January to mid-March the whale-watching boats also leave from here. Those wishing to observe the marine mammals in their element should contact Kim Beddall at the offices of **Victoria Marine** (tel: 538 2494), which is also on the Malecón.

When work on Arroyo Barril airport was delayed by the Government in 1996 for technical studies, the local people got tired of waiting to get their jobs back and formed the Comité *Samaná se Cansó de* Esperar *(Samaná's Tired of Waiting Committee).*

BELOW: whales "tailing" in Samaná's waters.
RIGHT: relaxing on the beach.

Welcoming cafes and restaurants line the promenade. With the green hills behind you and the sea in front, and the islets of **Cayo Vigia** and **Cayo Linares** on the horizon, you may wonder why you hardly ever see anyone on the picturesque footbridge linking the islands with the mainland.

The colourful side of Dominican life is to be seen at the **market** at the entrance to the town, behind the petrol station. Fruit, vegetables, meat, fish and clothing are all offered for sale, and the locals barter, argue, laugh and play *merengue* music for all they are worth. (Here you will also find *Públicos*.)

An excursion to **Cayo Levantado** ❺ will carry you back to the sun-sand-and-palm-trees scenario. However, it must be admitted that nowadays this exceptionally beautiful island in the bay only lives up to the desert island idyll early in the morning, during the evening and of course at night. During the day it is not easy to find a quiet corner between the stalls of grilled shellfish and fizzy drinks, and the lobster-coloured visitors.

As well as boats from the Malecón, a shuttle service to Cayo Levantado is operated by the hotel **Gran Bahía**, 10 km (6 miles) east of Samaná on the road to Las Galeras. A delightful complex built in the Victorian style, the private beach is relatively small, but the swimming pool is perched picturesquely on a hill.

Land's end – Las Galeras

Until recently, **Las Galeras** ❻, a tiny coastal village at the northernmost end of the peninsula, was devoted exclusively to the independent tourist. This meant that your neighbour's towel on the lovely beach lay mostly at a discreet distance from your own, and that, at night, total peace reigned, except for the noises of the tropics and the sounds issuing from the village's only bar. It also meant that each new arrival was eyed with friendly curiosity. If it transpired that a newcomer was a day-tripper, they would be invited to take a seat under a palm-frond roof by the seashore where, perched on a rickety bench and with their feet buried in the sand, they would be served freshly caught fish. If they wished to stay for a while, they would have the choice between three small hotels: the **Moorea Beach**, the **Club Bonito** and the **Villa Serena**. After a few days they would know everyone in the village.

Recently, however, mass tourism has made its appearance in Las Galeras. The all-inclusive resort **Casa Marina Bay** in the neighbouring bay offers visitors a choice of 250 rooms, two restaurants and a lively nightlife. The village itself is changing accordingly: a two-storey supermarket has opened up. And yet, Las Galeras is still the perfect setting for successfully doing nothing at all. You may go on a diving trip with **Dive Samaná** or visit **Moby's Whale Watch Restaurant** on the precipitous cliffs just before you enter the village. From here you can watch the huge marine mammals through binoculars without getting too close.

The magnificent beaches of **Rincón**, earmarked for a modern resort, **Playa Madame** and **Colorado**, whose sand shimmers with reddish hues, can be reached by boat, moped, on horseback or even on foot (in about two hours). ❑

Map on page 231

BELOW: cooling down in the midday heat.

NATURE'S HARVEST: THE ART OF THE CIGAR

The Dominican Republic is home to some of the world's finest traditional cigar makers. They have earned a reputation for producing quality smokes

Historical records suggest that the smoking of tobacco is not a modern pastime but an age-old pursuit practiced by some of Hispaniola's first settlers – the Taíno Amerindians.

Of the traditional crops grown in the Dominican Republic, including sugar, cocoa and coffee, tobacco is considered to be the oldest. And while the growing and export of the other crops has waned over the years the tobacco industry is still flourishing. The main tobacco growing and manufacturing region is Santiago in the north.

UP IN SMOKE

Cigar-making is complex and time consuming. As a rule it takes six weeks to germinate the tobacco seeds and a further six weeks before the plants are harvested. The dried out but still damp bundles of tobacco leaves are tied into bales and left to ferment in temperatures reaching as high as 60°C (140°F). This expels the ammonia and reduces the nicotine. The fermented tobacco is then left to age for up to two years, with some strains being left for as long as 10 years. A master blender creates a cocktail of aged tobacco which is hand-rolled into a cigar shape, cut and pressed into a mould. Finally the cigar is wrapped tightly in a specially selected fine tobacco leaf and secured with vegetable glue. The finished cigar is stored and aged for between one and six months before being boxed and shipped to stores throughout the country and around the world.

△ **THE PERFECT ROLL-UP**
At Don Esteban in Santiago, the tobacco is rolled by hand, pressed into a mould for an hour, before being wrapped.

◁ **CREATING A BLEND**
Sorting the tobacco leaves according to taste and strength. Up to four varieties can be blended together.

◁ FIELDS OF GREEN
Tobacco farmers tend their precious crop with care to avoid damage. Harvesting is a precise art with leaves picked in stages from the base up.

△ CUTTING THE TOBACCO
Once dried and fermented the tobacco's temperature is constantly checked. The prepared leaves are only cut when they have matured.

BIG CIGARS, BIG BUSINESS

During the 1990s the Dominican Republic became the world's largest exporter of cigars attracting tens of millions of dollars in foreign revenue. The agricultural belt of Santiago is the main growing region for tobacco because of its rich soil. There are also several cigar factories in the north. Specialist stores and street vendors can be found all over the country. Famous Dominican brands include Montecristo and Arturo Fuente. For a closer look at the history of tobacco the Museo del Tabaco (see page 241) near Parque Duarte, in Santiago, is worth a visit.

Cigars and their accoutrements are big business in spite of a vociferous international anti-smoking lobby. Choosing a cigar can be complicated: go for either a straight sided or figurado (shaped) cigar, from a corona to robusto, culebra to perfecto. Then there is the ring gauge (diameter) to consider, which affects the burn rate and smoking time.

The León Jiménez cigar factory located on the outskirts of Santiago, has fascinating, guided tours, even if you aren't tempted to buy.

△ FROM GREEN TO BROWN
Preparing the green tobacco for drying: during the process the green chlorophyll-filled leaves change to brown due to carotene production.

▽ FAMOUS NAMES
In the Dominican Republic some of the best-known and best-quality tobacco is grown for cigar-making, using plants grown from Cuban seed.

◁ DRYING OUT
Tobacco leaves are hung out to dry on poles for 1½ to 2 months. Each pole holds up to 100 leaves. Once dry the tobacco is bundled.

"LA HABANERA"
COMPAÑIA ANONIMA TABACALERA

THE CIBAO VALLEY

The real "gold" of the island was discovered early on in the rich, fertile soil of this northern region, where towns like Santiago still prosper after 500 years

Maps:
Town 240
Area 245

Paddy fields, banana plantations and fields of tobacco stretch out along both sides of the roads; cocoa trees and coffee bushes prosper on the rolling hillsides; lorries, heavily laden with sugar cane or oranges, thunder along the busy *Autopista* Duarte from Santo Domingo, heading for the bustling economic centre of Santiago. The Cibao region in the north of the island is the *República*'s bread basket: between Santiago, La Vega and Salcedo in particular, a thick layer of black fertile soil covers the ground. Rainfall is heavy in the southeastern section of the valley, which runs for 200 km (125 miles) between the mountain ranges of the Cordillera Central and the Cordillera Septentrional. That there is no shortage of water is due also to the rivers Yaque del Norte and Yuna.

The fertile valley has long been settled, and many plantation families have prospered over the centuries. Christopher Columbus called the beautiful landscape *La Vega Real*, the Royal Valley, and not long after his arrival, the *conquistadors* founded two settlements here – Santiago de los Treinta Caballeros and La Concepción de La Vega. The towns grew rapidly, but were destroyed by an earthquake in the 16th century. Both were rebuilt on different sites.

The **Ruta Turística** *(Carretera 25)* winds through the green hills of the Cordillera Septentrional for 50 km (30 miles) between Santiago and the north coast, passing numerous picturesque villages, and gives panoramic views over the Cibao Valley.

PRECEDING PAGES:
paddy fields
in Los Yayales.
LEFT:
rolling hills and
Constanza crops.
BELOW: Santiago
cigar makers Carlos
(left) and Don
Carlos Fuente.

Santiago – a proud city

Santiago de los Caballeros ❶ is one of the most important cities in the country, a fact which it owes to the *Autopista* Duarte, giving it a direct link to Santo Domingo *(see pages 169–190)* 155 km (96 miles) to the south. It is an important economic and business centre, and with its population of 700,000 it is also the second largest metropolis in the land after *La Capital* – there is keen rivalry between the two cities.

Described as being the "proudest" city in the Dominican Republic, Santiago seems less chaotic than Santo Domingo; the activity in the streets appears more purposeful. The inhabitants of Santiago are fond of mentioning that most of the country's presidents, along with numerous celebrities from the spheres of art and culture, have been natives of the city. The **Universidad Católica Madre y Maestra** is in an attractive spot on the southern section of the Avenida S. Estrella Sahdalá, and has an excellent reputation.

The original town of Santiago de los Treinta Caballeros was founded in 1495 by 30 Spanish aristocrats *(caballeros)*, along with Columbus's brother Bartolomé, a few kilometres to the northeast of the

city, near the village of **Jacagua**. The new arrivals were hoping to find more of the gold here which they had seen in the settlements of the Taínos. However, in 1562 the town was completely destroyed by an earthquake and was subsequently rebuilt in its present position on the eastern bank of the **Río Yaque del Norte**. Pirate raids during the 17th century, further earthquakes (in 1755, 1783 and 1842), not to mention a major fire during the *Guerra de la Restauración* (War of Restoration) in 1863, hampered the town's growth until it eventually expanded to become the economic centre that it is today.

Santiago is a city to visit for business, not for a holiday: executives from all over the world stay here in the efficient business hotels. The nightlife is quite lively, too, and shopping is considerably cheaper than in Santo Domingo.

Fortaleza San Luís ❹ (Fortress of St Louis) was built on a hill on the banks of the Río Yaque at the end of the 19th century. It was then used as a prison; today, the complex is occupied by the Dominican army, and it is only possible to get a glimpse of the inner courtyard. The road running along the top of the river bank lives up to its name of **Avenida Mirador del Yaque**, as from here there is an attractive view of the new section of Santiago to the south. Heading north you will find yourself in the city centre, where there's a wealth of Victorian and neoclassical buildings tucked between the modern ones.

Around Parque Duarte – the central square

The tall trees of **Parque Duarte** ❸ provide shade in which elderly men pass the time of day on benches, exchanging news and putting the world to rights. Ice cream, cold drinks and music cassettes are offered for sale at street stalls, and on the northern side of the square, the drivers doze in their horse-drawn carriages as

BELOW: view of Río Yaque del Norte.

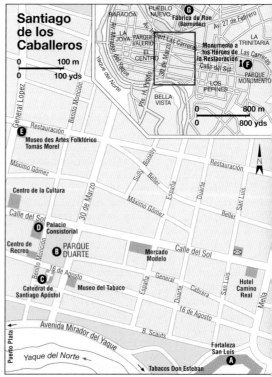

Santiago de los Caballeros

they wait for customers to take on a nostalgic tour of the city. In the centre of the little park is a small pavilion, behind which rises the **Catedral de Santiago Apóstol** ❸, built between 1868 and 1895 in a style which combines classical and neo-Gothic elements. Inside is an elaborately carved mahogany altar, decorated with gold leaf, and the beautiful stained-glass windows *(vitrales)* that were completed by the artist José Rincón-Mora during the 1980s.

The **Museo del Tabaco** (open Tues–Fri 9am–noon, 2–5pm; Sat am; entrance fee) next door was established by Dr Salvador Jorge Blanco. The exhibits provide a wealth of information about the tobacco plant, made all the more interesting because the tobacco industry is one of the most important economic factors of the region. The equipment, photographs and text are arranged in an illuminating manner throughout the museum, and an English guide is available.

The **Centro de Recreo**, on the western side of the square, was built at the end of the 19th century in the Mudéjar revival style, and stands in marked contrast to the mostly Victorian buildings in the historic city centre. Today, members of a private club gather beneath the exquisitely carved beams. You may be permitted to join a bingo session held here on Sundays.

The neighbouring building is an attractive and well-maintained example of Victorian architecture. Within the **Palacio Consistorial** ❹ (District Council Chambers), the **Museo de la Villa** (open Tues–Fri 9am–noon, 2–5.30pm; Sat and Sun 10am–2pm; entrance fee) displays the history of the city.

A few steps further on stands the **Centro de la Cultura** where there cultural and art exhibitions are held. In addition to the 500-seat **Teatro Nacional** and music school, in which concerts by local musicians or visiting stars from North America are held, there are also rooms for exhibitions by national and

Map on page 240

TIP

To find out what's on in Santiago and the surrounding area, drop in to the Centro de la Cultura in Parque Duarte, and look at the notice boards there, or call the local tourist office on 582 5885.

BELOW: a horse-drawn carriage waits at the Plaza de la Cultura.

The white marble Monumento a los Héroes de la Restauración de la República is referred to locally as "El Monumento".

BELOW:
José Manuel
Bermúdez with
his collection of
Trujillo classic cars.

international artists (open daily 9–noon, 2–8pm; free admission). And if your visit to Santiago does not fall during the month of February, when you can experience the colourful pre-Lenten carnival processions first hand, the next best thing is to see the brightly painted masks, especially the local variety known as *lechones* with long, sharp horns, that are worn in the parades along with other folkloric items at the **Museo des Artes Folklórico Tomás Morel** ❻ (opening times vary; free admission), which are displayed in a pretty Victorian wooden house in the Calle Restauración, at the corner of López.

Calle del Sol – a commercial thoroughfare

On your way back to Parque Duarte, a good place to stop for a snack is **Bar Colón** in Calle 30 de Marzo. Decorated in Spanish style, the cafe serves delicious coffee and sandwiches, but the long, curved wooden bar is often crowded, especially at breakfast time. Thus refreshed, you can face the crowds along **Calle del Sol**. A long, straight thoroughfare, lined on both sides with banks, shops of all kinds and temporary stalls, this road is the economic centre of old Santiago. In the side alleys, the dark entrances of the brightly coloured houses conceal repair businesses and a multitude of other small shops. The **Mercado Modelo**, on the corner of Calle España, sells all kinds of souvenirs, from jewellery to basketwork. From the floor-to-ceiling windows of the restaurant on the top floor of the **Hotel Camino Real**, near the Calle Mella, there is a spectacular panorama of the city.

On a hill at the eastern end of Calle del Sol is the city's most prominent landmark, the **Monumento a los Héroes de la Restauración de la República** ❺. It is 67 metres (220 ft) tall and was erected by President Rafael Leonidas Trujillo

n honour of the heroes of the War of Restoration. Those unfamiliar with the city should be grateful to the cruel dictator, for the monument can be seen from virtually everywhere, thus making it practically impossible to get lost. In the entrance hall you can inspect the *murales* by the artist Vela Zanetti, who died in 1998; his work also adorns the United Nations Building in New York. The top of the column, surmounted by an allegorical female figure, can be reached via a staircase, and there are wonderful views. Below the monument, in the district surrounding Calle R.C. Tolentino, numerous pubs and bars have sprung up, some of which have live music from time to time.

Tobacco and rum, coffee and cocoa

Beyond the city centre, you can take advantage of the opportunity to investigate at first hand the production of rum and tobacco. South of Santiago, 3 km (nearly 2 miles) along the *Autopista* Duarte, stands the **Tabacos Don Esteban** cigar factory. A couple of dozen workers are employed here in the manufacture of these exclusive cigars. The German manager, Oskar Nausch, speaks fluent English and provides an authoritative and humorous account of the various stages of production. (Call for a guided tour on 587 9976 or 583 3277).

Those who prefer their pleasures in alcoholic form can head for the **Fábrica de Ron Bermúdez** ❻ (tours Mon–Fri 9am–noon, 2–3pm) in the northwestern district of the city to taste the *República*'s pride and joy for themselves and see how it is made. The rum distillery is a long building on the Avenida J. Armando Bermúdez on the corner of Blanca Mascaro.

Moca ❷, the capital of Espaillat province, lies some 20 km (13 miles) to the east of Santiago. Clinging to a hillside, the little town was founded in the

Maps:
Town 240
Area 245

Camp David Ranch in the Gurabo district of Santiago (Carretera Luperón, Km 7.5, tel: 583 5230) is a restaurant with a breathtaking view of Santiago. Veteran cars which once belonged to the Trujillo family and a state carriage owned by the late President Balaguer are on display here.

BELOW:
Dominican rum is a well-kept secret.

THE STORY OF RUM

Christopher Columbus brought sugar cane seedlings to Hispaniola on his second voyage in 1493. The plant had spread from Asia via the Mediterranean to southern Europe, and the recently discovered "West Indies", with their subtropical climate, offered ideal conditions for its cultivation. Sugar soon became the "white gold" of the region, until the Europeans discovered sugar beet as an alternative source of sweetness.

The story of rum is almost as old as that of sugar cane itself. The principles underlying its manufacture have remained virtually unchanged, too. The best rum is made from molasses, the thick substance which remains after the crystallized sugar has been extracted. This by-product is thinned down and allowed to rest for at least 12 days. Then the rum is distilled and blended to obtain the best flavour. The blending is the most difficult part of the procedure, requiring the most skill. Before the amber-coloured liquid is bottled, it is matured in oak barrels for at least one year to allow it to mellow.

Compared with Jamaican rum, the Dominican version by Bermúdez, Barceló and Brugal has a lighter taste. But the export market is of secondary importance to Dominicans, as they prefer to keep their rum for themselves.

TIP

Time of the Butterflies
(1995) by Dominican
author Julia Alvarez
provides a lively and
penetrating portrait of
the brief lives of the
Mirabal sisters, who
were killed by the
ruthless dictator,
Trujillo, in 1960.

18th century; today it is a centre of coffee and cocoa production. Off the beaten track, it provides an ideal opportunity to absorb the atmosphere of a typical small Dominican town, although this one is richer than most. In the town centre there is a lovely neoclassical church, **Nuestra Señora del Rosario**, and the organ in the **Sagrado Corazón de Jesús**, whose tower dominates the region from the outskirts, is the only one of its kind on the island. Moca's Golden Age was during the early years of the 20th century, when the railway line between La Vega and Sánchez passed through it. A monument on **Plaza Viaducto**, depicting a small locomotive on rails, recalls those years. Moca seems to have played very little part in the history of the nation – except for the fact that, in 1899, the rebels who planned and carried out the fatal attack on the dictator Ulises Heureaux were from the town.

Revolutionary sisters

A well-maintained tarmac road leads for about 12 km (8 miles) through scenic farmland planted with bananas and cacao trees, divided up by little rivers, dotted with palm trees and trimmed with villages. **Salcedo** ❸ holds a bloody chapter in the nation's history. A small metal monument at the entrance to the town, and the portraits of the *Tres Hermanas Mirabal* painted on the wall recall the fact that the three Mirabal sisters – like many other political opponents and thousands of Haitians – were murdered by the henchmen of the dictatorial President Trujillo in November 1960, on their way home from visiting their revolutionary husbands in Puerto Plata prison. In the **Plazoleta de las Hermanas Mirabal** ❹, a small square a few kilometres further eastwards near the village of Ojos de Aguaon, lies the frame of the car in which the

BELOW: monument
to las Tres
Hermanas Mirabal.

outspoken sisters died and a 5-metre (16-ft) sculpture dedicated to their memory. The little **Museo de las Hermanas Mirabal** (the family next door will show you around for a small fee) stands on the right-hand side of the road some 5 km (3 miles) beyond Salcedo on the way to San Francisco de Macorís. The highly respected Mirabal family has dedicated the exhibition of photos and personal possessions of Patria, Minerva and María Teresa to the memory of the three young women.

Map below

Carnival in La Vega

The original La Vega, known as **La Vega Vieja ❺**, was founded in 1494 a few kilometres to the northeast of the present day La Vega. Its *raison d'être*, like that of Santiago, was gold. The *conquistadores* assumed from the tales of the Taínos that extensive deposits of the precious metal were to be found around here. The settlement rapidly grew in prosperity, not due to the modest amounts of gold discovered, but to the fertility of the valley, which enabled the Spanish to begin cultivating sugar cane right from the start. Nonetheless, towards the middle of the 16th century, many settlers abandoned the region. A number of them attempted to make their fortune prospecting for gold on the South American mainland, and in 1562 a severe earthquake almost completely destroyed the town. It was not until the 17th century that reconstruction began on the new La Vega, some 10 km (6 miles) to the south.

Carnaval masks can represent good or evil.

Today, **La Vega ❻** (also known as La Concepción de la Vega) is a quiet provincial town despite the proximity of the *Autopista* Duarte. Its 60,000 inhabitants mostly make a living from the extensive *zona franca*, the free industrial zone to the north. The historic buildings of La Vega which are still standing –

BELOW: keeping the peace at *carnaval*.

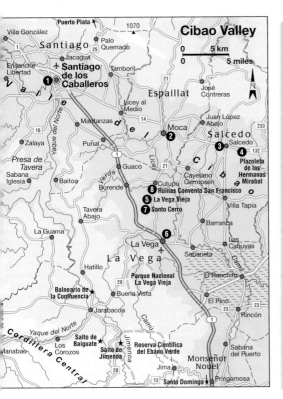

Map on page 245

the **Palacio de Justicia**, the **Teatro La Progresista** and the fire station, the **Bombería** – all date from the beginning of the 20th century, when the railway line to Sánchez created an economic boom for the town. The most recent architectural addition is the **Nueva Catedral**, at the junction of calles Independencia and Restauración, which was built of concrete in 1992. It is a building full of pomp and circumstance in which the Biblical number 12 is of great significance: 12 doorways lead into the interior, and 12 round windows provide light

February is the best month to visit the town, for then all hell is let loose every Sunday. Dominicans all agree that the pre-Lenten carnival in La Vega is the most magnificent in the land. *Diablos cojuelos* ("Limping Devils") in garish costumes dance through the streets. Their faces hidden behind gruesome masks, they take great delight in attacking innocent bystanders with pigs' bladders full of water.

Vision at Sacred Hill

The **Santo Cerro** ❼, or "Sacred Hill", can be found about 10 km (6 miles) north of La Vega and it is here that a legend, dating from the time of the *conquistadores*, was born. The story goes that in 1495, under the leadership of the *cacique* Guarionex, the Taínos went into battle against the Spanish. When they attempted to burn the cross which Columbus had erected, the *Virgen de las Mercedes* suddenly appeared and protected the Christian symbol from the flames. As a result the Amerindians were persuaded to accept its authority. "Is it possible that the cross was made of metal?" ask the cynics. The Dominicans deny this argument, for in the pilgrimage church of **Las Mercedes**, which was built in 1886, a splinter of wood from the historic cross is reputedly preserved for posterity. Whether you believe the story or

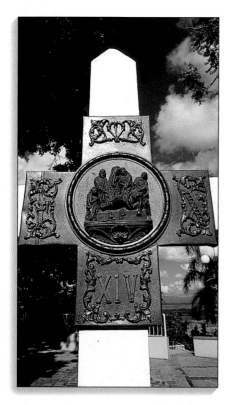

BELOW: cross detail on Santo Cerro.
RIGHT:
off to *carnaval* on a *motoconcho*, La Vega.

not, it's worth a visit because from behind the church there is a magnificent view of the valley, the forests of palms and the amapola trees which are a wonderful sight in February when they are covered in coral-red blossom.

On the other side of the Santo Cerro, a steep road winds down into the valley towards *Carretera* 21. At this point, if you turn left towards Pueblo Viejo, you arrive at the scant remains of La Vega Vieja. The next left turning puts you on the road to the **Ruinas Convento San Francisco** ❽, of which only a few outer walls can still be seen. You can make out the layout of the various components of the first monastery to be built on the soil of the New World: the chapel, well, cloister and enclosure. Beside the monastery is an old cemetery.

The open ruins of the **Fortaleza Nuestra Señora de la Concepción** can be found along *Carretera* 21. The fortress was built by the Spanish after their victory against the Taínos on Santo Cerro. Not much is left of the fortress today. The highest wall still standing is 2 metres (6 ft) tall but it was once part of a tower complete with embrasures. A tiny museum (open daily; entrance fee) displays everyday items dating from about 1500, including a large mortar described as a Spanish sugar mill – a true indication that the *conquistadores* grew sugar cane in the fertile valley even in those days. ❑

CORDILLERA CENTRAL

*The Dominican Alps offer panoramic views over lush valleys,
fertile farmland, dense forests and rapid flowing rivers,
perfect for hikers, cyclists and ecotourists*

Map
on page
253

Santo
Domingo

The Cordillera Central is a magnet to nature lovers, with beautiful alpine vegetation, clear mountain air and stunning panoramas of the surrounding rolling landscape. Hence it's attraction to active sports enthusiasts who flock to the area referred to affectionately as the "Dominican Alps", to hike, cycle and ride on horseback through the picturesque countryside and national parks. The Central range is vast – the largest of the five mountain regions in the Dominican Republic – running across the island of Hispaniola starting in Haiti and ending in the southern region of the Dominican Republic near **San Cristóbal**. The mountain peaks here offer cool relief from the heat and have the highest elevations in the entire Caribbean. Pico Duarte *(see page 255)* rises to an astonishing 3,087 metres (10,128 ft) and La Pelona reaches 3,082 metres (10,111 ft). Nestling at the foot of Pico Duarte are the two main towns, Constanza in the southeast and Jarabacoa towards La Vega *(see page 245)* in the northeast.

Overwhelmingly an agricultural and rural region, there is some industry in the area mainly due to the presence of mineral deposits such as nickel, silver and bauxite around Bonao: though it is a difficult task, Falconbridge nickel mine exploits the abundant mineral deposits. There are also several nature parks and scientific reserves with unique and luxurious vegetation and complex ecosystems, including the Parque Nacional José del Carmen Ramírez in the south, Parque Nacional Armando Bermúdez in the north and the Parque Nacional Valle Nuevo in the southeast.

These mountains are a dream come true for nature lovers, whether one visits simply to contemplate nature's wonders or to seek adventure in an adrenaline-rush activity. Guided excursions are available to Constanza and Jarabacoa from all the main tourist centres in the country. Jarabacoa is most commonly accessible by bus travelling northwest from Santo Domingo, which can take up to 2½ hours, or by taking a short ride from La Vega. If you plan to drive yourself you would be best advised to rent a four-wheel-drive vehicle to cope with the rugged terrain on excursions from either town.

Mountain adventures

Jarabacoa ❶ is a small town of 6,000 people in a lush valley 528 metres (1,732 ft) above sea level at the confluence of the **Río Jimenoa** and the **Río Yaque del Norte**. This is a rich agricultural and farming area producing fruits and vegetables as well as a wide variety of flowers. There are three main rivers in this area. The Río Baiguate flows into the Río Jimenoa and this in turn flows into the Río Yaque del Norte. There are rafting opportunities at various points on each river, depending on your level of expertise. At the meeting

PRECEDING PAGES:
the view over
Jarabacoa.
LEFT: the old bridge
at Salto de Jimenoa
has gone.
BELOW:
rafting down the
Río Yaque del Norte.

Locally grown fruit is used to make tasty fresh fruit juices served in the bars and restaurants.

place of the Yaque del Norte and Jimenoa rivers is **Balneario La Confluencia**, a shallow natural bathing pool north of Jarabacoa. There are several ranches in in the area which offer water-rafting tours and other action-packed activities such as tubing, canyoning, hiking and excursions through the countryside on horseback or in jeeps to **El Salto de Baiguate** (4 km/2½ miles) and **El Salto de Jimenoa** (entrance fee), which is 10 km (6 miles) outside of Jarabacoa. El Salto de Jimenoa is the more spectacular (and easily accessible) of the two, with waters tumbling down about 40 metres (130 ft) into a cool, rocky pool below. The route to the falls is well-signposted and there are parking facilities. In town visitors will find basic accommodation, but the best deals can be found on the outskirts where there a few hotels and cabins for rent.

Popular with vacationing Dominicans, the Cordillera Central is also a great place to try your hand at active sports. Though the Río Yaque del Norte is not as fast flowing or rough as others in the Dominican Republic, the journey down the river by inflatable raft can still get the blood pumping. River tours or mountain hiking tours can be booked through Rancho Baiguate (tel: 574 6890; www.ranchobaiguate.com.do), located just outside town, or through Iguana Mama in Cabarete (tel: 751 0908; www.iguanamama.com). Both companies will arrange everything from guides to camping equipment and mules; all you have to do is turn up, with a good pair of boots and suitable clothing.

Fruit and forests

BELOW: horse riding through the valley, Jarabacoa.

Cutting deeper into the central region and climbing higher from Jarabacoa is another beautiful valley, **Constanza ❷**. One of the highest valleys in the country at 1,200 metres (3,940 ft) above sea level, it has a temperate climate and

temperatures can drop to below zero in winter. The direct route which connects Jarabacoa to Constanza is rough and not recommended, it should be attempted only if driving a sturdy four-wheel-drive vehicle. The longer, but more practical route is to take the road back down to La Vega where you can pick up the *Autopista* Duarte back towards Santo Domingo, turning off at *Carretera* 12, which affords superb views of the mountains, forests and rivers, and leads to the town of Constanza. Here the combination of a mild climate and fertile farmland produces abundant crops of fruit and vegetables (mainly garlic, cabbages and strawberries) not usually grown in the Caribbean, and beautiful flowers for export.

The mountains surrounding the town are rich in timber-yielding woods such as mahogany and American pine, while the land down south to the **Parque Nacional Valle Nuevo** has a protected forest which includes cool streams and is excellent for birdwatching. Heading back along *Carretera* 12 towards Bonao is the **Reserva Científica del Ebano Verde**, a small forest which contains an amazing variety of plant and bird species.

East of Constanza in the mountains is **Bonao ❸**, capital of the **Monseñor Nouel Province**. Essentially a mining town, Bonao is the hometown of famous Dominican artist Candido Bidó, an award-winning painter whose art takes its inspiration from the rural landscape. His work is exhibited at presitgious galleries such as the Candido Bidó Galeria de Arte Moderno in Santo Domingo and throughout the world. Bidó established the Fundacion Bonao Para La Cultura, an art school for painting and crafts, including ceramics and pottery.

Fragrant frangipani.

Also in the district is the **Falconbridge Nickel Mine**, which for years has been one of the largest producers of nickel and iron for the export market. Although the mine provides the region with much-needed jobs for local

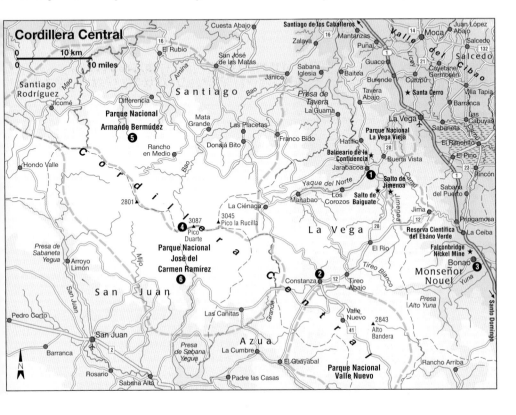

people, its effect on the environment has been a concern due to the pollution and degradation of the soil believed to be connected to the industry. In contrast much of the central range is being preserved in the form of national parks.

Through the parks

The Dominican Republic has 31 national parks and four scientific reserves and two of its main parks are in the Cordillera Central, created in the 1950s to protect the forests and wildlife they support. The two main national parks in the Cordillera Central, Parque Nacional Armando Bermúdez and Parque Nacional José del Carmen Ramírez, are in the foothills of the Antilles' highest elevation, **Pico Duarte ❹** *(see opposite page)*, and its neighbouring peaks La Pelona (3,082 metres/10,111 ft) and La Rucilla (3,045 metres/9,990 ft).

To the north is **Parque Nacional Armando Bermúdez ❺** (entrance fee) with its steep ground covered by native pine trees. The climate is alpine with cool weather dropping below freezing point during the winter months. In December and January the temperature can reach –8°C (18°F) during the night, and the rising sun reveals frost-covered bushes and vegetation, creating a type of ghostly scenery that is unexpected in the Caribbean.

Most organised tours begin at one of the small villages in the vicinity, including La Ciénaga, where there is a ranger station at the entrance to the park. If you are travelling independently this is a good place to book a qualified guide and buy an entry permit both of which are essential for exploring the land. An alternative jumping off point is San José de las Matas, a small and in parts modern, town southwest of Santiago. This is cattle country and though the roads are less than wonderful, they are passable in a four-wheel-drive vehicle.

There are a number of well trodden hiking trails through the park, up to the mountains and Pico Duarte. Most of the trails start at one of the ranger stations in the valley. Among the wildlife which populates the area are a rich variety of birds such as the *cotorra*, a small parrot indigenous to Hispaniola; the woodpecker; the *cigua palmera* (palm chat), the Dominican Republic's national bird, *papagayo*; and the *Guaraguao*, a rapacious bird that preys on small rodents.

The wild boar was hunted by the highlanders many years ago because they attacked domestic animals; it still roams the forests today. This is also the habitat of the mouse and the *hutía*, a small native rodent. Small snakes can be found in the lower areas of the woods.

South of Parque Nacional Armando Bermúdez and west of Constanza is **Parque Nacional José del Carmen Ramírez ❻** (entrance fee). Together the two national parks are home to more than ten of the Dominican Republic's main river systems and therefore have the most plentiful water resources in the country. The land gives birth to the rivers that irrigate the San Juan Valley, one of the most fertile in the country, known as the "south's granary". This is also the source of the **Río Yaque del Sur**, twin of the Río Yaque del Norte. Together the parks' rivers irrigate around 5,000 hectares (12,400 acres) of land. The rivers also provide the nearby communities with electricity by means of a hydro-power plant. ❑

Map on page 253

Most guides who lead tours through the national parks speak Spanish only, unless you book a trip through a tour group who will provide an English-speaking guide upon request. In the interest of safety carry bottled drinking water during a hike up to the peak.

BELOW: colours of Constanza.

Climb Pico Duarte

There was no attempt to climb Pico Duarte, at 3,087 metres (10,128 ft) the highest mountain in the Caribbean, until 1944. Today there are several trails leading to it. During his term as president, the dictator Trujillo christened the mountain Pico Trujillo, but with his fall the imperious peak was renamed after the founding father and 19th-century revolutionary Pablo Duarte. Even for experienced climbers "El Pico" is a challenge: the ascent leads through dense rainforest and extreme climate zones (from sunny and hazy to ice cold and windy).

The best time to climb is between March and October. Warm clothes, hiking boots, waterproofs and sleeping gear, a torch, a medical kit and food provisions are essential. As part of the Parque Nacional Armando Bermúdez on the northern border in the San Juan province, Pico Duarte is best reached from the little village of La Ciénaga, upriver from Jarabacoa. From there it is 23 km (14 miles) to the peak. Take an organised tour or employ a qualified guide (you pay the guide and provide provisions) for the trip, which will take three days on foot. The same journey by mule will cut the travelling time down to two days.

A good place to find a guide is at the rangers' station at the entrance to the park. To hike through the approaches and climb the peak you will need a park permit, which can be obtained at the park entrance on the outskirts of La Ciénaga.

At first, the trail follows the Los Tablones River. The first 4 km (2½ miles) bring a lush landscape of tropical broadleaf forest interspersed with wild cane. If you are tired, you can spend the night at a cabin nearby. The path climbs to La Cotorra (namesake of the Dominican parrot), passing fragrant almond trees, sierra palms and carpets of fern as it enters a wonderfully scented pine forest. At the designated rest area look up and see the fire-red *cotorra* swing through the crisp air. The view of the La Ciénaga valley is stunning.

Now the trail follows the ridge line for about 2 km (1 mile); after that the steep gradient reaches a side trail leading to the high mountain valley of Tetero. The neon-green grass meadows, reminiscent of the Swiss Alps, are an impressionist's dream. On to La Compartición, and the ascent of "El Pico" starts in earnest. It would be wise to stop and catch your breath before embarking on the steep and exhausting 14-km (9-mile) hike.

The Agüita Fría trail passes a large bog which is the source of the Río Yaque del Norte and the Río Yaque del Sur. The final ascent should begin before dawn. After a steady climb through pine forest the path leads through the Vallecito de Lilís, an open meadow with fields of lilies and a perfect view of both Pico Duarte and La Pelona. Continue, passing between massive boulders, until you reach the summit. There, a bronze bust of the national hero Pablo Duarte awaits. The views in all directions are spectacular and include the Caribbean Sea, Lago Enriquillo, the Cibao Valley and the mountains. ❏

RIGHT: ponies and mules can help carry hiking equipment, food and you, if you get tired.

WEST TO LAGO ENRIQUILLO

*Mountain ranges, desert landscapes and one of the world's
largest salt lakes provide stunning scenery in this, the poorest
and sparsely-populated part of the country.*

Map
on page
262

West of Santo Domingo's glitzy hotel resorts, the Dominican Republic
shows its more frugal side. Few people visit this arid land, interspersed
with oases of lush plantations. Close to the capital, families and city
dwellers flock to the beaches at the weekend, but hotels are few and far between
in the southwest. The journey to this neglected and poor area is through dramatic
scenery, with swathes of sugar cane, coffee bushes and banana fields giving
way to dry and barren mountains, tinged blue-green by the cacti growing here.
The road follows the spectacular coastline in places, indented with pretty bays
with shingle beaches or huge sand dunes. The region also contain's the world's
second largest salt lake – home to crocodiles and iguanas – and two huge
national parks where Amerindian caves and petroglyphs are poignant reminders
of the islands early inhabitants.

However, the closer you get to the Haitian border, the drier and more desolate
the landscape becomes, with correspondingly more impoverished inhabitants
and ubiquitous goats at the roadside.

Visiting the southwest can provide an unmissable adventure in a corner of the
country where you might not see another foreigner and so find yourself the
subject of curious stares, but you will not be unwelcome.

PRECEDING PAGES:
rural landscapes
beckon.
LEFT: friendly
smiles in Azua.
BELOW: statue of
the great *cacique*
Enriquillo.

Memories of bloody battles

History has left its scars in this region. The biggest
towns of San Cristóbal, Baní and Azua de Compostela
were all founded by *conquistadores* and the statues in
their little parks are carved memories of bloody battles
between Haitians and Dominicans, or between
Spaniards and Taínos. The deep spirituality of the
Amerindians is inscribed in the landscape near San
Juan de la Maguana and around Lago Enriquillo, where
the great *cacique* Enriquillo fought successfully against
the Spanish conquerors. The modern tyrant Trujillo left
architectural (and emotional) marks in and around his
birthtown of San Cristóbal.

In contrast to the east and north of the *República*,
where tourism dominates the economy, money comes
mainly from agriculture and mining. An international
airport, built to facilitate mass tourism, remains unused
by foreign airlines and there is still only one hotel suitable for package holidaymakers.

San Cristóbal – Trujillo's home town

Take the perfectly paved *Carretera* Sánchez from
Santo Domingo heading west, and the industrial
clouds of the Caribbean metropolis will soon fade into
the lovely scent of freshly cut sugar cane and aro-
matic herbs growing on the roadside. Endless sugar-
fine beaches and coconut palms are not to be found

Baní town flag mural.

here, yet the Dominican desert of scrub and organ pipe cacti, surrounded by massive mountain ranges, is fascinating in its own way.

Passing **Haina**, the main port of *la capital* which has the country's largest sugar-cane mill, **San Cristóbal ❶** emerges after 15 km (9 miles) on the banks of the **Río Nigua** like a mini version of bustling Santo Domingo. The industrial capital of the southwest with a swelling population of 170,000 is notorious as the birthplace of the 20th-century dictator, Rafael Leonidas Trujillo y Molina. It is hectic and polluted, and uninterested in tourists. *El Generalísimo* left numerous landmarks around town.

Recognising the first Constitution of the Dominican Republic, which was signed in the early 19th century after a rebellion against the Haitians in the local **Palacio del Ayuntamiento** (city hall), the dictator officially named San Cristóbal the "Meritorious City". However, today there is not much of meritorious value left here, and its sights will take only about two hours to visit. The city abandoned the dictator's label as soon as Trujillo was killed.

Close to the **Parque Duarte** stands the neoclassical church of **Nuestra Señora de la Consolación** (open daily 6–8am, 5.30–8pm; free admission), where you can see Trujillo's first tomb – his remains have been removed and he now lies in a Paris cemetery. The corrupt Trujillo spent a fortune on his home town, building the church in 1946 at an astronomical cost of US$4 million from government funds, along with the recently renovated plaza in front where, ironically, the city cannot afford to provide the fountains with water.

West of the town on a small hill lies the pompous **El Castillo del Cerro**, Trujillo's lavish six-storey villa, now no more than a ruined shell, stripped of its furnishings; you may be shown round by an armed guard for a tip. Costing

BELOW: Nuestra Señora de la Consolación houses Trujillo's tomb.

US$3 million from the government's coffers, the end result was so over the top that, apparently, when Trujillo's closest confidants criticised it for being tasteless he claimed that it was a gift from the people of San Cristóbal and declined to live in it. However, his family did reside at the villa and it is fascinating to see the remnants of their opulent lifestyle.

Instead he lived in another of his extravagant creations, the **Casa de Caoba** ❷ (Mahogany House) tucked away 5 km (3 miles) north of the town in the thicket. In the 1980s an attempt was made to restore the house to its former glory after it fell into disrepair, but concrete was used to replace the rotten wood which rather destroyed the look of it. Just a stone's throw away is the former private spring baths of *"El Jefe"*, the **Balneario La Toma** (open Mon–Fri 9am– 6pm, Sat and Sun 7am–8pm; entrance fee).

Petroglyphs and bats

The **Reserva Antropológica de las Cuevas de Borbón** ❸ is another 15 minutes along a bumpy dirt road north of Caoba. This is a series of 40 interconnecting caves, which include the **Cuevas de El Pomier** (open Mon–Sat 9.30am–5pm; fee for guided tours), where there are more than 5,000 petroglyphs and several thousand Amerindian wall paintings. The caves are also home to thousands of bats (don't forget the torch).

South of San Cristóbal, 15 km (9 miles) away on the coast, lies the sleepy village of **Nigua**. Right after the bridge over the **Río Nigua** are the old ruins of two sugar mills: the 18th-century **Ingenio Boca de Nigua** and the 16th-century **Ingenio de Diego Caballero**. A sign in front of the old factories describes the stages of sugar production.

Map on page 262

TIP

To avoid getting lost and to save time, it is advisable to take a taxi to visit Trujillo's El Castillo del Cerro and Casa de Caoba.

BELOW: the petroglyphs near the Casa de Caoba.

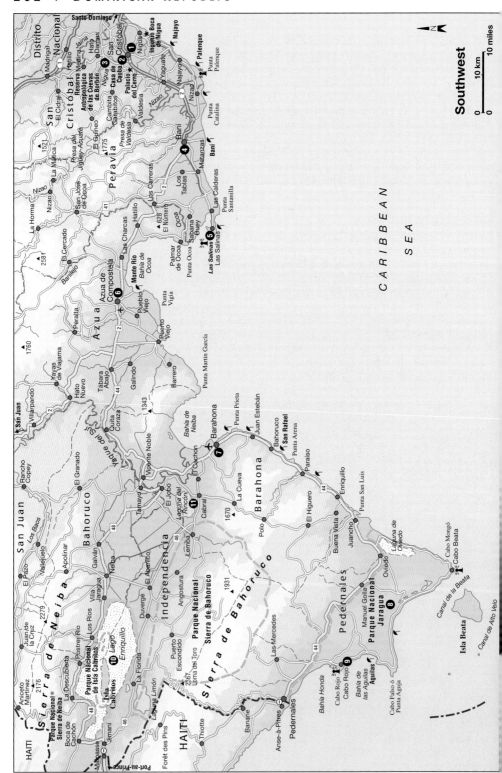

Southwest

0   10 km
0   10 miles

CARIBBEAN SEA

The scenic coastal road *Carretera* 10 leads westwards out of Nigua and passes the empty beaches of **Najayo**, where you can see the ruins of Trujillo's beach house, and **Palenque**. However, the mouse-grey sand and rotting rubbish around the palms may not appeal: the locals just love to slouch in those bright blue wooden sunchairs and snack on deep-fried cassava loaves and papaya juice. If you don't want to drive in the dark, you could stay at the Swiss-run Hotel Playa Palenque (tel: 243 2525) one minute away from the beach.

Map on page 262

Baní – birthplace of a liberation fighter

After a pleasant drive through a green landscape of waving sugar cane bordered by pastel-coloured huts, **Baní ❹** (pop. 40,000), also dubbed the "city of poets", is the next big town. The name Baní means abundance of water and, founded by immigrants from the Canary Islands in the 18th century, the town is friendly and sane. Except for the **Museo de Máximo Gómez** (open Mon–Sat; free admission), which honours the native 19th-century Cuban liberation fighter who was born here, there is not much to see, although coffee junkies should check out the **Museo del Café Dominicano** (open Mon–Sat 9am–5pm; entrance fee) where the Dominican wonder bean is documented. Great pictures can be taken at the lively **Mercado Modelo** near **Parque Central**. The city beach, **Playa Baní**, is difficult to reach, but definitely worth the bumpy ride.

From late May to early July, look out for stalls selling Baní's small but very sweet mangoes.

About 30 km (19 miles) further to the southwest, the salt gardens of the **Las Salinas Peninsula ❺** jut into the sea, and the area has been protected as a National Monument. To get there, follow the signs to Las Calderas naval base and turn left on to the dirt road. The bleach-white salt hills strike a surreal note, with the windy **Bahía de Las Calderas** to the right and panoramic **Sierra Martín García** behind. **Las Calderas Bay** is excellent for windsurfing, second only to Cabarete on the north coast, but the area is relatively undeveloped and there aren't many places to stay. For a pleasant swim in a beautiful setting, take the road north to **Palmar de Ocoa**. This quaint fishing village, which holds an annual fishing tournament, has a neat grey beach and some weekend *haciendas* for wealthy city folk.

BELOW: preparing salt at Las Salinas.

The scenery changes to an arid landscape of scrub and organ pipe cactus once back on the Carretera Sánchez (*Carretera 2*) towards Azua, 55 km (34 miles) west of Baní. In the spring, acacias and mesquite bloom on the mineral-rich soil. About 15 minutes before you reach Azua there is a military post that looks more like a miniature market in the middle of nowhere. Here poor children sell freshly roasted peanuts alongside toothless old ladies offering bundles of tasty shallots and dried chilli peppers. The wooden *pilones* (mortars) and *caña* brooms made from sugar cane are a particular speciality of the area.

Azua de Compostela ❻ (pop. 85,000) is another bustling city which lives off its flourishing agriculture (honeydew and watermelons). In 1504 the town was founded 17 km (11 miles) to the north by the Spanish soldier and colonialist Diego Velásquez (1465–1524), who later conquered and governed Cuba. He was granted a coat of arms by King Ferdinand in 1508. Yet the shipping metropolis, once home to the conqueror

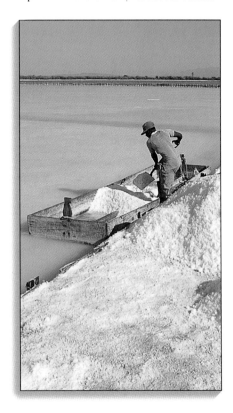

The Corral de los Indios is a large circle of stones 7 km (4 miles) north of San Juan de la Maguana, which was once a Taíno cult meeting place. In the centre is a tomb pillar, engraved with naive grimaces. La Maguana is the name of a Taíno tribe.

BELOW:
domino players can always find a game.

of Mexico, Hernán Cortés *(see page 186)*, regularly suffered heavy pirate attacks. In 1791, Azua was wiped out by an earthquake, and the town was rebuilt on its present site. Several times, Azua was burned to the ground, mostly by the Haitian army, until the gory battle of 19 March 1844 brought the Dominicans their long-awaited independence from Haiti. The battle, which is honoured by a monument in the **Parque Central**, took place 16 km (10 miles) away at **Puerto Viejo**, once one of the main ports of the island, where you can still see some colonial ruins, and where the great Taíno leader Enriquillo is said to be buried.

Alternatively, you can plunge into the lukewarm waves with the locals at the stony **Playa Monte Río** on the Bahía de Ocoa. Try the grilled fish there at the Restaurante San Miguel and enjoy the postcard-view of the lush green mountain **El Número** (628 metres/2,060 ft).

Barahona – gateway to a natural world

Returning westwards on the main coastal highway, the road gets steeper and more winding. Massive rocks as red as brick shoot up on both sides, and suddenly a breathtaking view of the **Bahía de Neiba** unfolds. Entering the fertile mouth of the **Río Yaque del Sur**, a bright green oasis of banana plants, *carata* palms and sugar cane flashes up in the otherwise barren land.

Barahona ❼ (pop. 160,000) is the next and last big town in the southwestern part of the *República* and is 80 km (50 miles) from Azua. It's hard to imagine this provincial port town ever being an El Dorado for the all-inclusive set, but the international airport has long been finished, though no planes land here, and the town planners are eagerly cooking up concepts for luxury resorts. It is only a matter of time before this untouched part of the island disappears under a sea of

development, but for the moment there are only a few neat hotels catering to tourists, and the locals are beginning to get used to *caritas blancas* (white faces).

The airport is named for one of the town's daughters, the Hollywood actress María Montez, whose real name was María Africa Gracia Vidal. Born in Barahona in 1912, she made more than 20 films in the 1940s, including *The Arabian Nights* and *Ali Baba and the Forty Thieves*. She died in 1951.

A favourite hideout for the notorious pirate Cofresí, Barahona was founded in 1802 by the Haitian liberation fighter Toussaint L'Ouverture *(see page 47)*. The town blossomed early as a major port for sugar export and, today, coffee, minerals such as gypsum, bauxite, wood and wax are handled here. There are no sights whatsoever in town, nor are there any decent beaches. But the people are really friendly and live life to the full, as you may see at the **Malecón** at night when the youngsters swing to *merengue* and show off their motorcycle acrobatics.

The real attraction of the town is its position at the top of the **Península de Pedernales** giving easy access to the beautiful national parks. Spend a day driving high up into the mountains of the **Sierra de Bahoruco** to the idyllic coffee village of **Polo** (Carretera 46 for 10 km/6 miles to Cabral, then turn left for 25 km/15 miles). The scenery is magnificent, as it is when you drive south from Barahona along the "Côte d'Azur of the Dominican Republic".

The well-paved, but winding Carretera 44 separates the lush green rainforest of the Sierra de Bahoruco to the right, while to the left cliffs rise steeply above the azure-blue Caribbean Sea. Numerous bays with endless pebble beaches and coconut palms interspersed with fishing huts line the road. Kids cool off in the crystal-clear waterfalls and rough and tumble in the rivers. The best place to stay in this area is at the pastel-coloured village of **Bahoruco**, 17 km (10 miles)

Map on page 262

The international airport is named after Barahona-born María Montez (above), who made it big as a Hollywood film star in the 1940s.

LEFT: street talk.
BELOW: view of the Bahoruco coastline.

*Casa Bonita
(tel: 696 0215, fax:
223 0548) is a
Moroccan-inspired
resort, built in 1998,
which some say
offers the best food
in the Dominican
Republic. The
thatched restaurant
also has a fantastic
view of the bay.*

south of Barahona. If you turn inland on a dirt track just south of **Las Filipinas** village and travel up into the mountains (four-wheel drive vehicle essential), you can see the nation's own semi-precious stone larimar being mined (open Mon–Fri (closed when it rains); free admission). This beautiful blue stone is mined by hand by some 450 miners working in a cooperative; conditions are basic. The men are helpful and friendly and will sell you uncut stones. **Playa San Rafael**, a little further on, is the most popular beach – where two freshwater pools fed by the **Río San Rafael** entice you in for a refreshing swim and *mamís* cook up tasty grilled fish in the shade.

Wildlife and archaeological treasures

At **Oviedo**, the massive **Parque Nacional Jaragua ❽** (1,400 sq km/540 sq miles) starts. The park spreads across the whole of the southern part of the Pedernales peninsula and includes the uninhabited islands of **Beata** and **Alto Velo** to the south. Once the "biotope" of the *cacique* Xaragua, it now attracts the attention of archaeologists and scientists. No wonder, since the park holds many pre-Columbian caves and even more archaeological treasures are still to be unearthed.

The wildlife includes 60 percent of all native birds. Even the endangered Hispaniola buzzard can still be seen gliding over the rough landscape of scrub, sharp "dogtooth limestone", cacti and desert palms. Exploring the labyrinthine park by yourself is prohibited. You must buy a permit at the ranger station at the park entrance (open daily 9am–5pm) at the **Laguna de Oviedo** and take an organised tour. The Laguna, a shallow, 15-km (9-mile) long saltwater lake, is the perfect spot to watch flamingos, pelicans and rhinoceros iguanas at close range.

Driving along the flawless but winding Carretera 44 to **Cabo Rojo ❾**, 48 km

BELOW: cacti and scrub landscape.

CROCODILES IN THE PARK

Alongside the giant rhinoceros iguanas (*Cyclura cornuta*) and the Ricord iguanas (*Cyclura ricordi*), a large number (some say around 500) of American crocodiles (*Crocodylus acutus*) can be seen basking in and around Lago Enriquillo in the Parque Nacional de Isla Cabritos. Since the early 1990s these prehistoric-looking reptiles have been the subject of a conservation study programme funded jointly by the Wildlife Conservation Society and the Swiss agency for Cooperation (Helvetas). Researchers have reported that sightings of crocodile nests rose from 14 in 1995 to 51 in 1996 – three nests were robbed by people in 1993 and only one in 1995. The main nesting grounds are on the Isla Cabritos, and, in recent years, nests have been spotted on beaches which are heavily frequented by tourists. Two nests have even been found right next to a trail on sandy ground, showing that the conservation work is helping to create a more peaceful co-existence between humans and crocodiles. After the eggs have hatched, the mother crocodile tends to ferry her newly hatched young away from the salty lagoon, out of harm's way, to the mouths of the freshwater streams that flow into the lake from the Sierra de Neiba and Sierra de Bahoruco.

(30 miles) across the peninsula on the western coast, you skirt the Parque Nacional de Jaragua on the left, with the **Parque Nacional Sierra de Bahoruco** to your right. On this road you can smell the heady aromas of the Dominican *macchia* that the Taínos used for their medicine. Named for the orange-red colour of its earth, which produces large amounts of bauxite, the fishing port of Cabo Rojo (red cape) is the second entrance to the Jaragua National Park. Following the bumpy dirt road southwards along the shore, you will discover untouched beaches scattered with large conch shells. The best beaches are in the **Bahía de las Aguilas** (a little-known hot-spot for scuba divers and snorkellers, although there are no facilities), which can only be reached in a four-wheel-drive or by boat. Ask the fishermen at the surreal cave-village **La Cueva** between Cabo Rojo and the bay: for a few US dollars they will take you there, as well as to the mosquito-infested islands of Beata and Alto Velo. At **Pedernales**, 20 km (12 miles) north on the border with Haiti, there are several checkpoints and little else.

A round trip to Lago Enriquillo

The extremely dry landscape surrounding **Lago Enriquillo** ❿ distinguishes the Dominican Republic from most of the other islands in the Greater Antilles. Almost every corner holds some historical value, since the legendary chieftain Enriquillo hid from the Spaniards with his men in the rocky mountains of the adjacent Sierra de Bahoruco and **Sierra de Neiba**, waging war for over 14 years. In 1533, on Isla Cabritos in the middle of Lago Enriquillo, he signed the first peace treaty between the Taínos and the colonials with an envoy of the Spanish king. The treaty guaranteed his people a reservation and himself the honorary title of "Don".

If you start early enough from Barahona (6am is perfect), you can make the tour

Map on page 262

TIP

Públicos and *guaguas* regularly ply the *Carretera* 44 between Oviedo and Pedernales and can take you to the ranger station at the entrance to the Parque Nacional Jaragua by the Laguna de Oviedo.

BELOW: view over Lago Enriquillo.

around Lago Enriquillo in eight hours. Follow Carretera 44 north out of the town for 12 km (7 miles), then turn left on to Carretera 48. After crossing **Río Yaque del Sur**, the road will take you through lush sugar-cane plantations where the squalid barracks of Haitian labourers stand, and children play naked in the dust.

After the *pueblo* Galván you come to **Las Marías** where the more foolhardy can jump into the sulphur hot springs from the surrounding oak trees. Then on through **Neiba** – which has a colourful market on Wednesday and Saturday – to **Villa Jaragua** and the shores of Lago Enriquillo, a 200-sq km (77-sq mile) inland sea, three times saltier than the ocean and lying almost 40 metres (130 ft) below sea level. Framed by statuesque coconut palms, with the Sierra de Neiba to the north and the Sierra de Bahoruco to the south, the lake was once part of a channel that linked the Bahía de Neiba in the east with the Baie de Port-au-Prince in the west, until it was cut off by tectonic movements of the earth's crust. You may find fossils, seashells and pieces of coral embedded in the soil.

The region's biodiversity is considered so significant that Lago Enriquillo has been declared a Wetland of International Importance. The wetland has a surface area of 20,000 hectares (49,421 acres), providing a habitat for three of the island's largest endangered reptiles and more than 65 species of domestic and migratory birds, of which five are threatened.

A walk on Isla Cabritos

The scenic road going northwest around the lake offers magnificent views, the most spectacular being at **Las Caritas** at the top of a steep 5-minute climb near **Postrer Río**. The *caritas*, or "little faces", are petroglyphs – faces carved by the Taínos into the coral rock, which has eroded into arches and overhangs to give

TIP

The animals at Lago Enriquillo don't like the hot sun. If you want to see them, visit Isla Cabritos in the early morning or in the evening. During the day they hide in the shade.

BELOW: on the road to Neiba.

Map on page 262

shade from the sun. The awnings may have served as a holy temple to the Amerindians and Enriquillo was said to have hidden from the *conquistadores* here.

About 500 metres (550 yds) further on is the entrance to **Parque Nacional de Isla Cabritos** (open daily 7am–7pm; entrance fee; tel: 224 9525). Walk through the shady tropical forest with iguanas larger than domestic cats to the boats that cross over to **Isla Cabritos** (Goat Island). The 12-km (8-mile) long island is home to some of the rarest animals in the Caribbean: crocodiles, rhinoceros iguanas and Ricord iguanas, large turtles and 62 species of birds, including flamingos, Hispaniolan parrots and spoonbills.

Back at the park entrance, the *balneario* **Las Barias** in **La Descubierta** is only a 10-minute drive away, providing an ice-cold dip in a shady oak forest. You can indulge in the oregano-seasoned *chivo guisado* (goat stew) at Señora Etamila. Next stop is the border town **Jimaní**. With the permission of the Haitian Embassy in Santo Domingo you can cross over to the "Other Hispaniola" in a private car (but not a rented one) and buy fake Nike sportswear at the duty-free market. Or take a trip to the saltwater **Etang Saumâtre** lake (*see page 298*) on the Haitian side of the border.

Returning to Barahona along Lago Enriquillo's south shore on the *Carretera 46*, the bronze statue of the lake's namesake, Enriquillo, stands at an intersection near **Duvergé**. Before you reach the town of **Cabral**, the country's second-largest inland lake, the **Laguna del Rincón ⓫** (47 sq km/18 sq miles), unfolds to your left. Here visitors may find flamingos and cormorants, and perhaps the endangered *jicotea*-turtle, languishing in and around the fresh water. The price you have to pay for this treat is an annoying, some might say strenuous, 20-minute tramp through damp hot fields. ❑

Lago Enriquillo was designated a Wetland of International Importance by the Ramsar Convention on Wetlands in 2002.

BELOW:
taking a mule ride home, Rincón.

HAITI

A detailed guide to the country, with principal sites
clearly cross-referenced by number to the maps

Haiti is not a typical Caribbean destination, no picture-postcard idyll of tropical charm. It is a land of startling extremes and contrasts, a place where grinding poverty is matched by extraordinary resilience, distressing squalor by great natural beauty, cruel inequality by individual warmth. It is a unique country, capable of provoking strong reactions and leaving few people indifferent.

Travelling within the country is a challenge; little goes according to plan. But the rewards are not measured in terms of comfort or familiarity. For what Haiti has to offer is precisely the unexpected. One thing is certain: you will not quickly forget this land of intense colours and insistent rhythms. Nor will you be able to ignore the ever-present imprint on today's nation of a proud history and a tragic past.

For a small country, there is astonishing diversity within its landscapes. Cactus-studded desert hillsides border lush green valleys; cool mountaintop villages are within half an hour of the sweltering city centre; a bustling capital of 2 million people seems a world apart from remote rural hamlets where electricity and piped drinking water are as yet unknown. And history has dictated that the North and the South – the two great peninsulas that reach out as if to seize the island of La Gonâve – have separate traditions and identities, reflected in their people as much as their architecture.

Port-au-Prince is the nerve centre and for a century and a half after independence the exclusive preserve of a commercial and governing élite, it is now home to a third of the population. The city is crowded, dirty and restless, but from its streets emerges a vitality born of the daily struggle. And with this comes the creativity that has made the impoverished nation so rich in artistic achievement. The capital's museums, art galleries and street markets bear witness to this creative impulse. Port-au-Prince's tireless activity is perhaps best experienced from the relative calm of its hillside neighbourhoods or from the mountain vantage-points above the graceful suburb of Pétionville.

The North is littered with the ruins of Haiti's momentous history: plantation houses, palaces and the the the awe-inspiring Citadelle La Ferrière. The South, traditionally the bastion of the wealthier mulatto minority, is a remote region of crumbling colonial towns and tiny fishing villages. In between lie the fertile Valley of the Artibonite, once the source of fabulous colonial wealth, and the desolate mountains that stretch towards the border with the Dominican Republic.

In the 1930s a bestselling and sensationalist book about Haiti was published entitled *The Magic Island*. The book's merits were debatable but the title undeniably well chosen, for that magic is still as powerful today. You may well fall under Haiti's spell. ❑

PRECEDING PAGES: sailboat lands in St Louis du Sud bay; a busy market day in Port-au-Prince; every *tap-tap* tells a story.
LEFT: carnival is fun time.

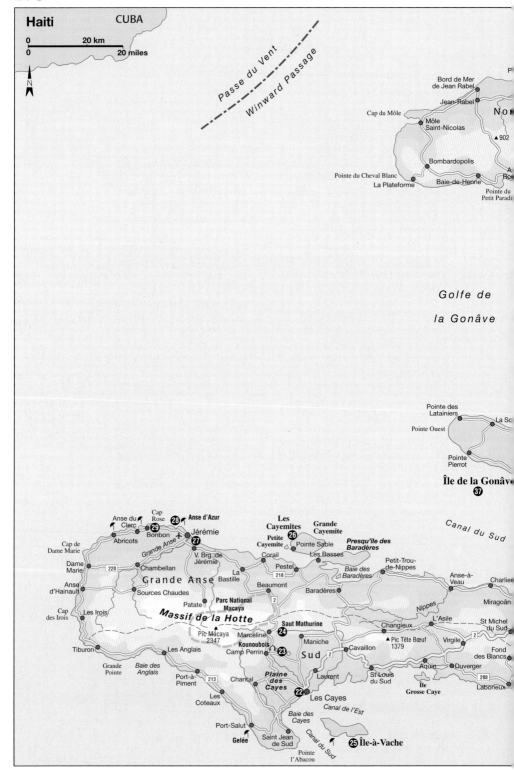

Haiti

CUBA

0   20 km

0   20 miles

N

Passe du Vent

Winward Passage

Golfe de
la Gonâve

Bord de Mer
de Jean Rabel

Jean-Rabel

Cap du Môle

Môle
Saint-Nicolas

No

▲902

Bombardopolis

Pointe du Cheval Blanc

La Plateforme

Baie-de-Henne

A
Ro

Pointe du
Petit Paradi

Pointe des
Latainiers

La So

Pointe Ouest

Pointe
Pierrot

Île de la Gonâv

37

Canal du Sud

Anse du
Clerc

Cap
Rose

28

Anse d'Azur

29

Bonbon

Jérémie

**Les
Cayemites**

**Grande
Cayemite**

Cap de
Dame Marie

Abricots

27

**Petite
Cayemite**

26

Pointe Sable

**Presqu'île des
Baradères**

Grande Anse

V. Brg. de
Jérémie

Corail

Les Basses

Petit-Trou-
de-Nippes

Dame
Marie

220

Chambellan

La
Bastille

Pestel

218

Baie des
Baradères

Anse-à-
Veau

Charlie

Anse
d'Hainault

Sources Chaudes

Beaumont

Baradères

Miragoân

Patate

**Parc National
Macaya**

2

Nippes

L'Asile

St Michel
du Sud

Cap
des Irois

Les Irois

Massif de la Hotte

Changieux

▲Pic Tête Bœuf
1379

Virgile

2

Tiburon

Pìc Macaya
2347

Saut Mathurine

24

Marceline

Kounoubois

23

Maniche

Cavaillon

S u d

2

Aquin

Duverger

Fond
des Blancs

208

Les Anglais

Camp Perrin

Laborieux

Grande
Pointe

Baie des
Anglais

Port-à-
Piment

213

Chantal

**Plaine
des
Cayes**

22

Laurent

St Louis
du Sud

Île
Grosse Caye

Les
Coteaux

Port-Salut

Gelée

Saint Jean
de Sud

Les Cayes

Baie des
Cayes

Canal de l'Est

25 **Île-à-Vache**

Pointe
l'Abacou

Canal du Sud

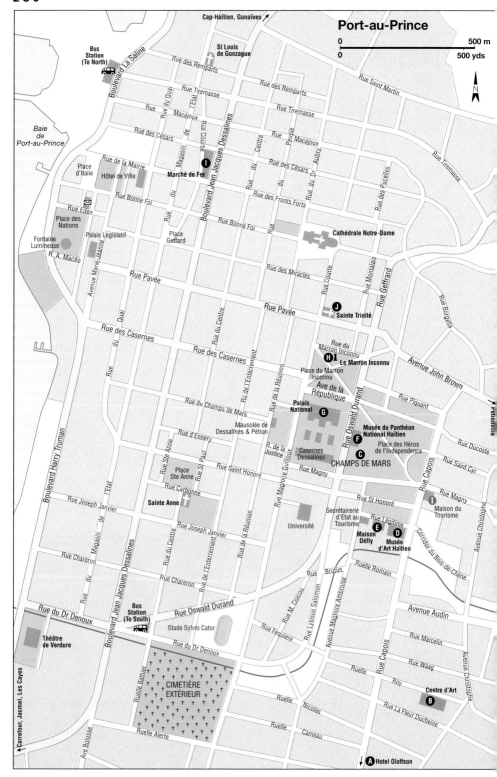

Port-au-Prince

Cap-Haïtien, Gonaïves

0 — 500 m
0 — 500 yds

Baie de Port-au-Prince

Bus Station (To North)

St Louis de Gonzague

Rue des Remparts
Rue des Remparts
Rue Saint Martin
Boulevard La Saline
Rue Tiremasse
Rue Tiremasse
Rue du Quai
Rue Macajoux
Rue des Césars
Rue des Césars
Rue Peuple
Rue Macajoux
Rue Tiremassa
Boulevard Jean Jacques Dessalines
Rue des Puicelles

Place d'Italie
Place de la Mairie
Hôtel de Ville
Marché de Fer 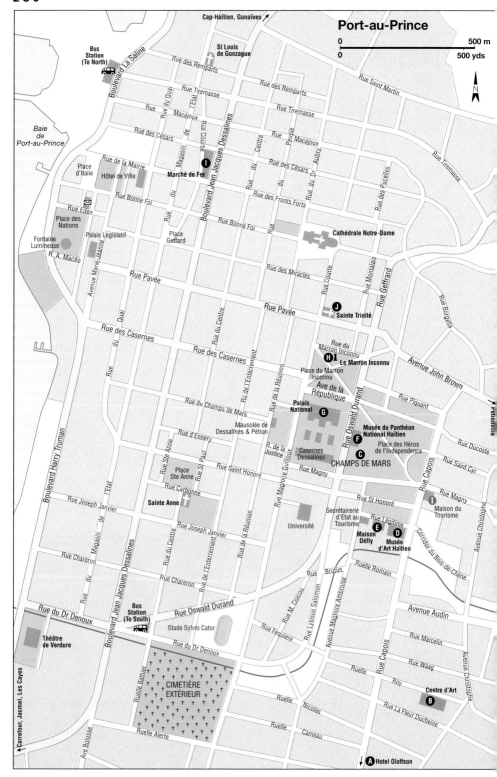 **I**
Rue Bonne Foi
Rue des Fronts Forts
Cathédrale Notre-Dame

Place des Nations
Place Eden
Fontaine Lumineuse
R. A. Macéo
Palais Législatif
Place Geffard
Rue Bonne Foi
Rue des Miracles
Rue Coupe
Rue Montalais
Rue Geffard
Rue Borgala

Avenue Marie-Jeanne
Quai
Rue Pavée
Rue Pavée
Sainte Trinité **J**

Rue des Casernes
Rue des Casernes
Rue du Centre
Rue du Marron Inconnu
Le Marron Inconnu **H**
Avenue John Brown

Rue du Champs de Mars
Rue de l'Enterrement
Place du Marron Inconnu
Ave de la République
Rue Piquant
Pétionville

Boulevard Harry Truman
Rue d'Ennery
Rue de la Réunion
Palais National **G**
Mausolée de Dessalines & Pétion
R. de la Justice
Casernes Dessalines
Musée du Panthéon National Haïtien **F**
Place des Héros de l'Independance
Rue Ducoste
Rue Saint Cyr
CHAMPS DE MARS **C**
Rue Oswald Durand

Rue Ste Anne
Rue St Paul
Place Ste Anne
Rue Saint Honoré
Rue Magny
Rue St Honoré
Rue Magny
Maison du Tourisme

Sainte Anne
Rue Carbonne
Rue Joseph Janvier
Université
Secrétairerie d'Etat au Tourisme
Rue Légitime
Maison Défly **E**
Musée d'Art Haïtien **D**
Avenue Christophe

Rue Joseph Janvier
Magasin de l'Etat
Rue Chareron
Rue du Centre
Rue de l'Enterrement
Rue Chareron
Ruelle Romain
Corridor du Bois-de-Chêne

Rue du Dr Denoux
Bus Station (To South)
Rue Oswald Durand
Boulevard Jean Jacques Dessalines
Stade Sylvio Cator
Rue du Dr Denoux
Rue M Coicou
Rue Lysius Salomon
Avenue Magloire Ambroise
Rue Brutus
Avenue Audin

Théâtre de Verdure
Ruelle Bathier
Rue Capois
Rue Marcelin
Rue Waag

Carrefour, Jacmel, Les Cayes
Ave Bolosse
CIMETIÈRE EXTÉRIEUR
Ruelle Alerte
Ruelle Nicolas
Ruelle Cameau
Roy
Centre d'Art **B**
Rue La Fleur Ducheine
Avenue Christophe

A Hôtel Oloffson

PORT-AU-PRINCE

The crowded and chaotic capital of Haiti can be a daunting experience, but it also offers unforgettable human interest as well as artistic and architectural treasures

Maps:
Area 278
City 280

Port-au-Prince

It is difficult to come to terms with the capital and largest city in Haiti whose population, now close to 2 million, was only 150,000 a few decades ago. Port-au-Prince, like all of Haiti, is a unique place full of constantly confounding contrasts and enigmas, fascination and mysteries.

The world press writes only of the negatives – crime, unrest and violence. But, in fact, Port-au-Prince is not as dangerous as it is portrayed, especially if you follow simple guidelines. As in any populous city anywhere in the world, there are basic precautions that go a long way towards ensuring safety. Some of these are so obvious that they're often overlooked. It's always best to keep as low a profile as possible, given that any tourist stands out in Haiti. And it may not be just skin colour. It's clothing, shoes, spectacles and jewellery. Your whole bearing will be like a flashing red light that says, "Look at me, I'm a tourist, a foreigner, I have money." The one essential: after dark, always take a taxi and never walk, especially in and around the city centre. Don't drive on the long side roads in Delmas. Extra caution is needed after dark because of the lack of street lights.

A wall of heat

There is nothing to prepare the visitor, even after several trips, for the physical reaction to the searing heat that strikes almost like an assault on that first step through the door after the plane has stopped on the tarmac. It's a momentary halt, then a brief half-step backward as though you've been smacked in the face. That initial surprise passes and you continue down the steps and into the teeming airport terminal, but it will take some time to adjust to the sometimes stifling and oppressive heat in the city, the sheer number of people, the stares and occasional expressions of surprise.

Skin colour in Haiti has always been a very complex issue, one that's undoubtedly difficult for a traveller to grasp. The term *blanc* (white) is used as a noun here, not an adjective, or as a title (instead of miss or sir, it's blanc). A *blanc* is anyone who is different, foreign, or who has achieved success, no matter how black the skin may be. And all *blancs* are believed to be rich with mounds of money and therefore should be separated from some of it. Your job is to spend only what you want. Think of it as a game. Just knowing this makes it much easier to keep things in perspective and retain a sense of humour. The truth is that visitors, by definition, will have more money in their pockets than most Haitians earn in a year.

Armed with understanding, preparation is easy. Leave jewellery and other valuables at home; dress conservatively; keep camera equipment out of sight until needed. Get as many of the smallest denomina-

BELOW: the markets of Port-au-Prince are always busy.

Detailed fretwork on the gingerbread architecture in Port-au-Prince and its suburbs such as Bois Verna and Pactot.

BELOW: the fading beauty of the Oloffson Hotel.

tion notes as possible because vendors and taxi drivers rarely have change. (Don't panic if, when making a purchase, the recipient walks away with the money; it is likely that he has only gone to look for change). Divide money into multiple small amounts in different pockets so as not to flash a big wad of notes for every purchase.

The layout of the city

Port-au-Prince ❶ crowns the middle of a large horseshoe-shaped bay at the top of La Gonâve Gulf. The very heart of Port-au-Prince for tourism is the Champs de Mars/Place des Héros de l'Indépendence area that includes the National Palace, statues of heroes including the *Marron Inconnu*, the Maison de Tourisme, Musée du Panthéon National Haïtien (MUPANAH) and Musée d'Art Haitien (Museum of Haitian Art). The Marché de Fer (Iron Market), Sainte Trinité Episcopal Church and the Cathedral of Port-au-Prince are also nearby.

The original colonial core of the capital, dating from the 1740s, is bounded by Rue des Remparts to the north and Rue Pavée to the south. Through this central district, laid out in a grid system, runs Boulevard Jean-Jacques Dessalines, the chaotic main arterial road that leads northwards towards Cap Haïtien and south towards Jacmel. Permanently clogged with traffic and teeming with street vendors, this is where much of the city's business is conducted – from the fierce haggling of the Marché de Fer to the offices and warehouses of Haiti's import-export firms. Don't expect to see much in the way of colonial architecture, however, since a succession of fires and revolutionary upheavals have long since removed the earliest buildings. Instead, the city-centre commercial district is comprised of rickety century-old stores and townhouses, interspersed with more modern concrete office

GINGERBREAD ARCHITECTURE

Many of the residences built between the 1880s and the 1920s were embellished with intricate ornamentation, turrets, steeply angled roofs and "widow's walks" – narrow balconies running all around the house, high up near the top. Unlike other cities around the world where most gingerbread houses were pulled down to make room for new construction, in Port-au-Prince the buildings seem to have been left as they were. A good number of gingerbreads have been renovated and turned into art galleries, schools and offices, and some are still homes. The best examples are in the winding hills of Pacot, in Bois Verna, and all along the Rue Lamartinière.

The Oloffson Hotel is a Port-au-Prince landmark and one of the best examples of gingerbread mansions. The once-stately green and white manse is close to the Champs de Mars yet a world away in Pacot. It has hosted the famous (and infamous) over the years and there is frequently an assortment of journalists and filmmakers, diplomats and politicians hanging about and trading stories. Authors Herb Gold and Graham Greene used it in their novels. Thursday night is usually a good night to go for dinner and enjoy the musical prowess of the owner, Richard Morse, and his band, RAM.

blocks. While high pavements are often shaded by colonnades, the numbers of street vendors with small stalls or piles of goods make life difficult for the pedestrian. Still, it is worth visiting central Port-au-Prince, if only to experience the sheer vibrancy and survival skills of this vast sea of humanity.

Continual growth has spread the city further and further east across the **Plaine du Cul-de-Sac** and into the foothills of **Massif de la Selle**, the semi-circular wall of mountains that protects the city's back. Moving out from the city centre, the next demarcation includes the suburbs built at the start of the 20th century. **Bois Verna** and **Pacot** are still mainly residential, displaying some of the elegance of those bygone times, with many streets brimful of mature trees and vibrant flowers in a riot of colours. The majority of the best remaining gingerbread buildings are peppered throughout, along with the Centre d'Art, art galleries, hotels such as the Oloffson and the Prince and a few small restaurants. The sprawling suburb of **Delmas** is the next division: small shops line the main road and the offices of many non-governmental aid agencies are sprinkled among the woodsy side roads.

The Oloffson Hotel

Celebrated as the inspiration for the sinister Hotel Trianon in Graham Greene's *The Comedians*, this masterpiece of gingerbread architectural exuberance stands at the southern end of Rue Capois. White, with bell turrets, a twin staircase and a cool verandah, the **Oloffson Hotel Ⓐ** is probably the best example of gingerbread style in Port-au-Prince. Set in spacious grounds, it was built at the end of the 19th century as a residence for the Sams, an élite Haitian family, before being turned into a military hospital during the US Occupation of 1915–34. Today, though faded, it remains Port-au-Prince's best-known hotel.

Maps:
Area 278
City 280

TIP

For tours contact the Republique d'Haiti Ministry of Tourism, tel: 223 2143/ 223 5631.
The tourism office can also direct you to Jacqualine Labrom at Voyages Lumière, for organised tours, tel: 249 6177; email: voyageslumiere@ haitelonline.com

BELOW: the streets are full of brightly coloured vehicles.

Every town and city has a cockfighting arena.

Centre of excellence

On the outskirts of the Champs de Mars, off Rue Capois on the corner, at 58 Rue Roy is the current home of the **Centre d'Art ⑬** (tel: 222 2018). The Pacot mansion, constructed in gingerbread style, is an elegant space for displaying art – ceramics, sculpture (including metal sculpture) and paintings are arranged along the original, wide, winding staircase and in a variety of rooms. The Centre is a popular venue for exhibitions of contemporary artists, just as the founders DeWitt Peters, an American teacher, and Selden Rodman, an art critic, had in mind when they first opened it in 1944 as a place for local painters to display their work.

Peters worked as an English teacher in Haiti during the 1940s and became enamoured with the country in general and *art naïf* paintings in particular. He is credited with promoting the work of Hector Hyppolite *(see page 100)*, one of the talented group of artists whose work earned the Centre a reputation for excellence. Rodman, who supervised the artists painting the murals in the Church of Sainte Trinité, also wrote several books on Haiti.

Now almost extensions of the city, places like **Pétionville** and **Kenscoff** were towns up in the cooler hills, where only those with financial means built homes to escape the blistering heat of Port-au-Prince. Pétionville forms the next ring out from the city centre. Next, continuing out to the perimeter of the semicircle are the still higher locations of Montagne Noire, Kenscoff, Fermathe, Forts Jacques and Alexandre and Boutilliers.

Port-au-Prince is always a highly charged, dynamic beehive of activity during daylight hours. (The number of residents continues to swell exponentially in towns throughout Haiti. As the rural, agrarian economy shrinks, farmers who were previously self-sustaining migrate to the towns in

BELOW: the streets are crowded in Port-au-Prince.

their droves in the hope of finding employment, only to learn that they're competing for limited resources with so many others in the same situation.) A result of this pattern is that where there were once beaches, the capital now has the world's largest shantytown. The area bordering the sea to the northern end of Port-au-Prince, La Saline, contains a vast, spreading expanse of slums, home to some 200,000 of Haiti's poorest people. The *bidonville* (shantytown) of Cité Soleil is particularly desperate, with no basic services, frequent flooding and a growing reputation for drug-fuelled violence. (This is the only place in all of Haiti that tourists should really avoid unless they have a resident as a guide.) The nearby port area, **Bicentenaire** (also called Cité de l'Exposition), was remodelled for the city's 1949 bicentennial. Almost everyone still calls the main road running through it by its old name, "Boulevard Harry Truman". This area is safe during the day, but should be avoided at night.

Colourfully painted *tap-taps,* buses and trucks serve as public transport throughout Port-au-Prince and its suburbs; they are usually so full of bodies that it's hard to imagine how those crammed inside will get out alive.

Touring the city centre

Champs de Mars ⊙, bounded by Rue Légitime, Rue Capois, Rue Mgr. Guilloux and Rue du Marron Inconnu/Rue Piquant, is described as a park, but it is easier to think of it as a group of park-like areas divided into sections by the roads that traverse them. Many of the main city-centre tourism sites fan out from Champs de Mars. The **Maison du Tourisme** (open Mon–Sat 8am–noon and 2–6pm) is at the corner of Rue Capois and Rue Magny, making it an excellent central reference point.

Map on page 280

The Champs de Mars also acts as a practice area for local driving schools. Watch out for VW Beetles being driven by novices around the monuments.

BELOW: plastic sheets used as innovative sails, Cité Soleil.

Standing at the Maison de Tourisme the expansive area spread out directly in front is the Champs de Mars. Turn left, and walk to the end of the park along Rue Capois to Rue Légitime (most likely there won't be a street sign), a narrow street, only one block long. Take care crossing the road as it's quite difficult to figure out exactly where any car in the intersection is heading. Try to cross near someone who looks familiar with evasionary tactics.

Art naïf

The unobtrusive, white building on the corner is the **Musée d'Art Haïtien ᴅ** (Museum of Haitian Art; open Mon–Sat 10am–4pm; entrance fee). It has one of Haiti's finest *art naïf* collections with work by Philomé Obin, Hector Hyppolite and Préfète Duffaut among others. Be aware that when the museum is showing one of its superb short-term exhibitions, the *art naïf* paintings are put away. If that happens, the Centre d'Art *(see page 284)* and major galleries are quite accessible. The museum has an interesting gift/handicraft shop with a good assortment of paintings, books and crafts for sale at reasonable prices.

Beyond the museum on Rue Légitime, a tall fence with a door hides a very large parking area. Just drive across the grass to where other vehicles are parked. This is also the entrance to the cafe and gift shop for those not visiting the museum. Don't be surprised if a young man approaches as you near the entrance. He is likely be an artist and will want to show his work. If you stop for a glance, a few more artists with paintings for sale will also gather round. They do not usually go for the hard sell, so a pleasant smile and friendly refusal should be sufficient if they don't have the masterpiece that catches your eye.

Behind the museum, in its private garden, the **Café du Jardin du Musée**

BELOW: *The Paradise* by Wilson Bigaud, Musée d'Art Haïtien.

(open Mon–Sat 10am–4pm) is a little hideaway, the museum's garden cafe and a good place to relax with lunch, a snack or a cold drink (try to sit at a table close to one of the fans). At lunchtime it's quite popular with French Embassy staff from across Rue Capois.

Continue on Légitime, and pass the museum's fence to reach the **Maison Défly ⑤** (tel: 222 4081), the pink house next door. It is currently a museum of créole life and antiques. Set back from the street, it has a little pink roundabout in the middle of a gravel parking area/entry in front, as if to allow visitors a moment to make the transition from the frenetic pace outside the gate to the more tranquil atmosphere inside. It was built by an army commander in 1896 in the Victorian "gingerbread" style.

The *pompiers* (firehouse) is just a bit further along Légitime, and next, behind a long wrought-iron fence, is the building housing the offices of the Haiti Ministry of Tourism. Don't be intimidated if you are ignored – just enter and ask at the desk, and if no-one is there, go up the large staircase (the gate on the staircase will probably be unlocked before 4pm) and ask the receptionist on the first floor. Try the Maison du Tourisme *(see page 285)* for a useful selection of leaflets and maps.

The end of Rue Légitime is just a few steps further; on the corner on the left is a small hotel catering mainly to Haitians who come to the capital to conduct business in that neighbourhood. Turn right on Avenue Magloire Ambroise; the sections of the park are on the right. All along the Champs de Mars, the fences are lined with second-hand books, interspersed with a wide variety of small items for sale, and vendors also sell sweets, food and drinks. You can go in to the park at the next entrance and wander around. There may be people filling huge plastic jugs with water from a pipe flowing into a big cement basin,

Map on page 280

TIP

When visiting the Ministry of Tourism it is best to make an appointment in advance, if you want to speak to someone at length.

BELOW: fresh produce on sale at a street market.

If you're curious to see a Voodoo show, ask at the Oloffson Hotel, but expect to pay a hefty fee to the officiating hougan. Alternatively you can wait until you go to Jacmel and make an appointment to see Mme Yclide La Guerre (see page 324)

or a group of young men playing football on an impromptu playing field – the long cement promenade.

At the second street look left to see a long, mustard-coloured building, the former army barracks **Casernes Dessalines** (no longer in use, and closed to the public). Enter the park and continue in the same direction to the Musée du Panthéon National Haïtien (MUPANAH). There are often groups engaged in lively discussions in this area of the park, reminiscent of "Speakers' Corner" in London's Hyde Park. The whole museum is underground except for a few architectural elements – a large fountain (that has never had water in it) and some fanciful, futuristic skylights, reminiscent of high-tech US architect Buckminster Fuller, which give the impression of a sculpture garden.

The **Musée du Panthéon National Haïtien** ⑤ has some informative historical exhibits about early Haitian leaders including diorama displays of clothing, Toussaint L'Ouverture's pocket watch, documents and an oil painting of King Henri Christophe by Welsh artist Richard Evans, who directed the monarch's Art Academy at Sans Souci Palace *(see page 310)*. The original anchor from Christopher Columbus's flagship, *Santa María*, which sank after hitting the reef near Cap Haïtien on Christmas Eve 1492, is also on display.

Place des Héros de l'Indépendence

BELOW: *Le Marron Inconnu with the Palais National in the background.*

Turning left at the museum exit, walk two blocks to the gleaming white **Palais National** ⑥. It dominates the large, open square and its tree-lined grounds include an incongruously green lawn. The palace resembles a gigantic spun-sugar wedding cake, which belies some of the egregious events that have taken place within its walls. President Aristide made a stand there during the

1991 coup and was barely saved from losing his life only by the timely arrival of the French ambassador. The present edifice was constructed in 1918 on the site of the previous one, which was blown up in 1912, with the then president still inside. The palace is not open to the public, but passers by are no longer made to walk on the other side of the square – as they were in the days of "Papa Doc" Duvalier.

Across the square, *Le Marron Inconnu* (The Unknown Slave) **H**, the striking statue by Albert Mangonès, depicts a man blowing the call to revolution on a conch shell. Other statues of Haiti's independence heroes – Dessalines, Pétion and Toussaint L'Ouverture – and an eternal flame dedicated to those who died for Haiti's independence complete the square.

Map on page 280

Try the Iron Market for wood sculptures and other crafts. Be sure to haggle to get the best price.

Mobile art

If one could just find a place to sit with a cool drink and watch the *tap-taps* passing, it would be like a moving psychedelic art gallery with messages in Kreyòl, English and French incorporated into themes from religion, sport, Voodoo and even purely geometric designs. Some of the designs could easily be displayed in any of the city's galleries. There are images of women, the Virgin and Child, motifs from nature, and humorous adages that manifest the Haitian wry sense of satire and religious proverbs.

Just as in many other parts of the Caribbean and Latin America, vans and buses used for public transport are given colourful monikers by their drivers, but Haitians have taken this form of indentification to a higher level. Don't be surprised to see a *tap-tap* approach you bearing the label: "*paix, amour*" (peace, love) or "*sans Jesus tout est nul*" (all is nothing without Jesus).

LEFT: onions for sale on a city street.
RIGHT: the People's Statue.

Marché de Fer

It seems impossible in a dry, dusty, often dirty city that *tap-taps* always look so gleamingly clean and shiny, yet they do. *Taps-taps* constantly congregate in front of the **Marché de Fer** ❶ (Iron Market), crossing and re-crossing paths as they ply Port-au-Prince with their passengers.

The market building, on the frenzied Boulevard Jean-Jacques Dessalines, is an iron structure topped by two minarets, painted a pleasing ochre. Legend has it that the structure was manufactured in France for the Turkish government, but that in the late 1880s, Haiti's President, Hyppolite, bought it when the pre-fabricated pieces were shipped to the Caribbean by mistake.

The several blocks surrounding the Iron Market throb with vitality. Hawkers of all ages pass with baskets of varying sizes balanced on their heads, heaped with a phenomenal assortment of items – giant steel-wool pads, bolts of fabric, piles of plastic plates and washing-up bowls. *Tap-taps* and private vehicles drop passengers here and there, start and stop in unpredictable places, or try to speed by, so great care and attention are vital in this area.

This is one place where it's good to have a fluent Kreyòl speaker with you. It's also one of the main places to be particularly protective of bags, cameras and any other obvious valuables. Keen photographers will find a host of colourful and often bizarre subjects in the market, but remember that Haitians are not keen on having their pictures taken, so it is always best to ask permission before lining someone up in your viewfinder. Alternatively bring a telephoto lens for your camera, or find an unobtrusive spot (next to impossible in the sea of curious humanity here), be discreet and choose your moment.

The entrances to the actual Iron Market building are obscured by the

BELOW: vendors at the Marché de Fer.

merchandise stalls standing cheek by jowl outside, but just pass through them at any small opening then find one of the doorways. To get your bearings before plunging into the warren of narrow aisles inside, stand facing the building. The left half contains mostly household items – kitchen goods and an amazing assortment of food – and it is basically a big open space with stands crowded everywhere. The right half is jammed with individual booths of 1 sq metre (9 sq ft) and separated from each other by high, dark, thin wooden walls. This is the section for paintings, sculptures, handicrafts and souvenirs.

Once inside, there is little light and even less air circulation. The smell of sweat, salted fish, spices and overripe fruit can be truly overpowering. The whole milieu feels very congested and the aisles are usually packed. Although a few stalls have a fan, it's really not the place for anyone who suffers from claustrophobia. Also be prepared for a crush of sellers trying to solicit business. They endeavour to take everyone to their stalls and failing that, tag along, resisting all attempts to shake them. Eventually only one is left and he sticks like glue, so that he'll get a commission on anything you buy because he tells the vendor that he brought you to them.

Among the profusion of art and artefacts, treasures and trash, it is possible to find some top-notch handicrafts, but it's good to have prior knowledge of comparative quality and prices elsewhere. If you are shopping for paintings, make sure they're original oils, not acrylics or copies. This is the place to buy soapstone sculptures, mahogany carvings, decorative wrought-iron items, and Voodoo prayer flags and accoutrements. While the prices here can be very reasonable, they will certainly be inflated by 50–100 percent for any tourist and it's imperative to bargain. Vendors think less of you, not more, if you don't haggle.

Map on page 280

Paintings produced by Adam Léontus and Jasmine Joseph in the 1960s decorate the panels around the choir gallery and the organ in the Sainte Trinité Episcopal Cathedral.

BELOW: the high altar in Sainte Trinité Episcopal Cathedral.

Map on page 280

Hector Hyppolite was a Voodoo priest and house painter when he was plucked from obscurity and his artistic work exhibited at the Centre d'Art.

BELOW: Port-au-Prince is colourful at carnival time.
RIGHT: buildings on the city streets are unmissable.

Eglise Sainte Trinité

The **Eglise Sainte Trinité Episcopal ❶**, about four blocks from the Champs de Mars, at the corner of Rue Courte and Rue Pavée, is a great place to watch the busy world go by and take photographs of *tap-taps*, without being as conspicuous as at the Iron Market. The church contains very impressive murals painted by some of Haiti's greatest *naïf* artists, including Philomé Obin, Castera Bazile and Rigaud Benoît. Traditional biblical scenes are peopled with Haitian faces the artists knew, and are set in Haitian backgrounds that they could recognise and identify with. These unique murals demonstrate that spirituality itself, no matter how it is expressed, is the most important factor in religious practice. The paintings should have gone a long way to resolving the debates about whether co-mingling Christian and Voodoo symbols diminishes one or the other. The artists were clearly interpreting religion from a Haitian view point. Today European-influenced catholicism and Voodoo practices originating in Africa are irrevocably joined, but unlike the time when the murals were created Voodoo is officially recognised *(see page 105)*.

High Art in Sainte Trinité

Works of art by famous Haitian artists line the walls of the church and stand proudly behind the altar. Most were painted between 1949 and 1951 and illustrate stories from the Bible. Displayed in the apse are *The Crucifixion* by Philomé Obin, *The Nativity* by Rigaud Benoît (left panel in the apse), *The Ascension* by Castera Bazile (right panel) and *The Angels* by Gabriel Lévêque (above the three apse panels).

On the south side of the building in the Lady Chapel are *The Miracle at Cana*, painted by Wilson Bigaud when he was just 22 years old, *The Flight Into Egypt* by Toussaint Auguste (above the east window), *The Visitation* by Fernand Pierre (above the west columns) and *The Anunciation* by Adam Léontus (on the outside of the Lady Chapel).

The South Transcept of the church houses *The Temptation of Adam and Eve* by Toussaint Auguste (above the transcept door), *The Temptation of Christ in the Wilderness* by Préfète Duffaut (above on the left) and the *Native Street Procession* also by Duffaut (above on the right). In the North Transcept you will find *The Casting out of the Money Changers* and *The Baptism of Christ*, both by Castera Bazile.

A small school is attached to the Eglise Sainte Trinité Episcopal, and there are occasional concerts of choral and classical music (for details tel: 222 5638). There is also a little gift shop in an adjoining building, selling a good range of books and postcards that you can send to the folks back home.

Three blocks down Rue Courte stands the larger, but less aesthetically appealing pink-and-white Catholic **Notre Dame Cathedral**. It was completed in 1915, and some say the twin-spired structure bears a passing resemblance to the Sacré Coeur in Paris. The cathedral contains a vast shrine to the Virgin Mary. On Sunday, there are huge crowds of fervent worshippers as well as a great many beggars, hoping to benefit from some Christian charity. ❏

HISPANIOLA'S TROPICAL FLORA AND FAUNA

The Dominican Republic offers a more spectacular variety of plants and wildlife than its neighbour. But there are still areas of natural beauty in Haiti

Much of Hispaniola has been devastated by deforestation, especially in Haiti where trees are felled to make charcoal or for firewood. The removal of the forests has reached danger level in some areas, laying waste to the land and exposing it to the harsh elements. In spite of this, both the Dominican Republic and Haiti remain gems of the Caribbean with bright, rare and exotic flowers. Samaná in the east of the Dominican Republic and the fertile central valley of Cibao – the nation's bread basket – sustain important agricultural crops such as sugar cane, tobacco, coffee and cocoa, while the Artibonite Valley in Haiti is that country's rice basket. Fruit trees laden with coconut, mango and orange grow everywhere, but cashew *(above)* and cacti thrive only in the dry regions.

FLORAL TRIBUTES

In Santo Domingo pink bougainvillaea adorns the walls of colonial homes. Tall palm trees line the Malecón and shade the city's parks, and the botanical gardens are brimming with fragrant flora.

Elsewhere, tropical flora flourish in the cool mountains and national parks such as southwestern Parque Nacional Sierra de Baoruco. In alpinesque Jarabacoa and Constanza there are mountainside meadows of wild flowers and pine forests at the foot of Pico Duarte. Hato Mayor, in the east, has a horticultural centre with a variety of exotic plants from anthuriums and bromeliads, and an aviary and butterfly house. Beautiful orchids grow in abundance; 300 species have been identified so far.

◁ **A GREEN EMBLEM**
The *cotica* (also called the green parrot) is the Dominican Republic's national bird. Spot it in the native palm forests.

▽ **BEAUTIFUL BUTTERFLIES**
Colourful butterflies can be seen flitting among the pretty mountain flora in the east near San Pedro de Macorís and in the botanical gardens in Santo Domingo.

△ **IGUANAS LOVE DRY HEAT**
The iguana, a protected reptile, inhabits hot, dry bush areas of Hispaniola including southern Haiti's Parc National Macaya.

▷ **LOUNGE LIZARD**
Crocodiles lounge around the salt water of Lago Enriquillo on the hot, arid Isla Cabritos and Etang Saumâtre, east of Port-Au-Prince.

⊲ **ON THE RÍO CHAVÓN**
Before hurricane damaged the trees on the right bank of the Río Chavón, forest land and vibrant wild flowers bordered a ravine below Altos de Chavón.

△ **BANANA BOUNTY**
The banana is believed to have been introduced to Hispaniola from the Canary Islands, but its name is thought to derive from West African Bantu.

△ **THE RARE HUTIA**
A rare endemic mammal, the hutia *(Capromys Pilorides)* lives in forests such as the Massif de la Selle, Haiti.

⊳ **FEARSOME CREATURE**
The rhinoceros iguana *(Cyclura Cornuta)* appears fearsome but in fact tends to be timid.

THE ANIMAL KINGDOM

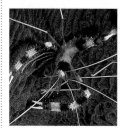

Many nature lovers are drawn to Hispaniola because of its rare wildlife. In the Dominican Republic the Parque Nacional del Este and Isla Saona in the southeast are home to great turtles and are ideal for spotting some of the rarest birds in the Caribbean such as the Hispaniolan lizard cuckoo. Deciduous forest and mangroves are the natural habitat of the endangered hutia, solenodon and the rhinoceros iguana. The hot dry conditions on Isla Cabritos make it ideal for crocodiles, iguanas and flamingos. The area around Etang Saumâtre, east of Haiti's capital, has similar wildlife to Isla Cabritos, and more than 100 species of waterfowl. Birdwatching is best in the Sierra de Bahoruco in the southwest of the Dominican Republic. Twenty-six of the country's 27 endemic birds can be found here. A variety of marine life call Antillean waters home, including the banded coral shrimp *(above)*. The humpback whale mates on the Banco de la Plata and in the warm waters around the northeast of the island (see page 156). There are no poisonous snakes on the island.

EXCURSIONS FROM PORT-AU-PRINCE

Map on page 278

To escape the heat and crowds of the capital take a hike over a mountain range, visit the cool hill-top retreats of the well heeled, or explore the workshops of Haiti's famed metalwork artists

Outside the capital, a hilly land unfolds which offers relief from the hustle and bustle and oppressive heat of the city. To the south are Pétionville and Kenscoff, which have fabulous views of the city landscape below. East of Port-au-Prince is Croix-des-Bouquets, and the beach resorts of the Côte des Arcadins lie to the north. At the present time there are few destinations recommended for tourism northeast of the city. Route Nationale 3 (RN3) to **Hinche** is actually 128 km (80 miles) of dirt track that requires a four-wheel-drive vehicle and takes at least five hours on a good day. The area around Hinche has been the axis for peasant unrest for a long time. Until the situation changes, it's preferable to visit other parts of Haiti that are still beautiful and are easier to reach.

Less than an hour's drive east of Port-au-Prince and still on the Plaine du Cul-de-Sac, **Croix-des-Bouquets ❷** is one of the country's little-known jewels. This small, neat town provides most of the wonderful metal sculptures sold in Haiti. The material looks like wrought iron, but is actually metal from recycled oil drums. Wander along the main street and down a few of the lanes to discover many interesting workshops and their artisan inhabitants who are happy to show off their designs. Some of the larger pieces with intricate cutouts and Voodoo symbols are truly exceptional. One caveat – almost everyone in the village speaks only kreyòl, so be sure to travel with a phrase book or an interpreter.

On the approach to Croix-des-Bouquets, just at the beginning of the main part of town, the large, fenced-in area on the right is a livestock market and abattoir where people bring their animals to be sold and slaughtered. There's a very lively market every Friday lining the streets in the vicinity.

Ville-Bonheur ❸, a small village on the Central Plateau, in the hills near **Mirebalais ❹**, attracts thousands of people for an annual pilgrimage every 15 July. Visitors include practising Catholics, Voodoo practitioners, and some who believe in both faiths. The 35-km (22-mile) trip from Port-au-Prince takes about three hours. The origins of the pilgrimage lie in events which occurred in 1884, when locals reported seeing an image of the Virgin Mary in a palm tree. They built a church to commemorate the spot.

The stunning waterfall, **Saut d'Eau ❺**, about 4 km (2½ miles) away, is a very sacred Voodoo site where believers bathe to purify themselves, before lighting candles to enlist the help of the ancient spirits believed to live there. The ceremony is one of many examples of overlapping Christian and Voodoo traditions and sites in Haiti.

LEFT: carrying baskets on the road from Port-au-Prince to Kenscoff.
BELOW: pilgrims at Saut d'Eau.

This pretty door detail is characteristic of Haitian architectural style.

There is considerable potential for the future development of environmentally friendly ecotourism at the inland saltwater lake, **Etang Saumâtre** ❻, but currently there is no real infrastructure. For the more adventurous and hardy who will go anyway, the north shore offers better opportunities for viewing birds and wildlife, including flamingos and rare American crocodiles. The habitats on the south shore have been affected by the nearby highway.

PÉTIONVILLE AND HILL EXCURSIONS

Some travel guides refer to **Pétionville** ❼ and the hill towns above it as "excursions" from Port-au-Prince. While these are separate and distinct destinations, their proximity to and short travel time from the capital make them more like suburbs. So Pétionville makes a satisfactory base when choosing a hotel for your sojourn.

Pétionville

BELOW: the hubbub of Place St Pierre. **RIGHT:** a colourful *tap-tap* is an everyday sight.

At 450 metres (1,500 ft) above sea level and several degrees cooler than downtown, Pétionville was once a refuge for the capital's élite. That hasn't changed, but now that it is more accessible, it is also a middle- to upper-class suburb. International aid organisations and embassies call it home, too. Named after the mulatto general, Alexandre Pétion, who unified Haiti's south during the early 19th-century revolution, Pétionville has many of Haiti's finest hotels and restaurants. There is also a casino, a 9-hole golf course and a few tennis clubs.

The town is teeming with trendy restaurants, and has numerous night spots, art galleries and boutiques. Most of them are within or close to a six-block area between the parallel north–south streets of Rue Lamarre and Rue Grégoire, and the

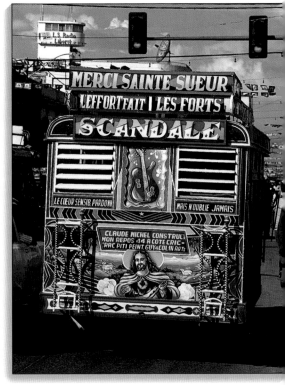

east–west Rue Panaméricaine (Avenue John Brown) and the Place St Pierre. Except for those few established places in Port-au-Prince that will always draw patrons and devotees, Pétionville is the place for anyone considering an evening out.

Three parallel roads lead up to Pétionville from Port-au-Prince. Route de Delmas (called Delmas), the northernmost, probably has the most traffic and minivan-type public transport. All streets that cross it are numbered (eg. Delmas 31, Delmas 60), making destinations in this populous district relatively easy to find. Street numbers are included in addresses and when giving directions. These numbered roads can be quite long. Some of them stretch between Delmas and the next main artery, Avenue John Brown, so it's important to determine exactly which main road is nearer your destination or it could be a long, hot walk.

Avenue John Brown is fun. First, everyone calls it **Lalue**. Second, it changes names part way up, at about Delmas 60, and becomes Rue Panaméricaine (or just Panaméricaine). Of the three, it has the most *tap-taps* and *publiques* (the shared taxis with a red ribbon on the rear-view mirror). In the middle of Pétionville, Rue Panaméricaine meets the end of Delmas, as well as Delmas 105 (right at the fork). Delmas 105 (also called Route de Frères) becomes Boulevard du 15 Octobre (the date Aristide returned to Haiti in 1994). It is a little longer leaving Pétionville this way, but it might bypass much of the city-centre traffic. It passes the airport, then intersects with RN1.

The southernmost road is Route du Canapé Vert (called Canapé Vert, literally meaning Green Canopy). This is the prettiest way to go from Port-au-Prince up to Pétionville, and it has the best views and the least traffic. Each bend in the road opens up a new vista as you make the scenic ascent. From **Champs de Mars** to Pétionville, depending on the traffic and driver, it is a fascinating 15-

Map
on page
278

TIP

Route Noailles in Croix-des-Bouquets contains some of the best metalwork workshops.

BELOW: Canapé Vert in the hills.

minute, animated drive with the opportunity to observe the tumultuous hub-bub of day-to-day life along the way. There's also the chance of the ultimate Port-au-Prince commuter experience – the hair-raising half second of pure panic when a fast-approaching vehicle threatens a head-on collision.

Head for the hills

Refreshing excursions into the cooler, serene hills above Pétionville merit one or two days of leisurely exploration. You will be rewarded with outstanding views of Port-au-Prince harbour, the city and the Plaine du Cul-de-Sac from the desti-nations themselves and the winding roads between them. However, if time is short, the visit could be condensed into a half day. If you are planning to use pub-lic transport, *tap-taps* and *camionettes* leave from near the Pétionville market.

Kenscoff is a small hill station with many beautiful summer homes and a weekly market. Fermathe hosts the Baptist Mission, which blames all of Haiti's ills on Voodoo. The museum here is called: the "history of this land, of this people and of serving Satan". Boutilliers has the best views. And Forts Jacques and Alexandre have cool pine groves along with excellent views. A recent addi-tion to these bucolic panoramas is the proliferation of construction sites in the hills and the profusion of multi-million dollar homes throughout the area. In a land of such stark poverty, the ostentatious wealth of the fortunate few seems particularly conspicuous in the heights overlooking steamy Port-au-Prince.

BELOW: an ersatz castle built for Barbancourt rum tasting.

Starting from Place St Pierre in Pétionville, drive past the police station and the surrounding swarms of people. Continue on Route de Kenscoff for about 10 minutes and turn right at **United Sculptors of Haiti**, which is worth a stop to look at woodcarvings. The road passes a large quarry and an enormous, ersatz

Map on page 278

castle. Built as a tasting room by the **Barbancourt Rum Company**, it has been mostly closed for years due to a dispute within the family.

Barbancourt still produces Haiti's fine rums at its distillery on RN1. The rums are made from sugar-cane juice rather than the molasses often used elsewhere. A visit to one of the cane juice distilleries on the Plaine du Cul-de-Sac is an excellent excursion that could be combined with a tour of former plantation sites on **La Route des Esclaves** (The Slave Route) and a trip to Croix-des-Bouquets *(see page 297)*.

The road to **Kenscoff** ❽ provides great views of Port-au-Prince as it twists and winds its way up to the cool hill resort at 1,500 metres (4,900 ft) above sea level. There are some beautiful country homes whose owners spend July and August here to escape the heat in the city. Hotel Florville has live music on weekends, and is a nice spot for refreshments or a meal but a basic place to stay. There are family-run restaurants which open only at weekends, sometimes with live music. Kenscoff has a small Friday market that is interesting because of the way it is spaced along the streets. The market is much less crowded and frenetic than most others, but you will still be expected to haggle for a bargain.

Kenscoff is difficult to surpass, yet for hikers **Furcy** is the next plateau. Because the road after Kenscoff is in poor condition, it may take considerable effort to reach the summit, which is distinguished by its radio mast. The panorama south over the pine and montane cloud forests that cover the **Massif de la Selle** ❾ makes the effort well worthwhile. Furcy is the jumping-off spot for the 5–6-hour hike down to the Arcadian **Auberge de la Visite** at secluded **Seguin** (50 km/30 miles) in **Parc National La Visite**.

Back on the main road, continue up winding switchbacks that present another

ABOVE: bars and restaurants have live music at the weekend.
BELOW: riding through the rolling hills.

Map on page 278

Independent Haiti had no navy, so in the event of an invasion the plan was to set the plains on fire and retreat into the mountain fortresses. There was never any need to test the plan, but the Caco guerrillas used some of the forts during the resistance against the 1918–20 US occupation.

BELOW: all smiles.
RIGHT:
an impression
of country life.

verdant vista around each turn, as the air becomes noticeably cooler. About 20 minutes later, just after a rather sharp turn, the **Mountain Maid Mission** appears on the right. If the car goes hurtling past a wall on the left covered with brightly coloured paintings, that's the spot, so slow down, turn around and go back to the mission. Some folks visit the Baptist-run mission in **Fermathe** just for lunch in the cafeteria because it serves American-style hamburgers, French fries and ice cream. A school in the complex teaches useful skills to underprivileged children, such as classes in crafts, farming and irrigation. The resulting orderly terraced hills, often shrouded in mist, can be admired from large, open windows in the cafeteria. It's mesmerising to sit and watch the changing tableau, from a bright, golden sun burnishing the green hills, to soft, hushed, grey-blue mist concealing the sky and mountain tops.

Much of the mission's output is sold in its two shops. One sells potted plants, seeds, some produce and excellent bakery goods. The other is a handicraft and souvenir shop with very good prices. Just outside the mission grounds, other handicrafts not available in the mission shop are for sale, and, of course, there are those paintings on the wall across the road.

The forts

Fort Jacques and **Fort Alexandre** ❿ were built by Haitians after they won independence from France, to guard against future invasion attempts. A turn-off near the mission leads to Fort Jacques 10 minutes away. The walls of the 1804 fortress are intact after restoration in the early 1990s. For a small sum, a young boy will unlock the entry gate, but there really isn't much to see inside. The main reason to visit is for the breathtaking views – west to Port-au-Prince and north over the Plaine du Cul-de-Sac. Fort Alexandre was never finished and very little remains of the original structure.

The other reason to visit the remains of the two forts (built on adjoining summits and said to connect underground) is to enjoy a cool, refreshing respite from the heat. The scent of pine trees is a rare pleasure and it is possible to picnic at either place.

On the way back to Pétionville, stop at another pleasantly cool spot 1,000 metres (3,300 ft) above Port-au-Prince. When the sky is clear, **Boutilliers** ⓫ has the best views of the city and its entire basin. And it is the most spectacular place to watch the sunset.

About an hour's drive north of Port-au-Prince is the **Côte des Arcadins** *(see page 342)*, best known for its resorts and beaches. The hotels that line the coast offer a variety of diversions including scuba diving, snorkelling and horse riding. These are not the best beaches in the Haiti but they are popular for a day out from the capital. The hotels have day passes for visitors to use their facilities and are often crowded with wealthy Port-au-Princiens and aid-agency workers. There are also public beaches. North of Cabaret is Montrouis and nearby the resort of Moulin sur la Mer, which is home to the **Musée d'Ogier-Fombrun**. The museum is especially significant to visitors following La Route des Esclaves because the display boards (in French) give a full history of Haiti from the Taínos and the slave trade to postwar times. ❏

THE NORTH COAST

Haunted by the legacy of its turbulent past, the area around Cap-Haïtien, the country's second city, is rich in history and dramatic scenery, combined in its spectacular palace and fortress

Maps:
Area 278
Town 309

Today the north coast is economically, politically and geographically remote from the capital, Port-au-Prince, but in the past it scooped most of Haiti's major historical events. The fertile Plaine du Nord, which surrounds Cap-Haïtien, was not so much the "bread basket" as the "sugar bowl" of the island during the colonial period, and the great northern plantations flourished by exporting their sugar to Europe. But the success of the plantations was directly proportional to the suffering of the slaves and consequently the north was the crucible of the slaves' revolt which led to Haiti's independence. The only discernible remnants of the grand plantations are isolated gate posts dotted around the northern landscape. There are many coastal forts in the area, constructed before and after independence. The flamboyant kingdom of former slave King Henri Christophe has endowed the area with more spectacular edifices, including the Citadelle and the Sans Souci palace. The coastline, especially to the west of Cap-Haïtien, is one of the most beautiful in Haiti and has many shipwrecks to explore. And Île de la Tortue, the island off the coast of Port-de-Paix, has a rich and colourful history due to the filibusters and buccaneers who used it as a hideaway during the 16th century.

PRECEDING PAGES: a view from the Citadelle La Ferrière. **LEFT:** the ruins of Sans Souci palace. **BELOW:** colourful Cap-Haïtien.

Cap-Haïtien ⓬ has a casual and relaxed atmosphere which acts as a counterpoint to the frantic pace of Port-au-Prince. The atmosphere is particularly enjoyable in the early evening as Cap-Haïtiens rest on their balconies, chatting, joking and fanning themselves. Cap-Haïtien is luckily bereft of the usual sharp hustlers and would-be guides, which makes strolling around town a pleasant experience.

The city has a homogenised architectural style owing more to Spanish than French influence. The streets are narrow, which always gives shade on one side whatever the time of day. The centre of town is laid out in a simple grid system and uses numbers and letters for identification. All the east–west running streets are numbered, from Rue 1 to 24, beginning at the southern end of the city. The north–south streets, parallel with the coastline, have been designated letters, from Rue A to Q. These start from the street closest to the Boulevard, the wide avenue which runs alongside the sea front.

Historically, the roots of Cap-Haïtien can be traced to a small settlement called Bas-du-Cap, established by buccaneers in the 17th century. The small town was renamed Cap-François by the French authorities and that was modernised to Cap-Français in the mid-18th century. Thanks to the extremely fertile Plaine-du-Nord that surrounded the city, Cap-Français became France's wealthiest colonial capital. It was soon celebrated for its opulent neoclassical architecture and referred to as the "Paris of the Antilles". After independence in 1804, the city was renamed, with

The utilitarian street names in use in Cap-Haïtien are a consequence of the 1915 US invasion. The US Marines refused to use the French street names as they were too difficult to pronounce preferring simply to rename them. Some of the older inhabitants still use the 19th-century names.

BELOW: passing the time of day at the cathedral.

good reason, Cap-Haïtien, which is usually referred to as Cap. The city has been devastated by two great fires in the 18th century, razed to the ground by Henri Christophe at the beginning of the 19th century and flattened by an earthquake later that century, so very little of its former grandeur remains today.

One of the finest vestiges of colonial architecture is the **Roi Christophe** , a hotel on Rue 24B that was originally built for the French governor in 1724. The style is more reminiscent of Spanish colonial than French, housing a shady central courtyard surrounded by pillared archways. Its marble-floored terraces look out onto a verdant walled garden, beyond which are the busy town streets. Continuing north from the Roi Christophe, across a small canal into the area called Carenage, the street eventually joins the coastal road which winds its way to **Plage Rival**, the dirty, litter-strewn city beach. The city's three old French fort sites are along this route. A couple of piles of rusty, hollow cannonballs on the left is all that remains of Fort Magny. **Fort Joseph** is perched on the edge of the cliff on the right, but access is prohibited. The most impressive site is **Fort Picolet**, where some of the staircases and walls are still standing and where a considerable arsenal of antique cannons can be seen.

The **Place d'Armes** Ⓑ, enclosed by rues F and H and rues 20 and 18, is a sleepy, spacious square in the centre of town. In the past it was the scene of a number of bloody showcase executions by the French. Many of the martyrs of the Haitian revolution died here. François Makandal, the maroon chief turned poisoner, was burnt at the stake here in front of an audience of thousands of slaves. Chavannes and Ogé, leaders of a mulatto uprising, were publicly tortured in the square and Boukman, the Voodoo priest who inspired the slaves to rebellion during a clandestine ceremony in Bois Caïman, was beheaded. Now young

Map below

students read books and eat ice creams in the shadow of the domed **Cathédrale de Notre Dame ⓒ**, built in 1774, and the Université du Roi Christophe, which was built on the ruins of a post-independence royal palace.

There is an iron market to the southwest of the Place d'Armes, bordered by rues I and K and rues 9 and 11, where women hawk a cornucopia of fruits, spices and vegetables. Further south, between rues I and K and rues 2 and 4, there is a more domestic market, selling pots, pans and everything imaginable that can possibly be moulded from plastic. At the point where Rue 17 hits the Boulevard there is a small craft market where paintings, embroidery and wooden carvings are on sale.

Philomé Obin, the north's most eminent painter, was born and lived in Cap-Haïtien, from 1891. His house still stands on the corner of Rue L, also known as Espanole, and is worth a visit. Further along Route Nationale 1, about 5 km (3 miles) south past the gaudy yellow city gates called **Barrière Bouteille**, is the district of **Vertières**. This is the historic site of Dessalines' victorious battle on 18 November 1803, which led to the capture of Cap-Français, the defeat of the French and liberty for the black slaves. There is a roadside monument dedicated to the heroes of the liberation, built in 1953 to commemorate 150 years of freedom.

During the colonial period there were more than a thousand vast plantations located on the **Plaine du Nord** to the south of Cap-Haïtien. Although most of the ruins are lost there are some reminders, such as the monument to Toussaint L'Ouverture on the site of the Bréda plantation. A society dedicated to the protection of Haiti's historical sites, ISPAN, is on Rue 15B. It can supply information about the various locations in the country.

Makandal was a maroon chief originally from Guinea. Expert in the skill of poisoning, he hatched a plan to eliminate the cruel colonists. Arsenic was his chosen toxin because it was a common insecticide, but he also used roots, berries, polluted earth and ground glass. His campaign of terror lasted for six years.

BELOW: in the historic quarter.

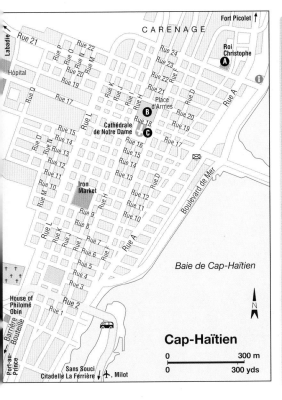

Some of the statues and monuments in the grounds of the Sans Souci palace have survived the 1842 earthquake and neglect.

BELOW: riding from Milot, overlooking Sans Souci.

Sans Souci Palace

Three years after independence, Henri Christophe, a former slave, crowned himself king of the northern province. He built nine palaces, eight châteaux and the most marvellous of his creations, the awesome Citadelle. Henri built palaces at Jean Rabel, Cap-Haïtien, and Petite-Rivière but the jewel in his crown was his elegant **Sans Souci** palace ⓭ (open daily; entrance fee) from which he held court to a newly created nobility. Even though Sans Souci was partially destroyed by the 1842 earthquake, which also flattened Cap-Haïtien, the skeleton remains and still conveys a sense of its original beauty. It is a startling apparition in the prosaic Haitian countryside, especially through the early morning mist.

Sans Souci can be seen on a day trip from Cap-Haïtien by taking the Rue de l'Aéroport to Milot, 20 km (12 miles) outside the city. It was commissioned in 1810, during the height of Henri Christophe's regal pretensions, and completed by 1813. With a burning desire to rival the grandeur of Versailles, he created the most ostentatious palace in the West Indies. It contained state chambers, banquet halls, ballrooms and even surreptitious spy holes through to the kitchens to check on the poisoning habits of his cooks. Cabinet makers, painters and stone masons were brought from Italy, France and England to contribute to the sumptuous decorations. There was even a basic under-floor cooling system, fed by nearby mountain springs. The palace itself was modelled on the Prussian palace at Potsdam in Germany, but the ornamental gardens were designed to resemble those in Versailles in France. The palace grounds covered 8 hectares (20 acres) and the outbuildings included a printing press, library, hospital, mint and barracks. This was the hub of Henri Christophe's northern administration, situated inland as protection against a sea-borne attack.

The Citadelle

Milot is the starting point for the trek, be it on foot or horseback, up to the **Citadelle La Ferrière** (open daily; entrance fee). The formidable Citadelle is a potent symbol of the severe paranoia within Haitian society during the early 19th century. The fear of re-invasion and further enslavement was deep-rooted and the Citadelle was built to combat any attack. The grim colossus sits on the peak of the 900-metre (2,950 ft) **Pic La Ferrière**, dominating the landscape. There is a car park near to Sans Souci where you can buy tickets for both the sites, costing around US$5, and another car park closer to the base of the Citadelle where horses can be hired. It is often better to employ a guide to prevent hassle from others, even if his information seems dubious. If you rent a horse a man will lead it and expect a tip. The 1.5 km (1 mile) hike to the summit of the Citadelle is quite arduous, so take a sun hat and plenty of water.

Work on the mighty Citadelle began in 1804 but it wasn't until 1817 that the last stone was dragged up the vertiginous Pic La Ferrière. An army of more than 20,000 conscripted former slaves hauled thousands of tons of stone, bronze cannons and cannon balls up to the site. The design was the work of Henry Besse and Henri Barre, an English and French architectural collaboration hired by Christophe. At first sight, the Citadelle resembles the prow of a gigantic modernist ship thrusting its way through the mountains. The shape is stunning and almost futuristic for its time. The fortress, with walls 4 metres (13 ft) thick and reaching a height of 40 metres (130 ft) in places, was impenetrable and held enough supplies to feed a garrison for over a year. From the apex the army could overlook Cap-Haïtien, the coast, the northern plains and the southern routes. The view of the **Chaine du Bonnet**, including the **Mount Bonnet à**

Map on page 278

Designed in part by the mulatto engineer Henry Besse, La Citadelle was Henri Christophe's final grand gesture and resting place. Partially paralysed by a stroke he shot himself in the head as Republicans converged on Sans Souci in 1820.

BELOW: the cannons still stand guard.

The use of the gourde as a unit of currency is a legacy of Henri Christophe. The gourde, the hard husk of the calabash fruit, was used for carrying water and fruit. Christophe nationalised the gourde, collecting over 200,000. He paid peasants in gourdes for an entire coffee crop which he was then able to sell to Europe for gold. Within a year Haiti had its own stable, metal currency known to this day as the gourde.

BELOW: the ruins of Fort Dauphin.

l'Evêque, is spectacular. It was within the royal suite of Sans Souci that Henri Christophe shot himself – some say in the head, others say in the heart – with a silver bullet in 1820 as his rebellious subjects rose up against his autocratic rule, but it was high within the confines of the Citadelle that his body was finally laid to rest encased in a vat of quicklime.

A one-horse town with a story

The road to **Fort Liberté** ⓯ is a left turn off the Route de l'Aéroport, a few kilometres out of Cap-Haïtien. It's hard to believe that this dusty one-horse and one-telephone town was once a historically strategic city. The only reminders are the remains of the old forts dotted around the wide bay. **Fort Dauphin**, built in 1732, is in the best condition and can be found by following the main road through the town gates and straight to the sea front. The red stone structure snakes around the bay and houses a powder room, arched vaults and the remnants of an old chapel. The town was called Fort Dauphin by the French but renamed Fort Liberté by Toussaint L'Ouverture when he captured it in 1796. In the 20th century, Fort Liberté was the site of the world's largest sisal plantation until the production of nylon killed the market.

The route between Cap-Haïtien and Fort Liberté passes through a small town called **Limonade** and close by the small coastal village of **Bord de Mer** ⓰. This is generally believed to be the site of **La Navidad**, the first European settlement built in the New World, though the only evidence which points to this conclusion is a wooden stake found on the site and carbon dated as originating from the 15th century. Columbus dropped anchor in the **Baie d'Acul**, which is west of Cap-Haïtien, on 21 December 1492. On Christmas Eve his flagship, the *Santa María*,

was sunk by coral further along the coast. The wreckage was used to build a settlement, La Navidad, where Columbus left a garrison of 40 men. A year later, it had been destroyed and the troops killed by the indigenous Amerindians.

West of Cap-Haïtien, on the northern coast of the cape, are some of the most beautiful beaches, bays and cliffs to be found in Haiti. The western continuation of Rue 21 from Cap-Haïtien forms the rough route into this area and takes about 20 minutes by car. The first accessible beach is **Cormier Plage**, which has a small hotel complex with diving and sailing facilities.

Further along is **Labadie Nord** ⑰, a walled peninsula leased by the Royal Caribbean International cruise line. Twice a week cruise ships deposit about 1,000 passengers here to jet-ski, swim, sunbathe and consume food and drinks. The headland is stunningly beautiful but probably best enjoyed on one of the quiet days when the entrance fee is around US$3.

The road continues for another 2 km (1 mile) past Labadie Nord to **Belli Beach** and water taxi access to Labadie Village, a simple fishing village, and many other hidden coves and bays. There are several basic hotels and restaurants where you can get a good fish lunch and a cold drink.

The only other major town on the northern coast is **Port-de-Paix** ⑱, a smugglers paradise where the honest men deal in second-hand mattresses from Miami. It's an oft-forgotten but very lively and interesting port. The wharf is the ideal place to absorb the character of the town and get a sense of the crazy world of Haitian commerce. The quayside can be piled high with second-hand fridges, bicycles, generators or T-shirts depending on the boat in dock. The whole area around the wharf transforms into a raucous street market when the ramshackle boats arrive. Historically, Port-de-Paix was the first capital of the

Map on page 278

BELOW:
a cruise ship
dwarfs a tourist
at Labadie Nord.

Map on page 278

The name filibusters originates from a 17th-century French translation of fly boats, which describes the small makeshift craft that they used for pirating. And their habit of curing their meat over large low fires, called boucans *by the Amerindians, gave the pirates the name buccaneers.*

BELOW: the beach and landscape around Labadie.

French colony of Saint-Domingue in 1665. In an attempt to settle the buccaneers the French authorities released 100 female prisoners, mainly prostitutes and pickpockets, and shipped them to Port-de-Paix. "I take thee without knowing, or caring to know, who thou art…" are recorded as the marriage vows in Port-de-Paix during this period. There are a couple of interesting churches, the attractive blue and white stucco **Cathedral** on Avenue Notre Dame and the dome-roofed **Église Montfort** just off Rue du Quai. There is a typical Haitian iron market primarily selling food off Rue Sténio Vincent and Rue La Forêt.

Haiti's poorest

From Port-de-Paix a rough road runs westwards towards the remote townships of **Jean Rabel** and **Môle St Nicolas**. Once a fertile agricultural area, the northwest is now the desolate site of Haiti's worst deforestation. Poverty and isolation have encouraged the development of a charcoal industry, with the result that almost all trees have been felled and turned into charcoal, which is then shipped to Port-au-Prince. A succession of droughts and near-famine conditions have turned the arid area into the country's poorest region, a situation made worse by occasional violent disputes between big landowners and landless peasants.

Heading back along the coast, boats leave for **Île de la Tortue** 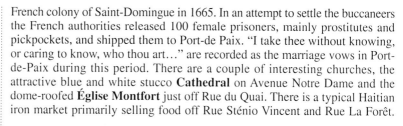 from **Saint-Louis du Nord**, 15 km (9 miles) east of Port-de-Paix. Passengers and their baggage are carried on to the boats on the shoulders of sailors as the wharf is almost a ruin, but the 10 km (6 miles) channel crossing is exciting and invigorating.

Within 30 years of the arrival of the Spanish in Saint-Domingue, French and English pirates or filibusters were setting up covert bases in the region from which they could attack passing ships. La Tortue (or Tortuga in Spanish) was soon recognised as the perfect spot from which to wreak havoc on the merchant ships and silver fleets. The island served as a haven for the buccaneers to divide the spoils, fix their boats and make merry. When sharing the plunder, the wounded were always paid off first, the amount according to the number of limbs missing. There are no relics of La Tortue's filibustering past, but the foundations of its biggest fortress, **Fort de la Roche**, can be found at a spring above **Basse-Terre**. The boats from Saint-Louis du Nord anchor off the small wharf at **Cayonne**, which although merely a coastal hamlet, sells soft drinks and food. There is a narrow concrete road ascending steeply to **Palmiste**, the main village on the island. Skilful negotiations are needed in order to secure a place in one of the very few cars on the island that run up and down the road. During this ride the views of the **channel** and mainland Haiti are beautiful.

Once in Palmiste rudimentary lodgings can be secured through the local Catholic priest, Bruno Blondeau. There is only one main road running east–west along the island and a couple of pickup trucks run back and forth all day long. The best beach is at **Pointe Ouest**, singled out as one of the top 10 beaches in the entire Caribbean. There are some caves containing pre-Columbian relics on the island that can be reached from Palmiste with the aid of a local guide. ❑

Empire Builders

La Citadelle, with 4-metre (13-ft) thick walls rising to almost 40 metres (130ft) above the crest of the 914 metres (3,000 ft) high Pic La Ferrière, is a colossal monument to both the Haitian revolution and the two black generals who, after leading the country to independence, became its first two monarchs.

By the time Jean-Jacques Dessalines read the declaration of independence in Gonaïves on 1 January 1804, he had long established a reputation for great courage and cruelty. Born circa 1760, "The Tiger", who came from a plantation near Grande Rivière du Nord, distinguished himself during the Night of Fire, which marked the beginning of the rebellion, by sawing people in half.

The massively built illiterate ex-slave who fought bare chested, rapidly rose to become Toussaint L'Ouverture's "most ferocious lieutenant". Although he lacked his beloved leader's intellect and gift for strategy, after Toussaint's capture it was The Black Fury's ruthlessness which brought swift victory.

Having symbolically torn the white from the French tricolor to make the Haitian flag, Dessalines emulated Napoleon, when he had himself crowned Emperor in 1805. Using the bayonet "for morale", he set about restoring the economy, seizing French- and mulatto-owned plantations for the state. He had a series of forts built in the mountains behind the major ports, to guard against invasion. Construction on La Citadelle, commanding the coast high above Cap-Haïtien, was begun in 1805. But the Emperor, with his taste for women and protracted banquets, did not have long to savour the imperial lifestyle. He was assassinated by the mulatto faction at Pont Rouge on 17 October 1806.

He was succeeded as provisional head of state by Henri Christophe, son of a black father and mûlatresse (mixed race) mother born either in St Kitts or Grenada circa 1767. Angered by the new constitution which limited his powers, Christophe marched on Port-au-Prince. After reaching stalemate with the mulatto leader Pétion, Christophe withdrew to set up the northern state which became the Kingdom of Hayti in 1811, when he was crowned Henri I.

Although an illiterate autocrat like Dessalines, Christophe had a high regard for culture and education. A confirmed anglophile, he invited English teachers to set up schools in the kingdom and created an aristocracy, complete with a Duke of Marmelade and a Count of Limonade.

His policy of enforced labour and the trade he developed with the USA and Britain gave him the wealth for a grandiose construction programme, aimed at establishing the new black state in the eyes of the world.

Work on the Sans Souci palace, in the foothills below La Citadelle, began in August 1811 and was completed by September 1813. The four-storey palace was made of brick plastered with yellow stucco, and red tile roofs. Among rooms of marble floors and hardwood panelling were banqueting halls, an audience chamber, an arsenal and chapel. It was here that the king shot himself, and the palace was stripped of its contents. ❏

RIGHT: rusty cannon balls lead the way to La Citadelle.

THE SOUTH

*Remote, undeveloped and often difficult to reach,
the wild southern peninsula has some of Haiti's finest beaches,
most extensive forests and friendliest towns.*

Map
on page
278

South of Port-au-Prince, splendid and sleepy, southern Haiti is a long, mountainous, sparsely populated peninsula of roughly 14,400 sq km (5,000 sq miles). An extensive coastline alternates between sheer, steep, rocky cliffs and isolated, white or black fine sand beaches that stretch for miles. It is the only place in Haiti where significant expanses of evergreen forest remain intact.

The mountain chain running from east to west along the middle of the peninsula divides it roughly in half. Here nature-lovers and hikers looking for ecotourism adventures will find one of the last uncrowded sanctuaries. The **Massif de la Selle** anchors the eastern end together with the highest peak in Haiti – **Pic La Selle** at 2,674 metres (8,770 ft). **Parc National La Visite** *(see page 301)*, with its majestic pine forest, montane cloud forest, steep waterfalls and immense limestone caves ready to be explored, also shelters some endangered bird species, including the beautiful Hispaniolan trogon *(Temnotrogon roseigaster)* and the White-winged warbler *(Xenoligea montana)*, as well as wintering migrants.

An undiscovered gem

At the western end of the mountains is the **Massif de la Hotte**. There are very few roads, so it is quite difficult reaching **Parc National Macaya**, but definitely worth the effort to enjoy the evergreen forests, and Haiti's other cloud forest atop **Pic de Macaya**; at 2,347 metres (7,700 ft), it is the national park's highest peak. Scaling the mountain is a challenging two-day climb in order to reach the summit and another two days getting back. It is home to 50 endemic varieties of orchids, and two mammals found only on Hispaniola. The Hispaniolan Hutia *(Plagiodontia aedium)* and the Solenodon *(Solenodon paradoxus)* called *"nez long"* (long nose), which is about the size of a small rat, both inhabit this wilderness *(see page 295)*. The park is also home to the rare Grey-crowned Palm Tanager *(Phaenicophilus poliocephalus)*, the Peregrine falcon *(Falco pergrinus)* and the black-capped petrel.

Relatively undiscovered, the South today lives like a colonial gem on the verge of a tourism explosion. It is known mostly for its charming towns sprinkled with once-lovely Victorian architecture, death-defying but magnificent mountains and difficult travelling conditions. The tropical climate at sea level sustains a breathtaking variety of flora including beautiful deep-purple bougainvillaea, bright hibiscus, orchids and a plethora of rainbow-coloured vines.

Grand plans to improve the transport system by building a coastal highway and roads to link perpetually isolated towns in the south have come to nothing because of a lack of finance.

PRECEDING PAGES:
boats off
Île de la Gonâve.
LEFT: carnival time.
BELOW:
statue and street
sign in Jacmel.

Papier mâché *animal masks are a speciality of Jacmel's artisans. People parade through the streets wearing these and other types of mask and colourful costumes at carnival time in the run up to Lent.*

BELOW: a beautiful balcony in Jacmel.

Travel by road

To reach the south from Port-au-Prince take Boulevard Harry Truman (also called Bicentenaire), to Route Nationale 2 (RN2) west towards Les Cayes. It parallels the coastline, traversing the populous, busy, slow-going Carrefour district of Port-au-Prince. The bypass road – which is under construction – will shorten the trip by an hour, but a completion date is still uncertain. In the meantime, enjoy the scenery, which includes a variety of unusual business names such as: Pharmacie Christ Vivant (Pharmacy of the Living Christ); L'éternel c'est mon Berger (the Eternal is my Shepherd) and Shalom Auto Parts.

After driving for 45 minutes, the lush, densely populated **Léogâne Plain** comes into view, allowing glimpses of rural life. Small villages dot the plain and bumpy byways intersect RN2. After crossing the stone-studded Momance River, turn onto any side road to take a brief detour and explore.

At the Carrefour Dufort intersection (Km 40) a short distance after Léogâne, the road ahead leads to Miragoâne and Les Cayes. Instead, turn south (left) onto a scenic road that snakes its tortuous way up and down the crests. As it passes through mountain-top market villages, there are glorious views of country life – cottages clinging precariously to the steep sides of cultivated hills and people walking along the road with all manner of items skilfully balanced on their heads.

Route Nationale 204, sometimes called **Route de l'Amitié** (the Friendship Route), was built by the French (some say to shorten the trip of their compatriots who often make the journey to their favourite beaches on the lush south coast). Rounding the final, dramatic curve, the bucolic river basin is spread out below with the first view of Jacmel harbour. Diminutive streets wind down small hills to a palm-fringed, dark-sand beach. Adjacent piers provide docks for both cruise

and commercial ships. The piers were constructed in time to welcome the 21st century, together with a convenient space for artisans whose workshops were previously hidden away in their homes, but still no cruise ships visit.

An enchanting town

The road entering **Jacmel** presents the most inviting approach to any town in Haiti. Immediately, everything looks cleaner, neater and less crowded than elsewhere. Turn right onto Avenue de la Liberté. After a few short blocks, it empties into the gated parking area of the white-washed **La Jacmelienne Hotel**. There's a striking view through the open, arched entry out past the sky-blue swimming pool, to a line of white, wooden lounging chairs, and, finally, to the sparkling harbour beyond.

Jacmel is an enchanting town, defined by a large, horseshoe-shaped bay. When the town was built in the late 19th century, wealthy coffee merchants imported cast-iron pillars and balconies from France or the United States to adorn their charming Victorian homes and New Orleans-style mansions. In the late 1990s, Jacmel was selected as one of three prime places for future tourism expansion. In addition to improved infrastructure, much of the Tourism Development Plan centres around restoration of the harbour and original architecture.

Jacmel's small size encourages exploration on foot. An easy stroll will reveal little hidden lanes, the beautifully restored area around Rue du Commerce and the lively commercial centre around the **Marché de Fer** (Iron Market). This, too, was built in Europe and imported in 1895. The hubbub, once reserved for Saturday's market day, now only stops on Sunday.

Map on page 278

With a limited telephone service in Jacmel, the Jacmelienne Hotel is an unofficial message centre. Almost everyone passes there when looking for someone, sometimes leaving messages. Delivery isn't guaranteed, however.

BELOW: a view over the market and cathedral in Jacmel.

TIP

If you are looking for a guide ask for Michel Jean, who speaks English and French. His detailed knowledge brings Jacmel alive and his bargaining skills will more than offset any tip for his services. All guides can also arrange a car and driver or horses and a local guide for a trip to Bassin Bleu.

BELOW AND RIGHT: bright murals and house painting reveal a creative community.

Exploring Jacmel

So many of Jacmel's sights are uncelebrated that it's well worth hiring a local guide to point them out. Traditionally, payment has been negotiable and guides work for tips as they are confident the visitor will be well pleased with their services. In general, it simplifies matters to ask in advance if there is a fee and to agree on payment before setting off.

Guides usually wait just outside the entrance gate at the Jacmelienne Hotel and that's often the only way to contact them. It is also a bit difficult to tell who is a guide and who is not, since they wear the same T-shirt and jeans ensemble as all the other young men in town. But there have been discussions about organizing the guides with official name tags and this system may be implemented at any time.

Visitors accompanied by a guide are usually protected from unwelcome solicitations. Tour guides from the capital employ a local guide, Michel Jean, when they organise a trip to Jacmel *(see Tip in margin)*. Please bear in mind that, while multiple offers of guide services may be vexing, the work provides a legitimate source of income in a country with high unemployment, so try to remain unruffled.

While exploring Jacmel, be on the lookout for murals – various signs and admonitions handpainted on walls that are artistic or whimsical – or discover a variety of striking Victorian buildings. Turning a corner, you may suddenly hear a band in full flight as it practises. In the middle of the square, the market women stand guard at their stalls and tables spread with shoes, blankets or trinkets, seemingly oblivious to the joyful sounds of the town. And there, in the centre of a small park, a costumed dance troupe may be practising their routines for the next festival parade.

Jacmel's main carnival remains one of the best and most popular in Haiti. It takes place a week before the one in Port-au-Prince (in the run-up to Lent) but it is more orderly and less overwhelming. As in Port-au-Prince, there are weeks of practise before the actual event, so it is possible to enjoy the flavour of the pre-celebrations even if your visit doesn't exactly coincide with the carnival. Creatively elaborate *papier mâché* masks, fanciful animal costumes and playful music distinguish the Jacmel carnival.

Map on page 278

Lenten celebrations with a twist

Rara (or Rah Rah) is another music-oriented celebration. Called the rural carnival, it takes place from Ash Wednesday to Easter and is anchored in ancient Voodoo traditions where revellers "raise the roof". At this time of the year, Rara bands can be seen on roads all over Haiti, playfully parading along to their hypnotic music, gathering followers like the Pied Piper of Hamelin.

Papier mâché masks and carved-wood animal figures are only two of the many handicrafts in the repertoire of Jacmel's artisans. Brightly painted objects – boxes, trays, toys and furniture – are another speciality. A typical shiny black lacquer-like base covered with parrots and/or flowers in vibrant colours makes an ideal souvenir to take home.

Colourful Caribbean bougainvillaea.

Like Préfète Duffaut, some of Haiti's best-known painters were born and raised in Jacmel, where Selden Rodman made his home and was one of the first people, along with DeWitt Peters, to promote Haitian *art naïf* (art which emphasises Haiti's African heritage, but with an overlay of classical French influences). Invariably there are less well-known – albeit superb – artists with small studios sprinkled throughout the town, waiting to be discovered.

BELOW: dressed up as devils at Jacmel's Carnival.

For a consultation with a *mambo* (voodoo priestess) in Jacmel, contact Madame Yclide La Guerre at 37 Rue de Cémitier, tel: 288 2420. The cost of a session can escalate quickly, depending on your questions and what remedies she suggests. You give her money for the ingredients, which are additional to her fee, so take along only the amount of money you are prepared to spend.

BELOW: a Haitian country boy.

Because many colonial buildings are still in use, it's easy to visit them. A former residence on Rue Seymour Pradel has been transformed into a North American-owned art gallery named **Salubria**. On leaving the gallery, turn left and walk up a small hill to the **Manoir Alexandre** (tel: 288 2711). This 19th-century patrician home is now a guest house with one of the best views in Jacmel and reasonable rates.

The Marché de Fer was erected two blocks east at Rue Veuve, Rue de l'Église and Rue Vallières. Smaller, and much more manageable than its Port-au-Prince cousin, it has no walls. Vendors sell mainly produce, meat and foodstuffs – no souvenirs in sight. The **Cathédrale de St Phillipe et St Jacques** stands in the middle of the block, directly across Rue de l'Église from the market.

Hidden behind the vendors at the corner with Rue Vallières sits the unprepossessing building where Simón Bolívar lived in exile and where the flag of Venezuela was created. Bolívar trained troops in Haiti and left from Jacmel on his voyage to liberate South America from Spanish rule. Later he was seemingly ambivalent about Haiti's independence because, it is said, he had agreed with Alexandre Pétion not to publicly acknowledge Haiti's support, since Pétion was fearful of renewed European aggression and reprisals.

The first part of Jacmel to be renovated was Rue du Commerce, a wide, pleasant, partly brick-paved street. Many of its 19th-century homes and warehouses are well preserved and have been turned into galleries or *artisanat* (handicraft) shops. The Boucard family home at the corner with Grande Rue is especially noteworthy, and the Vital family warehouse dates from 1865. In the middle of the block between Grande Rue and Avenue de la Liberté, the former residence of Selden Rodman stands out – truly a showplace with much of the original wrought-iron work still intact on stairways, balconies and bridges across the substantial, flower-filled courtyard. It was converted into a peerless haven for guests in 1999. Although there is no sign or number on the outside, it's easily found, right next to **Créations Moro**, the comprehensive lacquerware shop at number 40.

Back to nature

To get back to nature after exploring the city for a while, take Rue Roosevelt, passing some lovely old houses as well as new construction. After a short, easy walk to the top of a hill, there's a gently rolling meadow with several large shade trees and a wonderful, expansive view over all of Jacmel, the harbour and beyond. It has a remarkably rural feel, for a place that is so close to town.

Continue along the path for a grand circle tour of an area that will probably be filled with houses and shops in a few short years. Companions on the path might be either going to market or returning home, the women carrying large baskets on their heads brimming over with produce or charcoal, prodding their fully laden donkeys to get them to move. Men carry machetes or push wheelbarrows full of unwieldy items such as long tree branches and sugar-cane stalks.

To the beaches

Heading east, Jacmel's famous fine sandy beaches are close by. From Jacmel centre take Avenue Barranquilla east towards the airport, where **Le Rendez-Vous** restaurant stays open for snacks all day, seven days a week. Nearby **Fort Ogé** rates a brief stop. An obscure, virtually unknown relic of colonial days is the **Habitation Price**, where the ruins of a former plantation contain a unique steam engine (non-working). Built by the Scottish inventor and mechanical engineer James Watt (1736–1819), there is only one other engine like it in the world. They were used commercially in the sugar-cane industry when most other steam engines were busy pulling railway carriages. This might make an interesting stop for someone with plenty of time to spare and who enjoys a treasure hunt. Since there are no signposts, just turn left after the airport onto a bad road requiring a four-wheel-drive vehicle, especially during or after rain. Even if you find the place, there won't be a lot to see because the engine is in a poor state of repair.

Back on the road towards Marigot, *artisanat* shops in small houses beckon all along the route. After 7 km (4 miles) turn right down a side road to reach the beach, **Plage Cyvadier**, which is actually a little cove with a strip of sand and small rocks. An eponymous small hotel is situated high above the cove, with several buildings, housing the guest rooms, delightfully placed among the verdant gardens and lawns. A freshwater swimming pool graces one end of the grounds and there is a pleasant outdoor terrace (where the restaurant can serve your fresh lobster) under the bougainvillaea, near the steps leading to the pebble and sand beach. The hotel's owner donates part of the establishment's profits to a local school, so a stay at Plage Cyvadier can also help a good cause.

Map on page 278

BELOW: on the way to market.

TIP

When arranging a trip to Bassin Bleu:

● Agree on a price with your guide in advance.

● Be sure to rent horses in Jacmel – hiring them near the falls may prove more expensive.

● Take lots of small change for tips.

BELOW:
St Louis du Sud on the south coast.

Continuing east, the next beach sits right alongside the road 15 km (9 miles) from Jacmel. **Plage Raymond-les-Bains** has fine white sand and gentle waves that lap the beach, making swimming easy and keeping it a popular choice with local people, especially at the weekend. A bit further along, the small town of **Cayes Jacmel** is home to a unique craftsman. Worth a visit, Joseph Franck Pierre builds precise scale models of old sailing ships like the *Santa María*, *Cutty Sark*, and many others. There is also a little park commemorating Toussaint L'Ouverture's sojourn in town.

Plage Ti Mouillage, the next beach on the route, is a favourite with French expatriates. There are actually two beaches, the first of which has a basic restaurant and the second which offers small beach homes for rent. The expatriates often stay in **Marigot**, a little coastal village 10 km (6 miles) further east. From here, a steep, rough trail requires a good four-wheel-drive vehicle to complete the climb up to **Seguin** and on to Parc National La Visite. The area north of Marigot has a well-known hiking trail usually approached from Furcy *(see Excursions from Port-au-Prince, page 301)*.

Excursion to Bassin Bleu

Southwest of Jacmel there isn't much to see, but northwest of the town are the waterfalls of **Bassin Bleu** ㉑, a worthwhile excursion with some of the loveliest views in Haiti. The falls are actually a series of big, natural, deep, blue-green pools and three spectacular waterfalls, which descend in tiers through a fern-covered limestone gorge. An excursion from Jacmel takes most of a day, so don't be fooled if locals say it isn't far, or that it doesn't take much time to get there. And don't even think about going if it has rained.

The 12-km (7-mile) journey to Bassin Bleu is a memorable one. Although it is possible to hire a four-wheel drive vehicle for three-quarters of the trip, it is an extremely bumpy and noisy ride. A far more pleasant way of seeing the countryside is to hire horses or even hike if you are energetic (it takes 1½–2 hours each way), but remember to take plenty of water. If you choose to travel on horseback, you will find the animals to be small and docile, having been broken in at a very young age. Novices and experienced riders are welcome. The expedition should only be tackled with an experienced local guide and it is best to make arrangements in Jacmel, rather than Port-au-Prince. Always agree a price in advance.

The journey begins by crossing **Jacmel River**, where you may find local people washing themselves, their clothes, their animals or their vehicles. In the village on the other side of the river you may be treated as a curiosity, with children running out to stare or shout to the *blancs*. Reaching up into the hills you will be treated to fabulous views down to the Caribbean Sea.

A local guide always takes over from the Jacmel guide for the last kilometre, which is rough and very steep, so you need to be in good physical condition to attempt it. Arrival at the last waterfall requires the aid of a rope (and perhaps a little push from the guide), which means an additional small fee, or tip. Be aware that there will probably be more guides available than tourists, so they will all want to accompany you and all will expect a tip if they help you. Be precise about which man you wish to employ and make it clear that you only need assistance from one person. When you get to the falls you may discover that a local youth who plunges from the uppermost rock into the pool will also expect to be paid for his efforts, so take plenty of small change.

Map on page 278

Hundreds of different animal and plant species thrive in Parc National Macaya, including: 102 different kinds of fern; 99 mosses; 11 butterfly species; 57 types of snail; 28 kinds of amphibian; 34 reptiles, 65 bird species and 19 bats.

BELOW: washing clothes in the river next to the market at Cavaillon.

The far south and southwestern peninsula

All the way to Les Cayes from Port-au-Prince, RN2 provides a sufficiently smooth asphalt road in excellent condition and the scenic 200-km (120-mile) drive takes about 2½ hours. The road runs parallel to the north coast of the peninsula for the first hour. After Léogâne, the siren's call of the broad, beautiful beaches will be tempting, but keep going for another 20 km (12 miles) to a compact little town named **Grand-Goâve**. Bathing beaches between Grand-Goâve and its inaccurately named, much larger neighbour, **Petit-Goâve** (Little Goâve), are worth the wait. Petit Goave is a charming colonial town which sits at the head of a lovely harbour where small boats offer rides to **Cocoyer Beach**, the small sand island out in the bay.

Miragoâne overlooks the next cove, 26 km (16 miles) further on. Still a smugglers' port, it mirrors its larger siblings, Jacmel and Jérémie, with pretty, narrow streets winding down the hill to a bustling harbour. Rather than gold from looted sailing ships, the booty today is contraband from Miami – clothing, shoes and household supplies.

From Miragoâne, the main road turns south to **Les Cayes** ㉒, the site of an annual three-day music festival, the **Fête de Notre Dame,** held on the second weekend in August. The beachfront venue imparts a unique flavour, and competition is stiff because Petit-Goâve also hosts a festival on the same weekend. Entertainment includes top Haitian bands that have achieved stardom and notoriety in Europe, Canada and the US, including Tabou Combo, Ram and Ti Vice *(see More than Merengue page 111)*. Many young Haitians living abroad return home for the festival weekend, driving back and forth between the two towns.

John James Audubon, famous ornithologist and painter, was born in Les Cayes in 1785. Christened Jean-Jacques, he was the illegitimate son of a French naval officer and a Créole woman. Audubon went on to illustrate the monumental Birds of America.

BELOW:

preparing the land for planting in La Vallée.

Map on page 278

Les Cayes has beautiful beaches – calm water and sand like icing sugar – with a couple of basic hotels providing overnight shelter. The town has two other claims to fame – it is the closest town to **Parc National Macaya**, and it is the place where the best road and the worst road in Haiti meet. The best is the RN2; the worst is the RN7 or the RD214.

Sacred Voodoo sites

An extremely difficult road from Les Cayes to Jérémie in the north of the peninsula, RN7 allows access to the national park, the peak at Macaya, the **Kounoubois Caves ㉓** and **Saut Mathurine ㉔**, all near **Camp Perrin**. Camp Perrin still exhibits a few traces of its French colonial origins, such as **le canal de Davezac de Castera**, a canal built in 1749. The Kounoubois caves nearby are sacred Voodoo sites.

It takes half a day to reach the University of Florida base at Plaine Durand on the edge of Parc National Macaya. This very basic campsite remains the only place to stay in the park. It takes another two days each way to make the difficult trek up to the summit of the **Pic de Macaya** (2,347 metres/7,700 ft). Plan well in advance if you intend to make the hike, because you will need to employ an experienced local guide and take along sufficient supplies for the trip.

West of Les Cayes, road conditions are relentlessly bad and will remain so until completion of the coastal highway project. Driving is definitely not recommended after rain because the rivers are swollen and can be treacherous. From Les Cayes it takes about two hours (and possibly a flat tyre) to reach **Port Salut**, which is a great place to enjoy fresh seafood on the beach. A small island just off Macaya Beach, **Coq Anglade**, is little more than a coconut palm-

There was once a waterfall at Saut Mathurine but it was diverted in a hydro-electric scheme to provide power for the southern region.

BELOW: view over Corail to the ocean.

studded expanse of sand. It is possible to walk (or wade) out to reach it. Two other often deserted, undeveloped, palm-lined beaches nearby are **Gelée Beach** and **Pointe Sable**, which has a comfortable little hotel right near the beach.

The islands

The road from Les Cayes to Jérémie is so bad that most travellers usually fly to Jérémie from Port-au-Prince. The risky, 12-hour ferry ride to the southwestern town is not recommended.

Like Île de la Tortue (Turtle Island) up north, **Île-à-Vache** ㉕ (Cow Island) made a perfect pirate's refuge, thanks to numerous hiding places among indentations in the coastline's sheer rock cliffs. Pure white sand beaches bless the rest of the shoreline of this idyllic island near Les Cayes.

Henry Morgan, the infamous Welsh buccaneer who later became governor of Jamaica, used Île-à-Vache as a safe harbour. Here, too, he prepared for his siege of Panama, and in 1668 his ship exploded just off the island's coast.

Although Île-à-Vache is only a short boat ride from the mainland, the ferry schedule benefits workers in Les Cayes who live on the island. It leaves the island at 10am, returning from Les Cayes at 4.30pm, thereby precluding a day trip without organizing transfers from a local fishing boat. A local fisherman will probably be happy to take you across for a small fee, but luckily, there is an alternative solution.

The **Port Morgan** resort solves the lodging problem on Île-à-Vache. Guests can stay overnight and soak up the calm, peaceful atmosphere of the island. If arranged in advance, Port Morgan will pick up guests in its own boat. There is a small marina with shower facilities, a laundromat, fuel and internet access for yachties, making it a popular stopping-off point.

Les Îles Cayemites ㉖ lie off the north coast of the southern peninsula just north of **Pestel**, a pretty fishing village of pastel-coloured houses with a French fort. Thanks to its prime location midway between Miragoâne and Jérémie, Pestel is ideal for watersports and beach activities. **Grande Cayemite**, a large, inhabited and cultivated island, has two towns, an extensive necklace of tiny reef outcroppings and a lighthouse that flashes continually. **Petite Cayemite** is a small beach island. Distinctive from the air, a large stretch of land, the **Presqu'île des Baradères** (meaning almost an island), appears to be an island, but is actually attached to the coast at the western end.

BELOW: travelling by road in the south.

A bird's-eye view

Travelling to Jérémie by road is a long and arduous journey, with a none too safe 12-hour ferry ride as an alternative. If the budget allows, it would be wise to travel by air. Flights from Port-au-Prince to Jérémie feel almost like a tailor-made tour. All that's missing is the commentary. Some of Tropical Airways' aeroplanes have a window that bows out like a big bubble, just behind the cockpit on either side of the plane. If the flight isn't full and conditions are calm, some pilots may allow a passenger up front to stand at the window and shoot a few memorable photographs. The panoramic view of the land below is spectacular.

After take-off, the flight passes over Cité-Soleil shantytown and a boat-speckled Port-au-Prince harbour. The shimmering water below changes colour

Map
on page
278

from muddy brown, due to the run-off at the shore, to dark blue, then quickly to successively lighter, cleaner tones of turquoise as the shallow shoals and reefs surrounding **Île de la Gonâve** pass beneath the silver wings.

Flying slowly across the island, there is time to examine the aerial perspective of the reef system extending a good way out from land. Infinite colour variations of the water are apparent throughout the flight. Hues turn from almost white with just the slightest tinge of blue in shallows where the bottom is obviously sand, to sapphire blue where an edge of the reef suddenly drops away.

On the other side of Île de la Gonâve, flying almost parallel to the Îles Cayemites gives passengers a good look at crops in the fields, two small villages, and surrounding (known as fringing) reefs.

The city of poets

Jérémie ㉗ is in the midst of a renaissance, partly due to a re-awakening of civic pride after the scourge of the Duvalier years and their aftermath. Thanks in part also, to the increased number of flights landing here since Tropical Airways started service in 1999.

In 1964, Papa Doc Duvalier ordered the closure of Jérémie's port, in retaliation for local opposition to his dictatorial methods. With its coffee and cacao exports almost cut off overnight, the town fell into a protracted decline, and the road from Les Cayes literally crumbled away. For many years the town stagnated, living on its memories. Today, however, a measure of optimism is returning, and the population is growing once more, as Haitians who have lived and worked abroad return to build retirement homes and local farmers invest a lifetime's savings in houses in the town.

Jérémie was once a thriving coffee-producing centre but exports were sharply reduced during the 1960s when the town was isolated from the rest of the country by the dictator, Papa Doc Duvalier.

BELOW: at home in Grande Cayemite.

Haitian cacao produces chocolate using traditional methods.

BELOW:
coffee workers preparing beans.

By the beginning of the 21st century Jérémie, the once-booming coffee- and cacao-exporting centre known as the "City of Poets" (because of the town's notable poets such as Émile Roumer), remained undiscovered by most tourists. The neglected cast-iron-adorned Victorian buildings are beginning to be painted and renovated. Coffee growing and exporting are increasing; the production of coffee never stopped, but it was on a smaller scale because much of the land was given over to food crops during the hard times.

On the wharf and in large cement yards behind the warehouses, visitors can watch the start of the chocolate production process, virtually unchanged since production began. One man heaves a heavy sack on his shoulders; a second slits a corner of the sack. The first worker walks back and forth distributing the falling cacao beans in even rows, while the second rakes the beans to spread them for drying in the sun. Luckily for sweet-tooths, the September to February growing season for cacao makes chocolate available for Christmas and Easter. Even more fortuitous for Jérémie is the fact that a world shortage of chocolate has led companies like the US giant Hershey, with its cooperative in Dame Marie, to look to Haiti to fill the gap.

From the centre of Jérémie, Rue Roumer (named after the celebrated Haitian poet) becomes Rue Borges on the way up to the guest houses which sit above the central area, also called Borges. Driving up the pock-marked, rain-ravaged streets requires a sturdy four-wheel-drive vehicle and even those can barely make the climb. Almost everyone in Jérémie seems more friendly and open, and less guarded than in other places in Haiti. Perhaps because Jérémie has been isolated for so long and has had precious few visitors, residents have not yet had experiences to make them wary of strangers.

Another reason for the locals' openness is that most strangers who have been in the region recently have been there as part of international aid programmes. They continue to make tremendous strides in tackling health problems, particularly for women and children isolated in the mountains. The small clinic run by the Haitian Health Foundation is staffed by a team which includes multilingual doctors and North American nurses. The modern equipment is some of the best in Haiti.

Born in Jérémie, General Alexandre Dumas, the father of Alexandre Dumas *père* and grandfather of Alexandre Dumas *fils* would be proud of his native town. He rose to be a general in Napoleon's revolutionary French army, while his son wrote the famous novel *The Count of Monte Cristo*. The Dumas family typified the old light-skinned élite, educated in France, who dominated Jérémie and incurred Papa Doc Duvalier's wrath.

Party town

The use of generators, in the face of constant power cuts, has re-invigorated nightlife in Jérémie. Two of the many places to party are **Le Vertigo Beach**, a lively disco, and **Ma Folie**, a large spot with a restaurant on one level and dancing to bright flashing lights on the floor above. As in other places, such as Cap Haïtien and Jacmel, the **Alliance Française** offers a multitude of activities and classes. It has a restaurant and tennis courts, and is an excellent place to find out what's happening in town. The **Castillo Restaurant and Bar** opens at 7am for breakfast and continues until 3am the next morning when the disco closes.

Jérémie's most famous delicacy is *comparette*, a cake-like bread (also rolls) made from flour, cinnamon and ginger. Bring some as a gift to a Haitian anywhere else in the country and it is likely to be greatly appreciated.

Map on page 278

Some Peace Corps volunteers work way up in the mountains. There are no telephones, no electricity and no running water. It is a six hour walk, each way, to town.

BELOW: a country cottage.

Map on page 278

Much of Jérémie reveals spectacular views of the coastline. High regions provide uninterrupted vistas of steep cliffs that seem to run out to infinity. Empty white sand beaches sparkle in the sunlight and the startling, brilliant blue sea merges into frothy white clouds at the horizon. The colours of the sky are constantly changing. An early morning, pale pink tint as the sky awakens from slumber deepens to darker rose, melts into a golden glow that suddenly bursts into bright sunlight. Throughout the day the greens and greys, the muted or electric blues run through the rainbow's hues at the whim of the clouds. Sunsets are breathtaking. Night skies seem to reach down to enfold the observer, perhaps because the air is clear and there are no other lights to rob the stars of their brilliance.

Excursions from Jérémie

Anse d'Azur ㉘ is picture-postcard perfect. This scenic, sand beach lies halfway between Jérémie and the airport. Look for a small opening in the vegetation, then walk past the foundations of a building and down steep cement steps to the long, half moon-shaped cove. The calm, shallow waters, sheltered by the curve of the lush green, hilly coastline, are ideal for snorkelling. Just a short swim from the beach, the rusted metal frame of a sunken boat (with part of its engine intact) sticks up from the water. A variety of flourescent small fish dart in and out of the skeletal hulk. There's also a good-sized cave at the end of the beach, which you can enter by swimming or wading a short distance.

Further west around the coast is **Anse du Clerc**. The drive here is a bone-jarring, bouncing trip along the rock- and pothole-strewn dirt tracks and requires rocky river crossings. Along the way take a slight detour to **Bonbon** ㉙, a picturesque fishing village. It is not a place to buy souvenirs, but it provides a window in to the lives of rural Haitians, without having to hike for hours to an isolated mountain village.

Bonbon consists of a group of about 20 quite small and neat little mud houses painted in the bright blues, pinks and greens that are common in the Caribbean. There is a police commissary and a small schoolhouse with open sides and a line of benches where the children sit during lessons.

In an area set a little apart, local women sit on the ground to sell their wares – a few small fish, some fruit or vegetables and a few household items spread out before them. Carefree children run around happily in various states of undress. It's heart-wrenching to notice that some exhibit signs of malnutrition. However, they are unsurprisingly curious to look over any strangers who appear so far off the tourist track.

A scenic 7-km (4-mile) ride west from Bonbon over low mountains and around a scenic bay leads to **Abricots**, the centre of *artisanat* for the district. Literally the end of the road, only dirt tracks continue from here to the town of **Dame Marie** located at the western tip of the peninsula. Further still is Anse d'Hainault, which has a quiet beach and outside of town is a natural warm spring. ❏

BELOW: people from Jérémie are friendly. **RIGHT:** the hills dwarf a sailboat in St Louis du Sud.

CENTRAL HAITI, THE WEST AND THE ARTIBONITE VALLEY

Map on page 278

The centre of the country consists of vast grasslands, a fertile valley and a resort coastline, all divided by inhospitable mountain ranges, making travel by four-wheel drive imperative

Grass-covered savannah dotted with grazing cattle stretches as far as the eye can see over the Plateau Central, for this vast, flat, sparsely populated region, bordered by the Massif des Montagnes Noires to the south and the Chaine de la Grande Rivière du Nord to the north, is mainly an agricultural area. In the centre of it all lies the little town of Hinche, where the cows, goats, chickens and other livestock are brought to market twice a week. It is not an easy ride to Hinche, 171 km (80 miles) away from Port au Prince: the RN3 crosses the Plaine du Cul-de-Sac simply enough before climbing over the Montagnes du Trou d'Eau, then winding down to Mirebalais on the upper reaches of the Rivière de l'Artibonite. From here the road becomes rough and difficult, especially after rain and since Hurricane Georges caused the Barrage de Peligré (dam) to overflow in 1998, destroying much of the road system. It is advisable to travel in a four-wheel drive or expect a seven-hour bus ride.

PRECEDING PAGES: paddy fields in Haiti's rice basket. **LEFT:** rice drying in the sun. **BELOW:** Bassin Zim.

The Rivière de l'Artibonite flows west through a giant chequer board of paddy fields, known as the country's rice basket, which are home to a wide variety of egrets and many species of heron. Just over the mountain range to the south – "Behind the mountain there are more mountains" so the Créole saying goes – runs the Côte des Arcadins where Haiti's best beach resorts lie, washed by clear blue water, perfect for swimming and snorkelling. Opposite, three small sandy islands or cays, called the Arcadins, provide good diving around their coral reefs.

Hinche – a central market town

A quintessentially rural town, **Hinche** ㉚ (pop. 53,000) comes alive on market days. Peasants pour in over the bridge across the broad River Guayamoue, hoping to sell their cattle, pigs, goats and large basins full of turkeys balanced on their heads. The market is on Rue Stenio Vincent, east of the *tap-tap* depot, and it spills out into the surrounding streets, transforming the town. Here many small restaurants offer typical Haitian dishes of rice, beans and meat.

Rue J.J. Dessalines leads south from the bus station to **Place Charlemagne Péralte**. This dusty square is dedicated to the heroic son of Hinche, Charlemagne Péralte, who was the leader of the Cacos Resistance against the US military occupation in 1915. The Cacos were a band of black partisan irregulars from the Plateau Central who originally formed in 1867 in opposition to the Government. They survived, on and off, as a resistance force until their prodigious struggle against the US military and its practice of *corvée*,

*The Plateau Central
area around Hinche,
northeast of Port-au-
Prince, has been a
hotbed of peasant
unrest for some time.
The military
crackdown following
the 1991 coup
was especially
harsh here.*

enforced labour gangs for road building. After nearly two years of guerrilla warfare, Péralte was captured and executed by the US army which soon crushed the rebellion. The square is overlooked by Hinche's 16th-century cathedral whose interior easily rivals that of the modern one on Rue C. Heureuse.

About 15 km (9 miles) northeast of Hinche is **Bassin Zim ③**, a stunning waterfall which flows rather than cascades over a massive smooth rock into a 50-meter (164-ft) wide milky blue pool. It is a wonderful pool for swimming, although there are no changing facilities, just the odd rock to hide behind. From there a local guide (for a small fee) can show you the way, chopping away at the undergrowth with his machete as he goes, to the **Grottes du Bassin Zim**, about a 20-minute walk along a small path that requires some scrambling and climbing. The caves, hidden among rich green ferns and trees, are cold and dark and contain ancient wall drawings, thought to be relics of the indigenous Taíno Amerindians. Bassin Zim is at the end of a 5-km (3-mile) track past Papaye, off the road to Cap-Haïtien; a four-wheel-drive vehicle is essential as there are no buses. However, a *tap-tap* can take you to the hot springs at **Cerca-la-Source ③**, 30 km (19 miles) east of Hinche near the border – an experience in itself.

The fertile Vallée de l'Artibonite

The source of the Rivière de l'Artibonite lies across the border in the Dominican Republic. When it finally reaches the west coast of Haiti it has broadened into a grand and powerful navigable river, irrigating the fertile rice-producing region of the **Vallée de l'Artibonite**. The landscape around **Pont Sondé**, on RN1 is a patchwork of many small, intensely green, rice paddies delineated by a network of irrigation canals. Turning east you reach the small unassuming

BELOW:
bagging the rice
can be tiring work.

market town of **Petite Rivière de l'Artibonite** ㉝, where two blocks behind the restored church stands the **Palais des 365 Portes**, built by Henri Christophe as his provincial headquarters. There are actually only about 60 exterior doors and windows on this fascinating building, which has since been used as both a school and a town hall.

Continuing east, the road leads uphill to the remains of **Fort Crète-à-Pierrot** where, in 1802, Dessalines' army of slaves bravely withstood General Leclerc's French forces in a key battle in the blacks' struggle for independence. The view of the river is splendid from here. After rejoining RN1 at L'Estère, the road continues north to Gonaïves passing the dusty, desert-like region of **Savane Désolée**, strewn with brushwood and dotted with large cacti.

West coast blues

Although historically important as the spot where Haiti's independence was declared by Dessalines in 1804, **Gonaïves** ㉞ is notorious as the most charmless city in the country. Sprawling, flat and dusty, it lies beside slovenly, brackish beaches and much of the municipal architecture is modern and soulless. **Place de l'Independence** contains a monument to Dessalines, depicting him at the helm of a ship representing Haiti. An ugly, modernist cathedral dominates the square which doubles as an expansive bicycle repair yard, lined with stalls fixing and selling wheels, tyres and frames: the bicycle is king in Gonaïves. The **Memorial de l'Independence** stands on Rue Liberté to the west, leading down to the ramshackle, but busy, docks. Avoid the beaches just to the north of town, as they are believed to have been used as a dump for US toxic ash in 1988.

South of Gonaïves, 75 km (46 miles) away, you come to the lively port of

Map on page 278

Dessalines, about 20 km (12 miles) to the north of Petite Rivière along a rough road, was made Haiti's capital by the rebel leader after declaring independence in 1804. A hike into the surrounding hills with a guide will reveal the remains of the seven forts that Dessalines built to protect his stronghold.

BELOW: market day in Hinche.

Map on page 278

TIP

The spacious dockside Venus Restaurant, on the western edge of Saint-Marc's central park, is a perfect place for watching the cargo ships laboriously unload by rowing boat.

BELOW: a peaceful moment by the sea, Arcahaie.
RIGHT: mother and daughter returning home from market.

Saint-Marc ❸, an idiosyncratic, tumbledown town crowded with wooden, two-storey houses held together by corrugated iron, cardboard and hope. Saint-Marc was an important port during the colonial era and still handles and exports the sugar, bananas and rice produced in the Vallée de l'Artibonite. On the edge of town, small lard and soap factories provide more employment.

Smart resorts on the Côte des Arcadins

The **Côte des Arcadins** ❸ runs from Delugé, 16 km (10 miles) south of Saint-Marc, to Cabaret 45 km (28 miles) away, and has long, white beaches with safe, shallow waters for bathing *(see page 302)*. The coastline is backed by the denuded **Chaine des Matheux** mountain range and to the southwest, 5 km (3 miles) out to sea, lie **Les Arcadins**. These three sand cays are encircled by a clearly visible coral reef which provides endless entertainment for scuba divers. At the northern end, the small town of **Montrouis** has developed a good reputation for its tasty, cheap roadside food. The main road is lined with covered stalls serving a range of dishes from rice and beans, *mayi moulen* and fried *lambi (see page 138)* to fresh avocados and pineapples.

Most of Haiti's luxury beach resorts are located along the Côte des Arcadins and offer all-inclusive deals as well as day tickets for non-residents, which usually include a meal and the use of sports facilities. The resort of **Moulin sur la Mer** (tel: 223 5700), 3 km (2 miles) north of Montrouis, is built around a restored 17th-century building, housing a museum dedicated to the colonial period. An intact sugar press stands outside. The **Ouanga Bay Beach Hotel** (tel: 257 7889), 8 km (5 miles) south of Montrouis, has a warm and friendly atmosphere and has a nightclub with live music at weekends. Further south, the **Plage Publique** lies awkwardly, but promisingly, between the more upmarket, expensive all-inclusives of **Kaliko Beach Resort** (tel: 298 4609) and **Wahoo Bay Beach** (tel: 223 2950), which organises horse-riding trips into the mountains. The public beach was opened in 1997 by President Preval as a free beach for Haitians and has a lively atmosphere with impromptu bands dotted about, wild soccer games and people selling drinks and cheap food. The **Kyona Beach Club** (tel: 257 6863) is the most accessible resort from Port-au-Prince and therefore the busiest.

Ile de la Gonâve ❸, 20 km (12 miles) out in the Golfe de la Gonâve, is the largest of Haiti's coastal islands and is overpopulated by families trying to scrape a living fishing in the depleted waters, and farming in mostly arid and inhospitable conditions. Boats leave daily from a small wharf at **Carries**, north of Wahoo Bay Beach, which was once Baby Doc Duvalier's beach house.

The last major town before Port-au-Prince, 30 km (18 miles) away, **Cabaret** ❸ is a strange anomaly of Haitian architecture standing as a sad and desperate relic of Papa Doc's fragile ego. The town was conceived and partially built in 1961 as Haiti's answer to Brasília, and named Duvalierville. Recently renamed, all that remains of its Duvalierist legacy is an enormous, modernist cockfighting stadium. ❏

INSIGHT GUIDES
Travel Tips

✴ INSIGHT GUIDES Phonecard

One global card to keep travellers in touch. Easy. Convenient. Saves you time and money.

It's a global phonecard

Save up to 70%* on international calls from over 55 countries

Free 24 hour global customer service

Recharge your card at any time via customer service or online

It's a message service

Family and friends can send you voice messages for free.

Listen to these messages using the phone* or online

Free email service - you can even listen to your email over the phone*

It's a travel assistance service

24 hour emergency travel assistance – if and when you need it.

Store important travel documents online in your own secure vault

For more information, call rates, and all Access Numbers in over 55 countries, (check your destination is covered) go to **www.insightguides.ekit.com** or call Customer Service.

JOIN now and receive US$ 5 bonus when you join for US$ 20 or more.

Join today at

www.insightguides.ekit.com

When requested use ref code: **INSAD0103**

OR SIMPLY FREE CALL
24 HOUR CUSTOMER SERVICE

UK	0800 376 1705
USA	1800 706 1333
Canada	1800 808 5773
Australia	1800 11 44 78
South Africa	0800 997 285

THEN PRESS ⓪

For all other countries please go to "Access Numbers" at **www.insightguides.ekit.com**

* Retrieval rates apply for listening to messages. Savings based on using a hotel or payphone and calling to a landline. Correct at time of printing 01.03

(INS001)

powered by ✴ekit

"The easiest way to make calls and receive messages around the world"

CONTENTS

Getting Acquainted

Geography

The Dominican Republic has three main mountain systems: the Cordillera Central (Central Range), the Cordillera Septentrional (Northern Range) and the Cordillera Oriental (Eastern Range). The Central Range is the largest in area. Features of this range are Pico Duarte, the highest peak in the Antilles at 3,087 metres (10,128 ft), waterfalls such as Baiguate and Jimenoa, and several national parks and scientific reserves. The Central Range also gives rise to some of the country's most important rivers, including its longest river, Yaque del Norte, which is ideal for river rafting. The Northern Range runs parallel to the Central Range, separating the Cibao Valley from the Atlantic Coastal Plain. The highest elevation of this range is Pico Diego de Ocampo, which is also a scientific reserve. The amber mines near Puerto Plata are also in this mountain range. The Eastern Range is the shortest of the three ranges.

El Morro in Monte Cristi, in the northwest, is also noteworthy as are the Siete Hermanos (Seven Brothers) keys – ideal for scuba diving and fishing.

There are also five *sierras* or minor mountain ranges: Sierra de Samaná, Sierra de Yamasa, Sierra de Martín García, Sierra de Neiba and Sierra de Bahoruco.

Several rivers irrigate the Dominican Republic, some of which are used to generate electric power via hydroelectric dams.

Climate

The average temperature in the Dominican Republic is 25°C (77°F) year-round. The climate on the coasts is more tropical than in the central part of the country, where temperatures are cooler at higher altitude.

The average amount of rainfall varies depending on where you are in the country. On the northern coast the rainy season falls in Oct–April/May and in the south it is from May–Oct/Nov.

The northern and eastern towns have the most rain.

Average annual rainfall:

Puerto Plata	177 cm
Monte Cristi	68 cm
Santo Domingo	118 cm

Hurricane season runs from June through November.

Earthquakes of varying intensity are also a potential hazard, they tend to strike mainly in the north.

Economy

Four major industries sustain the Dominican Republic's economy: agriculture, mining, tourism and duty-free zones. In recent years tourism and duty free zones have been the most dynamic money-earners. Presently, tourism provides the greatest economic gain to the country, followed by duty-free zones in which textiles, electronic equipment, cigars etc are produced for export.

The main exports in the agricultural sector are coffee, cacao, sugar, pineapples, oranges, plantains, bananas, vegetables and flowers. The Cibao Valley region is not only rich in agricultural products but is also home to large deposits of ferronickel and the largest open gold mine on the continent, La Rosario Dominicana. Other mined exports are gypsum, marble and rock salt.

Government

Like other parts of Latin America, in the 20th century the Dominican Republic went through periods of political unrest, violent changes in its government and civil war. However, in the last four decades it has been able to develop into a representative democracy.

The Dominican Republic's democratic government is divided into three branches: Executive, Legislative and Judicial. Free elections take place every four years. The capital city and seat of government is Santo Domingo. The president names the provincial governors, who are his representatives in those provinces. The Senate elects the judiciary.

Planning the Trip

Visas & Passports

A visa is not required to enter the Dominican Republic for citizens and legal residents of Australia, Canada, Ireland, the European Union and the UK and the USA. Citizens of these countries require a tourist card (US$10) and must carry a valid passport and their residency card. They can stay for a maximum of 90 days. Citizens of all other countries need an entry visa.

Additional information from: Visa Section, Consular Department of the Foreign Office, tel: (809) 535 6280, ext. 326.

Customs

Articles classified as personal luggage will not be a problem for clearing customs. You are permitted to bring into the country 1 litre of alcohol, 200 cigarettes and gift articles with a value of no more that US$100. Your reception may depend on where your flight is coming from and the attitude of the inspector greeting you, but usually he or she will let you through with a friendly smile. Your luggage may be inspected.

Money Matters

The Dominican monetary unit is the peso (RD$). Coins are 1, 5, 10, 25 and 50 cents and 1 peso, and bills are in denominations of 5, 10, 20, 50. 100, 500, 1000 pesos. You will receive more for your dollars or pounds if you exchange them at a commercial bank upon your arrival in the country. By law, banks are required to place a slate in public view stating the daily exchange rate.

Health Precautions

The Dominican Republic is a safe destination provided you take the proper precautions. It is advisable to visit your GP prior to travelling to the island. Review your immunisation records with your doctor in order to verify what you need. The vaccinations recommended to all visitors to the tropical Caribbean islands are Hepatitis A and Hepatitis B.

Tap water is not safe to drink on the island. Visitors should drink bottled water or purified water which is available everywhere. For people travelling to major hotels and resorts, there are clinics available on the premises. Otherwise, local hospitals and clinics will treat independent travellers. In any case, make sure you have adequate health insurance.

Most hotels, restaurants and commercial establishments accept major credit cards and they are legally bound to use the correct exchange rate on them. US dollars are also widely accepted.

What to Bring

Light-weight clothes made of natural fibres are most comfortable while touring during the day. Be sure to pack bathing suits, sunscreen, sunglasses and comfortable shoes.

When visiting churches, men should uncover their heads as a sign of respect. Women do not need to cover their heads, though it is customary to wear a long-sleeved dress when attending a religious service. Entering a church wearing shorts may be interpreted as offensive.

Men attending a conference or on a business trip will occasionally need to wear a jacket and tie, and may need a tuxedo. On formal occasions a white suit is worn here and ladies wear evening gowns. On cool nights, from November to February, ladies may wish to carry a light shawl.

Getting There

Direct scheduled or charter flights from Europe depart from airports in London, Madrid, Barcelona, Berlin, Munich, Milan, Rome, Lisbon, Amsterdam, Bonn, Dusseldorf, Stuttgart, Brussels, Frankfurt, Helsinki and Paris, among others.

North American routes link the Dominican Republic with Toronto, Montreal, Ottawa, Quebec City, Halifax, Dallas, Minneapolis, Miami, Boston, Newark, New York and Detroit. There are also direct flights from Latin American cities including Caracas, Panama City, Lima, Santiago de Chile, Buenos Aires, Bogotá and Cancún.

Connections with neighbouring Caribbean islands are frequent with direct flights to and from Haiti, Antigua, the Netherlands Antilles, the French Antilles, Jamaica, Cuba and Trinidad and Tobago.

Over 60 charter airlines fly to the international airports of Puerto Plata, Punta Cana and Santo Domingo.

AIRLINES

From Europe: Martinair Holland, Iberia, Air Europa, Air France, LTU, Condor, Lauda-Air, Sobelair, Britannia Air, Leisure Air, Hapag Lloyd, Air 2000.

From North America: US Airways, American Airlines, Aerocontinente Dominicana, Air Atlanta, North American Airlines, Continental, Pan American, USA 3000 Airlines, Air Transat, Royal, Sky Service, Canair, Air Santo Domingo, Aeromar.

Inter-Caribbean: LIAT, BWIA, Air Jamaica, Tropic Air, Martinair Holland, Dutch Caribbean Express, Air Caraïbes, Air France, Iberia, Cubana de Aviación, Aeropostal, American Eagle, Transmeridian Airlines, Aerocaribbean, TCI Sky King.

From Central America: Aerocaribe, Copa.

From South America: Aeropostal, Copa, ACES, Aserca, Lan Chile, Air Plus Argentina.

Tourism Offices Abroad

In the UK:
Dominican Republic Tourist Board, 20 Hand Court, High Holborn, London WC1V 6JF. Tel: 020 7242 7778; Fax: 020 7405 4202 Email: inglaterra@sectur.gov.do. Or alternatively visit the Dominican Republic Tourist Board website: http://www.dominicana.com.do.

In the US:
Dominican Republic Tourist Board, 136 E 57th Street, Suite 803, New York, NY 10022. Tel: 212-588 1012; Fax: 212-588 1015 Email: newyork@sectur.gov.do 248 NW Le Jeune Road, Miami, Florida 33126. Tel: 305-444 4592; Fax: 305-444 4845 Email: miami@sectur.gov.do.

Tour Operators

SANTO DOMINGO

Caribbean Connections, Siervas de María 2, Naco., Santo Domingo. Tel: 549 4010; Fax: 566 8393. Email: James.garcia@codetel.net.do
Omni Tours, Ave. Lope de Vega 59, Santo Domingo. Tel: 565 6591; Fax: 567 4710. Email: Omni.tours@codetel.net.do
Turinter, Leopoldo Navarro 2, Gazcue, Santo Domingo. Tel: 686 4020; Fax: 688 3890. Email: manager@turinter.com Also has offices in Puerto Plata, Punta Cana and Juan Dolio.
Prieto Tours, Ave. Francia 125, Santo Domingo. Tel: 685 0102; Fax: 685 0457. Email: incoming@prieto-tours.com Offices also in Puerto Plata, Punta Cana, Samaná and Juan Dolio.
Temptation Tour and Travel, Plaza Francesca, Abraham Lincoln, Suite 229, Santo Domingo. Tel: 227 6651; Fax: 227 6696
Touridea, Leonor de Ovando 57, Santo Domingo. Tel. 685 7525; Fax: 682 0302. Email: Touridea@codetel.net.do

---

THE NORTH

Cocotours, Apartado Postal 4634, Santo Domingo. Tel: 586 1311; fax: 261 0004. Email: info@cocotours.com
Go Dominican Tours, Plaza Turisol 16, Puerto Plata. Tel: 586 5969; Fax: 586 8641. Email: godominican@codetel.net.do

Getting Hitched in the Dominican Republic

Tropical weddings in the Dominican Republic are increasingly popular with couples who want to combine the ceremony and honeymoon and bring friends and family along too. Whether you want to tie the knot on a picture-postcard beach or in a pretty Caribbean chapel, most tour operators, hotels and resorts offer all-in packages. Some hotels have dedicated wedding planners who can organise packages that include an indoor or outdoor ceremony, the services of a civil judge, wedding cake, champagne and flowers. Other services include music, photography and video.

Reservations should be made at least one month in advance.

Popular places to get hitched are Samaná, Punta Cana and Playa Grande, or lively Santo Domingo, Puerto Plata, Boca Chica and Playa Dorada.

Before the ceremony the couple must fulfil a three-day residential requirement and provide the following official documents translated into Spanish:
● a notarised statement of their country of origin, legalised in the Dominican Consulate, indicating their current marital status.
● legalised copies of any divorce papers.
● valid passports (also required for any foreign witness).
● an original birth certificate.

Practical Tips

Postal Services

The Dominican postal service (Inposdom) has offices in every city as well as in airports and resorts.

Telephone & Fax

The international dialling code for the Dominican Republic is **809**. The country has a modern telecommunications network via telephone, telex, cable, internet and fax, available 24 hours a day, every day. Public payphones are commonplace in towns and cities.

Two main telephone companies serve the entire country:
Cotedel, 8am–10pm daily. Services include internet access and fax.
Tricom, 9am–5pm Mon–Sat.

There are also several other smaller companies which provide a telephone service including Turitel and All America.
International access codes:
MCI: 1 800 888 8000; Sprint: 1 800 751 7877; AT&T: 1 800 872 2881

Embassies & Consulates

The following countries have diplomatic representation in Santo Domingo:
Canada: Ave. Máximo Gómez 30, tel: 689 0002 Email: e.canada@codetel.net.do
Haiti: Juan Sánchez Ramírez 33, tel: 686 5778; fax: 686 6096, Email: Amb.haiti@codetel.net.do
UK: 27 de febrero 233, tel: 472 7111; fax: 472 7574
USA: César Nicolás Pensón, tel: 221 2171; fax: 686 7437

International Organisations

Apostolic Nunciature
Máximo Gómez 27
Tel: 682 3773; Fax 687 0287
Email: nuncap.rd@codetel.net.do
UNESCO
Apartado Postal 25350
(Hotel El Ambajador)
Tel: 221 4575; Fax: 221 4581
Email: santo-domingo@unesco.org
UNICEF
Aybar Castellanos 165
Tel: 540 2868; Fax: 540 3905
Email: santodom@unicef.org

The Tourist Office

The main office of the Secretaria
de Estado de Turismo
(Department of Tourism) is on
Avenida México, Santo Domingo.
tel: 1-809 221 4660, 1-200-
3500 (toll-free in Dominican
Republic); fax: 682 3806;
email: sectur@codetel.net.do.
There are other offices on: Calle
Isabel La Catolica in the Zona
Colonial; in Puerto Plata, tel: 686
3858.

Disabled Travellers

The Dominican Republic is not yet
fully equipped to accommodate
disabled travellers, but it is
possible to find hotels that can
meet your needs. Consult your
travel agent, or one of the following
organisations that specialise in
advising disabled travellers:
Access to Travel Magazine Inc.
PO Box 43, Delmar,
NY 12054 1105, USA
Tel: 518 439 4146
Fax: 518 439 9004
Accent on Living
P.O. Box 700, Bloomington,
IL 61702, USA
Tel: 800 787 8444 or 309 378 2961
Fax: 309 378 4420
Email: acntlvng@aol.com
**Royal Association For Disability
and Rehabilitation** (RADAR)
12 City Forum, 250 City Road,
London EC1V 8AF, UK
Tel: 020 7250 3222

Fax: 020 7250 0212
Minicom: 020 7250 4119
Email: radar@radar.org.uk
**Society for Accessible Travel and
Hospitality** (SATH)
347 5TH Ave, Suite 610, New York,
NY 10016, USA
Tel: 212 447 7284
Fax: 212 725 8253
Email: info@sath.org

Women Travellers

Women travelling alone can move
around relatively safely in the
Dominican Republic. Stick to
populated areas by day and night.
And don't be surprised if local men
blatantly attempt to charm you.

Travelling with Children

Most larger hotels and resort
complexes offer facilities and a
range of entertainment activities for
children, as well as the services of
trained child minders.

Medical Services

There are clinics and hospitals in
most large towns and cities. Ask at
your hotel to recommend a doctor
or the nearest pharmacy.

Hospitals
Centro Cardiovascular
Josefa Perdomo 152
Santo Domingo
Tel: 682 6071
Hospital Jose Maria Cabral
Ave. Central
Santiago
Tel: 583 4311
Centro Médico Oriental
Sta. Rosa
Puerto Plata
Tel: 586 2210
Hospiten Bávaro
Carretera Higüey-Punta Cana
Tel: 686 1414

Media

There are five morning
newspapers and two afternoon
papers with nationwide
circulation, edited in Santo
Domingo: *El Caribe, El Nuevo
Diario, El Siglo, Hoy, Listin Diario,
El Nacional* and *Ultima Hora*. The
morning paper, *La Informacion*,
is edited in Santiago de los
Caballeros. There is also a
weekly English newspaper, *Santo
Domingo News,* with information
oriented towards tourists, and a
magazine, *Bohio Domincana*,
with international coverage and
specialising in tourist
information, published in English
and Spanish.
   There are 179 AM-FM radio
stations and 10 television
stations. Most hotels also offer
cable TV.

Security and Crime

In an emergency, dial **911**.
This 24-hour number will connect
you with the police, Red Cross, fire
service, civil defence and
emergency centres.
   Due to the authorities'
crackdown on drugs, the Dominican
Republic is one of the safest
destinations in the Caribbean.
However, it is important to be
cautious. Do not carry large
amounts of money on your person;
do not leave valuables unattended
at any time and avoid walking along
unlit streets after dark.
   The Department of Tourism has a
special security force called the
Politur or *Policia Turistica* (Tourist
Police). Officers provide information
and guidance to visitors on security
matters. For the national call
service contact: Tel: 686
8639/8301; 1-200 3500 (toll-free
in country of origin only).

Business Hours

In general shops and places of
business are open at the following
times:
Banks: Mon–Fri 8.30am–3.30pm

Public Holidays

January 1	New Year's Day
January 21	Day of Our Lady of Altagracia
February 27	Independence Day
March or April	Easter (variable)
	Good Friday (variable)
May or June	Corpus Christi (variable)
September 24	Day of Our Lady of Mercedes
December 25	Christmas Day

The following holidays are observed on the closest Monday to these fixed dates:

January 6	Epiphany
January 26	Juan Pablo Duarte's birthday
May 1	Labour Day
August 16	Dominican Restoration Day
November 6	Constitution Day

Government offices: Mon–Fri 7.30am–2.30pm
Commercial offices:
Mon–Fri 8.30am–12.30pm and 2.30–6.30pm, or 9.am–5.30pm
Shops: Mon–Fri 9am–7pm. Large stores stay open Saturday, and sometimes on Sunday, until 2pm.
Note: some shops and businesses close for siesta or a long lunch break between 12.30 and 2.30pm.

Tipping

In addition to a 12 percent tax restaurants add a 10 percent service charge to all bills, which is passed on to employees. It is customary to tip an extra 10 percent for good service.

Religious Services

Ninety-five percent of Dominicans are Roman Catholic, but other denominations include Anglican, Baptist, Evangelical, Seventh day Adventist and Mormon. Services in English are held in some city churches. The synagogue in Santo Domingo has a service on Friday evening.

Getting Around

From the Airport

The Dominican Republic has 8 international airports including Las Américas International, 20km (12 miles) east of Santo Domingo; Herrerra International (to be replaced by the new La Isabela airport) in the capital city; General Gregorio Luperón 18km (11 miles) from Puerto Plata; Punta Cana; La Romana; Cibao International in Santiago. The María Montez International in Barahona and the Arroyo Barril International in Samaná do not have a regular air service yet.

Most hotels and tour operators can organise transfers to and from the airport. But if you are travelling independently then your best bet would be to take a taxi. Always agree on a fee for the journey before entering the taxi.

By Air

Air Santo Domingo, a local airline, offers daily scheduled flights between the airports in or near the country's tourist and business centres.

Driving

Driving in the Dominican Republic can be hairy, so you are advised to drive defensively and with extreme caution. If you are involved in an accident, as a visitor, you will be expected to foot the bill for any repairs, even if the prang is not your fault. Ensure that any motor vehicle insurance you buy is fully comprehensive.

Remember to drive on the right and avoid driving at night.

CAR RENTAL

Car rental can be very expensive and involve bureaucratic form filling. To hire a vehicle drivers need to be at least 25 years old with a valid driver's licence from their country of origin (or an international licence) and have a major credit card. Hiring a motorbike (*motoconcho*) is an inexpensive and convenient alternative to a car for getting around town, but it can be dangerous and helmets may not always be provided.

If you plan to tour the island it would be wise to rent a 4-wheel-drive vehicle which can handle the sometimes rough, hilly country roads. While many roads are well-maintained others, especially in remote areas, appear to be little more than two-vehicle dirt tracks.

All the major car rental agencies, including Hertz, Avis, Thrifty, Budget and Dollar have a booth at the airports and in larger cities. Alternatively, book before you leave home.

Avis
Ave. Abraham Lincoln
Esq Sarasota
Santo Domingo
Tel: 535 7191
Antigua Autopista Duarte (km 2)
Santiago
Tel: 582 7007
Carretera Luperon (km 4½)
Puerto Plata
Tel: 586 4436
Casa de Campo Resort
La Romana
Tel: 221 0972
Marquez 35
La Romana
Tel: 550 0600

Budget
Ave. JFK Esq-Lope de Vega
Santo Domingo
Tel: 567 0177

Hertz
Mercantile Santo Domingo
Ave. Independencia 454
Santo Domingo
Tel: 221 5333
Fax: 221 8927

Casa de Campo Resort
La Romana
Tel: 523 8988
Fax: 221 8927

Nelly Rent-a-car
Ave. Independencia 654
Santo Domingo
Tel: 687 7997
Fax: 687 7263
Calle Estrella Sadhalá 204
esq. Proyecto
Santiago
Tel: 583 6695
Fax: 583 6698
La Union International Airport
Puerto Plata
Tel: 586 0505

Thrifty
Avenida 27 de Febrero 12
Santo Domingo
Tel: 685 9191
Ave. Duarte Esquina Maimón
Santiago
Tel: 583 5222

By Taxi

Private taxis are available 24 hours in Santo Domingo, Santiago and Puerto Plata and can be found outside the major hotels.

Not all taxis are metered so it is recommended that visitors always agree on a fare before getting into the vehicle so there will be no misunderstanding when you reach your destination.

Jumping on the back of a *motoconcho* (motorbike) taxi is a quick and inexpensive way to get around. **Note** that you are unlikely to be offered a helmet and your travel insurance will probably not cover you for accidents.

Public Transport

Public buses, *carros públicos* (public taxis) and minibuses offer an inexpensive and efficient way to get around Santo Domingo and other cities and towns. Fares are set by the government and are usually only a few pesos.

Where to Stay

Accommodation

The Dominican Republic has earned a reputation for its large, modern all-inclusive beach front resorts. There are, of course, smaller, simple hotels, charming guest houses and villas if that is your preference.

Children are usually welcome and some of the resorts have special programmes to keep them amused.

Below is a selection of the accommodation on offer. Rates and facilities are subject to change.

Hotel Price Guide

Room rates for two persons sharing:
- **Expensive:** more than US$60
- **Moderate:** US$30–60
- **Budget:** under US$30

Santo Domingo

Expensive
Meliá Santo Domingo
George Washington 365
Tel: 221 6666
Fax: 687 8150
Huge business hotel overlooking the Malecón, with pool, tennis, casino and night club that is popular at the weekends.
Palacio
Duarte 106, corner of Salomé Ureña
Tel: 682 4730
Fax: 687 5535
www.hotel-palacio.com
A colonial house in the old city with a modern wing and pool at the rear. Spacious rooms, tiled floors, portraits on the walls. Comfortable and popular, but no restaurant.

Sofitel Francés
Las Mercedes, corner of Arzobispo Meriño
Tel: 685 9331
Fax: 685 1289
A colonial mansion built around a courtyard in the old city. French-run, with wonderful French food served al fresco by the fountain or indoors.
Sofitel Hostal Nicolás de Ovando
Calle Las Damas 53
Tel: 687 3101
Fax: 688 5170
Restored colonial palace overlooking the river mouth with modern conveniences, including wheelchair access and pool.

Moderate
Casona Dorada
Ave. Independencia 255
Tel: 221 3535
Fax: 221 3622
Email: casonadorada@codetel.net.do
In Gazcue and convenient for the Malecón. Rooms small and basic with floral décor; some rooms sleep three. Air conditioning, TV, fridge and a murky pool. Good value.
Conde de Peñalba
El Conde corner of Arzobispo Meriño
Tel: 688 7121
Fax: 688 7375
www.condepenalba.com
In the heart of the old city on the corner of Plaza Colón. Rooms vary in price and size; the cheapest have no windows and the most expensive with balconies overlooking the plaza. Good bathrooms, TV, fridge and phone. Popular open air seating at the restaurant downstairs.
Duque de Wellington
Ave. Independencia 304
Tel: 682 4525
Fax: 688 2844
www.hotelduque.com
The best choice in this price range in this area. Adequate rooms, TV, fridge, bar and restaurant.
Hostal Nicolás Nader
Duarte corner of General Luperón
Tel: 687 6674
Nine beautifully furnished rooms in a colonial mansion decorated with modern art. The owners run one of the best art galleries in the Dominican Republic and Haiti.

Saint Amad
Arzobispo Meriño 353 corner of
Emiliano Tejera
Tel: 687 1447
Fax: 687 1478
Converted 300-year old mansion in
Zona Colonial. Comfortable rooms
with bathrooms are excellent value.
Internet access and a restaurant.

Budget
Aída
El Conde 464 corner of Espaillat
Tel: 685 7692
Fax: 688 9350
Cheap and cheerful, popular, family-
run hotel above a shop on a
pedestrianised shopping street.
Rooms vary in size, some sleep
three. Balcony and fan or air
conditioning. No smoking.

The Southeast

BÁVARO

Expensive
Barceló Bávaro Palace
Bávaro
Punta Cana
Tel: 686 5797
Fax: 688 5859
www.barcelo.com
The largest complex on the Costa
del Coco is one of five all-inclusive
hotels on the same property with an
18-hole golf course, lively nightlife
and several restaurants.
Catalonia Bávaro Beach Resort
Playas de Bávaro
Higuey
Tel: 412 0000
Fax: 412 0001
A large low-rise complex on the
pretty white sand beach. With a
nine-hole golf course, casino, pool
and bars and restaurants. Villas
with a terrace or balcony and air
conditioned suites. All-inclusive.

BAYAHIBE

Budget
Llave del Mar
Bayahibe
Tel: 833 0081
Fax: 833 0088
On the main street close to the dive

shop and restaurants. Simple, but
adequate. Rooms downstairs have
a fan; upstairs rooms have balcony
and air conditioning. No hot water.

Hotel Price Guide

Room rates for two persons
sharing:
- **Expensive:** more than US$60
- **Moderate:** US$30–60
- **Budget:** under US$30

MICHES

Budget
La Loma
Miches
Tel: 558 5562
Fax:553 5564
Perched on a hillside with fabulous
view of the coast. Light and bright
rooms with balcony, some with air
conditioning. Poor road access; a
four wheel drive vehicle is required.

LA ROMANA

Expensive
Casa de Campo
East of La Romana
Tel: 523 3333 or (800) 877 3643
Fax: 523 8548
www.casadecampo.cc
All-inclusive resort with rooms and
150 villas. Several swimming pools,
nine restaurants, a night club, and
a private airport. Two Pete Dye-
designed golf courses and a
Sporting Clay Centre. Reservations
required six months in advance.
La Reina Cumayasa
Near Soco
Tel: 555 7506
Fax: 550 8105
Above Río Cumayasa; reminiscent
of a Mediterranean castle.

Budget
Hotel Olimpo
Padre Abreu, corner of Pedro A.
Lluberes
Tel: 550 7646
Fax: 550 7647
Air conditioned rooms with private
bathroom. Swimming pool and
restaurant.

PUNTA CANA

Expensive
Club Mediterranée
Apartado Postal 106, Higuey La
Altagracia
Tel: 687 2606
Fax: 687 2896 or 685 5287
Features four multi-level U-shaped
blocks, three restaurants and a
huge swimming pool. All-inclusive.
Optional excursions.
Punta Cana Beach Resort
5 km (3 miles) south of Club Med
Punta Cana
Tel: 972 2139 or 221 2262
Fax: 541 2286
Email: reservas@puntacana.com
Villas and spacious rooms in 3-
storey buildings on the beach. All-
inclusive.

The Northeast

SAMANÁ

Expensive
Occidental Gran Bahia
Los Cacaos
Tel: 538 3111
Fax: 538 2764
Email: info.granbahia@do.occidental
hotels.com
All-inclusive, with 100 rooms,
pool, tennis court. The hotel
offers excursions to Cayo
Levantado and seasonal whale-
watching tours (January to March).

Budget
Docia
Samaná
Tel: 538 2041
Guesthouse above La Churcha with
a view over the bay. The upstairs
rooms are the best: large and airy
with good bathrooms, fan and hot
water.

LAS TERRENAS

Moderate
Las Palmas
Calle El Portillo
Tel: 240 6436
Fax: 240 6435
www.vamosalaspalmas.com
Twenty-three two-bedroom villas in a

pretty development across the track from the beach. Lovely flower gardens under palm trees.

Budget
Fata Morgana
Tel: 836 5541
Email: editdejong@hotmail.com
Dutch-run hostel popular with travellers on a tight budget. Away from the beach and off the main road down a track.

The North & West
PUERTO PLATA

Budget
Portofino Guest House
Ave. Hermanas Mirabal 12
Tel: 586 2858
Fax: 586 5050
Thirteen rooms in a one-storey building with swimming pool. With air conditioning, private bathroom, parking and inexpensive restaurant.

PUERTO DORADA

Expensive
Gran Ventana
Tel: 320 2111
Fax: 320 4017
www.victoriahoteles.com.do
One of the best of the all-inclusive hotels here. With a Central area around the pool for families and young couples or a quieter wing for people who want to relax. On the beach but close to the shopping centre and cinema too.

SOSÚA

Expensive
Piergiorgio Palace
Tel: 571 2626
Fax: 571 2786
www.piergiorgiohotel.com
Victorian-style hotel perched on cliffs with a stunning view of the bay. Good snorkelling off the rocks. Elegant, impeccable décor, luxury rooms with ensuite bathrooms. Romantic Italian outdoor dining.

CABARETE

Expensive
Velero Beach Resort
Calle La Punta 1
Tel: 571 9727
Fax: 571 9722
www.velerobeach.com
At the east end of the beach with an outlook on the windsurfers in the bay. Top of the range but good value apartments and suites.

Moderate
Villa Taína
Calle Principal
Tel: 571 0722
Fax: 571 0883
www.villataina.com
A friendly place in the centre of town with a pool, but also on the beach and close to the windsurfing schools. Restaurant on the beach.

SANTIAGO DE LOS CABALLEROS (CIBAO VALLEY REGION)

Expensive
Hotel Aloha Sol
Calle del Sol 50
Tel: 583 0090
Fax: 583 0950
Smart rooms and suites, the restaurant has local and international dishes.

Moderate
Hotel Gran Almirante
Ave. Estrella Sadhala
Tel: 580 1992
Fax: 241 1492
Comfortable rooms. At top end of this price bracket. Casino on site.
Hotel Matum
Ave. Las Carreras
Tel: 581 3107
Fax: 581 8415
Fifty well-kept rooms, cable TV, pool, night club and casino. Close to El Monumento.

Budget
Hotel Colonial
Salvador Cucurullo 115
Tel: 247 3122
Fax: 582 0811
The hotel is within walking distance

of the main square. Rooms with TV and balcony, hot water and a small restaurant on the property.

In the Mountains
JARABACOA

Moderate
Rancho Baiguate
Tel: 574 6890
Fax: 574 4940
www.ranchobaiguate.com.do
Rustic location in the countryside on the edge of the Baiguate river. Spacious rooms, no TV and no air conditioning needed up in the mountains. Lots of adventure sports including rafting, canyoning, horse riding and hiking.

CONSTANZA

Moderate
Alto Cerro
Tel: 696 0202
Fax: 530 6193
Email: c.matias@codetel.net.do
On a hillside overlooking the valley. Rooms or villas sleep up to seven, with balconies and a fire for cool evenings. Restaurant serves home-grown produce; there's a grocery store too.

The Southwest
BAHORUCO

Expensive
Barceló Bahoruco Beach Resort
Tel: 524 1111
Fax: 524 6060
www.barcelo.com
Large all-inclusive hotel on a stony beach. A buffet restaurant. Large, comfortable rooms and a pool.

Moderate
Casa Bonita
Carretera de la Costa KM16
Barahona
Tel: 696 0215
Fax: 223 0548
Rooms are adequate. Lovely setting on a hillside overlooking the sea. Good views from the thatched restaurant; open-sided lounge.

Where to Eat

The Dominican Diet

An integral part of the basic Dominican diet is rice, *arroz*, which is prepared in several different ways. For instance, *locrio* is a combination of rice with different types of meat; *moro* is rice with various vegetables or legumes (beans, peas, etc.), and *la bandera dominicana* (the flag) is the name given to the national dish – a simple plate of white rice, red beans, meat and *tostones* (fried green plantains).

In addition, each region has its own popular dish, such as goat with Creole sauce in the northwest, fish with coconut in Samaná and *Janiqueques* (pancakes, literally "Johnny cakes") in the eastern part of the country.

The recipe for *Cazabe* or cassava bread has been handed down through the generations from Hispaniola's Taíno Amerindians.

Meal Deals

Average price per person for a main course or buffet meal:
- **$$$** More than US$15
- **$$** US$8–15
- **$** Under US$8

Restaurants & Cafés

As well as plenty of places serving native Dominican dishes, there are restaurants specialising in Spanish, French, Italian, Swiss, Middle Eastern, Japanese and Argentine cuisine.

SANTO DOMINGO

La Briciola
Arzobispo Merino 152
Zona Colonial
Tel: 688 5055
Courtyard dining, Italian cuisine in a lovely colonial setting. Open for lunch and dinner. **$$$**

Museo de Jamón
La Atarazana 17
Zona Colonial
Tel: 688 9644
Not a museum but a Spanish restaurant, the ceiling is hung with hams. Great selection of *tapas*. Open daily for lunch and dinner. **$$**

Vesuvio I
Ave. George Washington 521
Tel: 221 1954
Traditionally the place to go for an elegant, expensive Italian meal. **$$$**

Mesón de Barí
Corner of Hostos and Arzobispo Nouel
Zona Colonial
Tel: 687 4091
Typical Dominican fare with merengue music at weekends. Open daily noon–1am. **$$**

Mesón de la Cava
Parque Mirador del Sur
Tel: 533 2818
Unusual setting in a cave, with live music and dancing. Good steaks. Very popular so reservations necessary. Open daily. **$$$**

Asadero Los Argentinos
Ave. Independéncia 809, between Ave. Abraham Lincoln and Máximo Gómez
Tel: 686 4060
Argentine food, great for meat lovers. **$$**

Les Fondues
Ave. Winston Churchill corner with Sarasota
Tel: 535 5947
Swiss fondues of all sorts, sweet and savoury. Wonderful chocolate fondue. **$$**

La Atarazana
La Atarazana 5
Zona Colonial
Tel:689 2900
One of several restaurants and cafés in this area. A popular place with criollo and international cuisine and seafood. **$$**

Sheherezade
Roberto Pastoriza 226
Tel: 227 2323
North African and Mediterranean cuisine. **$$**

El Conuco
Casimiro de Moya 152, corner with José Joaquín Pérez
Tel: 221 3231
Typical Dominican dishes served in a thatched barn. Large portions and a good place to try local specialities. Open for lunch and dinner with music in the evenings. **$**

Lumi's Park
Ave. Abraham Lincoln 809
Tel: 540 4755; 540 4584 (for delivery)
Dominican menu with outdoor dining under canvas. Try the *churrasco* or *mofongo* for a hearty meal. Popular, so if you can't get a table, get a takeaway or have your food delivered. Open daily for lunch and dinner until dawn. **$**

The Southeast

BOCA CHICA

Neptuno's Club
Tel: 523 4703
On the waterfront beside the Coral Hamaca Hotel. The bar is built into a replica of Columbus' caravelle, the *Santa María*, and seating is over the water. Mostly seafood but also meat and children's dishes. Open daily for lunch and dinner with live music on Wednesday and Sunday. **$$–$$$**

BAYAHIBE

Casa Eva
Calle Principal 1
On the seafront and a hub of activity, with an internet café. Main meals, salad and pasta. Open daily for breakfast, lunch and dinner. **$**

BÁVARO

Captain Cook
Playa El Cortecito
Punta Cana
Tel: 552 0645
On the beach and a welcome
change from all-inclusive dining.
Some hotels provide boat transport
to the restaurant. Spanish cuisine
and seafood including lobster and
huge shrimp. Try a lunch of mixed
fish, fried potatoes and salad,
washed down with a jug of sangría.
$$–$$$

In the Mountains

CONSTANZA

Antojitos d'Lauren
Duarte 17
Informal outdoor, but covered,
eating off plastic tables. menu
includes local specialities but
known for its pizza in the evenings
when families get together and
there is dancing. Open daily for
breakfast, lunch and dinner. **$**

JARABACOA

Vistabella Club Bar & Grill
Off the road to Salto Jimenoa
(5km/3 miles from town)
Open for lunch and dinner but best
during the day when you can enjoy
the view across the valley. Pool for
guests and a bar, popular with
Dominican families at weekends.
Local specialities include rabbit,
guinea fowl and *casabe con ajo* and
garlic cassava bread. **$$**

Rancho Restaurant
On the main road opposite the Esso
station
Cozy restaurant owned by Rancho
Baiguate but conveniently located in
town. Good food with local and
international dishes using locally-
grown ingredients. Open for lunch
and dinner. **$$$–$$**

The North Coast

MONTE CRISTI

El Bistro
San Fernando 26
Tel: 579 2091
Courtyard setting for lunch and
dinner with a varied menu of
sandwiches, pasta, salads, grills,
fish and seafood including good
value lobster. Open Mon–Fri
11am–2.30pm, 6pm–midnight,
Sat–Sun 10am–midnight. **$–$$**

PUERTO PLATA

Jungle Bar
Plaza Turisol 12
Tel: 261 3544
English-run with English menu
including a fried breakfast, toasted
sandwiches and curries. Very
popular with ex-pats and always full
around the bar in the evening,
particularly if there is a pub quiz.
Open daily 10am–10pm; the bar
stays open later with happy hour
5–7pm. **$**

Sam's Bar & Grill
José del Carmen Ariza 34
Tel: 586 7267
American-run with American menu
including burgers, spare ribs and
mouth-watering desserts. Open
daily for breakfast, lunch and
dinner; the bar is a popular meeting
place. Rooms are available. **$$–$**

SOSÚA

On the Waterfront
Calle Dr Rosen 1
Tel: 571 3024
Come here to watch the sunset and
for happy hour (4–6pm).
Spectacular location on a clifftop
overlooking the sea. Outdoor dining,
seafood, meat dishes and snacks;
live music most nights in season
and the occasional barbeque. Open
for breakfast, lunch and dinner. **$$**

CABARETE

Blue Moon
Los Brazos, 20 minutes from town
Tel: 223 0614
Reservations essential for this East
Indian restaurant where food is
served on banana leaves. Perfect
for a large group so you can try a
variety of dishes. **$$**

Ho La La
In the town centre
Tel: 571 0806
French and international food with
good pizza and seafood. Open
7am–11pm. **$$**

SAMANÁ PENINSULA

LAS TERRENAS

Casa Boga
Casa de los Pescadores
Tel: 240 6321
Fishermen's huts have been
converted into beachside
restaurants and this is probably the
best, serving excellent Basque
cooking. A huge variety of fish and
many ways to cook it. **$$–$$$**

Fast Food

Fast food in the Dominican Republic
is usually served by street vendors
or local shaded shack-style
establishments. Some of the tasty
morsels on offer include:

Chicharrones – strips of pork
crackling (skin), fried to a frazzle
(the chicken version is known as
chicharrones de pollo).

Pollo picante – chicken coated in
various spices and deep fried.

Janiqueques – pancakes fried in oil.

Pastelitos – deep fried pasties with
a beef, chicken or cheese filling.

Platanitos – hot plantain crisps.

Quipes – cracked wheat fritters with
a meat filling.

Drinking Notes

The national drink is rum and it is
so popular that many brands of the
amber nectar are distilled for the
domestic market and only a small
percentage is exported. Look out
for Brugal, Barceló and Bermúdez

rum which can be found all over the Dominican Republic.

The best-quality rums bear the inscription *ron añejo* or *extra viejo* – both meaning aged rum – or *gran reserva*. Whether you try this lubrication straight or in a cocktail be careful, it will have a kick – most Dominican rum is 40 percent proof.

Dominicans also consume vast quantities of beer. The market is dominated by Presidente and other brands, such as Bohemia and Quisqueya are less common.

Rum Cocktails

Almost every bar and club offers a staggering number of rum cocktails. And don't forget you can usually opt for a non-alcoholic version of any drink.

Cuba Libre is rum and coke with ice and a slice of lemon.

Daiquirí is rum with crushed ice and fruit.

Piña Colada is crushed pineapple, coconut cream and a dose of rum.

Coco Loco is fresh coconut mixed with rum and coconut cream.

Mamajuana is a delicious blend of rum, wine and honey infused with wood bark and herbs. Sold in a multitude of shapes and sizes of bottles on street corners or in markets.

Culture

Museums & Galleries

SANTO DOMINGO

Faro a Colón
Ave. Boulevard Alfaro
Tel: 592 5217
Controversial and phenomenally expensive museum (the name means Columbus's Lighthouse) which was built as a monument to, and mausoleum of Columbus. Exhibits include reproductions of historical documents. Open Tues–Sun 10am–5pm.

Museo de Arte Moderno
Pedro Henriquez Ureña
Plaza de la Cultura
Tel: 685 2153
Excellent display of contemporary Dominican art, well worth a visit. Open Tues–Sun 9am–5pm.

Museo de Historia Natural
Plaza de la Cultura
Tel: 689 0106
Disappointing exhibition of the natural world. The display boards are only in Spanish. Open Tues–Sun 10am–5pm.

Museo de Juan Pablo Duarte
Calle Isabel La Católica 308
Tel: 687 1436
Museum in the house where Pablo Duarte was born. Open Tues–Sun 10am–5pm.

Museo de las Atarazanas-Reales
Calle Colon 4
Las Atarazanas
Tel: 682 5834
Small maritime museum containing some interesting booty recovered from conquistadors' ships. Open Thur–Tues 9am–5pm and Sun morning.

Museo de las Casas Reales
Calle las Damas and las Mercedes
Tel: 682 4202
Once the home of the Royal Court.

Exhibits include colonial artefacts, coats of armour, antique coins and treasure from shipwrecks. Open Tues–Sun 9am–6pm.

Museo del Hombre Dominicano
Pedro Henriquez Ureña
Plaza de la Cultura
Tel: 687 3622
Many interesting artefacts and exhibits examining the Taíno, African and Hispanic influence of the present day Republic. Open Tues–Sun 10am–5pm.
www.museodelhombredominicano.org

Museo Mundo de Ambar
Arzobispo Meriño 452
Tel: 682 3309
Displays of Dominican mined amber and gems from around the world. A gift shop sells amber jewellery. Open Mon–Sat 9am–6pm.

Museo Nacional de Historia y Geographía
Cesar Nicolas Penson
Plaza de la Cultura
Tel: 686 6668
A museum which takes visitors on a short journey through history from the 19th century onwards. A lot of attention paid to Trujillo's dictatorship. Open Tues–Sun 9.30am–5pm.

Museo Numismatico
Pedro Henriquez Ureña and Leopoldo Navarro
Tel: 688 6512
Collection of coins and stamps. Open Tues–Sat 9am–5pm.

LA ROMANA

Museo Arqueológico Regional
Altos de Chavón
Excellently presented collection of Taíno relics and artefacts from the region. Open daily 9am–5pm.

SOSÚA

Museo de la Comunidad Judía de Sosúa
Calle Dr Alejo
Tel: 571 1386
Small museum displays the history of the Jews in the town. Open Mon–Thurs 9am–1pm.

PUERTO PLATA

Museo del Ambar Dominicano
Calle Duarte 61
Tel: 586 2848
Exhibits some good examples of ancient amber with fossilized inclusions. Open Mon–Sat 9am–5pm.
Museo de Arte Taíno
Calle Beller 22
Tel: 586 7601
The museum plots the pre-Columbian history of the Taínos with replicas. Exhibits include an excavated tomb. Open daily 10am–5pm.

SANTIAGO DE LOS CABALLEROS

Museo des Artes Folklórico Tomás Morel
Calle Restauración 174
Tel: 582 6787
Brightly coloured traditional carnival masks and costumes. Call ahead, opening hours are variable.
Museo del Tabaco
Calle 30 de Marzo
An insight into the history of one of the Republic's important industry's. English-speaking guides available. Open Mon–Fri 9am–5pm.

Plaza de la Cultura

Santo Domingo's Plaza de la Cultura is the city's cultural hub. On the plaza are several important museums, as well as the **Biblioteca Nacional** (National Library), the **Cinemateca Nacional** (National Film Library) and the **Teatro Nacional** (National Theatre).

Theatres

SANTO DOMINGO

Teatro Nacional
Plaza de la Cultura
Tel: 687 9131
Offers great performances of drama, contemporary dance, ballet and opera. There is a good view of the modern stage from anywhere in the theatre which can accommodate 1,700 people.
Palacio de Bellas Artes
Avenidas Máximo Gómez and Independencia
Tel: 687 2494
A beautiful building but only occasional drama and festival performances and art exhibitions.
Casa de Teatro
Arzobispo
Merino 14
Tel: 689 3430
Experimental theatre. Call for details and locations of performances.

SANTIAGO

Gran Teatro del Cibao
Monumento a los Héroes de la Restauración
Tel: 583 1150
Two concert halls, the larger auditorium seats 15,000, the smaller one is more used as a venue for merengue concerts and plays.

Carnival & Festivals

February is **Mardi Gras** time, one of the oldest traditions of the island. Each region has its own carnival and the season concludes with a colourful parade down Avenida George Washington (known as the *Malécon*) in Santo Domingo. Festivities in La Vega are considered to be the best but there are also carnivals in Santiago and Monte Cristi.

The famous two-week **Merengue Festival** which takes place in July in Santo Domingo, along the Malécon, is a lively fun event which attracts crowds of Dominicans from all over the country and foreign visitors too. In October Puerto Plata is the venue for the north's own Merengue Festival and cultural event.

Excursions

Guided Tours

In the Dominican Republic all of the all-inclusive resorts are affiliated with tour operators who offer their specialist tours to visitors. However, if you are travelling independently, you can book the tour of your choice with one of the following agencies:
Colonial City Tours
Tel: 687 5245
Fax: 685 1332
Tours around the Zona Colonial, Santo Domingo. Available in English, Spanish or French. Mon–Fri 8.30am–5.30pm, Sat 8.30am–noon.
Máxima Aventura
Rancho Baiguate, Jarabacoa
Tel: 574 6890
Fax: 572 4940.
Excursions to Pico Duarte, rafting, canyon trips, horse riding, trekking and quad rides; trips to Salto de Baiguate and Salto de Jimenoa.
Rum Runners Jeep Adventures
Puerto Plata
Tel: 586 8388
Fax 586 2729
Jeep safaris.
Iguana Mama
Cabarete
Tel: 571 0908
Fax: 571 0734
Specialists in mountain bike tours, also organises excursions to Pico Duarte, horse riding and whale watching in season.

Top Trips

Samaná–Cayo Levantado
In the northeast, you can drive through the countryside to the bay of Samaná. The waters around Samaná Bay are a whale sanctuary and every winter (15 Jan–15 Mar)

humpback whales mate close to shore. Once in Samaná, head to the Marina for a motorboat trip to Cayo Levantado (Barcardi Island) and its white sand beach. Contact **Victoria Marine** on the Malécon for whale watching tours, tel: 538 2588.

Santiago–Jarabacoa

A driving tour through the mountains of Jamao Al Norte. From the top of the mountains you have an impressive view of the lush Cibao Valley. Visit a coffee plantation near Moca/La Vega. Then drive on to Jarabacoa for a horse ride or take a jeep safari to the waterfalls. Don't forget your bathing suit and walking shoes.

Water Rafting

Raft through the rapids and canyons of the Río Yaque del Norte and see some mountain scenery in the Cordillera Central that's only accessible from the river.

Playa Grande and Laguna Gri-Gri

A trip to the Costa Verde, Río San Juan, where you can take a ride in a motor launch through the crystal clear waters of Laguna Gri-Gri, featuring mangroves and bird life.

Las Cascadas

Adventure trips by jeep through the sugar cane fields of Imbert to Las Cascadas with its caves and eight level waterfall. You can explore, dive, climb or just swim in the refreshing clear waters.

Santo Domingo City Tour

Cultural highlights of the capital city, founded in 1496 by Bartolomé Columbus (brother of Christopher Columbus), are the Palacio Nacional, Faro a Colón and the Zona Colonial (old Santo Domingo) including the first cathedral in the New World.

Nightlife

There is plenty of nightlife in the Dominican Republic, including discos, bars with live music, nightclubs and hotel floor shows. The following is a selection of popular night spots – nightclubs, café-bars and discos:

Santo Domingo

Bachata Rosa
La Atarazana 9
Tel: 616 0588
Live music.
Bar Marrakesh
Hotel Santo Domingo, corner of Ave. Independencia and Abraham Lincoln
Tel: 221 1511
Live music.
Guácara Taína
Paseo de los Indios
Ave. Cayetano Germosén
Tel: 533 0671
Live music and dance shows.
Jubilee Disco
Hotel Jaragua
George Washington 367
Tel: 688 8026
Dominican music.
Las Palmas
Hotel Santo Domingo, corner of Ave. Independencia and Abraham Lincoln
Tel: 221 1511
Live music.
Merengue Bar
Hotel Jaragua
George Washington 367
Tel: 221 2222
Live music.
Nightclub
Hotel Napolitano
Ave. George Washington 101
Tel: 687 1131
Live music.
Omni
Hotel Meliá Santo Domingo
Ave. George Washington 365
Tel: 221 6666.

Salón La Fiesta.
Hotel Jaragua
George Washington 367
Tel: 221 2222

Playa Dorada

Andromeda Playa Dorada
Heaven's Hotel
Tel: 320 5250, extension 851
Charlie's
Jack Tar Village Hotel
Tel: 320 3800, extension 2248
Crazy Moon
Paradise Beach Club
Playa Dorada
Tel: 320 3663
Hemingway's Café
Playa Dorada Plaza
Tel: 320 2230
Live music.

Language Schools

The country's two main language schools are in Santo Domingo.
AmeriSpan is an American programme. The course costs around US$1,250 for four weeks which covers 20 hours of one-to-one instruction per week, a private room with a host family, three meals a day and airport pick-up. For more information write to AmeriSpan at P.O. Box 4000, Philadelphia, PA 19106, USA; fax: (215) 751 1986; on the web: http://www.amerispan.com
Entrena also specialises in one-to-one tuition. Classes are for six hours per day, five days a week, and the course costs about US$375 for four weeks. Instruction is also offered on an hourly basis at US$10 per hour. Write to Entrena at Calle Rafael Bonnelly 26, Santo Domingo, Dominican Republic, tel: 567 8990; fax: 566 3492, email: entrena@codetel.net.do.

Shopping

What to Buy

Jewellery
Amber and larimar make authentic souvenirs and both gems can be bought all over the island. For guaranteed high quality, visitors are advised to try one of the Amber Museum's shops or Harrison's in Santo Domingo.

Crafts
A wide variety of crafts made by local artists can be found throughout the island, including pottery, ceramics, and items made of amber, larimar, horn, wood, leather or snail shells. Look out also for embroidered and locally manufactured cotton fabrics.

Art
Be wary of cheap, mock-Haitian artwork. The Dominican Republic has a long, rich art tradition and there is plenty of good Dominican art available in the country's numerous galleries.

Local artists, such as Candido Bido, produce work that is dreamlike and colourful. So a good place to start is Bido's own gallery in Santo Domingo: Galeria de Arte Candido Bido, Dr Baez #5 Ens., Gazcue, Santo Domingo, tel: 687 0115.

Sport

Outdoor Activities

SPECTATOR & PARTICIPANT

The Dominican climate is ideal for windsurfing, while the hilly terrain is great for hiking or horse riding. And then there is baseball, the national sport. Catch a game if you can.

Athletics
Practised at the Olympic Centre, Juan Pablo Duarte, tel: 540 4010. New facilities were added for the Pan American Games in 2003 (see page 146).

Baseball
Professional and amateur baseball is played from October to January. For information call **Liga de Baseball**, tel: 567 6371.

Basketball
Practised in the Olympic Centre and in private clubs year round.

Billiards & Bowling
Practised at Sebelen Bowling Centre, tel: 540 0101.

Boxing, Fencing, Judo, Karate
Contact the Carlos Teo Cruz Coliseum and hotels and sports clubs. Table tennis is also available at the Coliseum.

Golf
Most of the larger resorts have their own golf courses or access to established clubs. Some of the more spectacular courses on the Amber Coast overlook the sea. For information contact the **Asociación Dominicana de Golf** (Dominican Golf Association), tel: 476 4898.

Horse Racing
V Centenario Race Track, Autopista de las Américas, Km 14.5, tel: 687 6060.

Polo
Polo is played at the Casa de Campo resort near La Romana and elsewhere on the island. For information call: 523 3333.

Tennis
Amateur and professional tennis is played in the Olympic Centre, Juan Pablo Duarte, tel: 540 4010. There are also courts on the grounds of luxury resorts and at private clubs.

Fishing

For information on sport fishing, contact **Club Náutico de Santo Domingo**, Boca Chica, tel: 685 4940. For information on deep-sea fishing excursions with professional instructors contact **Actividades Acuáticas**, Boca Chica, tel: 523 4511; in Puerto Plata, tel: 320 2567.

Language

The official language in the Dominican Republic is Spanish, and although most people at the tourist resorts speak some English it is useful to know a few key words and phrases.

Useful Phrases

Yes *sí* (see)
No *no*
Please *por favor* (por fa-vor)
Thank you *gracias* (grass-ee-ass)
Excuse me/sorry *perdone* (pair-don-ay)
Please speak slowly *por favor hable despacio* (por fa-vor a-blay des-pasio)
Do you speak English? *¿habla usted inglés?* (a-bla oo-sted ing-lays)
I don't understand *no entiendo* (no en-t-en-do)
Hello/hi! *hola* (oh-la)
Good day/morning *buenos días* (b-wen-os dee-os)
Good night/evening *buenos noches* (b-wen-os noch-es)
Goodbye *adios* (a-dee-os)
See you *hasta luego* (as-ta lu-way-go)
How are you? (singular) *¿cómo está?* (com-o es-ta)
How are you? (plural) *cómo están?* (com-o es-tan)
Okay/fine *muy bien* (m-wee-bee-en)
Bill (check), please *La cuenta por favor*
How much? *¿Cuánto cuesta?*
You're welcome *De nada*
Can I see a room? *¿Puedo (Podemos) ver un cuarto?*
What is the rate? *¿Cuál es el precio?*
A single room *Un habitación sencilla*
A double room *Un habitación doble*
Key *llave*
Bathroom *Reterete, baño*

Further Reading

Background Reading

James Ferguson, author of the excellent *Traveller's History of the Caribbean* (Windrush Press/Interlink Books, 1998) and *Traveller's Literary Companion to the Caribbean* (In Print, 1997) and contributor to this guide, recommends some of the following books on the Dominican Republic and Haiti.

Dominican Republic

NON-FICTION

Emelio Betances, *State and Society in the Dominican Republic* (Westview Press, Boulder CO, 1995). An academic but readable analysis of the relationship between political and economic power.

Harry Hoetink, *The Dominican People* (Johns Hopkins University Press, Baltimore, 1982). Fascinating detail on where the country's culturally mixed population comes from and how its immigrants arrived.

David Howard, *Colouring the Nation: Race and Ethnicity in the Dominican Republic* (Signal Books/Lynne Rienner, Oxford/Boulder CO, 2000). Looks at troubled relations between the Dominican Republic and Haiti and analyses the Dominican obsession with race.

David Howard, *Dominican Republic in Focus* (Latin America Bureau/Interlink Books, London/New York, 1998). Very useful short introduction, covering everything from Columbus to bachata.

Frank Moya Pons, *The Dominican Republic: A National History* (Hispaniola Books, New York, 1994). An accessible history of the country by its foremost contemporary historian.

FICTION

Julia Alvarez, *In the Name of Salomé* (Penguin, 2000). A tale about a 19th century Dominican poetess and her struggle to overcome prejudice and political oppression, as seen through the eyes of her daughter.

Julia Alvarez, *How the Garcia Girls Lost Their Accent* (Plume-Penguin, New York, 1991). A perceptive story of a Dominican family caught between the US and La Isla.

Julia Alvarez, *In the Time of the Butterflies* (Algonquin Books, Chapel Hill NC, 1994). The horrors of the Trujillo period skillfully brought to life in a (real-life) tale of murder and heroism.

Junot Díaz, *Drown* (Faber & Faber, London, 1996). Tough and gritty short stories from the barrios of New Jersey and the Dominican villages left behind by the emigrants.

Manuel de Jesús Galván, *Enriquillo (1889)* (The Cross and the Sword, Victor Gollancz, London, 1956). The classic story of the Taino cacique and his impossible revolt against Spanish colonial rule.

Pamela Maria Smorkaloff, *If I Could Write This in Fire: An Anthology of Writing from the Caribbean* (New Press, New York, 1994). Excellent anthology, including work by the Dominican Republic's "national poet", Pedro Mir.

Mario Vargas Llosa, *The Feast of the Goat (La Fiesta del Chivo)* (Alfaguara, 2000). A story about the plot to end the Trujillo dictatorship, with all its cruelty and barbarity.

Haiti

NON-FICTION

Charles Arthur and Michael Dash (eds), *Libetè: A Haiti Anthology* (Latin America Bureau/Markus Wiener, London/Princeton). A comprehensive collection from and about Haiti, covering every imaginable topic.

CLR James, *The Black Jacobins:*

Toussaint L'Ouverture and the San Domingo Revolution (Allison & Busby, London, 1991). Classic 1930s account of the slave revolution and the birth of independent Haiti by the Caribbean's greatest historian,

David Nicholls, From Dessalines to Duvalier: Race, Colour and National Independence in Haiti (Macmillan, Basingstoke, 1995). The essential analysis of Haiti's trajectory from independence to dictatorship.

Ian Thomson, "Bonjour Blanc": A Journey Through Haiti (Penguin, London, 1992). A hair-raising and often hilarious account of travelling off the beaten track.

Amy Wilentz, The Rainy Season (Jonathan Cape, London, 1989). Atmospheric account of Haiti's troubled times in the aftermath of the Duvaliers.

FICTION

Alejo Carpentier, The Kingdom of This World (Penguin, London, 1980). The Cuban master of magical realism recreates the Haitian revolution and the bizarre building of the Citadelle.

Pierre Clitandre, Cathedral of the August Heat (Readers International, London, 1987). A surreal novel of poverty, political violence and spiritual redemption.

Edwidge Danticat, Breath, Eyes, Memory (Soho Press, New York, 1994). Sombre tale of alienation and political repression as experienced by a Haitian-American woman. Also author of Krik? Krak! (Soho Press Inc. 1995) and The Farming of Bones (Soho Press Inc. 1998).

Graham Greene, The Comedians (Penguin, London, 1984). The British novelist's unforgettable evocation of the evil and fear of the 'Papa Doc' Duvalier period.

Jacques Roumain, Masters of the Dew (Heinemann, London, 1978). Socialist-realist depiction of Haitian peasant life and the importance of collective action.

Getting Acquainted

Haiti

The République d'Haiti occupies the western third of the second largest island in the Caribbean (Hispaniola) which it shares with the Dominican Republic. The north coast is bathed by the Atlantic Ocean while the Caribbean Sea enfolds the south. The Windward Passage traverses the west coast, where Haiti is a mere 120 km (75 miles) away from Môle St. Nicolás.

Area: 17,142 sq. km (10,714 sq. miles) – the third largest Caribbean nation.

Landscape: Two-thirds of Haiti is mountainous, much of the rest is semi-arid, and the coastal areas are mild and humid.

Capital: Port-au-Prince

Population: 7 million.

Language: Kréyol and French.

Time Zone: Eastern Standard Time; GMT –5. Daylight Saving is not observed during summer.

Currency: Gourde (gd) and Haitian dollar.

Electricity: 110 volts, 60 cycles AC, as in the USA.

Literacy: 48 percent of males, 42.2 percent of females (1995 est).

International dialling code: 509

The Place

Anyone planning a visit to Haiti should understand that it is not a destination for everyone. It is a country of extreme contrasts where million-dollar (US$) homes are being built while the general economy is in shambles. Extreme poverty is pervasive, leading to poignant malnutrition in children everywhere, and crime. Democratic traditions are weak and the

Climate

Basically, there are two seasons – dry and rainy. The peak season, from November to March, sees temperatures ranging from 23–32°C (70–80°F) during the day and 15–27°C (60–70°F) at night. In July and August, searing temperatures hover around 32–36°C (80–95°F) with high humidity.

The two rainy seasons are roughly from April to June and September to October. Haiti sits directly in the hurricane belt and has been hit with devastating results such as the death and destruction caused by Hurricane Georges in 1998. Hurricane season is from July to October.

The temperatures in Cap-Haïtien are slightly lower than in Port-au-Prince, around 31°C (88°F) in the summer and 27°C (81°F) during winter. West of Port-de-Paix, the far west, has very low rainfall which has left it barren, arid and increasingly unable to support its rural peasant population.

tradition of a single, strong leader continues, whether elected or not.

Yet Haiti – as vibrant as the colours in its Art Naïf, as mysterious as its voodoo ceremonies, as exciting as its music, Carnival, and Rara festivities, as charming as its gingerbread architecture – can easily become addictive. It is a country for people who have travelled extensively and are therefore familiar with the complexities of the Third World. Visitors also need not be easily deterred by the exigencies of getting around when there are frequent delays, a barely functioning telephone service and a small tourism infrastructure.

Government

Haiti, the first Black Republic, and only the second Republic in the world (after the USA,) was formed in

1804 after a war of independence with France. The constitution was approved March 1987, suspended June 1988 and most articles were reinstated in March 1989. There was a coup in October 1991. And finally a return to constitutional rule in October 1994.

According to law, presidential and legislative (parliamentary) elections are to be held every five years, but elections were cancelled in 1997, 1998, and 1999.

In May 2000 Fanmi Lavalas (FL) won the legislative and municipal elections amid violence and harassment of opposition candidates. In November of the same year opposition parties boycotted the presidential elections, which were won by Jean-Bertrand Aristide for the Fanmi Lavalas, with 92 percent of the vote.

The country has universal adult suffrage over 18 years old.

The Départements

Haiti has nine regional administrative divisions known as départements just as they are in France. They are: • Artibonite • Centre • Grand'Anse • Nord • Nord-Est • Nord-Ouest • Ouest • Sud • Sud-Est

EXECUTIVE BRANCH

The chief of state is the president – currently Jean-Bertrand Aristide – who has been in office since February 2001. The president is elected by popular vote for a term of at least five years. The last election was held in November 2000.

The head of government is the prime minister. The prime minister is appointed by the president, then ratified by the congress. Former Senate President, Yvon Neptune, became Prime Minister in March 2002 following the resignation of the previous encumbent.

The cabinet is chosen by the prime minister, in consultation with the president.

The legislative branch is

bicameral, consisting of the national assembly: the senate which has 27 seats has a six-year term, with one-third elected every two years; the chamber of deputies has 83 seats, elected by popular vote for a four-year term.

The judicial branch of the government is the superior court (*cour de cassation*).

Currency

One US dollar (US$1.00) = 38 Gourdes (38Gds) at the time of writing. There is another, unofficial, currency system in use – the Haitian Dollar. One Haitian dollar (H$1) = 5 Gds. Therefore US$1 = about H$7.50.

Please note that when a price is quoted in dollars, be sure to ask, if it is Haitian or US dollars, otherwise you could be in for a nasty shock.

Business Hours

Banks are open 9am–1pm and 3–5pm Monday to Friday. Shops usually open 8am–4pm with an hour for lunch at noon. On Saturday, they are open 8am–noon.

Post offices open 8am–8pm Monday to Friday and 8.30am–noon on Saturday.

Government Offices officially open 7am–4pm Monday to Friday.

Language

Haitian *Kréyol* (Créole) and French are the two official languages of Haiti, but *Kréyol* is the main language of the country. Many people in larger towns, especially those involved in the tourism industry, speak some English, French, Spanish and/or French Créole. Still, the average person (around 85 percent of the population) speaks only *Kréyol*. While all Haitians understand and speak it some of the time, French (a necessity for professional career advancement) is limited to the "élite" and middle classes.

Since the 1990s there has been a major shift towards the increased official use of *Kréyol*. Radio

stations increasingly broadcast in *Kréyol*, musicians use it in their songs, authors write in *Kréyol* and some politicians give speeches in the language.

Religion

Eighty percent of the population are practising Roman Catholics and around 16 percent are Protestants. Of that 16 percent Baptists make up 10 percent, Pentecostalists 4 percent, and Seventh Day Adventists 1 percent. One percent of the total population are atheist and a further 3 percent are of unknown religion.

The influence of Voodoo is ubiquitous. Voodoo is a blend of religions from West Africa (mainly from Dahomey – present-day Benin and the Congo River basin), that permeates the everyday life of a large majority of the Haiti's citizens.

Voodoo acquired an overlay of Catholicism in colonial times when

Public Holidays

January 1	New Year's Day and Independence Day (1804)
January 2	Heroes of Independence Day/ Ancestors Day
Good Friday	March/April
Easter	March/April
April 7	Toussaint L'Ouverture Memorial Day
May 1	Labour Day
May 18	Flag Day
May 22	National Sovereignty Day
August 15	Assumption Day
October 17	in memory of the death of Jean-Jacques Dessalines
November 1	All Saints' Day
November 2	All Souls' Day
November 18	Vertières Day
December 5	Pan-American Discovery Day (celebrates Columbus' landing near Cap-Haïtien)
December 25	Christmas Day

slaves disguised their *loas* (spirits) as saints. Today major voodoo ceremonies often coincide with Catholic celebrations and some religious sites are visited by both Catholic and Voodoo pilgrims at the same time.

Class Differences

The origins of class struggle are, sadly, based on colour. Lighter skinned mulattos evolved over time into an élite ruling class after independence in 1804. They lived in the south, which became the Republic of Haiti. Ruled by the liberal mulatto general, Alexandre Pétion, centred in Jérémie and the area that later became Pétionville, The élite spoke French, studied and travelled abroad and were more educated than their black fellow countrymen in the north who had been forced back to work on plantations and denied education by the dictator Dessalines and his successor, Henri Christophe. Although Haiti was re-unified in 1818, there were then two ruling classes. The rivalry continued between the mulattos and the increasingly wealthy black middle classes.

Economy

Unemployment is estimated at 60 percent. Haiti has the lowest per capita income in the Western Hemisphere at US$480 in 2001, having declined by an average annual rate of 2.5 percent 1990–2001. About 75 percent of its citizens live below the poverty level and 70 percent depend on subsistence farming to survive. The rural community is being depleted as people move to the towns and away from agriculture.

In spite of the country's high unemployment, workers are regularly imported from the Dominican Republic, Cuba and the Philippines for major construction projects.
• **Unemployment**: 70 percent.
• **Main industries**: Sugar refining, flour milling, textiles, cement,

tourism, light assembly based on imported parts.
• **Agricultural products**: coffee, mangoes, sugar cane, rice, corn, sorghum and wood.
• **Environmental issues**: extensive deforestation (much of the remaining forested land is being cleared for agriculture and used as fuel), soil erosion; inadequate supplies of potable water.

Population

Haiti has a population of approximately 8 million. Ninety-five percent are direct descendants of black African slaves and 5 percent are mulatto and varying combinations other races. The following statistics are from 2001 estimates:
• 48 percent of the population is under 18 years old.
• The infant mortality rate is 93 deaths per 1,000 live births (2002).
• Life expectancy in Haiti at birth is 49.5 years old (2002).

Transportation

There are 13 airports; three with paved runways and 10 unpaved. There are ports and harbours in Port-au-Prince, Jacmel, Cap-Haïtien, Saint-Marc, Gonaïves, Jeremie, Les Cayes, Miragoâne, Port-de-Paix.
There are no railways in Haiti.

Planning the Trip

Visas and Passports

Citizens of Australia, Canada, the UK, and the USA require only a valid passport and a return or onward ticket. No visa is necessary for a stay of up to 90 days.
There is an entry tax of US$10 payable at the airport.

Customs

Visitors are allowed to enter the country with 250g (9 oz) of tobacco, and one litre (2 pints) of alcohol.

Health Precautions

Vaccinations against malaria, hepatitis, typhoid and polio are advisable. Rabies is also a potential hazard. Medical insurance is highly recommended as medical facilities are not often as well equipped as Western ones, and emergency airlift is very costly.
• Be careful what and where you eat, food poisoning occurs frequently among tourists.
• All water should be boiled, otherwise stick to bottled water.
• If you are on any medication be sure to bring it with you, pharmacists, though plentiful, are not always convenient.
Bring an insect repellent with the highest percentage of "deet" you can find. One brand found in the USA (available through REI stores, catalogues and website) is called *Jungle Juice*. It contains 99 percent deet. Be aware that this is a strong chemical and some people may be sensitive to it. An excellent alternative is called *Skin So Soft* made by Avon. It is actually a bath oil but when applied directly to the

skin it is a good deterrent and doesn't have an offensive smell.

Non-Deet products tested and validated by the London School of Hygiene and Tropical Medicine include Mosiguard, Jungle Formula and Autan.

HIV and Aids is prevalent among 6 percent of the population, so safe sex is always recommended.

A suggested personal medical kit would contain: sterile bandages, gauze, plasters, scissors, tweezers, cottonbuds, antiseptic, a suture kit; disposable syringes, antibiotic cream, antihistamines – internal and topical for allergic reactions or bites, insect repellent, sun screen, remedies for common headaches, muscle aches, diarrhoea.

One of the nicest things a visitor can do is to take (and leave) medical supplies that might be in short supply in Haiti. Contact an international aid agency for advice on what to bring.

Insurance

MEDICAL

Local doctors and hospitals often expect immediate cash payment for health services, so travellers are strongly recommended to take out a comprehensive travel insurance policy which includes medical repatriation by air in the event of serious illness. See your travel agent for advice. US citizens can find useful information about medical emergencies abroad, including overseas insurance programmes, in the brochure, *Medical Information for Americans Traveling Abroad*, available from the US Department of State's Bureau of Consular Affairs, auto fax: (202) 647 3000.

British visitors should consult the Foreign and Commonwealth Office website: www.fco.gov.uk, for useful information and travel health advice. It has links to the Department of Health Travel Advice (UK), www.doh.gov.uk/traveladvice.

Scuba divers can join DAN (Divers Alert Network). Besides being a non-profit organisation that funds

research, DAN has one of the best travel accident insurance policies.

THEFT

Theft outside the home is often covered under residential household insurance policies, check with your before you leave. A copy of the police report is usually required for any claim. If travelling with valuable equipment such as cameras and scuba gear, consider additional baggage insurance and/or a rider on just the most expensive items.

Money Matters

For several reasons, Haiti is one country where the preferred place to change money is a bank. Banks give the best exchange rate, they are more secure, and the notes are less likely to be counterfeit. A hotel is also good, but the rate will be lower than the bank's. Banks exchange only US dollars and US dollar traveller's cheques

The three banks with the best bureaux de change are Sogebank, Unibank, BNC (Banque Nationale de Credit), all have branches in the larger cities. Other principal banks in the country include the National Bank of Haiti (BNRH), Central Bank, Bank of Nova Scotia, Banque Populaire, Banque Nationale, Banque Nationale de Paris, Banque de L'Union Haitienne, Citibank, Promobank and Union Bank.

Always take along the receipt that came with the purchase of the traveller's cheques each time you go to the bank. This receipt, with the cheque numbers on it, is required in addition to a passport or photo ID, in order to exchange traveller's cheques at the bank. Without it, the traveller's cheques won't be cashed. Be prepared for long queues in most banks for any kind of service. Bank locations:
Promobank in Port-au-Prince, corner of Lamarre and Ave John Brown; Blvd du Quai; and Rue Eden.
Scotiabank in Port-au-Prince, Route de Delmas (beneath the Canadian

Embassy); and 360 Blvd Dessalines.
Citibank in Pétionville is open until 5pm, while the drive-in teller is open until 6pm.
Sogebank, **Banque de L'Union Haïtienne** in Cap-Haïtien: all are on Rue A between Rue 10th and Rue 11th.
In Jacmel there is a bank on Ave. Baranquilla Jérémie.

What to Wear

Clothing in Haiti is casual but discreet. Swimsuits and beachwear should not be worn in town. Only a few of the high class restaurants require formal dress for dinner.

Leave expensive jewellery at home and keep cameras out of sight until needed.

Tourist Information

Haiti has no Tourist information offices outside the country, but it does have some diplomatic representation.

HAITIAN EMBASSIES ABROAD

In Canada: 112 Rue Kent, suite 205, Ottawa K1P 5P2, tel: (613) 238 1628.
In the Dominican Republic: 33 Ave. Juan Sánchez Ramírez, Santo Domingo, tel: (809) 686 5778; (809) 686 6096.
In Jamaica: 2 Munroe Road, Kingston 6, tel: (876) 927 7595; fax: (876) 978 7638.
In the US: 2311 Massachusetts Avenue NW, Washington, DC 20008, tel: (202) 332 4090; fax: (202) 745 7215.
There are also Haitian consulates in: Miami, Florida; Boston, Massachusetts; New York; Chicago, Illinois and San Juan, Puerto Rico.

ON THE WEB

There are various websites online where you can glean additional information regarding Haiti. It is

What to Bring Checklist

- Insect repellent.
- An electronic mosquito repeller and mosquito coils to light at night.
- Sun block or tanning lotion (can be combined with "deet" for double action).
- Plastic "Ziplock" bags in various sizes.
- Photocopies of all documents – passport, credit cards, driver's licence, etc. Carry these and leave originals in the hotel safe.
- An international adaptor and a transformer if visiting from outside the US.
- Anti-itch remedies – Calamine lotion, antihistamines
- Decongestant, diarrhoea and motion sickness relievers.
- Ear plugs.
- Nasal spray.
- Anti-jet lag remedies.
- Liquid hand sanitizer
- Moist babywipes.
- Calculator.
- Small torch.
- Glasses/sunglasses.
- Small backpack.
- Lighter/matches.
- Paperclips.
- Small notebook.
- Sewing kit.
- Stain remover.
- Sellotape.
- Credit cards.
- Prescription medication and vitamins or supplements.

important to note, though, that travel information on many of the sites is not kept upto date. Below is a randomly selected list:

www.i-port.net/sd-hgv-port
www.haitionline.com
www.haitiglobalvillage.com
www.medalia.net/index.html
www.info.usaid.gov
www.haiti-info.com
www.doitcaribbean.com/haiti

Photography

Bring extras of anything that is difficult to replace, spare batteries and film. The current crop of strong airport x-ray machines can destroy or seriously damage film. Do not put any film – exposed or otherwise – into checked luggage. The machines at the security check points are not quite as bad, but the effects of multiple trips through these machine are cumulative. Carry all rolls of film in a zipped plastic bag and ask the security person to check it by hand. Sometimes they'll insist that it go through the machine, but each time it is hand-checked is a help.

Getting There

BY AIR

Airline schedules and routes in and to Haiti are constantly changing. New airlines start up and more airlines are adding or increasing service to Haiti.

Airlines servicing Haiti include: Aero Caribbean, Air Canada, Air d'Ayiti, Air France, Air Guadeloupe, ALM Antillean Airlines, American Airlines, Canada 3000, Copa, Dominair, Dutch Caribbean Express, Lynx Air, Surinam Airways, Tropical Airways.

Flying Times

New York to Haiti – 3 hours 20 mins
Miami to Haiti – 1 hour
San Juan to Haiti – 1 hour 10 mins
Santo Domingo to Haiti – 40 mins
Montreal to Haiti – 4 hours.

For information in the Port-au-Prince area contact one of the offices listed, which are at the airport unless otherwise stated:
Aero Caribbean, tel: 222 1792.
Air D'Ayiti, tel: 246 2300/5755/2692.

Air Canada, tel: 246 0441/0442.
Air France, Champs de Mars, B.P. 1161, tel: 222 4262; fax: 223 0172.
American Airlines, 29/31 Delmas, tel: 246 0100/0159/0205; 249 0311; Ave Marie-Jeanne, Bicentenaire
Canada 3000, tel: 257 2740.
Copa, tel: 246 0737/0778; Rue du Quai, 249 0203; tel: 249 1575.
Dutch Caribbean Express, 6 Rue Pavée, tel: 222 0900; fax: 222 8007.
Lynx Air. Tel: 262 1386.
Tropical Airways D'Haiti, Domestic and International, Rue Panaméricaine, PV, tel: 256 3626/7/8; fax: 256 3629/298 3445; Cap Haitien; tel: 262 1226; Jérémie, tel: 284 6989; Port-de-Paix, tel: 268-5770.
www.tropical-haiti.com

Routes include: American Airlines flights to Port-au-Prince from New York and Miami. There are also direct services to Port-au-Prince from Santo Domingo, Martinique and Guadeloupe.

Flights from Canada are available on Air Canada and the charter carrier Canada 3000. Tropical Airways flies between Port-au-Prince or Cap-Haïtien and Providenciales and Nassau. Dutch Caribbean Express flies from Curaçao, Miami and Sint Maarten. Sky King flies between Cap-Haïtien and Providenciales. Air D'Ayiti has regular flights to Miami.

Lynx Air run a regular commercial air service from Fort Lauderdale International Airport, Florida to Cap-Haïtien. For further information call (954) 772 9808 in the USA or 262 1386 at Cap-Haïtien airport.

There are domestic flights from Port-au-Prince. Caribintair run two flights a day between Port-au-Prince and Cap-Haïtien. The company has offices in Port-au-Prince, tel: 246 0737/0778; fax: 249 1575 and at Cap-Haïtien airport on 262 2300.

Departure Tax

There is a US$30 departure tax and a 10Gd security tax, both payable at the airport in cash only.

BY LAND

There are exit and entry fees to be paid in both the Dominican Republic and Haiti, travelling in either direction. Haiti requires a *laissez-passer* when leaving by road, in addition to the departure tax of US$10 plus 25Gds in cash.

The official border crossings with the Dominican Republic are at Jimaní in the south (the Santo Domingo–Port-au-Prince route) and Ouanaminthe in the north (the Santiago de los Caballeros–Cap-Haïtien route).

The Route Nationale 1 leaves the north of Port-au-Prince, passing through Saint Marc and Gonaïves before arriving at Cap-Haïtien. The journey takes about seven hours by car. In order to reach Port-de-Paix take Route 105 which leaves the Route Nationale 1 about 5 km north of Gonaïves. The drive takes about five hours and requires a 4-wheel-drive vehicle.

By Car

Rental cars cannot be taken over the border and the nuisance of police checks at roadblocks in Haiti makes driving yourself ill-advised anyway.

By Bus/Coach

In addition to the hot, overcrowded public buses that run daily between Port-au-Prince and Santo Domingo, and between Cap-Haïtien and Santiago de los Caballeros, there are air conditioned buses run by Terrabús and Caribe Tours; they will handle all border formalities for you.

Buses for Cap-Haïtien leave Port-au-Prince at the Estation O'Cap on Blvd La Saline and drop off near the city gates in Cap-Haïtien on Rue L. The trip costs around US$6 for a one-way trip. Tap-taps for Cormier and Labadie Plage leave from Rue 21 Q and cost about 5 gourdes each way. Buses and tap-taps for Milot and Fort Libertè leave from Rue Lapont south of the city and cost 15–30 gourdes per trip.

BY SEA

Other than the cruise ships that disgorge their passengers at a private beach at Labadie on the North Coast for about 8 hours, regular cruise ships ceased calling in Haiti after the 1991 coup.

Royal Caribbean Lines has three ships that stop for a day at Labadie Beach, near the Cap-Haïtien suburb, Cormier Plage. It is an isolated beach laden with amenities including watersports and shopping. Nearby Amiga (previously Rat) Island has wonderful snorkelling and offers an educational tour which looks at the making of artificial reefs. Scuba diving can be arranged through Jean Claude at Cormier Plage Hotel.

The three ships whose itineraries include this stop are *Enchantment of the Seas*, *Grandeur of the Seas*, and *Majesty of the Seas*.

Specialist Tour Operator

Trips Worldwide in the UK organise tailor-made holidays to the not so well-known Caribbean islands, Central and South America. For more information and a brochure contact them at:
14 Frederick Place, Clifton, Bristol BS8 1AS, United Kingdom, tel: 0117 3114 400; fax: 0117 3114 401.
Website: www.tripsworldwide.co.uk
Email: info@tripsworldwide.co.uk
Interchange Tour Operators specialise in tours to Haiti and Cuba. Contact them at:
Interchange House, 27 Stafford Road, Croydon, Surrey CR0 4NG, United Kingdom. tel: 020 8681 3612; fax: 020 8681 3613
Voyages Lumière (tel: 249 6177) operates from within Haiti, *see page 371*.

Embassies and Consulates in Haiti

The **Secrétairie d'État au Tourisme** is at 8 Rue Légitime, Port-au-Prince, Haiti, tel: 223 5631/0723, 221 5960; fax: 223 5359/5388; email: set@haititourisme.com; website: www.haititourisme.com
British Consulate, Hotel Montana, Rue F. Cardoza, Port-au-Prince, tel: 257 3969; fax: 257 4048.
Canadian Embassy, 1st floor, Scotiabank, Delmas 18, tel: 223 2358/8882; fax: 223 8720.
US Embassy, 5 Blvd Harry Truman, Bicentenaire, Port-au-Prince. For mailing purposes contact P. O. Box 1761, Port-au-Prince, tel: 222 0354/0368/0200/0612; fax: 223 1641.
US Consulate, 104 Rue Oswald Durand, Port-au-Prince, tel: 223 0989/8853/9324/7011; fax: 223 9965.

TRAVEL ADVISORIES

For travel advisories on vaccinations, visas and security before you leave home, contact:
US Department of State Overseas Citizens Services, tel: (202) 647 5225; **Canadian Travel Advisory Line**, tel: 800 267 6788; **British Travel Advice Unit**, tel: 020 7238 4503/4504; **Australian Travel Advisory Line**, tel: (06) 261 2093.

Practical Tips

It is worthwhile repeating, Haiti is a mutable country where everything is subject to change, almost from moment to moment. As such, prices, addresses and telephone numbers could change – possibly in the time between lunch and dinner on any day. It's part of what makes Haiti so frustrating... and so fascinating.

Etiquette

There are some general rules of etiquette that every visitor to Haiti should be aware of.
● Always acknowledge a greeting with a greeting in return. People usually greet each other in the morning with *bonjou* (bonjour) and *bo'swa* (bonsoir) in the afternoon or evening. If you prefer you can say hello or *salud* (pronounced "saloo") to people you meet along the way any time of day.
● Always greet people politely before asking directions or for help.
● Never assume that it's okay to take someone's photograph, ask permission first and don't be surprised if the subject expects a small payment in return.

Telephone and Fax

Haiti's country code is **509**. Local services and facilities are not particularly reliable, often making telephone contact difficult.

When trying to make a telephone call, be aware that a busy signal doesn't necessarily mean the recipient is on the phone, and a ringing tone doesn't necessarily mean that no one is there, or that there's a working phone in service

at that number. Be patient.

The entire country, including government offices, can be affected by an unannounced service disruption. A cellular telephone is the best way to avoid such problems, they can be rented at the airport upon arrival, or you can bring your own and have it connected for a fee check the system used in Haiti before leaving home.

Phonecards are an option for making calls from public telephones and can be purchased at the post office and from hotels. Cards include the MCI prepaid international telephone card which can be purchased in the US or Haiti. There is also an AT&T calling card account which must be activated before leaving the US.

There is a Teleco office on Rue 17 in Cap-Haïtien, close to the Boulevard, tel 262 0000 which is open 24 hours a day. Another office is in Port-de-Paix on Rue Estimé.

International access codes
AT&T: 183; MCI: 193; Sprint: 171

Postal Services

Post offices in the main towns are generally open 8am–4pm. All mail must be sent from a post office, although some hotels will organise a mail service for postcards. For larger items use an international courier, most have offices in the larger towns and the cities.

In Cap-Haïtien the post office on Rue 16–17 A is open Mon–Fri 8.30am–4pm, Sat 8.30am–noon.

In Port-de-Paix the post office on Rue Dessalines is open Mon–Fri 8.30am–4pm and Sat 8.30am–noon.

Media

Radio is by far the most popular medium and the country has a healthy mix of music and talk radio programming. Among the most listened to is *Radio Haiti Inter* which plays music and has news in French. Both the *BBC World Service* and *Voice of America* broadcast to Haiti.

Most newspapers and magazines are in French. Popular dailies

include *Le Nouvelliste* and *Le Matin*; weeklies *Haiti en Marche* and *Haiti Progrès*. *Libète* is a weekly paper produced in *Kréyol*. The US-published *Haiti Observateur* has some news stories in English.

Weights and Measures

Lengths
metric to imperial
1 millimetre (mm) = 0.04 inches
1 centimetre (cm) = 0.39 inches
1 metre (m) = 3.28 feet (ft)
1 kilometre (km) = 0.62 miles

imperial units to metric units
1 inch = 2.54 cm
1 foot = 30.48 cm
1 yard = 0.91 metres
1 mile = 1.61 km
1 int nautical mile = 1.85 km

Area
metric to imperial
1 sq cm (cm²) = 0.16 in²
1 sq m (m²) = 1.2 yd²
1 hectare (ha) = 2.47 acres
1 sq km (km²) = 0.39 mile²

imperial to metric
1 sq inch (in²) = 6.45 cm²
1 sq foot (ft²) = 0.09 m²
1 sq yd (yd²) = 0.84 m²
1 acre = 4046.9 m²
1 sq mile (miles²) = 2.59 km²

Volume/Capacity
metric to imperial
1 cubic cm (cm³) = 0.06 inches³
1 cubic decimetre (dm³) = 0.04 ft³
1 cubic meter (m³) = 1.31 yd³
1 litre (lt) = 1.76 UK pints/2.11 US pints
1 hectolitre (hl) = 22 UK gallons/26.4 US gallons
imperial to metric
1 cu inch (in³) = 16.39 cm³
1 cu foot (ft³) = 0.03 m³
1 fluid ounce (fl oz) = 28.41 ml
1 UK pint = 0.57 l
1 US pint = 0.5lt
1 UK gallon = 4.55 lt
1 US gallon = 3.78 lt

Mass
metric to imperial
1 milligram (mg) = 0.02 grain (gr)
1 gram (g) = 0.04 oz
1 kilogram (kg) = 2.20 lb
1 tonne = 0.98 UK tons
1 tonne = 1.1 US tons

imperial to metric
1 ounce (oz) = 28.35 g
1 pound (lb) = 0.45 kg
1 UK stone = 6.35 kg
1 ton = 20 cwt = 1.02 tonnes
1 US ton = 2000 lbs = 907 kg

Temperature
Centigrade to Fahrenheit
Multiply by 1.8 and add 32

Fahrenheit to Centigrade
Subtract 32 and multiply by 55

Tourism Offices in Haiti

There are three Maison du Tourisme offices (tourist information). Situated in the heart of the tourist areas, they are open 9am–4pm to provide information such as maps, details about tours and staff will answer questions.
In Port-au-Prince: corner of Rues Capois and Magny, tel: 221 5496.
In Jacmel: Avenue Barranquilla No. 165, tel: 288 3305.
In Cap-Haïtien: Rue 24 Boulevard, Cap Haitien: tel: 262 1061. Call ahead, opening times are erratic.

Travellers with Disabilities

Haiti still needs time to develop facilities which will make it accessible to disabled visitors. As the infrastructure improves the current situation is likely to change. For the present, it would be extremely difficult and uncomfortable for anyone with a physical disability to travel in Haiti.
Access to public transport and tourist attractions is severely limited. It seems as though there are construction sites everywhere in cities and towns.
In the countryside, a paved road is rare and it takes some effort,

even for the able-bodied, to reach notable landmarks.
Most hotels have steps to negotiate in order to pass from one area to another. Only hotels with more than three or four floors have lifts but power cuts make these unreliable.

Tipping, Taxes

Hotels and restaurants usually add a 10 percent service charge to the bill. Some hotels also charge a daily energy tax.
For exceptional service in restaurants you can give waiters a small additional tip (in gourdes). Taxi drivers do not expect a tip.

Religious Services

Many churches hold wonderful services with beautiful music. Ask at your hotel for suggestions.

Medical Services

Medical care, facilities, and supplies are limited and the level of sanitation is generally lower than in a developed country. One of the best x-ray facilities in Haiti is in a small clinic in Jérémie, which could be too far away in an emergency.

Medical Facilities
In Port-au-Prince: Hôpital du Canapé Vert, 83 Route du Canapé Vert, tel: 245 0281. 24-hour service.
In Cap-Haïtien: Hospital Justinien, Rue 17 Q, tel 262 0512. Situated high above the town; Clinic Antoni Constant, Rue 16 L No.46, tel 262 1577. Recommended by many of the hotels.

The Red Cross
The Red Cross in Cap-Haïtien can be contacted at Rue 17 P, tel: 262 0634. In Port-de-Paix contact: tel: 268 4141 and the general hospital on tel: 268 6264.

Security and Crime

The media publicises the car-jackings, armed robberies, and break-ins in Haiti but these offences are not directed exclusively at foreigners.
Use the same common sense you would use at home and try to be aware of your surroundings. Keep valuables out of sight (preferably in the hotel safe) and divide currency into small portions in different pockets. Be alert, especially on public transport and in crowded places. Keep car doors locked at all times, especially when sitting inside. Don't walk around Port-au-Prince after dark, and monitor potential danger areas by checking with the hotel and the embassy at home. Avoid travelling at night.
Visitors should exercise extreme caution when driving along Route Nationale 1, the airport road, in the port area and in Cité Soleil, as crimes involving vehicles occur regularly. While a lot of crime occurs in these areas, neighbourhoods in Port-au-Prince, such as the Delmas road area and Pétionville, formerly considered safe, have witnessed an increasing incidence of crime.
Holiday periods, Christmas and Carnival, especially, see a significant increase in violent crime.

Emergency Numbers

Police	Tel: 114
Fire	Tel: 115
Red Cross	Tel: 118

The Police
The police station in Cap-Haïtien is at Rue 25-26 A, Carenage tel 262 0951; in Port-de-Paix call 268 5383.

Getting Around

Orientation

Getting around Haiti can be difficult for a number of reasons, the main ones being language – non-*Kréyol* speakers may find it hard to make themselves understood – and a lack of tourist infrastructure. There are no scheduled sightseeing tours. Road conditions, especially in the mountainous interior, are poor. The fastest, safest, and most comfortable, albeit most expensive way to travel between Haiti's main cities is by air.

From the Airport

Taxis are usually available at the airports. There are three basic types of taxi: local **regular** taxis take individual passengers directly to their destinations, local **shared** taxis (the least expensive) stop briefly to drop off other passengers on the way to the furthest destination, and the **ACGH** (Association des Chauffeur-Guides d'Haiti – Haiti Association of Chauffeur-Guides) taxis. The latter are the same as regular taxis in terms of the type and condition of vehicles, but the drivers are accredited by the ACGH. They are supposed to have some training in tourism, wear the same type of white shirt-cum-uniform with an ACGH pin. Therefore these taxis are more expensive.

The government sets a scale of fares but this is not necessarily set in stone.

A good transport choice for groups is **Agence Citadelle** which runs a door-to-door air conditioned minibus shuttle which includes a "meet and greet" service at the airports in Port-au-Prince and Cap-Haïtien for around US$15 per person. Call the Port-au-Prince office in advance of the trip, tel: 222 5900, fax: 222 1792; www.agencecitadelle.com.

One of the regular tap-tap services can take visitors into the city centre usually dropping off at Rue 10 A.

By Air

It takes less than one hour to fly anywhere in Haiti from Port-au-Prince. Unless you have booked a private charter, flying between any two cities requires a transfer in Port-au-Prince.

Domestic Carriers

Air D'Ayiti has 5 flights per day to Cap-Haïtien and Port-de-Paix, as well as to Jérémie. Tel: 246 2300/5755.
Tropical Airways D'Haiti fly from Port-au-Prince to Cap-Haïtien, Jérémie, Port-de-Paix and Pétionville. The service is excellent, planes are comfortable and staff are friendly. Tel: 256 3626; fax: 256 3629, 298 3445; Cap-Haïtien, tel: 262 1226; Jérémie, tel: 284 6989; Port-de-Paix, tel: 268 5770.
Caribintair is a long-time carrier between Port-au-Prince and Cap-Haïtien, Jérémie, and Santo Domingo in the Dominican Republic. Tel: 510 8040; 298 3040/3041

By Car

TAXIS

Taxi fares will inevitably be inflated for visitors, except when there is a meter in the vehicle. And even if there's a meter in the taxi, don't assume that it's working, ask the driver before starting the trip. It's also wise to agree the fare for the journey in advance. Ask someone at the hotel what the typical fare is and then try to negotiate as close as possible to that.

Other than the *publiques*, taxis can't be flagged down, they must be called. A hotel is the easiest place to find a regular taxi, the hotel receptionist will usually telephone a reliable taxi service for anyone who asks, not just guests. Contact:
Nick's Taxi Service, Tel: 257 7777
Family Taxi, Tel: 511 3100.
Both are based in Pétionville and have metered radio taxis.
Akenssa Taxi, Rue 14B No. 178, tel 262-2210. An upmarket taxi hire firm in Cap-Haïtien.

City Street Names

Several major Port-au-Prince thoroughfares have two names, the official one used for maps and in the telephone book, and the unofficial one commonly used in conversation. Taxi drivers are often only familiar with the unofficial name. For example, Blvd Jean-Jacques Dessalines is called Grand Rue; Ave Lamartinière is known as Bois Verna (pronounced Bwa Vèna); Ave Jean Paul II is referred to as Turgeau (pronounced Too-joe or Tee-joe); Ave John Brown is called Lalue and as Pan Américaine in Pétionville; Ave Paul VI is referred to locally as Rue des Casernes; and Ave Martin Luther King is called Nazon.

Publiques

In Port-au-Prince *publiques*, with a red ribbon hanging from the rear-view mirror, are shared taxis that can be flagged down on the street. These taxis travel along a set route and the drivers speak only *Kréyol*. Be sure to ask if the *publique* is passing the desired stop. The destination of the first passenger in the taxi determines the route and the driver will stop to pick up and drop off others along the way. It is one of the best, fastest and least expensive ways to get around the city. The fare is usually 10 gourdes unless the destination is somewhere far out. *Publiques* stop working around 7.30pm.

In Cap-Haïtien local communal taxis charge about 12 gourdes for all destinations in town.

Chauffeurs-Guides

Chauffeurs-Guides are taxi drivers who cater to foreign visitors. They often wait outside the bigger hotels and at the airport. They can be used like regular taxis, hired by the hour or, for a half-day or day tour. Many of these drivers speak some French and/or a little English, and have some training to prepare them to work with tourists.

Book through the Association des Chauffeurs-Guides. Tel: 222 0330. The dispatch office is in Port-au-Prince city centre, 18 Blvd Harry Truman, near the US Embassy.

Driver-owned Taxis

Driver-owned taxis can be spotted easily, look for the double '0' painted on their doors, and a registration number painted on the bonnet.

Chauffeur-driven Rental

Secom, Pétionville, tel: 257 1913/2847. The auto rental company in will hire out a driver with their cars. The price for the service is very reasonable if it is only needed for a normal 8 hour day, but it can be expensive if a driver is required in the evening.

CAR RENTALS

If you're determined to drive, despite the warnings, then it's best to call ahead and reserve a vehicle in plenty of time as there are rarely enough rental cars to meet demand. A wide variety of vehicles can be rented from various agencies in Port-au-Prince and Pétionville. Daily rates are around US$60 to US$165 (for four-wheel-drive).

Ask for any special deals and discounts on offer; there are often special rates for rentals of a week or longer. Note that cars rented in Haiti cannot be taken over the border to the Dominican Republic.

Drivers with US, Canadian and European licences generally do not need to obtain a special licence for travelling around Haiti. Driving is on the right-hand side of the road.

Rental Agencies

Avis, tel: 246 4161/2696; fax:246 2640.
Budget, tel: 246 1366.
Hertz, tel: 246 0700. Also has an office close to the airport at the Centre Multidynamic tel 262 0369.
Secom, tel: 246 2799/257 1913; www.secomhaiti.com.

By Bus & Tap-tap

Camionettes (minibuses) and **tap-taps** (open-backed pickups with brightly painted wooden chassis) have fixed routes and fares. They are usually packed to capacity and therefore difficult to board with luggage. They generally stop running by 8.30pm.

To reach Pétionville from Port-au-Prince catch any of the tap-taps which run along Ave John Brown.

Tap-taps regularly run along two main routes in Cap-Haïtien on Rue L, from Rue 15 L to the city gates and along Rue A, from Rue 10 A to the airport. Each trip costs 3½ gourdes.

Tap-tap Art

Tap-taps are mini-vans, buses and trucks covered in brightly coloured geometric designs and delicately wrought art, inscribed with humourous mottos and religious messages in *Kréyol*, French and English. The pictures usually tell a story and some use images to make a social or political comment. Below are a few examples of tap-tap art:
● *Recherchez Le Bien de la Ville*
Look for the good in the city
● *Welcome to Don de Jesus*
Welcome to God's gift
● *Merci Manman*
Thank You Mother
● *Sans Jesus Tout est Nul*
All Is Nothing Without Jesus
● *Souv de mon Pere et ma Mere*
Remembrance of my Father and my Mother
● *Paix, Amour*
Peace, Love
● *Peuple D'Egypte. Oh! La Femme*
People of Egypt Oh! The Woman

Driving

Road conditions in Haiti are very poor and paved roads in Port-au-Prince and the major provincial capitals are littered with potholes. Most roads in the countryside are unpaved and unlit. Traffic laws are similar to those in the US but are not generally enforced.

Port-au-Prince traffic is congested most of the day as a result of the poor roads, undisciplined driving, badly maintained vehicles, a plethora of street merchants, itinerant mechanics and so many pedestrians.

The utter chaos and poor road conditions are an unnerving, white-knuckle, hair-greying experience. It isn't easy to determine who has the right of way in any traffic situation. Vehicles have been known to pass stationary traffic by mounting the pavement. And when there are roadworks, there is rarely any warning or detour signage.

Excursions

Most organised tours are pre-planned for groups only, so try to make arrangements well in advance.

TOUR OPERATORS & TRAVEL AGENCIES

Agence Martine
17 Rue de Miracles, Port-au-Prince; 18 Rue Oge at Geffrard, Pétionville, tel: 257 2740; fax: 257 2824.
Voyage Chatelain 76 Rue Geffrard, tel: 223 2400, 222 0130; fax: 223 5065.
Agent for the Terra Bus to Santo Domingo.
Sans Souci
Ave. John Brown, tel: 245 6395/6980/6407.
Cap Travel
Rue des Miracles and Bicentennaire, tel: 222 3150/9774; fax: 223 9452.
Napolitano
24 Ave. John Brown, tel: 223 8426/9796/9826; fax: 223 8498.
Omni Tours

34 Rue des Casernes, tel: 223 8870/8981; fax: 222 8351.

SPECIALIST TOURS

Some unique cultural, historical, environmental and adventure tourism is developing in Haiti.
Agence Citadelle S.A. and **American Sightseeing Haiti**
35 Place du Marron Inconnu, Port-au-Prince
Mailing address: PO Box 41, Port-au-Prince, Haiti, tel: 222 5900/223 5900; fax: 222 1792;
www.agencecitadelle.com.
The largest tour company in Haiti provides: a "meet greet" and transfer; Airport Express; sightseeing tours around Port-au-Prince and to Cap-Haïtien; Intercity tours to the Dominican Republic. All tours are on air conditioned buses and minibuses.
Voyages Lumière
Delmas 75, Ave Fragneauville, Rue M. Esteve, Port-au-Prince, Haiti, WI
tel: 249 6177; 557 0753 (cellular); email:
voyageslumiere@haitelonline.com
www.voyageslumierehaiti.com
Jacqualine Labrom, an Englishwoman living in Haiti, specialises in Gingerbread House tours for small groups and knows Jacmel and Port-au-Prince like the back of her hand. She can also arrange tours elsewhere in Haiti, book hotels and internal flights.
Résidence Pauline
Résidence Pauline once belonged to Napoleon's sister, Pauline. There are usually two group tours (minimum of 10 people) per week, on Tues and Thurs and perhaps another on Sat with a full lunch or tea. Individuals can join a pre-booked tour depending on the type of group. Contact: PO Box 30, Cap-Haïtien, Haiti, tel: 262 2098.
Destination DjonDjon
Maison du Tourisme, Cnr of Rue Magny and Rue Capois, Port-au-Prince, tel: 222 8896.
A network of groups providing an alternative view of Haiti.

Where to Stay

Hotels

A 10 percent room tax is added to all hotel bills. An energy surcharge of about US$5 per day and a service charge may also be added.

Despite the decline in tourism and the lack of facilities for tourists, hotel prices in Haiti are relatively expensive, although in many places it is possible to negotiate.

Port-au-Prince & The West

PORT-AU-PRINCE

Expensive
Hôtel Oloffson
60 Avenue Christophe
Tel: 223 4000/4102; fax: 223 0919.
A city landmark – preserved old gingerbread mansion in a quiet residential area, yet close to the centre. Most rooms have air conditioning and ceiling fan, restaurant, bar, pool and a small souvenir shop. Unique ambiance created by Haitian-American musician-owner, Richard Morse, utilising Haitian art and antique furniture. His band, RAM, usually perform at the hotel on Thursday. A favourite haunt of journalists, photographers and politicians. **$$$**
Prince Hotel
30 Rue 3, corner Ave. N, Pacot
Tel: 245 2764/5; fax: 245 2756, 222 2765, 221 8604
A hotel in a quiet residential neighbourhood three blocks from the Oloffson. Rooms with air conditioning, restaurant, bar, pool. The original building is filled with eclectic art and antique furniture while the newer wing has modern motel-type furnishings. **$$$**

Moderate
Le Plaza
10 Rue Capois, Champ de Mars
Tel: 223 9800/9783/8697; fax: 223 7232;
email: hiplaza@ acn2.net
Sometimes referred to as the Holiday Inn. A large hotel built around a lush tropical garden, convenient for the city centre. With 80 air conditioned, rustic rooms, pool, restaurant and bar. Has its own generator. **$$**

Hotel Price Guide

Room rates for two people sharing:
● **$ = Budget** under US$25
● **$$ = Moderate** US$25–50
● **$$$ = Expensive** over US$50

PÉTIONVILLE

Expensive
Hotel El Rancho
Ave. Panaméricaine
Impasse José de St. Martin
Tel: 257 2080/81/84, 257 9623; fax: 257 4134
Hotel in a Spanish-style building set on a large lush property with mature trees and flowering plants. Large air conditioned rooms and 5 suites, pool, tennis courts, gym, casino, disco, restaurant and bar. The Presidential Suite has its own dining room and beautiful antique furniture, another suite features a red Victorian bath. **$$$**
Hotel Kinam
Place St Pierre, at corner of Rue Lambert
Tel: 257 6525/0462; fax: 257 4410;
www.hotelkinam.com
Gingerbread-style hotel in an excellent location on the main square with friendly staff. The restaurant overlooks the pool and there is an intimate bar. Comfortable, charmingly decorated rooms in tropical style. Rooms at the back are quieter than those at the front. **$$$**

Hotel Montana
Rue Cardozo
Tel: 257 4030, 257 1920/21; fax:
257 6137;
email: htmontana@aol.com
Uninspiring architecture but
spectacular view of Port-au-Prince
and the bay from the poolside
restaurant. Spacious, well
appointed, air conditioned rooms
are decorated in bright tropical
colours. Two restaurants, a bar and
a souvenir shop. **$$$**

Villa Creole
Ave. Panaméricaine
Impasse José de St Martin
Tel: 257 1570/71, 257 1609, 257
8106, 257 7228; fax: 257 4935;
www.villacreole.com
Large welcoming family-run hotel in
attractive Spanish architectural
style, spread among courtyards and
gardens with good views. Antique
mahogany furniture, original
paintings and a beautiful pool.
Indoor and al fresco dining. All 72
air conditioned rooms have cable TV
and telephone with voice mail.
Internet access to guests. **$$$**

Moderate

Caraïbe Hotel
13 Rue Léon Nau
Tel: 257 2524
Charming, good value, quiet and
simple hotel built in the 1920s.
Rooms with air conditioning, large
baths, bar, restaurant, TV lounge
and pool. **$$**

Hotel Ibo Lélé
Rue Borno, on the way to Montagne
Noir, above Pétionville
Tel: 257 5668/1695; fax: 257 8012
Built in the 1950's the hotel has a
spectacular view over Port-au-
Prince. Reminiscent of an American
motel, rooms have private bath,
telephone and terrace. Restaurant,
pool and jacuzzi. Has its own
generator. Dancing at weekends. **$$**

Budget

Ife Hotel
30 Rue Gregoire
Tel: 257 2168/0737
Modest, charming little refuge in
the busiest part of Pétionville. No
food service but it's close to excellent restaurants and nightlife. **$**

Sunset Suites
15 Route Ibo Lélé
Tel: 257 0553
Small, quiet hotel about a 15-
minute walk uphill from Place St
Pierre. Six rooms with bath and
hot water, TV in the lobby, and a
pool in the garden. Meals can be
ordered from Café des Arts (same
owner). On the weekend during
summer and holidays loud music
comes from the nearby Ibo Lélé
nightclub. **$**

Hotel Price Guide

Room rates for two people
sharing:
● **$ = Budget** under US$25
● **$$ = Moderate** US$25–50
● **$$$ = Expensive** over US$50

GUEST HOUSES

Moderate

Doux Séjour
32 Rue Magny
Tel: 257 1560
Simple accommodation on quiet
street five blocks from Place St
Pierre. Weekly rates for rooms with
fan and bathroom. **$$**

Villa Kalewes
99 Rue Grégoire
Tel: 257 0817
Rooms in a villa, with a pool, near
Place St Pierre and at the upper,
quiet end of the street. **$$**

Budget

Marabou
72 Rue Stephen Archer
Tel: 257 1934
Just behind St Pierre church. The
owner, Mme. Odette Weiner, puts
on folkloric shows. **$–$$**

CÔTES DES ARCADINS

The beach resorts on the north
side of the Gulf of La Gonâve
are open to non-guests for day
use and for meals. The biggest
choice of food will be
available on the weekend when it
is busier.

Expensive

Kaliko Beach Club
Km 61, Route Nationale 1
Côte des Arcadins
Tel: 298 4607; 222 8040 (Port-au-
Prince); fax: 298 4610
Medium-sized hotel with 40 air
conditioned rooms, restaurant, bar,
tennis courts, pool. The beach is
part sand, part pebbles. Pegasus
scuba diving run by José Roy; boats
too. **$$$**

Moulin sur la Mer
Km 77, Route Nationale 1
Tel: 222 1918, 245 1013 (Port-au-
Prince); 278 6700/05; fax: 278
6720; www.moulinsurmer.net
Large resort set in a restored
18th century plantation house
with a large pond and pretty
gardens. A modern extension has
large air conditioned rooms and
filtered water. Guests use golf
carts to get around the 20-hectare
(50-acre) property. Dine in **Le
Boucanier** restaurant at the
beach. Lots of outdoor activites
including pedal-boats, snorkelling
and scuba diving. Busy at the
weekends with day visitors from
Port-au-Prince. The Oratory is used
for weddings and a small building
on the property houses the **Ogier-
Fombrun Colonial Museum**, one of
the best museums detailing the
history of the colonial period in
Haiti. **$$$**

Wahoo Bay
Km 64, Route Nationale 1
Tel: 223 2950, 222 9653; fax: 222
5332
Beach resort with garden,
restaurant, pool and watersports.
$$$

Moderate

Kyona Hotel Beach
Km 60, Route Nationale 1
Tel: 222 6788 (Port-au-Prince);
257 8663/9137; fax: 257 6850
Beachfront hotel in lovely location
the closest to Les Arcadins,
small uninhabited islands
surrounded by coral reefs
protected in a marine preserve.
Rooms are basic with cold water,
but have ceiling fans; restaurant
and bar. Great for snorkelling.
Near the fishing village of Luly. **$$**

Ouanga Bay Beach Hotel
Km 65, Route Nationale 1
Tel: 234 0430; fax: 222 4422
Delightful beachfront hotel with
friendly staff, balconied rooms and
watersports. Live music at the
weekend. **$$**

The North

CAP-HAÏTIEN

Expensive
Roi Christophe
Rue 24 B
Tel: 262 0414
An elegant, colonial building set in a
leafy, walled garden in the centre of
town with a decent restaurant. air
conditioning, private bathroom and
breakfast included. Credit cards
accepted. **$$$**
Hotel Mont Joli
Rue B, Carenage
Tel: 262 0300; 222 7764; fax: 262
0326;
email: montjoli@aol.com
Elevated position to the north of
town commands great views of the
city and bay. All rooms have a sea
view, air conditioning, TV and
private bathroom. Lively pool side
restaurant and friendly bar. Credit
cards accepted. **$$$**

Moderate
Pension Brise de Mer
4 Carenage
Tel: 262 0821
Overlooking the sea at the north
of the city, a family run
idiosyncratic hotel furnished
with period furniture. Veranda
with rocking chairs and terrace
restaurant. All rooms have
private shower and price
includes breakfast and evening
meal. **$$**
Les Jardins de l'Océan
90 Blvd de Mer
Carénage
Tel/Fax: 262 1169/2277
A lovely white-washed house
converted with 8 guest rooms of
different sizes (all with private
baths). Also two air conditioned
rooms and 10 more planned.
French restaurant, terrace bar and
a beautiful view of the harbour. **$$**

LABADIE

The road ends at Labadie and there
a growing number of delightfully
isolated properties which are only
accessible by boat.

Expensive
Cormier Plage
Tel: 262 1000
Just outside Labadie Nord this
attractive beach resort is located
on a beautiful stretch of sand with a
fine restaurant and sporting
facilities. **$$$**
Habitation Labadie
Tel: 223 5900;
email: Lablab@hotmail.com
Built on Pointe Sauvage, a
small island off the coast of
Labadie only accessible by boat.
Suite accommodation, excellent
cuisine, a small beach, beautiful
pool, a pool bar and friendly
ambiance. **$$$**

Setting Standards

Association des Micro-
Enterprises Touristiques du Sud-
Est (AHMETS), 40, Rue d'Orléans
Tel: 288 2840
The association sets standards –
which members must comply to
in order to join – and follows up
Jacmellians who rent rooms to
tourists in their homes. It is an
excellent programme and a good
way to meet Haitian families.
Single and double rooms are
available from AHMETS. **$**

Budget
Belli Beach Bar
Plage Belli
Tel: 262 2338
A group of small rooms and
restaurant overlooking a tiny cove,
beach and fantastic view. **$**
Norm's Place
Tel: 262 0400
Secluded and atmospheric
beachfront hotel near Labadie
village. Originally a 16th century
French fortress. Good food in the
restaurant. Accessible only by water
taxi. **$**

PORT-DE-PAIX

Moderate
Hotel Le Plaza International
Rue B Sylvain
Tel: 268 5448
Tourist class hotel on the sea front
about 5 minutes out of town by car.
air conditioned chalets and a good
restaurant. **$$**
Figuier Guesthouse
Île de la Tortue
No phone. Leave a message for
Victor on: 257 8400 ext. 6412
Simple lodgings with bathroom on
the eastern side of the island.
Sailing trips to Pointe Ouest beach
can be arranged. **$$**

Budget
Bienvenue Hotel
Rue Stenio Vincent 92
Tel: 268 5138
Central hotel with clean rooms with
private bathrooms. **$**

GONAÏVES

Gonaïves is the closest town to
Soukri and Souvenance ideal for
visitors attending Voodoo
celebrations and pilgrimages. There
are a couple of hotels for people
who prefer to stay in traditional
accommodation rather than in the
peasant houses at the sites.

Budget
Family Hotel
Route des Dattes
Carrefour Laborde
Tel: 274 0600
Large, simple hotel with pool and
secure parking. Some rooms have
air conditioning, triple rooms also
available; request meals in
advance. **$**

The South

JACMEL

Expensive
Hotel la Jacmelienne
Rue St-Anne, on the corner of Ave
de la Liberté
Tel: 222 4899, 288 3451; fax: 288
3453.

Hotel in an excellent location on a broad beach near the cruise ship pier and close to the centre of town. Rooms with bath, fan and minimal furnishings; a few have air conditioning; restaurant, bar and pool. Outdoor patio dining is popular but the service can be lackadaisical. **$$$**

Hôtel de la Place
3 Rue de l'Église
Tel: 288 2832
This hotel is popular with Haitian business people visiting Jacmel. Some of the rooms have air conditioning. **$$$**

Moderate

Hotel Florita
29 Rue du Commerce
Tel: 288 2805; fax: 288 3182
An unusual American-owned hotel. The magnificent property has been a coffee exporting house in the late 1880's and the former home of the critic and *Art Naïf* promoter, Selden Rodman. It retains its original ironwork features such as circular stairs and charming balconies. Same owner as budget-priced **Guy's Guest House** on 52 Grand Rue, tel: 288 3421. Next door to Baruk's artisan shop with the beautiful lacquered and painted wood items. **$$–$$$**

Budget

**La Coquille Restaurant
& Guest House**
Rue de la Mandou
Small place in an interesting part of town, quiet and safe. Basic rooms with private bath in a separate building behind the restaurant. Screened windows, but bring mosquito repellent anyway. **$**

Manoir Alexandre
Rue d'Orléans
Tel: 288 2711
Beautiful gingerbread-style mansion with an incomparable view over Jacmel and its bay. Rates are per person not for the room. All rooms share baths. **$**

JACMEL ENVIRONS

Expensive

Hôtel Cyvadier Plage
Ave Barranquilla
Tel: 288 3323
Small hotel in lush gardens which overlook the cove. Restaurant with a terrace. **$$$**

Hotel Price Guide

Room rates for two people sharing:
- **$ = Budget** under US$25
- **$$ = Moderate** US$25–50
- **$$$ = Expensive** over US$50

ÎLE-Á-VACHE

Expensive

Port Morgan
Tel: 286 1600
www.port-morgan.com
Large complex with marina and bungalow accommodation. Excellent beaches nearby. **$$$**

LES CAYES

Moderate

Hotel La Cayenne
Presqu'île des Caques
Tel: 286 0379
Simple, but comfortable hotel by the beach; with pool, some rooms have air conditioning. **$$**

Budget

Hotel Le Meridien
Carpentier
Tel: 286 0331
A small place with air conditioned rooms just 5 minutes from town. The hotel has a generator. **$**

JÉRÉMIE

Budget

Auberge Inn
Rue Roumer
The refurbished inn has an open porch and beautiful, original mahogany detailing and is furnished with some lovely antiques. A few of the rooms have a shared bath. The

property stretches back to the next street, Rue Brouet. **$**

Hôtel La Cabanne
A pink building with flowers. The rooms, with fans, are rather neglected. Has a conference room-cum-dining room/bar. Well-maintained exterior. **$**

JÉRÉMIE ENVIRONS

Budget

Anse du Clerc
Small, basic bungalows with a bed and table, no fans or toilets. Fresh water comes from the property's own spring. In a beautiful, bucolic setting on remote, expansive bay. Hammocks to relax in and solar electricity for about 12 hours a day.. Price per person, including breakfast and dinner. **$**

Where to Eat

What to Eat

Créole food is a combination of French, tropical, and African flavours using local spices. Most meat dishes are fried, such as *taso* (fried beef), *kabri* (goat) *griyo* or *grillot* (fried pork), *poule* (fried chicken) and *lambi* (conch) – often served with *Kréyol sòs* (tomato sauce). *Langouste* (local lobster) is a speciality at the beach.

Hot sauces are common – *piment oiseau, ti malice* – and *banan peze* (fried plantain) are a frequent side dish or snack. *Djon djon* is a small, dried Haitian mushroom that adds flavour to many dishes. When served with rice the dish is also called *Djon djon*.

Haiti grows some of the most delicious tropical fruit. Fruit can usually be purchased where it grows or in the city at markets and from vendors along the roads. There are plantains – from the banana family – which cannot be eaten raw and should be fried or boiled. Then there are small, very sweet bananas that melt in the mouth (figs). Other fruits include mangoes, watermelon, kumquats, Corosol (soursop), sweetsop and custard apples. Sugar cane can be peeled and the juice sucked directly from the stalk.

Where to Eat

It is very difficult to standardise a restaurant rating system in Haiti because there is so much variation between restaurants which would otherwise be in the same category. There can even be a noticeable difference from one day to the next within the same restaurant. Price does not necessarily reflect quality of food, service or ambience. Some of the eateries mentioned below are simple places with good food, but no phone, so turn up and tuck in.

PORT-AU-PRINCE

Port-au-Prince has no real top-of-the-line restaurants. Except for Chez Rose, the distinctly limited dinner choices are in hotels, in Pacot.

Aux Artistes
Institut Français d'Haiti
Blvd Harry Truman at Rue des Casernes
Tel: 222 3720
Good for a snack after attending an event or visiting the library at the institute. Open 10am–4pm Tues–Fri, 9am–5pm Sat. **$–$$**

Café Jardin du Musée
2 Rue Légitime
(behind the Musée d'Art)
Tel: 222 8738
French and Haitian cuisine which is a favourite lunch spot of French Embassy staff. **$–$$**

Café Terrasse
11 Rue Capois at Rue Ducoste
Tel: 222 5648/5025, 221 2956
Lots of staff from international aid agencies lunch here. **$**

Chez Rose
Corner of Rue Quatre and Bellevue
Pacot (near the Prince Hotel)
Tel: 245 5268
Very good Haitian/Créole food.
Open Mon–Sat noon–9/10pm. **$$**

Chez Yvane
19 Blvd Harry Truman
Tel: 222 0188/7676
Créole food in an air-conditioned restaurant. Lunch only. **$**

Jerry's Subs
Rue Capois
Great sandwiches. **$**

Le Bec Fin
Rue des Miracles, below Grande Rue
(Blvd. Jean Jacques Dessalines)
Good, simple Haitian-style food at very reasonable prices. **$**

Le Plaza (at the Holiday Inn)
Rue Capois
Inexpensive and expansive buffet lunch. **$–$$**

Rotisserie Lifran
Ave Delmas (near Imperial Cinema and Citibank)
Excellent barbecued chicken. **$**

Tiffany
12 Blvd. Harry Truman
Bicentenaire
Tel: 222 0993/3506
French, Haitian, American. **$**

Restaurants in Hotels

Hotel Oloffson
60 Avenue Christophe
Open for lunch and dinner. Serves Haitian and international food. There is an al-fresco dining area on the verandah. **$$–$$$**

Le Plaza Restaurant
(in Le Plaza Hotel)
10 Rue Capois, Champs de Mars
Tel: 222 0766
Good restaurant with a lunchtime buffet during the week. **$$–$$$**

Snacks and Ice Cream Parlours

Crème Maison
Ruelle No.4
Turgeau
Tel: 245 5592
Ice-cream parlour.

Red Rose Ice Cream
Ave John Brown 261
Tel: 245 6062
Ice-cream parlour.

Price Guide

Approximate cost of a main course per person:
- **$ = Inexpensive** US$5
- **$$ = Moderate** US$5–10
- **$$$ = Expensive** over US$10

PÉTIONVILLE

Cassagne
8 Rue Borno, corner of Louverture and Mettelus
Tel: 257 1223; fax: 246 0410
Haitian menu in a large old manor house with beautiful decor in a lovely setting. Excellent ambience and service. Bar and music. **$$**

Chez Gérard
17 Rue Pinchinat (near Place St Pierre)
Tel: 257 1949
Can be one of the best, but the French and Haitian food is inconsistent. Beautiful setting in a nicely landscaped courtyard. The bar for pre-dinner drinks is also

where dinner orders are taken from the blackboard *carte du jour*. Some vegetarian dishes available. **$$$**

Guess Who
49 Rue Gregoire (at Rue Louverture)
Tel: 256 3256
Nice setting for a casual lunch on a rooftop patio in the heart of Petionville. Creative dishes – anything from grilled brochettes to ravioli with cheese and basil. Service can be slow. A local hot spot during the evening when the bar is open and the menu is limited. Music on Thursday. **$$$**

La Plantation
Impasse Fouchard, off Rue Borno
Tel: 257 0979
A bit difficult to find, but definitely worth the search. The French chef prepares French and Haitian food. Relax with a drink in the bar-reception before moving on to beautifully landscaped indoor or outdoor dining area. Extensive menu but choices may not always be available. The Grand Marnier "pouch" is one of the best desserts. Excellent service. **$$$**

La Souvenance
8 Rue Gabart at Aubran
Tel: 257 7688
Gourmet French cuisine prepared with local and imported ingredients. Consistent quality food. Friendly hospitable owners and excellent service. Drinks in the small lobby bar. **$$$**

Les Cascades
73 Rue Clerveaux at Ogé
Tel: 257 7589/7597/6704
Relaxing ambience; paintings by local artists hang on the walls. The Haitian and French food can be excellent, especially if the proprietor is in the kitchen. Lobster bisque, veal chop (imported) and bananas flambé or crêpes suzette prepared at the table. Very good service. **$$$**

Café des Arts
19 Rue Lamarre
Tel: 257 1131/7979
French restaurant located below and owned by the Galerie Monnin. The atmosphere is reminiscent of eating places on the Left Bank in Paris. Open 7pm until late. regular live music.**$$–$$$**

Nature et Delices
49 Rue Grégoire
Tel: 257 4613
Deli and health food store with freshly made sandwiches using the best ingredients. Wide variety of imported health foods and snack items. Good place for food to take on a picnic. **$$–$$$**

Le Coin des Artistes
59 Rue Panaméricaine (beneath the Festival Arts Gallery)
Tel: 257 2400
Simple, often crowded place with a casual atmosphere. Fresh seafood from the neighbouring fish market and the grilled fish can be excellent. **$$**

Le Prince de Liège
89 Rue Grégoire
Tel: 257 8522
Belgian-owned. International dishes with local ingredients; good cheeses. Cuban and Dominican cigars. Open Mon–Sat 7pm–11pm. **$$**

Parasol Cafe
Choucoune Plaza
Tel: 257 4007/4008.
In the **Promenade complex** which is a small group of shops in the Choucoune Plaza above the Post Office on Rue Grégoire at Lamarre and Chavannes. The Promenade includes a bookshop, boutiques and a branch of Agence Citadelle travel agency. The cafe is one of two eating establishments. **$$**

Fabrizio
126 Rue de Louverture
Tel: 257 8433
Good Italian food, admirable quality pizzas and pastas in huge portions. Regular tables in front section and a less formal, large family-style back room with big-screen TV. Casual, friendly and great value. When ordering red wine, ask in advance if you prefer it room temperature, or it will be served chilled. **$**

Il Fior di Latte
Choucoune Plaza
Tel: 256 8474
Serves sandwiches, salads, pizza, carpaccio and outstanding Italian-style *gelatos* on a nicely landscaped patio below the shops. Very fresh ingredients. Good for lunch and evening meal. **$**

Muncheez
Rue Panaméricaine, corner with Rue Rebecca
Tel: 256 2177
Very popular place with some of the best pizza in Haiti. Take out or eat on the patio overlooking the hubbub of this busy street. **$**

St Pierre
Place St Pierre
Bustling bar and restaurant that is a favourite hangout of the French-Canadian expat crowd. Extensive menu ranges from pizza and steak to Greek dishes. **$**

Price Guide

Approximate cost of a main course per person:
- **$ = Inexpensive** US$5
- **$$ = Moderate** US$5–10
- **$$$ = Expensive** over US$10

Restaurants in Hotels

La Ville Belle
(at Villa Creole)
Ave Panaméricaine
Impasse José de St Martin
Tel: 257 1570/1571/1609
Excellent Continental food in a relaxing covered, open-air setting overlooking the beautifully landscaped grounds and pool. Friendly bar and private seating areas which often attract the business and diplomatic crowds. One or two innovative dishes daily compliment the interesting if limited regular menu. On Sunday Prime Rib nights and Monday barbecues, the regular menu is not available. Breakfast and lunch alongside the pool under a huge almond tree. **$$$**

Continental/Gourmet
(at El Rancho)
Route El Rancho
Tel: 257 2080/2082.
The El Rancho Hotel has three different places to eat but the food all comes from the same, uninspired kitchen. There are tables around the pool which make a pleasant setting. Inside there is a dark dining room or a more atmospheric and pricier restaurant next door. Service is slow and inattentive. **$$$**

Hotel Kinam
Place St Pierre
Tel: 257 0462/6525
Haitian and Continental food served in an attractive setting overlooking the pool. Food and service in the restaurant are inconsistent. This is unfortunate because otherwise the hotel staff are friendly and very helpful. Go for drinks or a snack and enjoy the atmosphere. **$$**

Fast Food
Dominos Pizza, 91 Rue Panaméricaine near the turn for Villa Creole and El Rancho.
Tel: 257 5151
Pizza from an international chain.
Fabrizio Pizza, Delmas, next to Radio Shack
Tel: 246 3558.
Three locations.
Les Délices Burger, 97 Rue Gregoire
Tel: 257 8468
Large, American-style burgers, fries and pizza.

OUTSIDE PÉTIONVILLE

Altitude 1300
Boutilliers
Open weekends for excellent Créole cuisine in refreshing mountain environment. **$**
La Florville
Kenscoff
Very good Haitian and international food with live music. **$**
Mountain Maid Inn
Baptist Mission, Fermathe
Tel: 255 9807
Cafeteria-style American lunch and snacks of burgers, fries, and ice cream. **$$$**

CAP-HAÏTIEN

The restaurant and nightlife scene in Cap-Haïtien has shifted to the increasingly popular Carenage area (the northern end of Boulevard). Most restaurants serve the usual Créole and French mélange, the only exception being a couple of pizza bars.

Éclipse
Rue du Boulevard
Carenage
Tel: 262 3523
Excellent bar and restaurant specialising in high-end traditional Haitian food, run by a lovely French couple. Relaxed, romantic atmosphere. Live music several times a week. Open Mon–Sat noon–midnight.
Mont Joli
Rue B, Carenage
Tel 262 0300
Classical Haitian/French fare at poolside restaurant with live music in the evenings. Attentive and friendly staff and a good selection of cocktails. **$$$**
Roi Christophe
Rue 24 B
Tel 262 0414
Excellent French/Creole menu. The horseshoe-shaped bar is excellent for meeting people. **$$$**
Cap 2000
Rue 5 Boulevard
Popular seafront restaurant serving Haitian food, sandwiches and ice-creams. Open 7am–11pm. **$$**
Les Jardins de l'Océan
90 Carenage
Classic French cuisine downstairs. Freshly made pizzas on the roof terrace bar. **$$**
Marina Anacoana
Rue 13–14 Boulevard
Traditional food and drinks served at the jetty side cultural centre. **$$**
Advantage Bar Restaurant
Rue 18 K
Haitian fare in sweet local restaurant with bright murals. Open 6am–10pm Mon–Fri. **$**
La Caille
Rue du Boulevard
Carenage
Bustling open-air locale. The patio dance floor is always crowded as are the tables teeming with customers enjoying the serve-yourself snacks. **$**
Ozan Nan Na
46 Rue 18 A
Great cheap bar and restaurant overlooking craft market, Serving sandwiches and Haitian *plat complet*. Open 9am–2am daily. **$**

PORT-DE-PAIX

Most of the hotels in town have restaurants which are worth investigating.
Capitol Restaurant
Rue Estimé
Typical Haitian food. **$**
Chez Ketia Bar Restaurant
Rue Stenio Vincent
Small cheap restaurant. **$**

JÉRÉMIE:

Alliance Française
In addition to a restaurant, there are tennis courts and this is the best place to find out what's happening in town. It's also a staple of the expat social life.
Chez Patou
Rue Monseignor Beaugé
In a red and white, two-storey building. Also a snack bar and a good place for a cold beer and ice cream.
Castillo Restaurant and Bar
28 Rue H Merlet
Tel: 284 5658/5659
Elaborate wrought-iron outside and in – a beautiful spiral staircase leads to the second-floor restaurant. Open daily 7am until the last person leaves. Serves breakfast, lunch, dinner and snacks. A balcony over the entryway is a nice place for an afternoon or evening drink. The menu is varied.

JACMEL

La Crevette Resto Club
Rue St Anne
Tel: 288 2834
Excellent location near wharf. Good seafood. Live music at weekends.
La Jacmelienne
Rue St Anne
Tel: 222 4899
Al fresco dining is popular but the service is inconsistent.
Hôtel de la Place
3 Rue de l'Église on Place d'Armes
Tel: 288 2832
Haitian and American fast food served in a busy lively atmosphere. The terrace is a great place to enjoy a drink and watch the world go by.

Drinking Notes

Most international liquors and liqueurs are available in night clubs, and the top-end restaurants offer French wine. Distillers in Haiti make fine Barbancourt rum and the local "fire water" Clairin, made from sugar cane, flows liberally at Voodoo ceremonies. "Culligan" is the name used generically for filtered, sterilised and bottled water.

Bars & Nightclubs

Below is only a small selection of Haiti's nightlife. Most of the action is dotted around the main towns with concentrations in the Port-au-Prince environs and Jacmel.

Pétionville

Cheers at 14 Rue Villatte in Pétionville has a good bar and good food. It's popular with locals and visitors with money to spend.
Bash at El Rancho, Route El Rancho, Pétionville. Live jazz on Saturday evening.

Jacmel

Chez Dimicaté Bar
Ave. Baranquilla, facing Teleco
Congo Plage on Rue St Anne in Jacmel is a small inexpensive restaurant and bar in front of the Jacmelienne Hotel. It is usually lively on weekends.
Platinum Resto Bar on Rue du Commerce.
Samba in Jacmel is a very large indoor and outdoor space which has live music for dancing every night.The performers include local group Les Invincibles and international bands. Open 9pm–3am Mon–Fri, 7pm–3am Sat.
Yaquimo Plage in Jacmel is an open-air disco/club and restaurant.
Distraction Bar on Rue B H Jeune in Cayes Jacmel is actually a small basic guest house which serves food and drink accompanied by Haitian music in the evening.

Culture

Haitian Art

An original Haitian *art naïf* painting in bright, vivid colours makes a wonderful, but not inexpensive, gift for someone back home (*see Haitian Art page 99*).

In addition to the well-established artists whose work commands prices commensurate with their fame, there are many top-quality artists yet to be discovered.

In general, the well-known galleries are the best places to purchase art. However, there are excellent, undiscovered artists who display their work elsewhere because they are not represented by the galleries.

It is always a good idea to have an idea of prices before making a purchase. This can be complex in because many of the better-known galleries show only the handful of artists.

If you want to buy an original artwork then it would be wise to take a good look around before making a purchase. It will soon become obvious which pieces are mass-produced imitations. You can also visit artists in their studios and check out the Musée d'Art Haïtien in Port-au-Prince, as well as the smaller shops.

Check that the painting is done in oil, not acrylic and that it is on canvas. Also be sure to ask if the picture you are buying is actually a painting and not a print.

Remember that haggling (negotiating) to secure a good price is not only tolerated, it is expected. If you want to buy several things then negotiate for everything together as a group and you may get a good deal.

Art Galleries

PORT-AU-PRINCE & ENVIRONS

Pacot is the lovely neighbourhood in the outskirts of the capital. It is filled with flowering old trees and Victorian homes that surround the Prince and Oloffson hotels as well as some excellent art galleries.
Le Centre d'Art
58 Rue Roy, Pacot
Tel: 222 2018
An elegant space in a former mansion that supports artists by exhibiting their works in keeping with the intent of founders, DeWitt Peters and Selden Rodman.
Galerie Issa
17 Ave du Chili, Pacot
Tel: 222 3287
Issa was the model for "the Syrian Connection" in Graham Greene's novel, *The Comedians*. It probably has more paintings than a warehouse and at good prices too. A good place to visit after narrowing down your preferences.
Galerie Carlos Jara
28 Rue Armand Holly, Debussy
Tel: 245 7164
This gallery has a fine art collection. Located ten minutes drive from Pacot.
Georges Nader Gallery
18 Rue Bouvreuil, Croix Desprez
Tel: 245 0565; and also at 50 Rue Grégoire, Pétionville
Tel: 257 5602/0855
Email: gnader@haitiworld.com
Gallery open Mon–Sat, 10am–7pm.
Damballa Art Gallery
Rue Magasin de l'État 243
A wonderful hole-in-the-wall gallery.
Dantor
77 Rue Fonts-Forts, across the little park from the main Post Office

PÉTIONVILLE & ENVIRONS

Expressions Galerie d'Art
55 Rue Metellus
Tel: 256 3471
www.expregal@haitiworld.com
Exhibits handicrafts as well as art and sculpture.

Galerie Marassa
17 Rue Lamarre
Tel: 257 1967/5424; fax: 257 8981
Has the work of modern artists and different media. Moro's lacquer ware from Jacmel exhibited here.
Galerie Monnin
19 Rue Lamarre
Tel: 257 4430
A family-owned gallery displaying painting and sculpture. Open Mon–Fri 10am–6pm, Sat 10am–2pm.
Galerie Bourbon-Lally
23 Rue Lamarre
Tel: 257 6321
Rainbow Art Gallery
9 Rue Pierre Wiener, Bourdon
Tel: 245 6655/6039
Displays and sells handicrafts as well as paintings.

JACMEL

Domond Artist Studio
76 Portail Léogane
Parizot Domond is an artist and a Voodoo *oungan* (priest). One theme of his art is the particular use of *Voodoo* symbols and colours that draw the viewer into the dreamworld he unveils. Domond comes from a rom a family of artists, all three walls of his one-room, open-front gallery are covered from floor to ceiling with their works. He speaks only Kréyol, so bring along a translator.

CAP-HAÏTIEN

Philomé Obin, Cap-Haïtien's most famous *art naïf* painter established the **École du Cap-Haïtien** (Cap-Haïtien School). Much of the art from Cap-Haïtien is inspired by the artist's neighbours going about their daily lives among the town's distinctive pastel-coloured buildings.
Galerie Toussaint L'Ouverture
Rue 16–17 B
Small gallery with good selection of local art and crafts.

Museums

Musée d'Art Haïtien
Rue Légitime
Port-au-Prince
Tel: 222 2510
One of the finest *art naïf* collections on the island. The museum makes space for travelling exhibitions by shelving some of the permanent displays, so call if you are visiting only to see the *art naïf*. Mon–Sat 10am–4pm.
Musée du Panthéon National
Port-au-Prince
Tel: 222 3167
An underground museum with interesting historical exhibits and artefacts.
Musée d'Ogier-Fombrun
Moulin sur la Mer, Montrouis
A compact but worthwhile museum, which plots Haitian history from Taíno times.

Tour the Forts

Haiti's ruined forts on the coast were built by the French or English in the 17th and 18th centuries, while inland fortresses were built by the Haitians after independence in 1804.

In the north, Cap-Haïtien shelters the ruins of three French forts: **Magny**, **Joseph**, and **Picolet**. They overlook the harbour entrance and the Atlantic Coast for as far as the eye can see in all directions. The remains include cannons, cannonballs, and parts of the foundations and walls.

Fort Dauphin in the town of Fort Liberté, east of Cap-Haïtien, dates from the 1730's. It is in fairly good condition and would make an interesting visit. There is no other reason to be in Fort Liberté.

The incomparable **Citadelle** (*see page 307*) is a massive mountaintop fortress that took 20,000 men 13 years to build. It is 19 km (12 miles) from Cap-Haïtien and can be seen from almost anywhere within a 32-km (20-mile) radius. It is an effort to reach the spectacular monument. The impressive building offers unparalleled 360° views.

Fort Jacques built by Pétion in the 19th century and **Fort Alexandre** are located in the beautiful hills above Port-au-Prince.

Festivals

CARNIVAL

Throughout Haiti, the finale of Carnival month are the three days before Ash Wednesday. **Jacmel**'s festivities are the most popular because of the tradition of elaborate, imaginative masked costumes and lively fun. However the music is considered better in **Port-au-Prince**. There are free open-air concerts all over the city during the three or four weekends prior to carnival when bands are preparing for the final event. Few people wear costumes in the capital any more and the floats have less decoration than they formerly had. Still, nothing can compare with the experience of the explosion of music blaring from the stands and floats, together with the exuberant dancing and chanting crowds. There's a good view from the stands and it's safer too.

RARA

Rara, the "peasant carnival", runs from Ash Wednesday to Easter. Rara bands tour the countryside in brightly coloured attire, playing homemade wind instruments, beating drums, dancing and singing. Their antics can attract a following of a thousand or more people, and considerable drinking adds to the merriment. Léogane is one of the best places to experience Rara.

SAUT D'EAU

During July and August, local festivals – both traditional and religious – are held in many towns, including Petit Goâve, Souvenance, Soukri, Limonade, Plaine du Nord, and Ouanaminthe. The ceremonies at Soukri (near Gonaïve) are unique in that they honour the Congo loas (spirits) only.

Sport

Outdoor Activities

Though Haiti is no sporting mecca there are things to do for the more energetic visitors and sport to watch for the rest.

COCKFIGHTING

Cockfighting is a an activity that transcends race and class. Virtually every Haitian town has a cockfighting arena patronised by the poor and wealthy alike.

FOOTBALL

Football is a popular sport in Haiti, take in a game at the Sylvio Cator Stadium in Port-au-Prince or Parc St Victor in Cap-Haïtien.

WATERSPORTS

Cormier Plage
Labadie Nord
tel 262 1000
The luxury beach resort can organise a variety of watersports including scuba diving, snorkelling and sailing for guests and non-guests.
Pegasus Diving Services
B.P. 15785
Pétionville
Tel: 298 4621 (dive shop); 238 2471/3140 (workshop).
José Roy can organise dives in the waters along the Côte des Arcadins, which he knows like the back of his hand.

Shopping

Artisanat

Haiti is famous for its high-quality and unique arts and crafts. Papier mâché carnival masks and animals, brightly painted black lacquerware, unusual carvings and exceptional ironwork – from small *bibelots* to large decorative doors. Wall hangings of exquisite faces fashioned from leather, soapstone carvings, and items associated with Voodoo ceremonies are just a few of the possibilities.

All of the excellent outlets are too numerous to mention, so the main streets in which to meander are listed below, in addition to a sampling of the shops.

PORT-AU-PRINCE CENTRE

Marché de Fer (Iron Market)
Blvd Jean-Jacques Dessalines
Port-au-Prince
Mon–Fri 8am–4pm, Sat 8am–noon. Haggling (bargaining) is expected and highly recommended even if a quoted price seems reasonable, the visitor can be sure that it is at least twice what the seller expects to be paid in the end.

The hot, crowded, covered market is crammed with a huge variety of items of varying quality. Soapstone and wood carvings, paintings, leatherwork, ironwork, printed fabrics, straw hats, *Voodoo* flags and small souvenirs all vie for attention. As well as shoes, clothing and foodstuffs. Note that salesmen and middlemen may almost come to blows as they compete to escort the shopper to their own or other stalls where they will be paid a commission for the introduction and subsequent sale.

PORT-AU-PRINCE ENVIRONS

Pacot has a wealth of handicraft shops and a visit to the area makes a delightful day out to enjoy the architecture, painting and sculpture.
Comité Artisanal Haïtien
29 Rue 3
Pacot
Tel: 222 8440
Open Mon–Fri 9am–4pm, Sat 10am–noon. Excellent cooperative with reasonably priced handicrafts from all over Haiti. Another shop sits right across the street. Go to the corner, turn left and walk three blocks, (passing the Hotel Oloffson) to Rue Capois for more shops.
Ambiance
17 Rue M
Pacot
Tel: 245 2494
A gingerbread home with fine examples of Haitian and international handicrafts, jewellery and pottery.
Gingerbread
52 Ave Lamartinière
Bois Verna
Tel: 245 3698
Open Mon–Fri 10am–4pm, Sat 10am–1pm. Sells ironwork, papier-mâché, *Voodoo* flags, horn carvings and other artisania.

PÉTIONVILLE AND ENVIRONS

Rue Clerveaux and around **Bourdon** are good places to explore, and the listing below shows a few places to start. Almost anyone in the smaller towns outside the capital will be able to point out studios, workshops and galleries.
Capeline Nap Nap
81 Rue Grégoire
Above the post office and The Promenade. Hand-painted household items, many from Cap Haïtien.
Ceramic Art
Thomassin 35, Laboule
Tel: 255 7799
Fleur de Canne
34bis, Rue Gabart, Pétionville
Tel: 257 4266
Specialises in objects for the table.

Everything is either made by them or for them. Items made to order.

Le Grenier
74 Ave Panaméricaine
A small eclectic antique shop.

Pierre Pierre
85 Bis
Route de Delmas
Tel: 246 5277

Sunny Home
393 Route de Delmas
Tel: 257 3230

CROIX DES BOUQUETS

Officially part of Port-au-Prince, this small town about an hour from the capital is worth a visit. See where most of the artisans have their workshops.

JACMEL

Moro's on Rue du Commerce has an extensive selection of beautiful lacquerware and the friendly proprietors will ship the goods anywhere. Look around in the small shops in **Rue St Anne**, **Portail Léogane** and at **Zoo Art** in Rue Triscotte.

CAP-HAÏTIEN

On Rue 17 near Boulevard there is a small group of sheds where artisans sell their crafts.

JÉRÉMIE

Abricots is a small town, about 7 km (4 miles) from Jérémie, which is the artisan centre for the district.

Comperettes is a delicious bread which is found only in Jérémie.

Rum

Taking some local rum home is a great idea. Try **Barbancourt** which is considered the best for export. **Clairin** is made from sugar cane and is used in *Voodoo* ceremonies. A good gift for friends who enjoy the unusual.

Language

Kréyol

Kréyol (Créole) is pronounced phonetically. E's are pronounced as an acute unless they have a grave accent. So *pase* becomes pas-ay in speech. Another point to note is that me is written simply as *M* but is pronounced um

USEFUL PHRASES

Greetings
Hello *Bonjou*
Good-bye *Orevwa*
How are you? *Ki jan ou ye?*
What's up?/
What's happening? *Sak pase?*
What's new? *Ban m nouvèl ou!*
I'm okay *M la*
And you *E ou menm*

In conversation
What is your name? *Ki jan ou rele?*
Allow me to introduce myself *Kite m prezante m*
My name is Paul *M rele Pòl*
I'm very happy to meet you *M bien kontan fè konesans ou*
Do you speak Kréyol? *Ou pale kréyol?*
...English? *anglè?*
...French? *fransè?*
...Spanish? *pannyòl?*
Yes, I speak Kréyol *Wi, m pale kréyol*
No, I don't speak Kréyol *Non, m pa pale kréyol*
Speak slowly, please *Pale pi dousman, sivouple*
Do you understand? *Ou konpran?*
I understand *Mwen konprann*
I don't understand *M pa konprann*
Please *Sivouple!*
Thank you *Mèsi*
Thank you very much *Mèsi anpil*
Don't mention it *De ryen*

I'm sorry *M regrèt*
Be careful! *Pinga!*
What would you like? *Sa ou ta vle?*
I'd like... *Mwen ta vle...*
I'd like to learn Kréyol *Mwen ta vle aprann kréyol*
I'd like orange juice *Mwen ta vle ji zoranj*
What do you need? *Sa ou bezwan?*
I need... *Mwen bezwan...*
I'd rather... *M pito...*
How much is...? *Konbyin pou...?*
How much is the book? *Konbyin pou liv la?*
It is $5.00 *Senk dola pou liv la*
What time is it? *Kilè li ye?*
It is 1pm *Li inè*
It is 2pm *Li dezè*
I'm hungry *Mwen grangou*
I'm thirsty *Mwen swèf*
It's hot *Li fè chò*
It's cold *Li fè frèt*

About town
Where is Main Street? *Ki kote Granri ye?*
You go straight ahead *Ou prale tou dwat*
You go straight along this street *Ou pran ri sila a tou dwat*
You turn right *Ou vire a dwat*
You turn left *Ou vire a goch*
I am lost *M pèdi*

ART & PHOTO CREDITS

Tony Arruza 30, 66, 72, 90, 93, 95, 200, 284, 302
AKG London 23, 26L, 33, 42, 45, 46, 47, 48, 49
Steve Bly 12/13, 137, 143, 172L, 199
Bill Boyce 154, 272/273, 276, 282T, 287, 289L/R, 298R, 300, 316/317, 319, 322L, 325
Bridgeman Art Library 20, 29, 32, 36, 38, 40, 44, 50
Michele Burgess 310
Skip Brown 4, 144L, 152, 195, 203R
Thomas Conlin/Aquatic Adventures 150
Nancy Crampton 126
Editions d'e Art Daniel Derveaux 18/19
Gregory Drezdzon 140
Jean-Leo Dugast/Panos Pictures 125, 288, 289T, 308, 309, 310T
Sarah Errington/Hutchison Library 70, 292
Yves Fonck front flap top, spine top, back cover center left, back cover center, 2, 2/3, 5, 6/7, 17, 21, 51, 71L, 73, 74, 76/77, 87L/R, 88, 92, 94, 99, 103, 107L, 131, 147, 270/271, 274/275, 290, 297, 298T, 298L, 299, 304/305, 306, 311, 313, 314, 320T, 321, 322R, 326, 327, 329, 330, 331, 333, 334, 335
Marc French/Panos Pictures 67, 75, 104, 285, 338, 340
Eduardo Gil 28
Leah Gordon/Axiom 68, 106L, 123, 148/149, 323, 328, 341, 342
Leah Gordon 1, 100, 105, 108, 116, 127, 128, 130, 133, 283, 286T, 291, 307, 312, 315, 318, 320, 336/337, 343
Ronald Grant Archive 265T
Andreas M. Gross 35, 37R, 59, 69, 83, 119, 172R, 174, 178, 182, 188, 190, 208T, 211L, 212T, 213T, 215, 227, 323T, 331T
J. Hatt/Hutchison Library 109
J. Henderson/Hutchison Library back flap top, 71R, 282
David Hoey 164, 201L
Jeremy Horner/Hutchison Library 180/181

Jamaica National Library 34, 28
Catherine Karnow back cover right, 4/5, 14, 23L, 52, 56/57, 58, 62, 63, 85, 86L, 91, 110, 122, 134, 138R, 139, 160/161, 162/163, 169, 186, 187T, 194, 202R, 204/205, 224/225, 226, 228, 229, 231T, 239, 240, 241, 242, 252T, 255, 263T
Monika Latzel 86R, 144R, 153, 168, 176, 210, 211T, 233, 242T, 245T, 245, 247, 248/249, 251, 344
M+W Fine Arts/New York/Jose Martin 31
Nancy Durrell McKenna/Hutchison Library 80, 82, 243, 263
Paul Murphy 39, 96/97, 171, 209T, 211R
P. Regent/Hutchison Library 135
Wolfgang Rossig/APA 5L, 24, 25R, 56/57, 114, 151, 173, 176, 177, 183, 184, 202L, 208, 209, 214, 218, 220, 221, 244, 258, 259, 260, 261, 266, 267, 171T, 172T, 174T, 210T, 220T, 253T, 260T, 303
Elizabeth Saft (courtesy of New York Public Library) 22
Kay Shaw Photography 339
Robert Smith 10/11, 111, 112, 113, 115, 117, 120, 121
Sean Sprague/Panos Pictures 132
Martin Thomas front flap bottom, back flap bottom, back cover bottom center, 8/9, 60, 61, 81, 118, 124, 129, 136, 141, 142, 145, 146, 155, 158/159, 184T, 185, 189, 192/193, 196, 197, 201R, 206, 207, 216/217, 219, 222, 223, 230,

232R, 236/237, 238, 246, 250, 252, 254, 256/257, 264, 265L/R, 268, 269
Topham Picturepoint 232L, 332
Mireille Vautier 53, 64/65, 89, 98, 101, 106R, 107R, 138L, 281, 284T, 286, 293, 296, 301T, 301, 324
Ilona Weöres 191, 196T, 199T
Phil Wood/APA title, 102
Philip Wolmuth/Hutchison Library 78/79, 84, 175
Norbert Wu/NHPA 179

Picture Spreads

Pages 54/55 Top row, left to right: M. Thomas, Yves Fonck, Maurice Harvey/Hutchison Library. Centre row, left to right: Yves Fonck, Wolgand Rossig/APA, Yves Fonck. Bottom row, left to right: Catherine Karnow, Yves Fonck, Yves Fonck.
Pages 156/157 Top row, all: Mark Cowardine. Centre row, all: Mark Cowardine. Bottom row, left to right: Mark Cowardine, Monika Latzel, Tom Conlin.
Pages 234/235 Top row, left to right: Monika Latzel, Nancy Durrell McKenna/Hutchison Library, Nancy Durrell McKenna/Hutchison Library, Monika Latzel. Centre row, left to right: Monika Latzel, Nancy Durrell McKenna/Hutchison Library. Bottom row, left to right: Monika Latzel, Andreas M. Gross, Wolfgang Rossig/APA.
Pages 294/295 Top row, left to right: Andreas M. Gross, Steve Bly, Nancy Durrell McKenna/Hutchison Library, B. Jones & M. Shimlock/NHPA. Centre row, left to right: Wolfgang Rossig/APA, Daniel Heuclin/NHPA. Bottom row, left to right: David Hoey, Yves Fonck, Wolfgang Rossig/APA, Martin Harvey/NHPA.

Map Production: Phoenix Mapping
©2004 Apa Publications GmbH & Co
Verlag KG (Singapore Branch)

INSIGHT GUIDE
DOMINICAN
REPUBLIC & HAITI
Cartographic Editor Zoë Goodwin
Production Linton Donaldson
Design Consultants
Carlotta Junger, Graham Mitchener
Picture Research Hilary Genin,
Britta Jaschinski, Natasha Babaian

Index

Numbers in italics refer to photographs

The two countries are included in the following index. To identify the location of each placename, follow the key:

(DR) = Dominican Republic
(H) = Haiti

A
B
C
E
F
G
H
I
J
a
b
c
d
e
f
g
h
i
j
k

Insight Guides Website
www.insightguides.com

Don't travel the planet alone. Keep in step with Insight Guides' walking eye, just a click away

INSIGHT GUIDES

The world's largest collection of visual travel guides

INSIGHT GUIDES

The classic series that puts you in the picture

Alaska
Amazon Wildlife
American Southwest
Amsterdam
Argentina
Arizona & Grand Canyon
Asia's Best Hotels
&Resorts
Asia, East
Asia, Southeast
Australia
Austria
Bahamas
Bali
Baltic States
Bangkok
Barbados
Barcelona
Beijing
Belgium
Belize
Berlin
Bermuda
Boston
Brazil
Brittany
Brussels
Buenos Aires
Burgundy
Burma (Myanmar)
Cairo
California
California, Southern
Canada
Caribbean
Caribbean Cruises
Channel Islands
Chicago
Chile
China
Continental Europe
Corsica
Costa Rica
Crete
Croatia
Cuba
Cyprus
Czech & Slovak Republic
Delhi, Jaipur & Agra

Denmark
Dominican Rep. & Haiti
Dublin
East African Wildlife
Eastern Europe
Ecuador
Edinburgh
Egypt
England
Finland
Florence
Florida
France
France, Southwest
French Riviera
Gambia & Senegal
Germany
Glasgow
Gran Canaria
Great Britain
Great Gardens of Britain
& Ireland
Great Railway Journeys
of Europe
Greece
Greek Islands
Guatemala, Belize
& Yucatán
Hawaii
Hong Kong
Hungary
Iceland
India
India, South
Indonesia
Ireland
Israel
Istanbul
Italy
Italy, Northern
Italy, Southern
Jamaica
Japan
Jerusalem
Jordan
Kenya
Korea
Laos & Cambodia
Las Vegas

Lisbon
London
Los Angeles
Madeira
Madrid
Malaysia
Mallorca & Ibiza
Malta
Mauritius Réunion
& Seychelles
Melbourne
Mexico
Miami
Montreal
Morocco
Moscow
Namibia
Nepal
Netherlands
New England
New Orleans
New York City
New York State
New Zealand
Nile
Normandy
Norway
Oman & The UAE
Oxford
Pacific Northwest
Pakistan
Paris
Peru
Philadelphia
Philippines
Poland
Portugal
Prague
Provence
Puerto Rico
Rajasthan
Rio de Janeiro

Rome
Russia
St Petersburg
San Francisco
Sardinia
Scandinavia
Scotland
Seattle
Shanghai
Sicily
Singapore
South Africa
South America
Spain
Spain, Northern
Spain, Southern
Sri Lanka
Sweden
Switzerland
Sydney
Syria & Lebanon
Taiwan
Tanzania & Zanzibar
Tenerife
Texas
Thailand
Tokyo
Trinidad & Tobago
Tunisia
Turkey
Tuscany
Umbria
USA: On The Road
USA: Western States
US National Parks: West
Venezuela
Venice
Vienna
Vietnam
Wales
Walt Disney World/Orlando

INSIGHT GUIDES

The world's largest collection of visual travel guides & maps